MENTAL MODELS

Edited by
DEDRE GENTNER
ALBERT L. STEVENS
Bolt Beranek and Newman Inc.

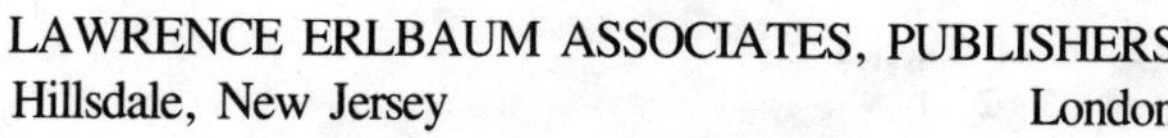

LAWRENCE ERLBAUM ASSOCIATES, PUBLISHERS
1983 Hillsdale, New Jersey London

Lawrence Erlbaum Associates, Inc., Publishers
365 Broadway
Hillsdale, New Jersey 07642

Library of Congress Cataloging in Publication Data

Main entry under title:

Mental models.

(Cognitive science)
Includes bibliographies and indexes.
1. Cognition. 2. Comprehension. 3. Knowledge, Theory of. I. Gentner, Dedre. II. Stevens, Albert L. III. Series: Cognitive science (Lawrence Erlbaum Associates)
BF311.M446 1983 153 82-21113
ISBN 0-89859-242-9

Printed in the United States of America
10 9 8 7 6 5 4 3 2 1

Contents

Introduction

A typical piece of mental models research is characterized by careful examination of the way people understand some domain of knowledge. For example, Patrick Hayes (1979) has analyzed the concepts involved in understanding the behavior of liquids. This understanding enables people to predict when a liquid will flow, stand still, or spread into a thin sheet on a surface. Using Hayes' analysis, we can model the way in which people imagine liquids moving through time from one of these states to another: for example, a glass of water spilling on a table, flowing over the edge, hitting the floor, and then dripping through a crack. Hayes' attempt to represent this knowledge is extremely explicit. He has carefully described the inferences a person can draw from each of these different liquid states.

What is the point of research on mental models? Why attempt to lay out human understanding of a domain so explicitly? Clearly, this research has applied utility. For example, Hayes' work on liquids would be relevant to understanding why operators of nuclear plants do not always correctly interpret their instruments. Similarly, in order to train seamen about how a steam ship works, the better our models of exactly what kind of knowledge is involved in liquid flow and phase transitions, the better we would be able to simulate, teach, and test for this knowledge.

But, as important as these applied consequences are, they are not the fundamental goal of mental models research. Mental models research is fundamentally concerned with understanding human knowledge about the world.

Dimensions of Mental Models Research

There are three key dimensions on which to characterize mental models research: the nature of the domain studied, the nature of the theoretical approach, and the nature of the methodology.

Domains. Our first efforts to capture naturalistic human knowledge must necessarily center on the simplest possible domains. We need to choose domains for which there exists some normative knowledge that is relatively easy to detail explicitly. Therefore, mental models research focuses on simple physical systems or devices. The naive physics of liquids, although it may seem an intimidating topic to a nonphysical scientist, is a considerably more tractable domain than, for example, interpersonal relations—it is very easy to tell an expert from a novice in a domain like Newtonian mechanics, and very difficult to tell the expert from the novice in a domain like marriage. The reason that mental models research has focused on seemingly technical domains is precisely because those domains that have proved the most tractable to physical scientists are the ones for which there exists the best explicit normative models.

The domains studied are simple physical or mathematical systems, or artificial devices—for example, naive mechanics, naive theories of heat, or naive theories of liquids. The emphasis is on dynamic phenomena, so most of the devices or phenomena studied involve changes of state, often causally connected changes.

Theoretical Approach. The approaches towards knowledge representation are based on computational semantics as developed by the artificial intelligence community, rather than on mathematical formalisms. Data and process tend to be represented in the same formalism. For example, constraint networks, production rules, networks with attached procedures, and other such formalisms tend to be used.

Methodology. The methodologies used are eclectic: they include protocol analysis, traditional cognitive psychology experiments, developmental studies, expert-novice studies, simulation of possible psychological models and comparison of the results of that simulation with what humans do, field observation, comparison across cultures, comparison across time within the same culture (i.e., historical comparisons), and what might be called designed field observation, in which an artificial domain is constructed that has interesting relevance to the real domain under consideration.

Interdisciplinary Aspects

Mental models research is a confluence of two major lines of research that have developed individually to the point where an extremely productive synergy is possible. The first line includes cognitive psychology and the related disciplines of linguistics, anthropology, and philosophy. This line has expanded the range of techniques for investigating what is going on in the human mind, so that it is now possible to be extremely ambitious about testing complex theories of how people understand naturalistic information. Most cognitive psychologists, even those who stay carefully within one or two paradigms and whose conclusions seem extremely conservative, bound to particular parameters, are closet naturalists. Most of us really want to understand the mind. We really want to know how someone thinks about the way the world works. We feel that the accumulation of careful knowledge and methodology arising out of our experimental investigations is now ready to be tried again in service of the central goal. In order to accomplish this, a formal language of sufficient power to describe knowledge and thought processes is necessary.

This brings us to the second line of research, artificial intelligence. This line has provided powerful formalisms in which to explicitly notate theories of human knowledge representation and processing. Three decades ago, Piaget, a powerful and intuitive observer of human mental phenomena, had only mathematical models to use as a formalism for knowledge representation. He theorized, for example, that the kind of thought processes that are acquired in adolescence constitute 16 boolean algebraic relationships. This kind of representation was a limitation in theorizing about the richness of Piagetian phenomenology. It does not permit us to capture anything like the complexity of human knowledge representation, particularly the representation of dynamic knowledge. Nor does it allow us to explicitly represent human thought processes. In the last decade, computational models have moved from early models which emphasized information flow and channel capacity to exceedingly rich, finely structured formalisms for representing both data and processes in a uniform framework.

The combination of a rich variety of psychological techniques and a new and seemingly apt formalism for representing human knowledge and processes has led us to believe that the time is ripe for developing theories about how people understand the world. The chapters in this book represent several researchers' attempts to develop such theories.

From what we have said so far, it is clear that the ideal mental-models researcher would be a combination of cognitive psychologist, artificial intelligence researcher, anthropologist, linguist, and philosopher, and certainly a knowledgeable practitioner of the domain being studied. In addition to all of these things the researcher should also have good field intuition. At present, most of us fall well short of this ideal composite. But, as we hope is evident in the chapters that follow, the technique adopted in mental models research is one of "overlap and conquer." Although no one person is expert in all the areas necessary, the researchers share their central domains of expertise; and they endeavor to learn enough about the companion techniques so that their work can interact with work in other disciplines. Out of this collaboration may come the kind of powerful unifying theory that we would all like to have.

AN OVERVIEW OF THE CHAPTERS

The chapters in this volume show a remarkable degree of eclecticism. There is in every case a central focus that can be characterized as either primarily a deep domain theory (a knowledge representation for a domain), or a phenomenological theory of human processing. Traditionally, these two directions would involve very different methodologies; the canonical methodology for a deep, explicit domain representation would be the development of a knowledge-representation network, perhaps with a computer simulation; the canonical methodology for a processing theory would be psychological experimentation. Here, however, we find that in addition to the canonical methodology, in almost every case the authors have borrowed other methods, even methods that are supposed to belong to other disciplines.

The authors who are primarily concerned with deep domain theories are Forbus, de Kleer and Brown, and Bundy and Byrd. Each of these three efforts involves serious computer simulation. Forbus has simulated a well-defined subdomain of spatial knowledge, using qualitative local rules which include both entities and inference processes. Yet he has also drawn on his field observations to refine a theory and to make it compatible with what can be discovered about psychological processing. De Kleer and Brown have concerned themselves with competence models: with what is the essential set of shared structural constraints that an ideal model of a domain must have. They have produced an elegant simulation of expert knowledge of electronic circuit analysis. This simulation was based in part on extensive interactions and protocols of expert circuit analysts. The Bundy and Byrd chapter presents a simulation of a particular method of integration in integral calculus which reflects heuristics that are taught to mathematics students in the course of learning calculus.

Many of the chapters in the book have as their central concern some combination of psychological theorizing and psychological phenomenology, with different emphases in different cases. In these cases, we might expect that their primary method of investigation would be laboratory experiments, and indeed some of the authors have relied primarily on experiments; but in almost every case there have been other techniques used as well. Five of the studies rely on psychological experimental techniques as their major methodology. These are the chapters by Larkin, McCloskey, Clement, Gentner and Gentner, and Greeno. Larkin compares how expert and novice physics practitioners represent a domain in which they are trying to solve problems. She demonstrates that the two groups differ in the accuracy and speed of their solutions, and traces these differences to differences in the way in which they cognitively approach the problems. She designs a program to simulate these processes, and compares the program, with its explicit series of knowledge rules, with the performance of her subjects. This allows her to test whether the hypothesized differences in knowledge representation really do lead to the observed differences among the subjects. Gentner and

Gentner propose a theory of the way in which analogies are psychologically processed, and then use both protocol analysis and the results of experimental manipulations to show that different analogies do lead to the predicted differences in understanding of the topic domain. Greeno reviews the results of several different lines of experimentation in order to try to develop some major rules for determining how a person's knowledge representation—particularly the parsing of a domain into entities and processes—will affect his performance in a domain. Clement and McCloskey are both concerned with people's understanding of naive mechanics. McCloskey compares experts and novices in their solutions to problems presented experimentally. He then relates the differences that he finds in his experiments to the historical differences found among comparable naive theories of mechanics that flourished in the 16th century physical theories, using protocol analysis of his current subjects as further evidence for the similarity of their thinking with that of the 16th century academicians. Clement, studying very similar phenomena, relies even more upon protocol analysis, as well as on the results of experimental comparisons, to demonstrate that there is surprising commonality in the deviant, or normatively incorrect theories that college students have about the way objects move and collide.

Three of the chapters in the book rely primarily upon observation in a natural situation and on protocol analysis: the papers by Williams, Hollan and Stevens, by Young, and by diSessa. The Williams, Hollan, and Stevens chapter uses protocol analysis to trace the development of a theory of heat exchangers from a naive stage in which the model has very little structure and important variables are conflated through a series of discoveries to a considerably more sophisticated model. Young compares different models of hand calculators, and uses protocol analysis to support his theoretical arguments that different models should lead to different kinds of performances: different errors, different orders of acquisition, and so on. He buttresses his protocol analysis with observations of people using these calculators. DiSessa adopts the interesting technique of field observation in an artificial domain. He presents subjects with a computer simulation of an ideal Newtonian world, and asks them to perform simple manipulations. By observing their behavior he can discover the extent to which ideal Newtonian laws are in fact puzzling and opaque, even to MIT physics students.

The chapters discussed so far have used certain comparisons to gain leverage on the major issues of interest. These comparisons have been comparisons of different models of the same domain or comparisons of different developmental stages in understanding a given domain, including both developmental comparisons and expert-naive comparisons. The two chapters yet to be considered use a more ambitious, broader scale sort of spatio-temporal comparison. One of the studies is cross-cultural, the other cross-historical; in both cases, very disparate approaches to the same domain, either by two different cultures existing at the same time, or by the same culture at two different periods of time, are used to gain knowledge on what must be universal in human cognition concerning the world and what is free to vary. The Hutchins chapter concerns the theories of space that underlie navigation in the Solomon Islands, and compares these theories with Western theories. He uses field observation, and to some degree, protocol analysis, to guide his theorizing. He finds that the Solomon Islanders, using a mental model radically different from our western model of spatial navigation, nevertheless routinely perform extremely difficult navigation tasks. The Wiser and Carey chapter is a historical protocol study. They present persuasive evidence, both from the scientists' journals and from examining the types of experiments that these academicians conducted, that their model of the heat domain differed from ours not only in the processes postulated but also in the kinds of entities that were assumed to exist in the world. Both the impressive successes of these early scientists and also their bafflingly wrong conceptions provide an intriguing framework against which to compare the development of heat concepts in present-day children.

Thus there is represented among the authors in this volume both a considerable variety in background and techniques, and a unity of central concern. It is these together which give to mental models research the promise it holds for creating a deeper and more comprehensive understanding of human knowledge.

Albert L. Stevens
Dedre Gentner

REFERENCES

Hayes, P. J. "*Naive Physics 1—Ontology for Liquids.*" Memo, Centre pour les etudes Semantiques et Cognitives, Geneva, 1979.

1 Some Observations on Mental Models

Donald A. Norman
University of California, San Diego

One function of this chapter is to belabor the obvious; people's views of the world, of themselves, of their own capabilities, and of the tasks that they are asked to perform, or topics they are asked to learn, depend heavily on the conceptualizations that they bring to the task. In interacting with the environment, with others, and with the artifacts of technology, people form internal, mental models of themselves and of the things with which they are interacting. These models provide predictive and explanatory power for understanding the interaction. These statements hardly need be said, for they are consistent with all that we have learned about cognitive processes and, within this book, represent the major underlying conceptual theme. Nonetheless, it does not hurt to repeat them and amplify them, for the scope of the implications of this view is larger than one might think.

In the consideration of mental models we need really consider four different things: the *target system,* the *conceputal model* of that target system, the user's *mental model* of the target system, and the *scientist's conceptualization* of that mental model. The system that the person is learning or using is, by definition, the *target system.* A *conceptual model* is invented to provide an appropriate representation of the target system, appropriate in the sense of being accurate, consistent, and complete. Conceptual models are invented by teachers, designers, scientists, and engineers.

Mental models are naturally evolving models. That is, through interaction with a target system, people formulate mental models of that system. These models need not be technically accurate (and usually are not), but they must be functional. A person, through interaction with the system, will continue to modify the mental model in order to get to a workable result. Mental models will be constrained by such things as the user's technical background, previous experiences with similar systems, and the structure of the human information processing system. The *Scientist's conceptualization* of a mental model is, obviously, a model of a model.

Some Observations on Mental Models

My observations on a variety of tasks, with a wide variety of people, lead me to a few general observations about mental models:

1. Mental models are incomplete.
2. People's abilities to "run" their models are severely limited.
3. Mental models are unstable: People forget the details of the system they are using, especially when those details (or the whole system) have not been used for some period.
4. Mental models do not have firm boundaries: similar devices and operations get confused with one another.
5. Mental models are "unscientific": People maintain "superstitious" behavior patterns even when they know they are unneeded because they cost little in physical effort and save mental effort.
6. Mental models are parsimonious: Often people do extra physical operations rather than the mental planning that would allow them to avoid those actions; they are willing to trade-off extra physical action for reduced mental complexity. This is especially true where the extra actions allow one simplified rule to apply to a variety of devices, thus minimizing the chances for confusions.

Let me now expand upon these remarks. In my studies of human error and human-machine interaction, I have made reasonably extensive observation of people's interactions with a number of technological devices. The situations that I have studied are quite diverse, including such tasks as the use of calculators, computers, computer text editors, digital watches and cameras, video cameras and recorders, and the piloting of aircraft. Some of these have been studied extensively (the computer text editor), others only in informal observation. I conclude that most people's understanding of the devices they interact with is surprisingly meager, imprecisely specified, and full of inconsistencies, gaps, and idiosyncratic quirks. The models that people bring to bear on a task are not the precise, elegant models discussed so well in this book. Rather, they contain only partial descriptions of operations and huge areas of uncertainties. Moreover, people often feel uncertain of their own knowledge—even when it is in fact complete and correct—and their mental models include statements about the degree of certainty they feel for different aspects of their knowledge. Thus, a person's mental model can include knowledge or beliefs that are thought to be of doubtful validity. Some of this is characterized as "superstitious"—rules that "seem to work," even if they make no sense. These doubts and superstitions govern behavior and enforce extra caution when performing operations. This is especially apt to be the case when a person has experience with a number of different systems, all very similar, but each with some slightly different set of operating principles.

Observations of Calculator Usage

Let me briefly review some of my observations on people's use of calculating machines. I observed people using hand-held versions of four-function, algebraic, and stack calculators while they were solving a series of arithmetic problems. They were asked to "think aloud" as they did the problems and I watched and recorded their words and actions. When all problems were complete, I questioned them about the methods they had used and about their understanding of the calculator.[1] Although the people I observed were all reasonably experienced with the machines on which I tested them, they seemed to have a distrust of the calculator or in their understanding of the details of calculator mechanics. As a result, they would take extra steps or decline to take advantage of some calculator features, even when they were fully aware of their existence. Most of the people I studied had experience with several different calculators, and as a result they mixed up the features. They were often unsure which feature applied to which calculator, and had various superstitions about the operations of the calculator. Finally, their estimation of the amount of mental workload required by various strategies often determined their actions; they would perform extra operations in order to reduce the amount of mental effort. Let me provide some examples.

One of the subjects I studied (on a four-function calculator) was quite cautious. Her mental model seemed to contain information about her own limitations and the classes of errors that she could make. She commented: "I always take extra steps. I never take short cuts." She was always careful to clear the calculator before starting each problem, hitting the clear button several times. She wrote down partial results even where they could have been stored in the machine memory. In a problem involving "constant sums," she would not use the calculator's memory because:

---

[1]The inspiration for these studies came from Richard Young's analyses of calculator operation, presented at the conference that led to this book. However, his work did not include any studies of what people actually believed of the calculators or how they used them: hence my investigations. I made up problems that required only simple arithmetic operations—addition, subtraction, multiplication, and division—but some required storage registers, writing down of partial results, or planning of the sequence to avoid the need for writing or storage.

Since performing these studies and writing the paper I have learned of the closely related observations and analyses made by Mayer and Bayman (1981).

> I would not have done that because often when you play with the memory and the clear button, if you are not really clear about what it actually clears you can clear out the memory and it—it—I'm too cautious for that. I would be afraid that I'd mess up the memory.

All the people I observed had particular beliefs about their machines and about their own limitations, and as a result had developed behavior patterns that made them feel more secure in their actions, even if they knew what they were doing was not always necessary. A major pattern that seemed to apply to all my calculator studies was the need for clearing the registers and displays. The four-function calculator did need to be cleared before starting new problems, but the stack and algebraic calculators did not. Yet, these people always cleared their calculators, regardless of the type. Moreover, they would hit the clear button several times saying such things as ''you never know—sometimes it doesn't register,'' or, explaining that ''there are several registers that have to be cleared and sometimes the second and third clears do these other registers.'' (The four-function calculator that I studied does require two depressions of the CLEAR button to clear all registers.)

In an interesting complement to the excessive depressing of CLEAR to ensure that everything got cleared, during a problem with the four-function calculator where it became necessary to clear the display during the solution of a problem, one person balked at doing so, uncertain whether this would also clear the registers. All the people I observed expressed doubts about exactly what did and did not get cleared with each of the button presses or clear keys (one of the algebraic calculators has 3 different clear keys). They tended toward caution: excessively clearing when they wanted the calculator to be restarted, and exhibiting reluctance to use CLEAR during a problem for fear of clearing too much.

A similar pattern applied to the use of the ENTER button on the stack calculator. They would push it too much, often while commenting that they knew this to be excessive, but that is what they had learned to do. They explained their actions by saying such things as ''It doesn't hurt to hit it extra'' or ''I always hit it twice when I have to enter a new phrase—its just a superstition, but it makes me feel more comfortable.''

These behaviors seem to reflect some of the properties of mental models, especially the ease of generating rules that have great precision and of keeping separate the rules for a number of very similar, but different devices. The rule to hit the CLEAR button excessively allows the user to avoid keeping an accurate count of the operation. Moreover, it provides a rule that is functional on all calculators, regardless of design, and that also makes the user resistant to slips of action caused by forgetting or interference from other activities. All in all, it seems a sensible simplification that eases and generalizes what would otherwise be a more complex, machine specific set of knowledge.

When people attribute their actions to *superstition* they appear to be making direct statements about limitations in their own mental models. The statement implies uncertainty as to mechanism, but experience with the actions and outcomes. Thus, in this context, superstitious behavior indicates that the person has encountered difficulties and believes that a particular sequence of actions will reduce or eliminate the difficulty.

Finally, there seemed to be a difference in the trade-off between calculator operations and mental operations that the people I studied were willing to employ. For problems of the sort that I was studying, the four-function machine was the most difficult to use. Considerable planning was necessary to ensure that the partial answers from the subparts of the problem could be stored in the machine memory (most four-function calculators only have one memory register). As a result, the users seemed to prefer to write down partial sums and to do simple computations in their heads rather than with the machine. With the stack machine, however, the situation is reversed. Although the machine is difficult to learn, once it is learned, expert users feel confident that they can do any problem without planning: They look at the problem and immediately start keying in the digits.

On Modeling a Mental Model

Consider the problem of modeling some particular person's mental model of some particular target system. Let the particular target system be called *t*. Before we can understand how a person interacts with a target system, we need to have a good conceptualization of that system. In other words, we need a conceptual model of the system: call the conceptual model of *t*, *C(t)*. And now let the user's mental model of that target system be called *M(t)*.

We must distinguish between our conceptualization of a mental model, *C(M(t))*, and the actual mental model that we think a particular person might have, *M(t)*. To figure out what models users actually have requires one to go to the users, to do psychological experimentation and observation.[2]

In order to effectively carry out such observation and experimentation, we need to consider both representational and functional issues. Let me discuss three of the necessary properties: belief systems, observability, and predictive power.

[2]Let me warn the nonpsychologists that discovering what a person's mental model is like is not easily accomplished. For example, you cannot simply go up to the person and ask. Verbal protocols taken while the person does a task will be informative, but incomplete. Moreover, they may yield erroneous information, for people may state (and actually believe) that they believe one thing, but act in quite a different manner. All of a person's belief structures are not available to inspection, especially when some of those beliefs may be of a procedural nature. And finally, there are problems with what is called the ''demand structure'' of the situation. If you ask people why or how they have done something, they are apt to feel compelled to give a reason, even if they did not have one prior to your question. They are apt to tell you what they believe you want to hear (using their mental models of your expectations). Having then generated a reason for you, they may then believe it themselves, even though it was generated on the spot to answer your question. On-line protocols generated while in the act of problem solving and that give descriptions of activities rather than explanations are much more reliable.

These three functional factors apply to both the mental model and our conceptualization of the model, to both *M(t)* and *C(M(t))*. They can be summarized in this way:

Belief System. A person's mental model reflects his or her beliefs about the physical system, acquired either through observation, instruction, or inference. The conceptual model of the mental model *C(M(t)),* should contain a model of the relevant parts of the person's belief system.

Observability. There should be a correspondence between the parameters and states of the mental model that are accessible to the person and the aspects and states of the physical system that the person can observe. In the conceptual model of the mental model, this means that there should be a correspondence between parameters and observable states of *C(M(t))* and the observable aspects and states of *t*.

Predictive Power. The purpose of a mental model is to allow the person to understand and to anticipate the behavior of a physical system. This means that the model must have predictive power, either by applying rules of inference or by procedural derivation (in whatever manner these properties may be realized in a person); in other words, it should be possible for people to ''run'' their models mentally. This means that the conceptual mental model must also include a model of the relevant human information processing and knowledge structures that make it possible for the person to use a mental model to predict and understand the physical system.

On the Relationship between Conceptual and Mental Models

Conceptual models are devised as tools for the understanding or teaching of physical systems. Mental models are what people really have in their heads and what guides their use of things. Ideally, there ought to be a direct and simple relationship between the conceptual and the mental model. All too often, however, this is not the case.

That a mental model reflects the user's beliefs about the physical system seems obvious and has already been discussed. What is not so obvious is the correspondence that should hold between the mental model and a conceptual model of the physical system, that is, between *M(t)* and *C(t)*.

In the literature on mathematical learning models, Greeno and Steiner (1964) introduced the notion of ''identifiability.'' That is, they pointed out that a useful model will have a correspondence between the parameters and states of the model and the operation of the target system. I find that these remarks apply equally well to the problems of mental models. It is important that there be a correspondence between the parameters and states of one's model and the things one is attempting to describe. This restriction does pose some strong constraints upon the nature of the mental model. Certain kinds of mental models will be ruled out if the identification cannot be easily made.

A major purpose of a mental model is to enable a user to predict the operation of a target system. As a result, the predictive power of such a model is of considerable concern. Although great stress is laid in this book to the notion of "running" a conceptual or mental model, it should also be possible to make predictions by straightforward inference, a declarative form of predictability, rather than the implied notion of procedural running of a model. Whatever the mechanism, it is clear that prediction is one of the major aspects of one's mental models, and this must be captured in any description of them.

The System Image

In the ideal world, when a system is constructed, the design will be based around a conceptual model. This conceptual model should govern the entire human interface with the system, so that the image of that system seen by the user is consistent, cohesive, and intelligible. I call this image the *system image* to distinguish it from the conceptual model upon which it is based, and the mental model one hopes the user will form of the system. The instruction manuals and all operation and teaching of the system should then be consistent with this system image. Thus, the instructors of the system would teach the underlying conceptual model to the user and, if the system image is consistent with that model, the user's mental model will also be consistent.

For this to happen, the conceptual model that is taught to the user must fulfill three criteria:

Learnability
Functionality
Usability

What good is a conceptual model that is too difficult to learn? Or a model that has little functionality, failing to correspond to the system image or failing to predict or explain the important aspects of the target system? Or what of a conceptual model that cannot easily be used, given the properties of the human information processing structure with its limited short-term memory and limited ability to do computations?

Alas, all too often there is no correspondence among the conceptual model of the system that guided the designer, the system image that is presented to the user, the material in the instructional manuals that is taught to the user, and the mental models of the user. Indeed, for many target systems, there is no single conceptual model that was followed in the design. The stack calculator gives us a good positive instance where a conceptual design was neatly implemented into a consistent physical device, with the operations and instructions all based around the same basic model. It should be no surprise, therefore, that in my studies, users of this calculator were most confident of their abilities.

Summary

The moral of this story is that it is important for us to distinguish among several different kinds of models and conceptualizations. Our conceptualization of a target system should not be confused with the mental model that a user creates of that system. The designer's conceptualization may also differ from the image that the system itself presents to the user. In the ideal world, the system image will be consistent with the designer's conceptualization, and the user's mental model will thereby be consistent with both.

People's mental models are apt to be deficient in a number of ways, perhaps including contradictory, erroneous, and unnecessary concepts. As designers, it is our duty to develop systems and instructional materials that aid users to develop more coherent, useable mental models. As teachers, it is our duty to develop conceptual models that will aid the learner to develop adequate and appropriate mental models. And as scientists who are interested in studying people's mental models, we must develop appropriate experimental methods and discard our hopes of finding neat, elegant mental models, but instead learn to understand the messy, sloppy, incomplete, and indistinct structures that people actually have.

ACKNOWLEDGMENT

This research was conducted under Contract N00014-79-C-0323, NR 157-437 with the Personnel and Training Research Programs of the Office of Naval Research, and was sponsored by the Office of Naval Research and the Air Force Office of Scientific Research. I thank Sondra Buffett for her suggestions for the manuscript.

REFERENCES

Greeno, J. G., & Steiner, T. E. Markovian processes with identifiable states: General considerations and applications to all-or-none learning. *Psychometrika,* 1964, *29,* 309–333. (An easier treatment is provided in the chapter on identifiability in Restle, F., & Greeno, J. G., *Introduction to mathematical psychology*. Reading, Mass.: Addison-Wesley, 1970.)

Mayer, R. E., & Bayman, P. Psychology of calculator languages: A framework for describing differences in users' knowledge. *Communications of the ACM,* 1981, *24,* 511–520.

2 Phenomenology and the Evolution of Intuition

Andrea A. diSessa
Massachusetts Institute of Technology

INTRODUCTION

In axiomatic mathematics it has long been recognized that beneath all the complex of definitions and theorems must exist a special layer which serves as foundation for the rest. Elements of this layer, undefined terms or axioms, etc., have the property of being primitive in the sense that they are not explicitly explained or justified within the system. Quite evidently the selection of this layer plays a fundamental role in determining the character of the system. In science as well, though somewhat less prominently displayed, selecting the primitives of a theory is an important and complex process.

This chapter is about primitive notions which similarly stand without significant explanatory substructure or justification. The system of which these primitives are a part, however, is cognitive, not a scientific theory or axiomatic system. We are after simple knowledge structures which are monolithic in the sense that they are evoked as a whole and their meanings, when evoked, are relatively independent of context. Because of this character we shall naturally find such primitives, like axioms, at the root of many explanations and justifications. In addition to explanation and justification, however, we are concerned with the important issue of control in human reasoning, not only what are the basic terms in which a situation will be viewed, but how does one come to view it in that way? The context of exploring these ideas is physics, specifically the evolution and function of primitives in physics understanding, from naive to novice to expert.

Goethe gave an account of the development of scientific explanation which can serve to bring out the main features of the sketch of development in understanding which we shall propose. Goethe's claim is that scientific explanation begins with common sense observation, a principal characteristic of which is its appearance as disparate and isolated special cases. What follows is a process of sifting through the cases, finding successively the more and more general and fundamental ones which serve as principles, explaining the more special cases. In the end, one reaches the highest level which Goethe insists cannot be purely abstract, but still must be phenomenological. Below, Goethe (1978) describes these ultimate explanatory elements:[1]

> We call these primordial phenomena, because nothing appreciable by the senses lies beyond them, on the contrary, they are perfectly fit to be considered as a fixed point to which we first ascend [in the process of finding what is fundamental], and from which we may, in like manner, descend to the commonest case of everyday experience. [p. 72].

Something very much like primordial phenomena, we prefer the terminology "phenomenological primitives" (p-prims for short), are the central elements in the examples and analyses to follow. In brief the pattern we see is as follows. In the course of learning, physics-naive students begin with a rich but heterarchical (none being significantly more important than others) collection of recognizable phenomena in terms of which they see the world and sometimes explain it. These are p-prims. Some of these are compatible with the formal physics and are thus "encouraged," acquiring what we might call a higher priority than the others in terms of being readily used in physical analyses and explanations. In contrast to Goethe's philosophy of science, we do not propose that any of these are in themselves laws of physics. Instead they can serve a variety of cognitive functions in a physicist's knowing physics; for example, they can serve as heuristic cues to specific, more technical analyses. Typically, a process of abstraction including an expansion of domain of applicability accompanies this increase in priority and attachment to "textbook" concepts. In complementary manner, some p-prims lose status, very often being "cut apart," explained in terms of more fundamental, higher priority ideas.

What we wish to take from Goethe is the sense that direct experience in only mildly altered form can play a significant role in the understanding of "abstract" matters and his sense of continuity from naive to scientific apprehension of the world. The notion of evolution along the dimension of selecting some naively recognizable phenomena for more systematic and general application as knowledge structures will also be important. What we wish to leave behind are assumptions that phenomenology must be manifest in explicit science. Indeed, it will appear in most of our examples that the work being done by p-prims is covert, perhaps necessarily so.

---

[1]An article along lines similar to this paper, though not cognitively motivated, is Zajonc (1976).

At another level entirely, that of cognitive modeling, the choice of primitives in this chapter warrants comment. In particular, the process of recognition of phenomena is central. In addition to being motivated by the examples to follow, there is a significant body of experimental data which suggests recognition is a fundamental operation of the human cognitive apparatus. Recent work in facial recognition even suggests specific neurophysiological support (Carey & Diamond, 1980). Thus we consider it a good candidate for a "black box" to be used in theorizing about more complex cognitive activities. The points we make relate to what is recognized when, and how that contributes to physical reasoning; the process of recognition itself remains opaque.

The empirical basis for this work comes mostly from a series of in-depth interviews (about a dozen 1-hour sessions per individual) with four M.I.T. undergraduates taking freshman physics. The interpretations we offer motivate and explain the ideas we propose; they are not offered in proof. For these purposes, citations from protocols are paraphrased to increase clarity and brevity, and we also use informal observations made outside the study.

SPRINGINESS

M. was proposed the following problem:

> If a ball is dropped, it picks up speed and hence kinetic energy. When the ball hits the floor, however, it stops (before bouncing upward again). At that instant, there is no kinetic energy since there is no motion. Where did the energy go?

To a physicist, the analysis is straightforward: The ball and floor are mutually compressing on impact. That compression, just like the compression of a spring, stores energy in mechanical distortion. That is where the energy goes when the ball comes to a stop. The distortion, in fact, is what pushes the ball back up into the air on rebound.

M. was a quite respectable physics student whose analysis of the falling ball, gravitational potential energy gradually converted into kinetic, was clear. She had herself made the observation that a bouncing ball must stop at some point before its rebound upward. Further, she had an unequivocal commitment to conservation of energy and accepted the question about what happens at the bottom of the fall as a natural, even obvious one to ask.

M. quickly discarded gravitational potential energy as a repository for the "lost" energy and proceeded with the working hypothesis that the floor or earth must get the energy. As she appeared to be ignoring the role of springiness, the interviewer tried to prompt her by focusing on the rebound—the compression "pushing back"—thinking that a salient feature of springiness. "What causes the ball to acquire a velocity after it has stopped?" This involved her in elaborate rationalizations for the energy not staying in the floor. The gist of her clearest argument was that the floor is essentially an infinite mass (the earth) which in its resistance to moving could not permanently "accept" the energy and therefore "returned" it to the ball. She had enough sense of physical mechanism to be disturbed by her own almost animistic explanation, but could not offer any other.

Seeing no progress in this line, the interviewer offered a straightforward explanation. "Think of a situation with a mass on the top end of a spring, where the mass and the spring fall to the floor." M. spontaneously continued the explanation; spring compresses, stores energy, pushes mass back up. Then the interviewer continued. "The ball is really the same thing, with the 'squishing' of the ball replacing the spring's action."

Although the mechanism of spring and mass was clear to M., she countered that, though a tennis ball might bounce in that way, she did not really believe bouncing could generally work like that. "What about a ping-pong ball? It doesn't squish."

The interviewer responded that it really did, but only a very small amount. However, if one took a strobe photograph and analyzed it carefully, one would see compression.

M. was undaunted. "How about a steel ball bearing?" The interviewer had to admit that depending on the materials involved, it might be the floor that did the squishing to absorb energy. But the principle would be the same.

M.'s final example to refute springiness was a glass ball on a glass plate which she knew to bounce very well—and yet glass would surely shatter rather than squish. Running out of time (and arguments) the interviewer terminated the session assuring that springiness was really there.

The next week M. was again asked about the bouncing ball. During the week the physics class had started kinetic theory, and she said she had a clearer idea where the energy was because of that; it must be in the internal kinetic energy of the molecules of the ball and/or floor! She did not mention springiness. (Though it is possible that energy could be transformed to internal kinetic energy of this sort, heat, that cannot account for bouncing. There is no mechanism to return the energy to gross motion.)

Rigidity and springiness are the p-prims at issue here. M. does not see springiness in the ball bounce. Moreover, her counterexamples show this is no accidental oversight. She is used to thinking about "hard" objects as being rigid and appeals to her common-sense characterizations of everyday phenomena as self-evident justification: steel is hard (rigid); glass is also hard and, in fact, responds to attempts to deform it by breaking. Within her intuitive frame there is little point in asking why steel is rigid and even less in asking for a justification of the applicability of the concept to the world at all. Rigidity is simply a property which she knows, by example, some objects have.

In contrast, physics experts have a much lower priority attached to the phenomenon of rigidity, although it will be assumed in restricted contexts, typically in making geometric calculations. This low priority is principled: relative rigidity is an effect explained by much higher priority ideas such as forces (e.g., intermolecular electrostatic forces). Physicists have a strong and particular sense for physical mechanism which includes the fact that looking at the world in terms of forces is fundamentally the right kind of explanation for physical phenomena.[2] A physicist views rigidity as irrelevant to any deep explanation of how things happen.

Springiness is another matter. It is not only consistent with the highest priority (Newtonian) physical ideas, it provides a convenient organizing conception which frees one from the necessity of always treating spring-like phenomena in terms of idiosyncratic situational details such as how and where exactly physical deformation is taking place. It serves as a macro-model which summarizes the causality (deformation → restoring force → rebound) and energy flow (deforming force drains energy into potential energy which is liberated as the deformation relaxes).

For the expert, springiness is a more powerful explanatory concept than rigidity, but it has definite limits. In the physical world there is no system that has exactly the properties needed to match the idealization, e.g. energy content dependent only on displacement (not velocity). Thus a physicist is not surprised if a numerical prediction made with the concept is in error by a few percent. Even more, his understanding of how springiness relates to more fundamental concepts alerts him to circumstances when it will fail drastically. For example, a long steel rod bouncing on concrete involves wave motion internal to the rod rather than simply uniform compression. This means internal energy during the bounce does involve significant kinetic energy of the molecules, albeit in a coherent form rather than M.'s "kinetic gas" image. An observation like this is sufficient to cause an expert to abandon macro-springiness and begin to construct a more elaborate special model.

Control of reasoning is an important issue here, and it is worth abstracting the function of springiness in expert thought with regard to this. By seeing the phenomenon of springiness in a situation, an expert brings to bear a default macro-model, sparing a great deal of situation-specific reasoning. The more "clever" the mechanism which cues springiness to recognition (triggering it only when it is a good approximation), the better off is the expert. But as we assume that the cuing mechanism is relatively simple so as to be quick, its pattern matching will not be perfectly reliably correlated with circumstances under which springiness will prove useful. Hence, although it has a relatively high priority, under certain circumstances it will defer, likely to higher priority concepts (in this case probably micro-modeling on the basis of discrete masses and intermolecular forces or some continuum approximation thereof).

---

[2]To explain how this sense is encoded is part of the point of this paper. Our proposal, in brief, is that explanatory knowledge of a certain type has a particular place in a priority hierarchy.

Implicit in these observations is a two-fold structuring of the concept of priority. First of all, we must differentiate flow of control to and away from the use of springiness. The former, which we call *cuing priority,* has to do with how likely the idea is to be profitable. Springiness is much more consistent with a Newtonian world view than rigidity, so in expert thought it will be used with less provocation than rigidity—it has a higher cuing priority than rigidity. Once cued, the resistance to abandonment is a second kind of priority which we call *reliability priority*. This second kind of priority is closer to being a proper technical sense for the notion of "more fundamental." Springiness, as we pointed out, is abandoned by experts relatively easily compared to such perspectives as provided by, for example, force and energy.

The second structuring of priority comes from the simple observation that specifics of the situation are relevant to deciding the priority of the use of an idea. In other words, priorities are context-dependent. In this sense, it is even clearer that there is a difference between M.'s priorities as regards springiness, and an expert's. M. certainly views a spring as springy, yet it does not occur to her at all to see a bouncing ball in terms of springiness. M.'s perception of springiness must change to become like an expert's specifically with respect to enlarging the set of contexts which cue the idea. In a similar way, reliability priority must change. Although it is not demonstrated by the protocol, M. does not know very much about the circumstances (context) under which even a spring should not be regarded as springy.

The context dependency of priorities allows us to make more apt descriptions of the class of "fundamental" ideas. The high reliability priority of conservation of energy is better described as "in a context where energy is applicable, one must heed conclusions drawn within its perspective." In contrast, conclusions drawn on the basis of springiness might be ignored even if it seems the concept is applicable, particularly if those conclusions are in conflict with those of a higher reliability perspective.[3]

It seems extremely plausible that the knowledge which structures reliability priority should regularly point to specific alternatives or refinements based on context. This kind of chaining of control pathways will be important in later examples. For now we can illustrate the idea by hypothesizing that one way the context which cues springiness could be augmented is that another p-prim present in naive students, "bouncing," comes to defer very readily to springiness. Bouncing never comes to have a very high reliability priority, but serves its function as a rapid heuristic control link to springiness. Because of its low

[3]The language used here, "drawing conclusions," "ignoring," and "heeding" is unnecessarily anthropomorphic and suggests a relatively elaborate reasoning process. In reality, of course, what goes on is likely unconscious and too quick and simple to be dignified by such high level terms. We are after low level control of reasoning mechanisms, and short of developing a technical vocabulary here, we rely on metaphoric use of these familiar, but higher level terms.

reliability priority, an expert would be unlikely to appeal to bouncing in any explanatory way, and its effect might well be consigned to the "junk category" of intuition or "just knowing" e.g. that springiness is involved.[4,5]

The kind of development proposed here poses interesting pedagogical problems. Reorganization and change of function of knowledge structures seems less obviously amenable to external manipulation than "giving students new knowledge." The case in point is M.'s resistance to seeing a bouncing ball as a spring. How could one convince her that one should do so? In the absence of a more elaborate theory, we propose only that the process must be an extended one in which the coherence and success of the evolving new control system gradually compels reorganization of priorities.

M. gave additional force to her arguments against springiness by appealing to other well-known phenomena characterized in common sense terms. Harder objects typically bounce better. If the "give" of objects accounts for bouncing, how is it that things with a lot of give, soft things like clay, don't bounce at all, and things with little give, hard things like ball bearings, bounce so well?

From a physicist's point of view, M. is making a mistake here which is common in naive and novice students—confusing softness (a small modulus of elasticity) with lack of reversibility (hysteresis) which causes smaller rebound. There is no necessary correlation between the two. In everyday objects with everyday forces, however, softer objects undergo greater deformation which, in turn, is often associated with more loss of energy, greater hysteresis; objects with more give generally bounce less well.

Though it is tempting to reify this conclusion (softer objects bounce less well) into part of a naive concept of springiness, M.'s protocol here showed a pattern of examples first (clay, steel, etc.) with conclusions following. This is in contrast to the issue of whether bouncing involves springiness where examples followed pronouncements and were apparently drawn up in an attempt to justify her impressions. Her mistaken understanding of the character of springiness here would seem to be emerging from on the spot reasoning based on well-known phenomena. The following interpretation suggests itself: M. perceives a family resemblance among the various cases of objects giving when stressed, a naive p-prim which we might call "squishiness." In order to elaborate her own understanding of the phenomenon, she examines a few typical cases of it and concludes rebound decreases with softness. It is important that hysteresis, lack of

---

[4]Cuing and reliability priorities are very general control constructs, and we do not mean to reserve them for phenomenology. But they seem particularly well adapted to explain control of reasoning where a large number of competing perspectives might apply. Motivated by some of the same considerations, Clemenson (1981) has developed a control system which one can understand as a particular version of structured priorities in the context of a computer-implemented problem solver.

[5]Incidentally, one sees an important coherence in the naive acceptance of a world including rigid objects and the acceptance of bouncing as a primitive which needs no mechanistic explanation.

reversibility, is not salient for her, and that she does not pursue the question of *why* such a correlation holds. It seems plausible she might now simply remember the conclusion. But even if she does not, her vocabulary of phenomena and typical examples thereof means she would likely rederive the result on future occasions.

A final excerpt from a protocol points to intermediate stages in the change of function and reorganization of priorities on the road from naive springiness and rigidity to those of the expert. T. was given the following problem after demonstrating that he was clearly beyond M.'s belief in rigidity and unrefined sense of springiness.

> A pencil can be balanced horizontally on a finger. The interesting fact is that the configuration is stable under small pertubations; when pushed, it returns to horizontal. Why?

The problem is tricky because it is very tempting to assimilate it to a "standard balance" geometry, an object pivoting on its center of mass. The pencil pivot is not only not at the center of mass, but even moves as the pencil rolls back and forth on the finger. Applying standard methods of energy, etc., with the false assumption of pivot at center of mass does not predict stable balancing.

Some students take stable balancing as a primitive phenomenon, "that's the way balancing works," and never bother using textbook physics on the problem. At best they appeal vaguely to sanctioned principles like symmetry. T. was also more advanced than that. Though he fell into the trap of the false geometric model, that slip allowed a good glimpse of his rather well-developed, though not quite expert-like notion of springiness.

T. started with a fairly long, of course unsuccessful, attempt at using forces, torques and detailed energy considerations. Searching for another way to look at the problem he focused on the process of pushing one end down a bit, thus doing work on it, and then on the conversion of the "stored" energy into kinetic energy as the pencil is released to swing back to its horizontal position. T. described the situation as "like a spring." More than a description, he proposed that analogy as an explanation, we would say appealing to springiness as a primitive explanatory phenomenon. When queried about how comfortable he was with that as physics explanation, he indicated that he really was a bit reluctant to make it and suspected there might be a better way to explain it.

T. has evidently abstracted springiness to the level of macro-model for energy storage and restoring. We also would interpret the fact that he thinks to use it in this nonspring situation as indicating he has expanded, perhaps too much, the contexts in which he appeals to the idea. Possibly T. directly recognized springiness in the pattern of response of the system to pertubation ("oscillation" cues "springiness"), or possibly at the abstract level of energy storage. Either way, this suggests his cuing priorities have advanced, and he is not just bringing springiness to bear without first seeing its relevance. His tentative use of the concept as an explanation also indicates a substantial reliability priority, probably more than a naive person, but that priority is clearly not structured like an expert's. An expert would be looking for a deformation to decide whether springiness was relevant.

In summary, we see the development of the p-prim springiness from naive to novice to expert in the following way. The everyday phenomenon of springiness gradually becomes abstracted and modified from a root "squishiness" to a model[6] of an idealized spring-like causal and energy storage mechanism which helps physicists avoid unnecessary, detailed, situation-specific considerations. Cuing mechanisms to springiness become changed, specifically broadening to include all bouncing, and specifically made narrower to exclude large hysteresis examples like clay. An expert will use the phenomenon in some cases as a primitive explanation, but also must defer to other ways of viewing the situation if he is being careful, i.e., if he is requiring his analysis involve only notions with the highest reliability priority.

OHM'S P-PRIM

> Think of a vacuum cleaner whose intake nozzle you hold in your hand. If you put your hand over the nozzle, will the pitch of the sound you hear from the motor go up or down?

There are three common classes of answers to this problem. (In this case we do not deal with expert solutions.)

1. Some subjects do not understand enough of the mechanism of sound production to answer reasonably. Typically an analogy is made to the tuning of a musical instrument and pitch is assumed to be related to length of pipes, etc., instead of directly to the speed of the motor. This class will be of no interest. The other two classes draw opposite conclusions about the change of pitch, interestingly for essentially the same reason.

2. The second class has the pitch (speed) of the motor reduced. This is attributed to an interference with the action of the motor by the hand and is occasionally explicated with reference to examples like an electric drill slowing down when the bit is inserted in wood. Almost never is there any explanation beyond that.

---

[6]In contrast to other kinds of models, this type is not constructed on the spot; its usefulness is in serving as an archetype. Furthermore, it is essentially monolithic and not generally open for inspection in terms of more primitive elements. Some researchers call similar knowledge structures "schemata."

3. Others answer that the motor must speed up—the motor is being interfered with, and the motor must "work harder" (or some equivalent phrasing) because of the interference.

We explain both of these answers using a primitive explanatory phenomenon we call Ohm's P-prim. (The reason for the terminology will become apparent.) It comprises three elements, an impetus, a resistance and a result. The impetus acts through the resistance to produce the result somewhat as schematized in Fig. 2.1. These elements are related through a collection of qualitative correlations such as an increase in impetus implies an increase in result, an increase in resistance means a decrease in result, etc. Recognition of the phenomenon in the vacuum cleaner situation is compellingly simple. The motor provides a model impetus, the hand a clear blocking interference, and the spinning of the motor coupled to the flow of air is the result. Class two answers appeal directly to Ohm's P-prim as an explanation for the slowing of the motor. The features of the situation are so obviously those of Ohm's P-prim, that some subjects report remembering that the pitch goes down. (In fact, it goes up.) Like the low-level processing which causes visual illusions by responding to cues which are not always associated with genuine features of an image, the p-prim can cause a "conceptual illusion," so that the person perceives interference where there is none.

Class three explanations draw the correct conclusion, that the motor speed and pitch go up, based on the same Ohm's P-prim illusion, but adding an anthropomorphic feedback loop: As the interference (resistance) increases, the motor must increase its effort as if to make up for increased resistance. Anthropomorphism of this sort is frequently offered by physics-naive people as a primitive explanation, but its priority in the context of purely mechanical situations drops quickly as technical sophistication increases. In many cases, it appears that this anthropomorphism is forced as a rationalization for what they remember, speeding up, in view of the evident Ohm's P-prim which predicts slowing down. Some of these subjects admit sensitivity to anthropomorphism's defects. Some even spontaneously wonder out loud how the motor "knows" what's going on, or comment on the lack of a mechanism for a motor to "want" to produce some result. To support our contention that class three explanations are composite Ohm's P-prim plus anthropomorphism, some subjects after questioning and rejecting their own anthropomorphism are left with Ohm's P-prim and begin to question their remembrance that the pitch goes up.

FIG. 2.1. The Ohm's P-prim.

We take Ohm's P-prim to be a very commonly used, high priority p-prim. Contexts of application range from pushing harder in order to make objects move faster, to modeling interpersonal relations such as a parent's offering more and more encouragement to counter a child's offering increasing resistance. Although we think it provides a qualitative model and, at early stages in learning, a self-contained explanation for many more formal concepts in physics, we will focus on only one, Ohm's Law, I = E/R: the current flow in a circuit, I, is proportional to the voltage (also called potential), E, and inversely proportional to the resistance, R. The interpretation of I = E/R in terms of the Ohm's P-prim is straightforward and a good match with other characteristics of the physical quantities. Voltage is an independent impetus which causes a dependent amount of current to flow as a result. Resistance modulates current flow in the appropriate way.

This interpretation of I = E/R is so natural that it is easy to mistake it for understanding the equation. But, though physics texts implicitly and sometimes explicitly invoke it for its mnemonic effect and because proper attachment of the Ohm's P-prim to the equation makes qualitative reasoning about varying quantities quick and easy, still the interpretation is only an interpretation. What follows is a typical textbook invocation of the p-prim and a warning that it (particularly its causality) is not inherent in the physics (Ford, 1968).

> A simple way to look at the law is to picture the potential as the "motive power" (the British word for potential, "tension" is suggestive), the current as the resulting effect. Doubling the potential across a circuit element causes a doubling of the amount of charge that flows through it in one second. This assignment of cause and effect, of course, is only an aid to visualization, and has no deep meaning. [p. 551].

The author deliberately uses the metaphor "motive power" to enforce the impetus interpretation of potential, and he describes current as the resulting effect before warning that this too is metaphorical. His remarks also remind us that these associations were almost certainly in the minds of the scientists who first discovered such laws and then codified their interpretations in technical terms chosen to convey the sense, like "tension" and "resistance."

In terms of our theory sketch we can summarize as follows: The Ohm's P-prim becomes profitably involved with the physical Ohm's Law as a model of causality and qualitative relations compatible with it. It initially serves novices as an explanation of the law and comes to be cued in circumstances were I = E/R is applicable providing rapid qualitative analysis. With experts the p-prim is still useful,[7] but has low reliability priority; it will not be identified with the law or used to explain it (except as a deliberate analogy).

---

[7]One might think experts would drop such interpretations, except for pedagogical purposes. On the contrary, at least in some circumstances they invent more of them! Electrical engineers often

ROLLING AND PIVOTING

Consider two identical coins with markers to distinguish up from down as in Fig. 2.2a. If the bottom coin is held fixed and the top rolled without slipping around to the bottom of the fixed coin (2b), which way will its arrow point?

Subjects answering this question often suffer the false intuition, at least initially, that the arrow will point downward whereas the correct answer is that it will point upward. Figure 2.3 depicts a one-to-one correspondence argument, joining points of the coins where they touch, which indicates that in rolling, the top of the moving coin must wind up touching the bottom of the fixed coin. The only way to satisfy this constraint is to have the final position of the rolling coin with the arrow pointing up.

I believe there are two routes to the false intuition that the arrow will point downward. The first is to see the coin's gross motion as a movement of 180° around the center of the fixed coin, then to somehow link or confuse that motion with the rotation of the coin about its center. This route is not interesting here, and we will not pursue it.

To explain the second route, we begin by considering an archetypical analysis of a rolling situation as illustrated in Fig. 2.4. The analysis is basically an image of the disc or wheel "laying off" its circumference on the ground. Thus distance rolled on the ground is the same as the length around the circumference which has touched the ground. This makes evident a simple proportionality between distance rolled and amount of turning of the wheel as shown in the last frame of Fig. 2.4. Though simple, this is an important analysis which is used (and probably learned) in elementary physics courses.

The hypothesis is that this analysis, once learned, is cued by the simple recognition of "rolling." Thus subjects presented with the coin problem recognize rolling and apply the analysis. (Whether "applying" means simply to assert the result or run through the analysis anew in the archetypical situation is moot.) Many subjects report straightforwardly that "the moving coin rolls off half its circumference and thus must have turned 180°."

In moving toward expert-like understanding, we can imagine developing other analyses to debug the faulty one, possibly with new phenomenological cues to their use. If one imagines a coin rolling on a square as in Fig. 2.5, one recognizes a new phenomenon at the corner, pivoting. This phenomenon ordinarily has a lower priority than rolling, but is naively recognizable, at least in its pure form.

The analysis which could be cued by pivoting is that, in pivoting around a

---

speak of a resistor as a kind of transformer which converts current flow into voltage. "A known current causes a potential drop IR in flowing through a resistance." This causality, which is the reverse of the Ohm's P-prim interpretation, is equally metaphorical. It will be assumed when convenient, but ascribed no deep meaning.

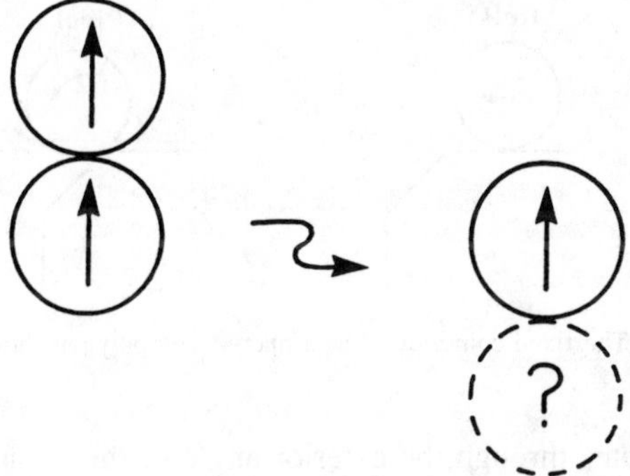

FIG. 2.2. Rolling a coin about a fixed one.

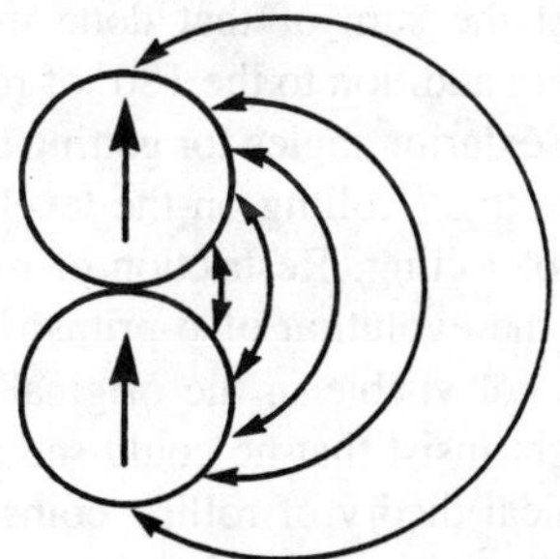

FIG. 2.3. Joining points which touch.

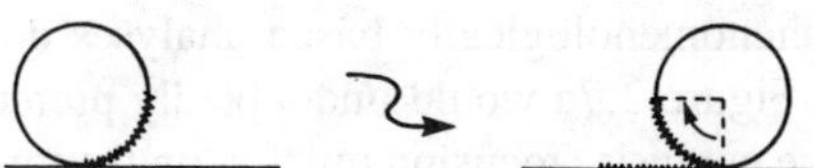

FIG. 2.4. A wheel ''laying off'' its circumference in rolling.

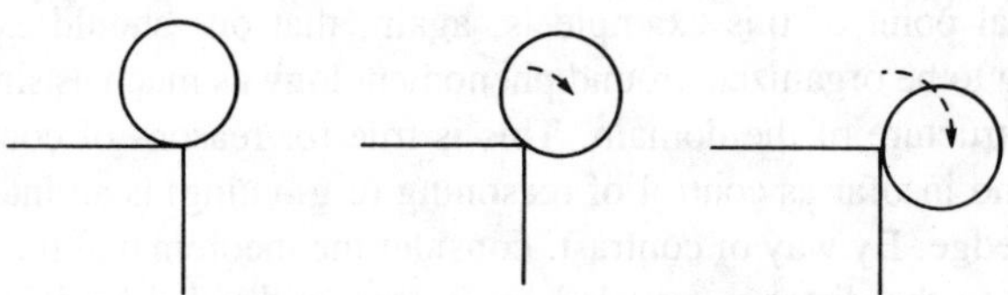

FIG. 2.5. A coin pivoting on a corner.

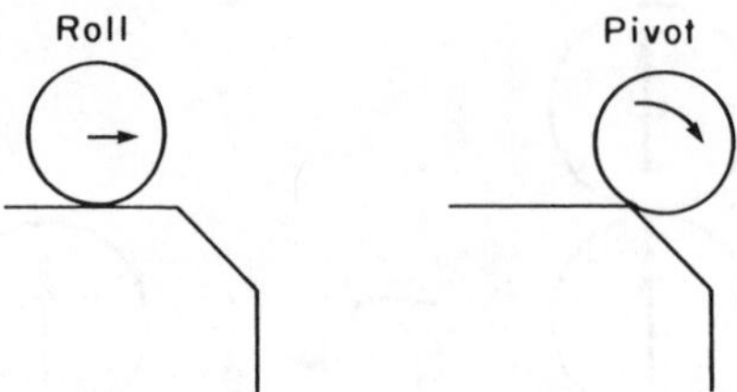

FIG. 2.6. The fixed coin viewed as a many-sided polygon shows pivoting.

corner, a coin rotates through the exterior angle of the corner, 90° in Fig. 2.5. (Watch the tangent to the coin at the vertex to see this clearly.)

Figure 2.6 shows a slight modifcation of the original coin problem which makes evident pivoting as well as rolling. Simply consider the fixed coin's perimeter to be a many-sided polygon instead of an exact circle. In fact, the net turning of the coin is just the sum of that done in rolling and that done in pivoting. One can see that in addition to the 180° of rolling, pivoting contributes 180° (that is the sum of the exterior angles for getting around half the fixed coin's circumference). Notice that this ''rolling-on-the-level'' is a restricted version of the original phenomenon of rolling. Restriction of meaning like this should be expected to be typical of the evolution of p-prims. Notice also that to the untrained eye, pivoting was not visible in the original coin problem, although a coin-rolling ''expert'' might insist that he could see it; it *has* to be there. More than that, a more economical theory of rolling coins might see even rolling as pivoting (consider the *rolling* coin as well to be a many-sided polygon). One could have a theory of rolling coins based only on pivoting. In that case the initially more salient phenomenon of rolling would be drastically reduced in priority.

It is interesting to play with variations on this problem as domains of applicability of these phenomenologically based analyses do not precisely match their cuing contexts. Figure 2.7a would undoubtedly preferentially cue the one-to-one correspondence analysis (focusing quickly on the top point of the top coin matching the bottom point of the fixed coin). Figure 2.7b might cue pivoting (two turns of 180°) rather than rolling even for naive subjects. Neither of these would likely cue rolling, although 7b with its visual emphasis on 90° might provoke the false 180° intuition through the gross motion/rotation confusion.

The general point of this example is, again, that one should expect expert understanding to be organized around phenomenology as much as simply around the abstract structure of the domain. This is true for reasons of continuity with naive ideas and insofar as control of reasoning (e.g. cuing) is an integral part of expert knowledge. By way of contrast, consider the theorem that the turning of a coin is equal to the distance traveled by its center divided by its radius. This theorem subsumes, but also hides, both pivoting and rolling.

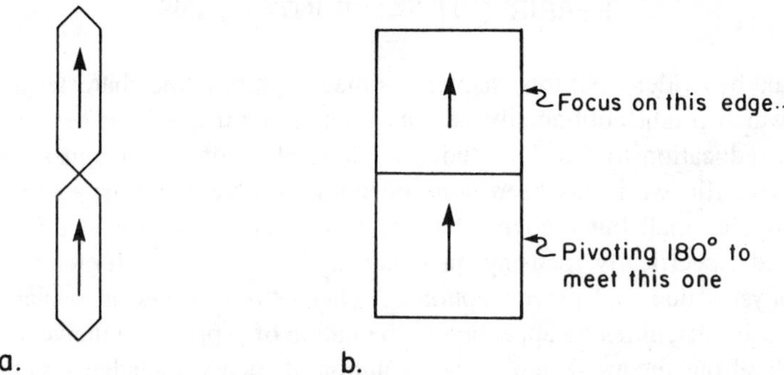

FIG. 2.7. Versions of the coin problem cue different analyses.

A NOTE ON ABSTRACTION

We have said little about the process of "abstaction" through which naive phenomena become changed to serve as expert p-prims. So as not to leave this box entirely black, consider a thought experiment. A novice has been learning about potential energy, perhaps even in the context of springs, and decides to run through a squish-unsquish cycle in his head. He imagines his hand slowly pushing the coils of the spring together realizing his agency and the work he is doing on the spring—pumping energy into it. Simultaneously he feels that the spring "wants" to cause his hands to fly apart. The energy is not gone and in releasing the spring one can feel the work it is doing, now on his hand.[8] (M. probably had gotten this far; she understood springs. But as far as priorities, her "squishiness" dominates in contexts other than literal springs.)

Notice how the elements of the interpretation, in particular the set of features to be attended to, are mostly drawn from common sense, and yet the combined effect is to serve as the model of causality and energy storage which is the function proposed for the expert p-prim. The thought sequence binds together in an appropriate way the elements of previous knowledge which serve as basis for the interpretation. The structure of that combination is the new element for the student. That structure is locally justified because it is seen merely as a description of a known phenomenon, the action of a spring.

The abstraction going on here is essentially the selection of a conventional interpretation of an everyday event. It is abstract only in that the "actors" in the phenomenon (e.g., person, spring) are subordinated to become instances fulfilling their "role" in the interpretation (e.g., cause of squishing, thing that deforms).

[8]Though this thought experiment was fabricated, in the time since this paper was originally written several students have recounted strikingly similar episodes. These should appear in future publications.

PERSISTENT FALSE INTUITIONS

It should be evident that this chapter is aimed at probing the character of knowledge which might colloquially be called intuition. It has long been a goal of physics education to develop students' physical intuition, though surprisingly little scientific work has been done on intuition of either novices or experts. Recently, a small but recognizable wave of interest roughly in this area has appeared, specifically focusing on systematic difficulties with elementary college physics due to "preconceptions." This section offers an explanation of three such difficulties by appealing to the notion of p-prim and the very coarsest outlines of our theory-sketch of the evolution of such knowledge structures. To wit, we identify p-prims likely to be responsible for each of the difficulties in the sense that the p-prims involved are all high priority naive phenomena which require drastic reduction of priority or rearrangement of priority structure to allow expert-like understanding.

"Dying Away" Aristotle explicitly cited the dying away of certain actions like the dying away of sound from a bell (his metaphor) as a primitive element of analysis that one does not seek to explain but simply is so. Despite the fact that friction is a named and relatively well-known cause for many forms of this dying away, we think that humans early in their lives take the phenomenon as a p-prim, effectively adopting a stance similar to Aristotle's toward it. Reducing the priority of this idea, and in particular having it defer to dissipative mechanisms, is not a simple task. Such mechanisms are hardly salient in a rolling ball or in a struck bell. Taking "dying away" as the natural way of things causes or at least contributes to the well-known tendency of naive and even novice students to assume a constant force is needed to maintain a constant velocity, and other such nonphysical analyses (Clement, 1979; Cohen, 1974; Viennot, 1979).[9]

"Force as a Mover" Another relatively well-documented (diSessa, 1982; White, 1981) false intuition of naive and novice students is that a force causes motion in the direction of the force, ignoring the effect of previous motion (Fig. 2.8a). We propose to explain this by assuming that the most commonplace situation involving forces, pushing on objects from rest, becomes abstracted as the highest priority p-prim that one will use to predict motion in general circumstances. (No doubt various instances of "carrying," where intention and motion of the agent match the direction of the moved object, serve roughly the same

[9]None of the responses cited in these references are pure "dying away," but also involve at least the "force as mover" p-prim as well (see text). I believe many behaviors claimed to exemplify naive concepts should be cut apart as combinations of "smaller" structures like p-prims. Moreover, the context sensitivity as far as cuing of these ideas is concerned tends to be underestimated, and as a consequence spurious debates arise about which is *the* naive theory of motion. See McCloskey, Caramazza and Green (1980) and McCloskey (this volume). It's time to abandon metaphors like "theory" for more precise descriptions of intuitive knowledge structures.

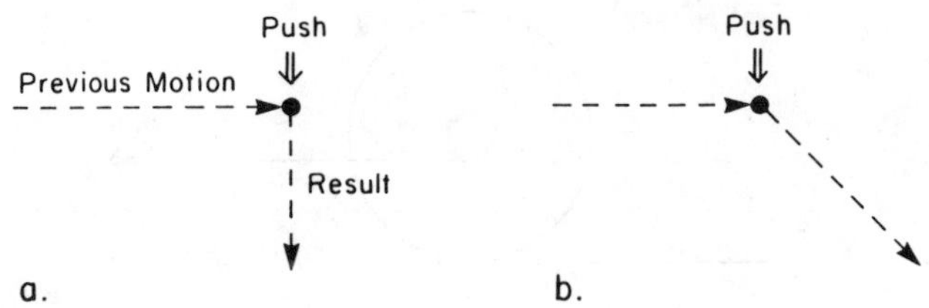

FIG. 2.8. The "force as a mover" and "force as a deflector" phenomena.

purpose.) The abstracted features are object, push and result (not including previous velocity). One sees how critical it is exactly what set of features of the world is selected as part of the p-prim. Like rolling, the absence of other equal priority understandings contributes to an over-extension of the contexts of invocation. More speculatively, we might suppose that the development to more expert understanding involves raising the priority of a competing primitive analysis. In the case of rolling, an earlier section suggests pivoting as a possible competitor. Deflection as in Fig. 2.8b offers such competition in the case of "force as a mover."

One of the surprising things about naive physics is that people will indeed recognize a phenomenon like deflection to exist, if one makes the circumstances compelling enough. It simply is not referenced for ordinary situations. The notion of priorities helps to explain this. Pivoting is another such case. Though it is recognizable in its pure form, it takes some time before novices confidently "see" pivoting in problems like coin rolling where the rolling, though an incomplete analysis, is manifest.

"Force as a Spinner" That pushing an object off-center causes it to spin is a phenomenon recognized by young children. Because beginning mechanics treatments almost always focus on point particles or pushing through the center of mass to illustrate F = ma, the priority claim of "force as a spinner" to explain what happens when one pushes off-center is unaffected. Though F = ma is learned as the way to understand the effect of force in moving a body, a very common mistake when students first encounter pushing off-center is to assume only torque (spinning) analyses are relevant. At best the sense is that because such a force causes *both* spinning and moving, its effect in moving (acceleration) should not be as great as if the force were applied *only* to cause moving. (There seems to be kind of a conservation of effect also implied in this intuitive argument, multiple effects each drain away part of the efficacy of a force. In fact, students often appeal, speciously of course, to conservation of energy or some other conservation to try to justify disbelieving F = ma in these circumstances.)

A good situation for cuing force as a spinner is as follows: A yo-yo resting on a table is pulled as in Fig. 2.9, but not so strongly as to cause it to slide on the table. Which way does the yo-yo roll? Quite evidently, the tug on the string will cause the yo-yo to spin counterclockwise. That results, in turn, in the yo-yo

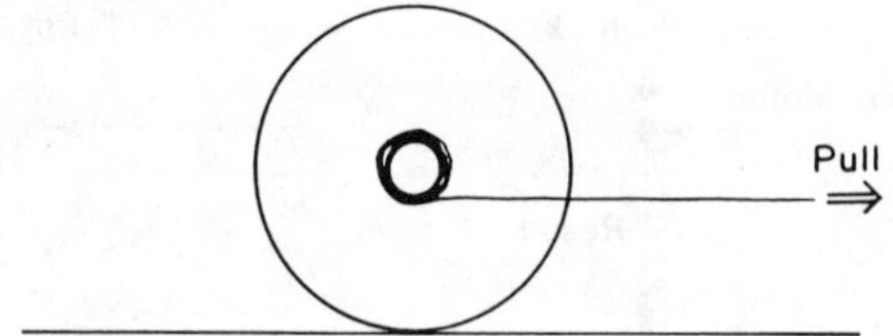

FIG. 2.9. Which way will the yo-yo roll on being pulled?

rolling away from the tug—toward the left. In reality, that analysis is exactly wrong; the yo-yo rolls toward the right. Even some physicists will make the wrong prediction and attempt to justify it by technical arguments about torque which we strongly suspect are cued by force as a spinner in expert thought. Note that, were it cued, even the primitive force as a mover would suggest the correct answer, and at least cause second thoughts about the force as a spinner prediction. The fact that this almost never happens with naive subjects indicates the goodness of match between the problem and the cuing structure to force as a spinner. It also indicates the priority of force as a spinner over force as a mover in situations where both apply.

SUMMARY AND CONCLUSION

P-prims are relatively minimal abstractions of simple common phenomena. Physics-naive students have a large collection of these in terms of which they see the world and to which they appeal as self-contained explanations for what they see. In the process of learning physics, some of these p-prims cease being primitive (and are seen as being explained by other notions), and some may even cease being recognized at all. But many become involved in expert thought in very particular ways. We have tried to highlight two ways in our examples: p-prims serve as elements of analysis, we might say models, which partially explain and provide rapid qualitative analysis for similar but more formal ideas; the recognition of p-prims can serve as a heuristic cue to other, typically more formal, analyses.

In becoming useful to experts, naive p-prims may need to be modified and abstracted to some extent. In particular they will need to be recognizably applicable to a different, usually more general set of contexts. Just as important, they will not often serve the same naive role, self-explanatory analysis, and must defer to other analyses for that purpose. We have developed the idea of structured priorities to refer to the complex of mechanisms which determine when a p-prim is recognized in a situation and when it is abandoned from consideration, perhaps in deference to some particular other view of the situation. This theory-sketch highlights a difference between novices and experts, indeed between common sense and scientific reasoning, which is not so much the character or even content of knowledge, but rather its organization. Experts have a vastly deeper and more complex priority system. Physics-naive people's knowledge system is structurally incapable of supporting any strong, principled commitment to a particular interpretation of a physical phenomenon.

On a higher level this theorizing is an attempt to understand the potentially pervasive and fundamental function of recognition in human cognition, the recognition of a large collection of events as like some particular one. In the same vein, the notion of p-prim suggests how another relatively primitive operation, the remembrance of an interpretation of some event such as the compression and relaxation of a spring, complete with selective focus on particular features, can have important and far reaching effects when integrated into an elaborate control system which "knows" when and when not to see a situation as like that particular event. Finally, we have suggested that it is important to know about a naive person's repertoire of p-prims and how easily their priorities can be molded when considering how one should explain advanced notions in such a way as to be understandable at the student's level, but just as important, in such a way as to develop naturally into expert understanding.

ACKNOWLEDGMENT

The author gratefully acknowledges the continuing support of the Spencer Foundation on this work.

REFERENCES

Carey, S., & Diamond, R. Maturational determination of the developmental course of face encoding. In D. Caplan (Ed.), *Biological studies of mental processes.* Cambridge Mass.: MIT Press, 1980.

Clemenson, G. *A case of dependency directed problem solving,* (unpublished Ph.D. thesis). Cambridge Mass.: M.I.T. Department of Mathematics, January, 1981.

Clement, J. *Common preconceptions and misconceptions as an important source of difficulty in physics courses.* (Unpublished Working Paper). Amherst Mass.: University of Massachusetts, Amherst Cognitive Development Project, July, 1979.

Cohen, H. The art of snaring dragons (MIT AI Memo 338), Cambridge Mass.: M.I.T. A.I. Laboratory, 1974.

diSessa, A. Unlearning aristotelian physics: A study of knowledge-based learning, *Cognitive Science,* 1982, *6,* 37–75.

Ford, K. W. *Basic physics,* Waltham Mass.: Blaisdell Publishing Co., 1968.

Goethe, W. v. *Theory of colours* [translated by C. L. Eastlake], Cambridge Mass.: MIT Press, 1978.

McCloskey, M., Caramazza, A., & Green, B. Curvilinear motion in the absence of external forces: Naive beliefs about the motion of objects, *Science,* 1980, *210,* 1139–1141.

Viennot, L. *La raisonnement spontane en dynamique elementaire.* Paris: Hermann, 1979.

White, B. Y. Designing computer games to facilitate learning, (MIT AI TR-619), Cambridge Mass.: M.I.T. Artificial Intelligence Laboratory, February 1981.

Zajonc, A. G. Goethe's theory of color and scientific intuition. *American Journal of Physics,* 1976, *44,* 327–333.

3 Surrogates and Mappings: Two Kinds of Conceptual Models for Interactive Devices

Richard M. Young
Medical Research Council, Applied Psychology Unit, Cambridge, England

Although it is widely accepted that people's ability to use an interactive device depends in part on their having access to some sort of a mental model (e.g., Moran, 1981a), the notion of the "user's conceptual model" (UCM) remains a hazy one, and there are probably as many different ideas about what it might be as there are people writing about it. The common ground covers something like a more or less definite representation or metaphor that a user adopts to guide his actions and help him interpret the device's behavior. The purpose of this chapter is to help clarify the notion of a UCM by examining the mental models appropriate for a number of different designs of pocket calculator.

As this book amply demonstrates, one can usually study mental models of different phenomena in many different domains. I would like to argue that the investigation of UCMs of interactive devices has certain special properties that allow it to complement these other approaches in important ways. Foremost among them is that the analysis of interactive devices forces one to respect distinctions that other approaches can afford to ignore. Figure 3.1, for example, depicts the situation of someone using a pocket calculator to solve an arithmetical problem, and illustrates some of the entities that must be distinguished. The example shows firstly that the domain of the *task* can be distinct from that of the *device*. In the case of physical systems, whether natural (e.g., Larkin, this volume) or artefactual, this distinction is often not appropriate, as the goals of the task are normally expressed in terms of the system itself. The example also helps clarify what it means to be a *user* of a device, and thus exactly whose mental models are being discussed. Particularly for the topics of mathematics (e.g., Bundy, this volume) and physics (e.g., diSessa, this volume), where the systems under discussion do not admit of a "user" in the familiar sense, it can be much harder to specify the relationship between the system and the owner of the mental model.

A further point suggested by Fig. 3.1 and often overlooked is that each of the four agents (drawn in boxes) has his/its own version of the UCM. This statement requires some clarification. I am not merely making the point that the Designer and the Psychologist will have their own representations of the device, and that these are likely to differ from the User's. Rather I am saying that even when it comes to considering the *User's* conceptual model, the Designer and the Psychologist may disagree about its form and content. To consider each agent briefly in turn: The User has a UCM which is his as a matter of definition. There is no need to say more about it here as it is, in a sense, what most of this book is about. The reason for distinguishing between the User's own UCM and the Psychologist's version is not to argue for some philosophically contentious difference between the UCM the Psychologist thinks the User has and the one he *really* has, but in order to clarify the role that the UCM is meant to play. The distinction can perhaps be best understood by asking for whose benefit the UCM is intended. Is the purpose of the UCM to help the User employ the device more easily and effectively, or to help the Psychologist make better predictions of the User's behavior? Although these aims are not necessarily contradictory, we have to allow for the possibility that their differing requirements will shape the UCM in different ways.

Whether the Designer can, or should, share the same UCM as the Psychologist (or the User) is at present unclear. One can argue (as does Moran, 1981b) that the Designer should be encouraged to do so in order to achieve a satisfactory interface design. Alternatively, one can believe that for the model to remain tractable, the Designer will need to employ a cruder UCM which incorporates assumptions about the tasks to be tackled and the methods to be employed in a

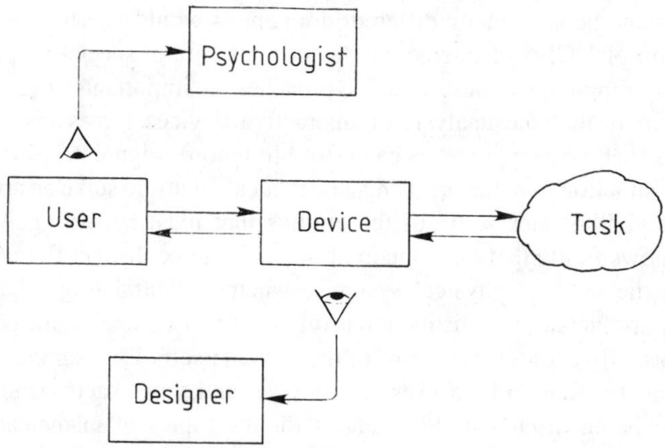

FIG. 3.1. Performing a task with an interactive device.

way which invalidates it as a psychological model. At present we simply do not understand the issues well enough or have enough evidence to choose between these opposed views. Indeed, the formulation of the question in these terms is itself quite new.

Finally, it might seem strange to suggest that the device can have its own version of the UCM, and for devices as simple as pocket calculators it is clearly not so. But once the device achieves the complexity and aspirations of a computerised tutor or ''Intelligent Teaching System'' (Sleeman & Brown, 1979), where it has to adapt to the user in complex ways, then it needs its own model of the user's knowledge about the device (the ''student model'': see Self, 1974). However, such models will not be considered further in this chapter.

DIFFERENT KINDS OF MENTAL MODELS

To help bring some order to this diversity of usage, it is necessary to have some agreed basis for discussing and evaluating different ideas about UCMs. Table 3.1 offers some suggested criteria that a UCM should try to meet. It should be stated immediately that this list is put forward only tentatively as a starting point for discussion. I hold no brief for this particular collection of criteria, and will make no attempt to justify them individually or defend them against sensible alternatives. Just a couple of points need to be made. It should be noted that apart from the ''design'' criterion, the Table assumes that we are dealing with a Psychologist's UCM, i.e., that the purpose of the UCM is that of helping us understand how the user does what he does. It should also be noted that the different groups

TABLE 3.1
Proposed Criteria for a Conceptual Model:
The User's Conceptual Model Should Help Explain
These Aspects of the Use of a System

Performance
- Choice of method
- Details of performance (e.g., fine structure of timing)
- Locus and nature of (certain types of) errors

Learning
- Generalizations and over-generalizations
- What retained and what forgotten over long term
- Long-term memory distortions

Reasoning
- Predicting the response of the system
- Inventing a method
- Explaining the system's behavior

Design
- Providing guidelines for a good design

of criteria implicitly assume the existence of a range of different kinds of tasks that can be undertaken with the device. As well as actually *using* the device for its intended purpose (the Performance criteria), the user can also be asked to *learn* to use a device, or to *predict* its response to specified input, or to *explain* its behavior, and so on.

Table 3.2 summarizes eight different suggestions as to the nature of UCMs. As before, the tentative nature of these proposals needs to be stressed. As with Table 3.1, the list is put forward as a starting point, and makes no claims to completeness. Nor are the different proposals necessarily mutually exclusive. Although some of these individual suggestions might on closer analysis turn out to be untenable, the list as a whole serves to illustrate the diversity of possible viewpoints.

It is not within the scope of this chapter to attempt a detailed presentation and discussion of each of these kinds of mental models. The following remarks will have to suffice:

The *Strong Analogy* model is probably familiar to the reader. A common example is that "a video display unit (VDU) is like a typewriter," so that knowing how to type tells one (to some extent) how to use a VDU (Carroll & Thomas, 1980). It should be noted that this is not an "ultimate" view of a UCM, since it says nothing about how the more familiar device (D′) is itself represented.

A *Surrogate* model is essentially a "mechanistic" account of how the device works. Surrogate models are discussed further in this chapter.

Mapping models (more precisely, *Task/Action Mapping* models) focus on the fact that the role of a UCM is to mediate between the task the user is trying to perform and the actions he must take. They are discussed further in this chapter.

TABLE 3.2
Eight Views of a Conceptual Model (M) of a Device (D)

Strong Analogy:	D is sufficiently similar to another device D′ that a representation of D′ can serve as a M of D.
Surrogate:	M is a physical or notational analogue of the mechanism of D, and can be used to answer questions about D's behavior.
Mapping:	M is the core of the mapping between the user's actions on D and what D does.
Coherence:	M is the (Bartlettian) schema that provides long-term stability in memory for the user's skills and knowledge of D.
Vocabulary:	M is the set of terms in which knowledge about D is encoded.
Problem Space:	M is the problem space in which problems about the use of D are formulated.
Psychological Grammar:	M serves the same role for behavior concerning D as the "grammar in the head" does for one's native language.
Commonality:	M is constructed by the observer, and results from positing a common data structure accessed by all behaviors concerning D.

The *Coherence* model relies on the general observation about human memory that it is hard to remember accurately a set of incoherent facts about the same topic. Instead what remains, after a time, is a structuring of the facts round a schema (Bartlett, 1932). Individual facts may be distorted either to fit with the schema or to contrast with it, or else may be forgotten. This memory schema is proposed as a UCM.

The *Vocabulary* model (Newell, 1980) draws attention to the mental terms in which the user encodes information about the device. It suggests a distinction between the learning of a new item of information in terms of the existing vocabulary, which is a matter principally of assimilation and memory, and the acquisition of a new term, which is more akin to the formation of a new concept. This proposal suggests, for example, that it will be easier to learn certain facts (i.e., those which can be expressed in the existing vocabulary) than others, so that some aspects of the device may get learned and others not. It points to a possible source of errors during learning, as the attempt to encode a new fact in the existing vocabulary may well result in *mis*information of various degrees of subtlety. It might also explain the principal way that Strong Analogies have their effect, by supplying a ready-made vocabulary.

The main limitation of the *Problem Space* model should be immediately apparent: It is unclear that much use of the device is "problem solving" in the relevant sense (Newell & Simon, 1972). Most of it is more plausibly analysed as "routine cognitive skill" (Card, Moran & Newell, 1980, in press), or some other mode of behavior yet to be identified.

One of the main purposes of the UCM is to explain how the user employs the device in tasks that go beyond anything he has been explicitly taught, and how much of this behavior is guided not by rational analysis but by a "feeling" that "that's the way one uses this device." These two phenomena, of *productivity* and *regularity*, are in psycholinguistics part of what fuels the drive to explain language behavior in terms of a *Psychological Grammar* (e.g., Bresnan, 1978). By analogy, such an analysis may be appropriate for UCMs also. (For an application of this kind of model in practice, see Reisner, 1981.) The main disadvantage of this line, it seems to me, is that it seeks to clarify a potentially concrete and tractable idea by replacing it with a vague and contentious one. A better scientific strategy would be first to understand UCMs in their own right, then perhaps to use them to illuminate the notion of a psychological grammar.

Finally, the *Commonality* model arises from the desire of the Psychologist (of Fig. 3.1) to explain all the User's actions concerning the device in terms of processes accessing a single, shared data structure. This structure, of course, would be the UCM.

A thorough analysis of each of these suggestions would be a large undertaking. The aims of this chapter are more modest: To explore just two of the kinds of UCM and test them against the criteria offered in Table 3.1. The next two sections present a summary of the research reported in Young (1981), which should be consulted for further details.

SURROGATE MODELS

Recently I have spent some time trying to understand the nature of users' conceptual models of different kinds of pocket calculators as a logical preliminary to psychological experiments (Young, 1981). In the course of this investigation I explored two types of model which fall respectively into the categories referred to as *surrogates* and *mappings* in Table 3.2.

A surrogate model S of a device D is essentially just the familiar notion of a "working model" which explains how D functions as a mechanism. Typically S presents a highly simplified account of D, so that it has more the flavor of a fictional "cover story" than an elaborate engineering description. S can be a physical model, i.e., an analogue—a "scale model" of an airplane, or a maze of colored liquids and glass tubes to represent the national economy—but more commonly it will exist only on paper, written in some informal or formal (e.g., mathematical) notation. S is called a surrogate because it can be used in place of D for answering questions about D's behavior. In addition to their ubiquitous use in science and engineering, surrogate models have been used as a way of providing novice computer programmers with a picture of how the programming language interpreter behaves (du Boulay, O'Shea & Monk, 1981; Mayer, 1981).

I will content myself with just one further remark about surrogate models at this level of generality, to point out that they are inherently biased towards the "prediction" criterion of Table 3.1. S is primarily a simulator of D. Given the inputs to D, it will foretell D's response. S may also help with some of the other tasks by providing a structure for the workings of D which can be reasoned about. But as a surrogate, S functions in its preferred direction from the given inputs to the unknown output.

A Reverse Polish Calculator

Certain designs of calculator employ what is known as Reverse Polish Notation (RPN). The defining characteristic of RPN is that arithmetical operators, such as "+", are written *after* their operands. Thus to express the sum of 2 and 3, where ordinary algebraic notation would write "2 + 3" RPN writes "2 3 +", and the more complex expression

$$2 \times (3 + 4)$$

becomes

$$2\ 3\ 4 + \times.$$

It happens that the standard introduction to RPN calculators (e.g., in the manufacturer's instruction manual) is built round the explicit presentation of a surrogate model of the machine. For the particular calculator I analyzed (Young, 1981) the model consists of a *stack* of four registers each capable of storing a number (Fig. 3.2a). The registers are called X, Y, Z, and T, and it is always the

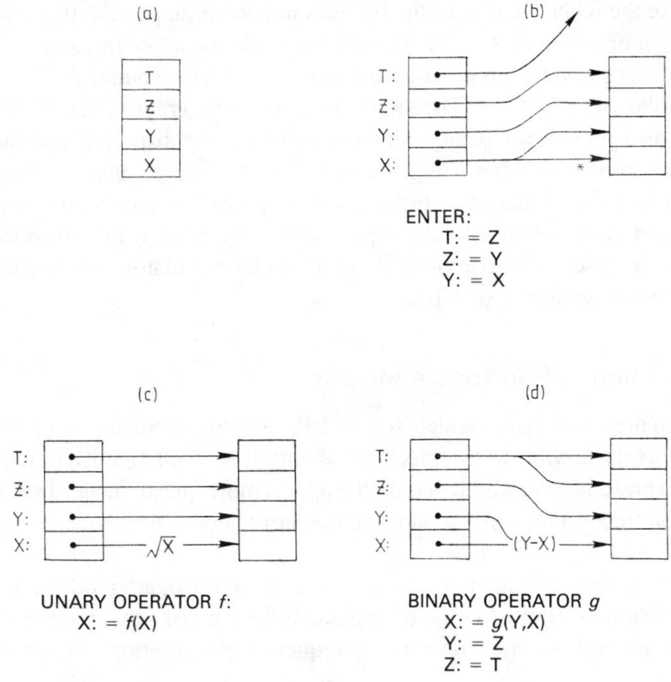

FIG. 3.2. Stack model for the RPN calculator.

number in X which is displayed. The stack is used to specify the effects of the various operations. Figure 3.2 shows the behavior of the ENTER key (used for separating numbers), of a unary operator (square root), and a binary operator (minus).

This stack provides an elegant illustration of what a surrogate model can be. Once a few small details have been attended to, the stack model is adequate to account for the behavior of the calculator. Furthermore, it has the perhaps unexpected property of predicting its response to *any* sequence of inputs. An arbitrary series of numbers, ENTERs, and unary or binary operators can be run through the model to determine the resulting state of the machine.

A Simple Four-Function Calculator

The second calculator to be discussed is representative of the simpler, cheaper machines available. It is "algebraic" in the sense that it uses ordinary infix notation, but it has no brackets and no built-in hierarchy among the operators. Apart from the keys for typing in numbers, there are just the "=" key and the four arithmetic functions. It is thus appropriate to call it a "four-function" (FF) calculator.

Unlike the RPN calculator, the FF does not come supplied with a ready-made conceptual model, and the derivation of a suitable model in the same style as that for the RPN provides an entertaining detective story (Young, 1981). The outcome is shown in Fig. 3.3. The model has two internal registers, called X and Y, as well as a pointer to specify which number will be displayed and into which register a typed-in number will go. The diagram also gives rules for the functioning of this notional machine. For present purposes the details are unimportant. Relevant is the fact that, like the stack model for the RPN, this surrogate model provides an essentially complete account of the calculator and predicts its response to any sequence of inputs.

Shortcomings of Surrogate Models

Although these surrogate models for the RPN and FF calculators can be shown to be objectively faithful to the machines themselves, their fidelity to the psychological representations employed by the user is more questionable. In this section I mention three objections to taking these surrogates seriously as psychological models.

The first objection applies also to many other surrogate models, and lies in pointing out their limited range of applicability. For tasks that require deliberate problem solving (such as devising a sequence of operations to achieve some

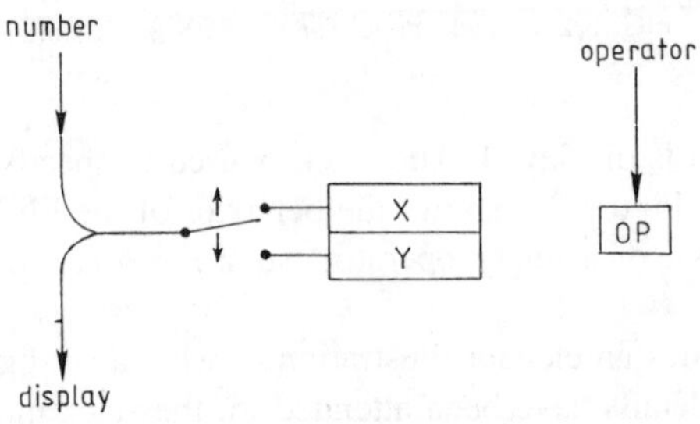

Initialise:	X := Y := 0	
	OP := "+"	
	SW → X	;i.e. switch points to X
Input number N:	@SW := N	;store N in register SW points to
Press operation f:	if implied "=" then do sequence for "="	
	OP := f	
	Y := X	
	SW → Y	;set switch to Y
Press "=":	X := OP(X,Y)	
	SW → X	;set switch to X

FIG. 3.3. Register model for the Four-Function calculator.

desired effect—the "invention" task of Table 3.1), the surrogate may perhaps be usable as the mental representation on which the problem solving is based. But for the more performance-oriented tasks the surrogate seems practically irrelevant. It is arguable that someone who had never seen a calculator before and never read the instructions might perform his first few calculations by painfully deriving an input sequence from first principles. But thereafter he will quickly learn some familiar sequences that short-circuit the problem solving. Such sequences lie, in principle, beyond the compass of surrogate models.

Even as a basis for problem solving the psychological validity of these models is doubtful. The model of the FF calculator given in Fig. 3.3 can hardly be called complicated, yet it is near the limits of what can comfortably be manipulated in the head. The reader who tries using Fig. 3.3 to predict the response of the FF calculator to the input sequence "3 + 5 ÷ = 6 =" will soon find himself wishing for pencil and paper.

The second objection is that the surrogate models fail to capture several salient characteristics of the calculator. It was already pointed out, for example, that both these models treat their input as an unstructured series of numbers, operators, and "="s (or ENTERs). Yet with the FF calculator, say, the input sequence is clearly experienced by the user as having a definite structure, consisting of a series of units each of which is a run of alternating numbers and operators terminated by an "=". Surrogate models can in principle say nothing about such structure.

Another aspect not captured by the FF model is a certain area of confusion encountered in the use of the machine. Although the answers given by the calculator conform to one's expectations for sequences such as "2 + 3 =", "2 + 3 + 4 =", and "2 + 3 = + 4 =" (results 5, 9, and 9 respectively), users are frequently surprised by its response to "2 + 3 = 4 =" (result 7) and even more to "5 ÷ = =" (result .2). What happens in these cases is that the input of an operator interacts with the default value used for its second argument, in ways that are not easy to grasp. Immediately after the sequence "2 + 3 =", for example, another "=" will give an answer of 8 whereas pressing "+ =" yields 10. The surrogate model, although it gives the same answer as the machine to all these sequences, throws very little light on the difficulty. There is no way to examine the model and have it exhibit the cause. One can only "run" it, just as one can use the machine itself, and watch the problem emerge. This particular failing has important practical implications, insofar as it means that the surrogate model of the FF calculator, which *looks* as clean and simple as that for the RPN, is *in fact* positively misleading as a basis for design. Thus it fails to meet the "design" criterion of Table 3.1.

The third shortcoming of surrogate models is best illustrated by another kind of calculator, a fully-fledged algebraic machine (ALG). Unlike the FF calculator, it provides keys for left and right brackets, so that expressions such as

$$(2 + 3) \times (4 + 5) =$$

can be keyed in directly as they stand. The ALG calculator also offers operator precedence, so that multiplications and divisions are performed before additions and subtractions. What sort of surrogate model could one offer for this machine? In principle it would be possible to elaborate the kind of analysis performed for the FF machine and develop a picture of its inner workings. But such a route would lead rapidly to a complex model with a variety of internal stacks, registers, priority tags, and so forth. If we were to pursue that path, it would be appropriate after a while to remind ourselves that the purpose of the exercise was to develop a conceptual model for the person operating the calculator, not an implementation design for the engineer building it. I have suggested (Young, 1981) that a preferable alternative is simply to summarize the function of the machine in a *statement* to the effect that:

> *"You type in an expression. The machine examines it, analyzes it, and calculates the answer according to the rules of arithmetic."*

Such a statement is deliberately vague about many details, yet I argue that its inexplicitness may be precisely correct. The internal structure of the calculator is complicated enough that the user does not have (and normally should not need) a detailed picture of what is happening inside. In which case the very superficiality of the "statement" makes it superior to a surrogate as a conceptual model.

All three of these shortcomings arise from the fact that a surrogate model by its very nature focuses exclusively on the device itself, taking no account of the task or user. They suggest that a better conceptual model should pay more attention to the relationship between the user's actions and the task being carried out. This hint is followed by the second kind of model to be considered.

TASK/ACTION MAPPING MODELS

The task/action mapping model derives from ideas in the "Command Language Grammar" of Moran (1981b), which presents a technique for describing the interface between a user and an interactive computing system at a number of levels of detail. The use of a calculator can be viewed from at least two different perspectives. The performance of a particular calculation, such as the addition of 2 and 3, can be described in terms of the arithmetical *task domain* as the numerical evaluation of an expression consisting of the binary operator "+" applied to the two operands 2 and 3. In the *action domain* of keypresses and readouts from the calculator, the same calculation can be described as the typing of the key sequence "2 + 3 =" followed by the reading of the result from the display. Obviously these two descriptions are not unrelated, and the task/action mapping model is a way of characterising the correspondence between them.

The mapping analysis (which is illustrated for the FF calculator later in this section) begins by trying to describe the structure of the task and action domains in such a way that there is a simple and direct mapping between their corresponding parts. Normally it will not be possible to achieve this over the whole of the domains, so one or more central *core* tasks and their *core* action sequences are chosen which can be put into close correspondence. The links between these core entities form the *core of the mapping*. Other tasks are mapped into their corresponding actions by first expressing them as variants of the core task, then using the core of the mapping to transfer to the action domain, and finally translating to the appropriate action sequence.

The structure of this linkage, which means that the core of the mapping acts as a kind of "communication channel" carrying all the mappings between the two domains, provides a layered organisation to the mapping as a whole. Between items within the core the correspondence is direct. Between more peripheral items the correspondence is indirect, having first to pass into the core before making the jump across to the other domain. And between still more distant items, for which there is no effective route to the core, there is (within this analysis) no mapping at all.

Because the cores are, by definition, subareas of the domains between which there exists a simple and direct mapping, it follows that these core entities are of closely similar internal structure, i.e., isomorphic. They can therefore be seen as realizations in the different domains of the same, more abstract, structure. This higher-order commonality between the cores of the domains (referred to in Young [1981] as their "abstract prototype") provides a coherent, integrative characterization of the overall functioning of the device. The FF calculator, for example, can be seen as essentially a *machine for performing basic calculations* (see Fig. 3.4). The Algebraic calculator can be characterised as being (more or less) a *machine for evaluating formulae*. And the RPN calculator can be viewed as a device for computing a third kind of calculation (called a *locally structured binary* (LSB) calculation—the term will be needed again shortly).

A number of consequences follow from this analysis, some of them leading to empirically testable predictions about the user's behavior (Young, 1981). Several of them, such as those concerning the relative merits of ALG and RPN calculators, are of interest primarily to calculator enthusiasts, but others address the shortcomings of surrogate models discussed earlier and are worth describing here.

Understanding the FF Calculator

In contrast to the surrogate model, the mapping for the FF calculator exhibits explicitly the origin of the confusion experienced in its use. The analysis proceeds as follows. The core task is the evaluation of what I call a *basic calculation*, i.e., the application of a binary operator to its two operands (Fig. 3.4a).

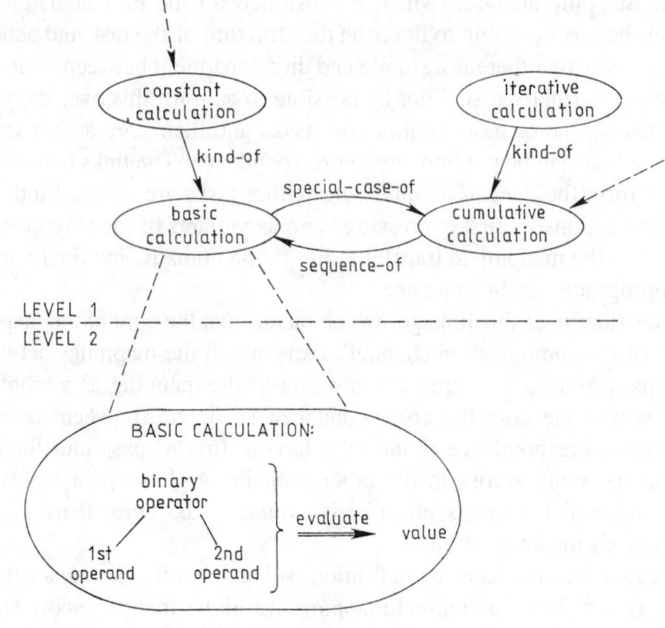

(a) TASK DOMAIN

‹calculation-sequence› : := ‹terminated-calculation›*
‹terminated-calculation› : := ‹main-part› ‹operation›*? =
‹main-part› : := ‹1st-number›? |
‹main-part› ‹operation›* ‹2nd-number›

where:

‹operation› : := + | − | × | ÷
‹1st-number› : := ‹number›
‹2nd-number› : := ‹number›

N.B. "|" means "or"
Symbols tagged with "*" can be repeated one or more times
Symbols tagged with "?" can be optionally omitted

(b) ACTION DOMAIN

FIG. 3.4. Task and action domains for the Four-Function calculator.

Other kinds of calculation are treated as variants of the basic one. A *cumulative calculation* for example, in which a "total so far" is repeatedly combined with a new number, is treated as a series of basic calculations where the result of one step is used as the first operand for the next. An *iterative calculation* (such as summing a column of numbers) is a special kind of cumulative one. In the action domain (Fig. 3.4b), the possible sequences are described by a grammar (cf.

Task Domain		Action Domain
basic calculation	↔	‹terminated-calculation›
operator	↔	‹operation›
1st operand	↔	‹1st-number›
2nd operand	↔	‹2nd number›
evaluation	↔	"="
value	↔	answer on display

FIG. 3.5. Mapping of the basic calculation task for the Four-Function calculator.

Reisner, 1981; Moran, 1981b). The core sequence is of the form "Number Operator Number =," and other sequences are cast as repetitions and variations, following the options allowed by the grammar.

So long as the calculator is being used for basic calculations, the mapping between domains is simple and straightforward, as shown in Fig. 3.5. For a basic calculation, the grammar generates the sequence

‹1st-number› ‹operation› ‹2nd-number› =

and each of these components corresponds directly to a part of the task. For other sequences, however, the mapping is more complicated, especially for those calculations that involve the defaulting of the second argument (Fig. 3.6). Firstly, the grammar itself imposes a dependence between the second number and the operation, so that a second number can be input only if a new operation is input also, even if that operation is the same as the one last given and is therefore what the default would be anyway if the new operation were omitted. Secondly, keying the operation changes the default used for the second argument from its previous value to the value of the first argument.

The complexity of the mapping, especially of the interaction between the operator and the second argument and the conditionality of the defaulting, is what accounts for the confusion found in using the calculator.

Induced Structure of Action and Task Domains

The search for a description of the domains yielding a close correspondence between the core entities means that the mapping analysis imposes a structuring on the domains that reflects the properties of the particular device. That is to say, from a more psychological point of view, it *induces* a structure in the user's representation of the domains. Thus the analysis predicts, for example, that users of different types of calculator will carve up the space of calculations in different ways.

In the action domain, in contrast to the unstructured sequence expected by the surrogate models, the input is governed by the grammar of Fig. 3.4b. All inputs

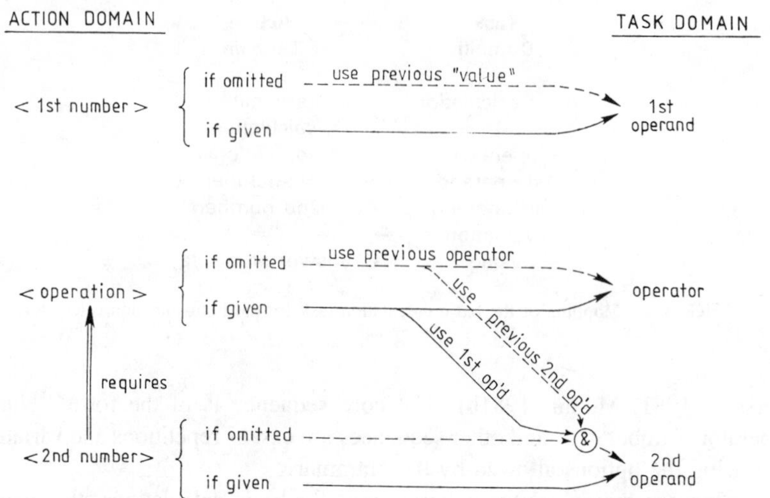

FIG. 3.6. Mapping between task and action on the Four-Function calculator.

to the FF calculator are cast as variants of the core sequence, resulting in a structuring of the input in the way described earlier.

Figure 3.7a shows again the task structure for the FF calculator, with the basic calculation at the center and the other tasks related to it directly or indirectly. *Constant calculations* are a series of basic calculations with one of the arguments held fixed. An *upside-down division* is a division of a single number by a more complicated expression, and can be handled by the FF only in an obscure way as a kind of constant calculation. The quotient 6 / (3 + 5), for example, has to be evaluated by the input sequence "3 + 5 ÷ = 6 =". A *left-branching LSB* is, roughly, a calculation whose structure corresponds to a left-branching binary tree, and so can be evaluated as a cumulative calculation. (For further details, see Young, 1981.) A *left-associative formula,* such as (((3 + 5) × 7) − 4), can be mentally parsed into a left-branching LSB and treated accordingly. Other formulae cannot be handled by the FF as they stand.

For comparison, Fig. 3.7b shows the structure for the ALG machine. This time formula evaluation is at the center, the other tasks having to be treated as special variants. Because constant calculations inherently cannot be cast as formulae, they are effectively in a separate world of their own. Figure 3.7c shows the task domain for the RPN calculator, with all calculations having to be transformed into LSBs. Written formulae have to be *parsed,* for instance, before they can be input to the calculator.

It should be noted how different these task structures are. They vary both in what kinds of objects they contain as well as in how those objects are related. The task domain for the FF calculator, for example, contains some bizarre objects—

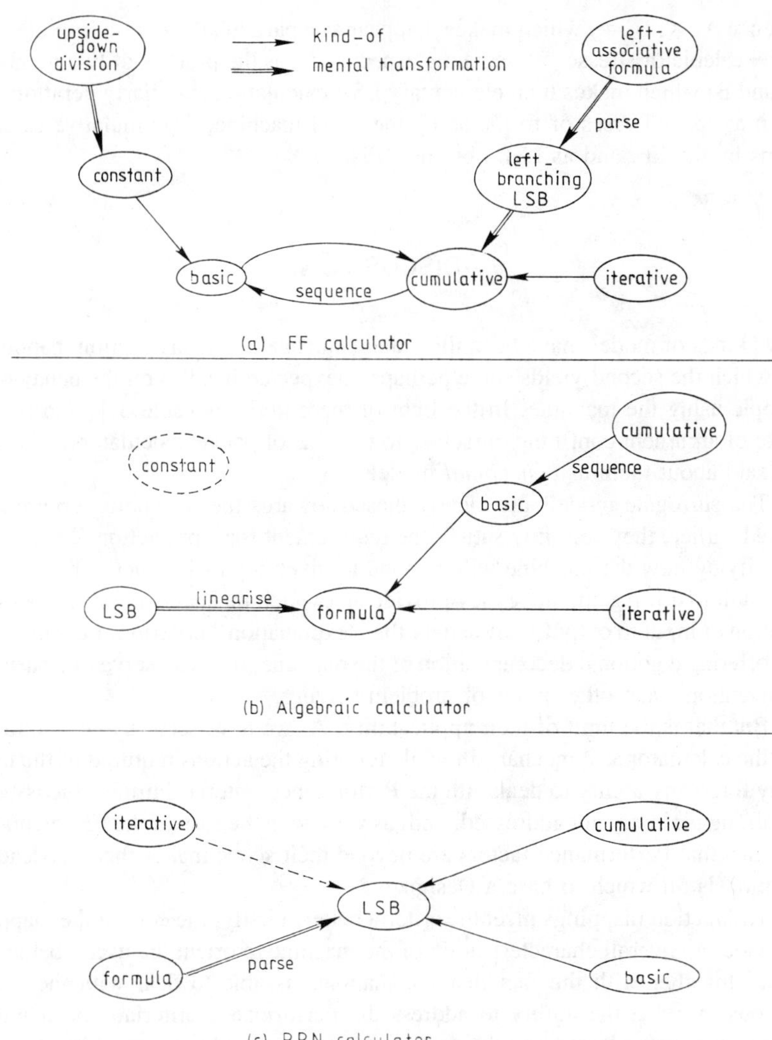

FIG. 3.7. Structure of the task domains for the three calculators.

left-associative formulae, upside-down divisions—which have no separate existence for the other machines. Conversely the ALG calculator, although providing a facility for constants, has no constant calculations in its main task domain. Even when the same objects appear, they may be differently connected. The simpler kinds of calculation are especially labile. The basic calculation, for example, is seen by the FF calculator as the core exemplar of what a calculation really is. The ALG calculator emphasises its linear structure (i.e., as the sequence A, ×, B, =) which makes it appear as a particularly simple formula. The RPN calculator stresses its semantic aspect (i.e., as the product of two numbers, A and B) which makes it an elementary LSB calculation. Similarly iterations are seen as special cases of formulae by the ALG machine, as cumulative calculations by the FF, and as LSBs by the RPN.

DISCUSSION

Two kinds of models have been illustrated, surrogates and task/action mappings, of which the second yields some perhaps unexpected handles on the behavior of people using the machine. In the light of the criteria in Table 3.1, and for the sake of argument confining ourselves to the case of pocket calculators, what can be said about them as *conceptual* models?

The surrogate models are clearly biased towards the Reasoning criteria. As noted earlier, they certainly satisfy the requirement for "prediction," insofar as specifying how the machine will respond to given inputs is exactly the job they are built to do. Again, since they provide an explicit mechanism for the transformation of input to output, they satisfy the "explanation" criterion. Less directly, by offering a notional decomposition of the machine, they can serve as a basis for "invention" and other kinds of problem solving.

But that is the limit of their applicability. As we have seen, by concentrating on the calculator as a mechanism while ignoring the actions required of the user, they forgo any ability to deal with the Performance criteria. Further, the issue of Learning is simply not addressed, and, as we saw in the case of the FF calculator, the fact that Performance factors are beyond their scope makes them misleading as models on which to base a Design.

Task/action mappings meet the criteria better. Firstly, the core of the mapping provides an overall characterization of the machine to orient the user's behavior. That, together with the fact that the mapping is able to deal with the user's actions, gives it the ability to address the Performance criteria. The mapping directs the method used and the details of its execution by virtue of its ability to set up a correspondence between the structures of the task and the action sequence (Fig. 3.5). The question of errors is less well explored, but it is clear that having an inappropriate model can be a source of systematic confusion.

The mapping says nothing directly about the process of Learning, so its relevance here is restricted. Nevertheless it does offer a basis for generalization, insofar as only very little data is needed in order to establish its core. On the ALG calculator, anyone familiar with arithmetic needs to be shown only a few examples such as "2 + 3 =" and "2 × (3 + 4) =" in order to be able to apply the mapping freely and generally. (This is presumably the basis for the ALG calculator's strong initial appeal: so little needs to be learned.) The mapping can similarly lead to overgeneralization. The same learner is liable to transcribe unary functions such as *sin, log,* or *sqrt* as prefix (instead of postfix) operators when he first meets them.

The position with regard to the Reasoning criteria is more complicated. Some of the tasks here, such as "explanation," clearly belong in the home territory of the surrogate models and are handled poorly by the mappings. Just as the surrogate models tend to focus too narrowly on the calculators themselves, so the task/action mappings tend to pass them by. Nevertheless some of the Reasoning tasks can be carried out in the task or action domains. Although mappings are unable to predict the effects of arbitrary input sequences, for example, if a sequence can be decomposed into a concatenation of familiar units then its effect can be foretold in terms of a series of corresponding steps in the task domain. Similarly, a method can be devised for certain novel tasks by arguments based in the task domain, i.e., by essentially arithmetical reasoning.

Lastly, mappings look promising as a basis for good design. The case has not yet been worked out in detail, but I have suggested (Young, 1981) that the overall "shape" of the mapping provides a guide to the designer. With realistically complicated machines, for example, the mapping is likely to consist of a number of submappings, and once that happens the relationships between them become crucial. If the submappings overlap, for instance, then certain tasks fall within the domain of two or more of them. For the machine to appear "consistent" it is then important that those tasks translate into the same actions no matter which route is chosen.

This chapter has illustrated just two of the types of model put forward in Table 3.2. Exploration of and comparison with the others will have to wait for a longer, more thorough investigation. However, the final point to be made here requires us to anticipate one of the outcomes of that future enquiry. In the fuller analysis it will almost certainly turn out that one of the major distinctions between models is their position on a dimension of assimilation–accommodation. Models at the assimilatory end tend to view the device in terms of its relationships to other systems already familiar to the user (e.g., the Strong Analogy models of Table 3.2). At the accommodatory end the emphasis is more on an understanding of the device in its own right. In terms of this distinction, both of the models considered here are located near the accommodatory pole. The surrogate model and the mapping both take as their starting point the actual behavior of the machine. I suspect this comes about because of the precisely specified and highly specialized nature of the job that calculators perform. Seeing a calculator as being like a typewriter (you press keys to make it work) or a slide rule (it helps you with calculations) may well color our attitude towards it and be important for certain sociological aspects of its use, but such analogies are nowhere near specific enough to guide its actual operation.

REFERENCES

Bartlett, F. C. *Remembering*. Cambridge, Eng.: Cambridge University Press, 1932.

Bresnan, J. A realistic transformational grammar. In M. Halle, J. Bresnan & G. A. Miller (Eds.), *Linguistic Theory and Psychological Reality*. Cambridge, Mass.: MIT Press, 1978.

Card, S. K., Moran, T. P., & Newell, A. Computer text-editing: An information processing analysis of a routine cognitive skill. *Cognitive Psychology,* 1980, *12,* 32–74.

Card, S. K., Moran, T. P., & Newell, A. *The Psychology of Human-Computer Interaction*. Hillsdale, N.J.: Lawrence Erlbaum Assoc., in press.

Carroll, J. M., & Thomas, J. *Metaphor and the cognitive representation of computing systems.* Yorktown Heights, N.Y.: IBM Research Report RC-8302, 1980.

du Boulay, J. B. H., O'Shea, T., & Monk, J. The black box inside the glass box: Presenting computing concepts to novices. *International Journal of Man-Machine Studies,* 1981, *14,* 237–249.

Mayer, R. E. The psychology of how novices learn computer programming. *Computing Surveys,* 1981, *13,* 121–141.

Moran, T. P. An applied psychology of the user. *Computing Surveys,* 1981, *13,* 1–11. (a)

Moran, T. P. The Command Language Grammar: A representation for the user interface of interactive computer systems. *International Journal of Man-Machine Studies,* 1981, *15,* 3–50. (b)

Newell, A. Personal communication, 1980.

Newell, A., & Simon, H. A. *Human Problem Solving*. Englewood Cliffs, N.J.: Prentice-Hall, 1972.

Reisner, P. Using a formal grammar in human factors design of an interactive graphics system. *IEEE Transactions on Software Engineering, SE-7,* 1981, 229–240.

Self, J. Student models in CAI. *International Journal of Man-Machine Studies,* 1974, *6,* 261–276.

Sleeman, D. H., & Brown, J. S. Editorial: Intelligent tutoring systems. *International Journal of Man-Machine Studies,* 1979, *11,* 1–3.

Young, R. M. The machine inside the machine: Users' models of pocket calculators. *International Journal of Man-Machine Studies,* 1981, *15,* 51–85.

4 Qualitative Reasoning About Space and Motion

Kenneth D. Forbus
Massachusetts Institute of Technology

1. INTRODUCTION

People reason fluently about motion through space. For example, if two balls are thrown in to a well they might collide, but if one ball is always outside and the other always inside they cannot. The models we use in this qualitative kind of reasoning seem to be simpler than formal mechanics and appear to be based on our experience in the physical world.

One way to test theories about how we reason about a class of situations is to build a program that can answer the same sorts of questions we might ask about those situations. Writing a program requires explicit consideration of how the knowledge involved is used as well as just what must be known. If it works, the program provides a strong argument that the theory it embodies is sufficient for the domain. The behavior of the program can be compared to human performance on the questions of interest to see how well the theory it embodies explains what people do. Some of the details necessary to make a program run may suggest more precise experiments on human subjects.

There are several limitations to this methodology. Programs that do any reasoning at all are usually at the limits of current technology. Not all of the details of what the program does are relevant to what people do—they are a consequence of the different types of hardware available for the task (see (Marr, 1976). Worse yet, Computer Science is very young—much like chemistry before the periodic table, and certainly before biochemistry. Nevertheless, the ways of thinking about processes that it provides are the most precise we have.

The focus of this work on formalizing common sense knowledge is much in the spirit of the Naive Physics effort of Hayes (Hayes 1979a). However, Hayes ignores computational issues such as the use of a diagram and the "style" of reasoning, which are considered here. My approach is very different from the efforts described in (Bundy, 1976; Novak, 1976, and McDermott & Larkin, 1978), which are mainly concerned with modeling students solving textbook physics problems. When learning physics, students are forced to relate the new information to the physical knowledge they already have. It is only the latter kind of knowledge that is examined here.

1.1 The Domain and The Program

To explore the issues involved in reasoning about motion a program called FROB (Forbus, 1981a) was written. FROB reasons about motion in a simplified domain called the "Bouncing Ball" world. A situation in the Bouncing Ball world consists of a two dimensional scene with surfaces represented by line segments, and one or more balls which are modeled as point masses. A typical situation is depicted in Fig. 4.1. These assumptions allow us to avoid dealing with complex shapes and the third dimension. Only motion through space and momentary collisions with surfaces are considered; sliding, rolling, spinning, and other types of motion are ignored. Gravity is the sole external influence considered, for we wish to ignore air resistance and such complexities as charged or magnetic balls.

A scene is specified by a diagram containing a description of the surfaces. Given a scene, FROB analyzes the surface geometry and computes qualitative descriptions of the free space in the diagram. The person using the program can describe balls, properties of their states of motion, request simulations, and make global assumptions about the motion. FROB incrementally creates and updates

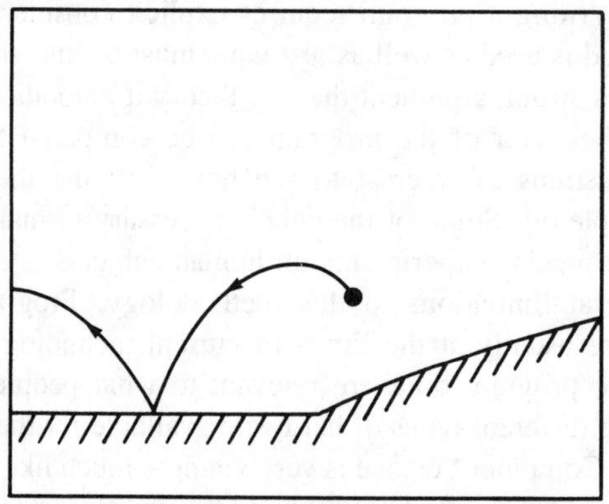

FIG. 4.1. *A typical scene from the Bouncing Ball world.* A situation in the Bouncing Ball World consists of a diagram that specifies surfaces and one or more balls. This drawing only shows the geometric aspects of the descriptions involved.

its descriptions to accommodate this information, complaining if inconsistencies are detected. Questions may be asked by calling procedures that interrogate these descriptions.

1. What can it (a ball) do next?
2. Where can it go next?
3. Where can it end up?
4. Can these two balls collide?

1.2 Main Ideas about Motion and Space

There are several theories concerning reasoning about motion and space that FROB illustrates. To summarize:

1. A quantitative "analog" geometric representation simplifies reasoning about space. It does so by providing a simple method for answering a class of geometric questions. Qualitative spatial reasoning can be thought of as manipulating a set of symbolic descriptions of space, defined in terms of the underlying analog representation.

2. Describing the motion of an object can be viewed as creating a network from descriptions of qualitatively distinct types of motion. They are linked by descriptions of the state of the object before and after each of these motions. This network can be used to analyze the motion and in some cases can be constructed by a process of simulation.

3. The result of envisioning (de Kleer, 1975, 1979) can be used as a device to assimilate assumptions about global properties of motion and in checking the actual motion of an object against these assumptions. The assimilation process makes heavy use of qualitative spatial descriptions and basic properties of motion.

2. SPATIAL DESCRIPTIONS

We do not yet know why people are so good at reasoning about space. Theorem proving and symbolic manipulation of algebraic expressions do not seem to account for this ability. Arguments against theorem proving may be found in [Waltz & Boggess, 1979], while the sheer complexity of algebraic manipulations argues against it as a basis for our spatial abilities. I conjecture that people find diagrams useful because they allow certain spatial questions to be decided by interpreting the results of perception. The marks in a diagram reflect the spatial relations between the things they represent, which allows us to use our visual apparatus to interpret these relationships as we would with real objects. In this case, perception provides a simple (at least for the processes that use it) decision procedure for a class of spatial questions.

People also can reason about space using less detailed representations than that of a diagram, as the well example discussed in the beginning of the paper illustrates. My conjecture about qualitative spatial reasoning is that it involves a vocabulary of PLACES whose relationships are described in symbolic terms. By PLACE, I mean a piece of space (point, line, region, volume, etc.) such that all parts of it share some property. The nature of a domain determines the notion of place appropriate to it. There might be more than one useful way to break up space even within a single domain, and the results of qualitative spatial reasoning must be integrated with other knowledge. This suggests embedding the place vocabulary in a more quantitative, analog representation.[1]

2.1 The Metric Diagram

We do not yet understand the complexities of human vision, so we do not know precisely what people compute from a diagram or how they do so. The role of a diagram can still be studied by building a representation that has some simple way of computing the answers to relevant questions. A type of geometry representation that I call a *Metric Diagram* was used in FROB to explore these issues. The geometric aspects of a problem are represented by symbolic elements whose parameters are numbers, embedded in a bounded global coordinate system. The vocabulary of elements required for the Bouncing Ball world consists of points, line segments, regions bounded by line segments, and pieces of vertically oriented parabolas. The mathematical simplicity of the elements and the availability of numerical parameters means analytic geometry can be used to calculate answers to most kinds of geometric questions.

In constructing the program three kinds of questions proved important. They will be called *identity, parity,* and *intersection.* Identity questions concern the relationship of the geometric elements with the descriptions of the objects whose geometric aspects they represent. Aside from being necessary for interpreting the results of the processes associated with the diagram, indexing the elements by what they represent can speed up searches that use the diagram. For example, detecting possible collisions with surfaces is much faster if only the surface geometries need to be tested against the trajectory as opposed to testing all elements in the diagram.

A geometric element divides space up into different pieces, which can be considered as "sides." Parity questions concern on what side of some element a

[1]By contrast, Hayes (see Hayes, 1979b) explicitly avoids the use of metric representations for space. I suspect that a metric representation will be required to make his concept of a history useful, in that to compare them requires having a common coordinate frame.

point is, and what sides of one element another is on. For example, to detect that a ball is placed inconsistently inside a solid requires being able to detect that the point which represents the ball at some point in time is inside the region that represents the solid.

Intersection questions are very important, because for physical things to interact they must "touch." They are answered by solving the equations attached to the elements to find possible points of contact and filtering the results with parity operations to account for the limited spatial extent of the elements. One use of intersection questions is finding out if a ball hits a particular surface, and if so, where.

2.2 The Space Graph

In FROB the *Space Graph* provides the vocabulary of places. Because all balls are point masses and are subject to the same forces, the Space Graph is independent of them and depends only on the surface geometry. Free space is divided into nonoverlapping regions in a way that simplifies the description of possible motions, as will be discussed in section 4. These regions and the edges that bound them are the Metric Diagram elements that form the nodes of the Space Graph. These nodes are connected by arcs that are labeled with the name of the relationship between them (such as LEFT or UP). Any other place required for

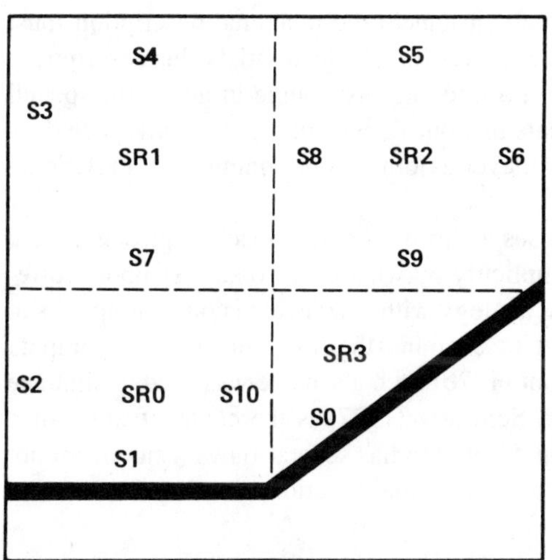

SREGION0
left: SEGMENT 2
right: SEGMENT 10
up: SEGMENT 7
down: SEGMENT 1
class: SREGION

SEGMENT 1
up: SREGION0
connecting-region: SREGION0
class: SURFACE

SEGMENT 2
right: SREGION0
left: SPATIUM-INCOGNITO
connecting-region: SREGION0
class: BORDER

SEGMENT 10
left: SREGION0
right: SREGION3
class: FREE

FIG. 4.2. Space Graph for a scene. The free space in the diagram is broken up into regions in a way that simplifies the description of the kinds of motion possible. The labels on the pointers indicate the spatial relationships between the nodes.

qualitative reasoning can be described by composing these places. The graph structure provides a framework for efficient processing (see sections 4 and 5). An example of the places in a scene and the graph structure they produce is contained in Fig. 4.2.

2.3 Comparison with Other Spatial Descriptions

The Metric Diagram has much in common with the descriptions used as targets for language translation of Waltz and Boggess (1979) and the imagery theory of Hinton (1979). It is quite different from the traditional "pure relational" geometric representations used in AI and the "naive analog" representations used by Funt (1976), and Kosslyn and Schwartz (1977). Both of these schemes are inadequate, but for different reasons.

Reasoning about space with just relational descriptions can be difficult. Transitive axioms such as

$$\text{Left-of}(X, Y) \wedge \text{Left-of}(Y, Z) \Rightarrow \text{Left-of}(X, Z)$$

are often needed to answer parity questions, and their use can lead to combinatorial searches, as pointed out in [Waltz and Boggess, 1979]. Relational systems are very weak models of space.[2] For a fixed vocabulary of predicates and relations there is only one full relational description (all possible relations and predicates are asserted) up to isomorphism between object names for any Metric Diagram, but for a relational description there can be infinitely many Metric Diagrams. In drawing a diagram from a relational description (as is often done in solving physics problems, for instance) the relational description must first be filled out and then actual parameters found which satisfy this description. The fact that people are willing to go through this trouble in generating pencil and paper diagrams seems to indicate that our fluency in dealing with space does not come solely from a set of very clever axioms for reasoning with a relational description.

The "Naive Analog" scheme uses an array to model space, representing the location and extent of an object implicitly by what cells contain symbols corresponding to that object. By explicit analogy with low-level vision, a simple local process called a "retina" is used to examine the array in order to compute answers to spatial questions. In Funt (1976) such a scheme was used to simulate falling blocks and in Kosslyn and Schwartz (1977) is the central feature of a theory of mental imagery. This representation has several flaws (aside from not corresponding to the facts available about retinal function). Putting the process-

---

[2]Hayes [Hayes, 1979a] notes that the axioms for the geometry of blocks in many problem solvers can be satisfied by modelling a block as an ordered pair of integers, one component for the number of blocks below it, and one component for discrete locations on the table. This is far from the intuitive notions of space they are intended to capture.

ing in the "retina" leads to performing searches to answer most questions. To place an object into an array requires choosing parameters for its location, scale and rotation and then turning on the correct cells in the array. The instantiation of a Metric Diagram element requires only the first part of this process, and since it can be used to answer the questions the array becomes superfluous. Hinton (1979) argues against the use of array based representations in mental imagery on the same grounds. For some geometric questions a fully parallel array scheme could have certain advantages, such as determining intersections in constant time. The tradeoffs involved in such a scheme, however, have yet to be determined.

3. DESCRIBING A PARTICULAR MOTION

When people watch an object move, they generally couch their description in terms of a sequence of qualitatively distinct motion types. I call a network built from descriptions of motions linked by descriptions of the state of the object before and after each motion an *Action Sequence.*[3] The knowledge associated with each type of motion allows it to be further analyzed, the consistency of the proposed description to be checked, and permits making predictions about what will happen next. A drawn trajectory of motion in the Bouncing Ball domain and the schema of its associated Action Sequence is illustrated in Fig. 4.3.

The two basic types of motion in the Bouncing Ball world are flying and colliding. We denote occurrences of these motions by elements in the Action Sequence called FLY and COLLIDE. Flying up and flying down are separated into distinct acts because different things can happen after each of them. Acts that represent transitions to motion outside the domain of the Bouncing Ball world are CONTINUE for leaving the space enclosed by the diagram and AMBIGUITY-SLIDE/STOP, AMBIGUITY-SLIDE/STOP/FALL, and STOP when a ball interacts with a surface for any amount of time. Each act in the Action Sequence describes where it is occurring as well as when.

The description of a ball's state contains a parameter indicating the instant it applies to. It includes quantitative parameters such as the ball's position (specified by a point in the Metric Diagram), speed, and heading at that time. The kind of motion that will occur next, and what the ball is touching at that instant are other important parameters.

A description of the motion in terms of a qualitative state is also provided within the Action Sequence. The qualitative state of a ball includes the type of motion, position abstracted to a PLACE, and heading abstracted to a symbolic description, such as (LEFT UP). These qualitative states link the description of a

---

[3]The Action Sequence may be viewed as the *history* of a ball (in the Naive Physics sense of the term) since it contains explicit spatial and temporal limits.

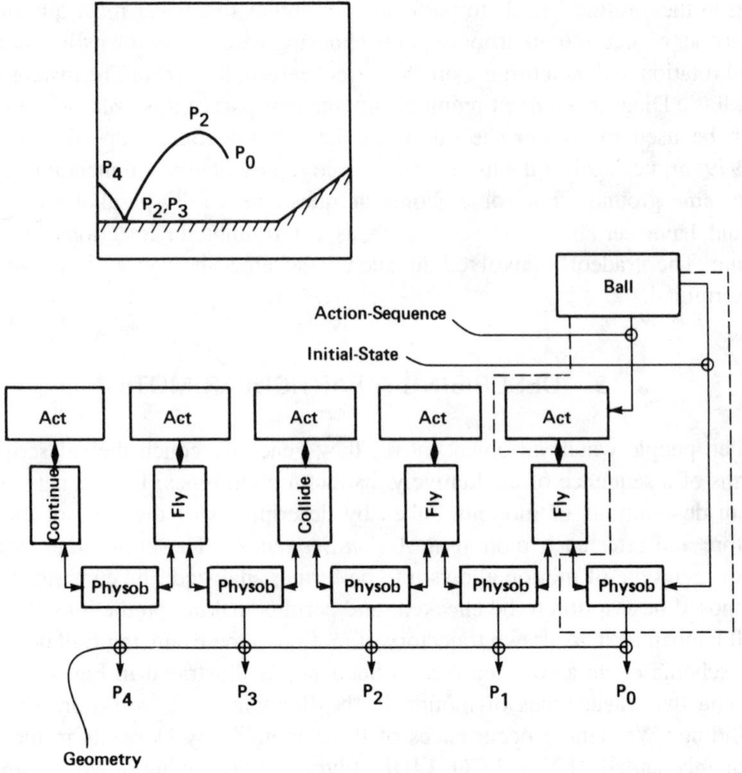

FIG. 4.3. Action Sequence Schema for Bouncing Balls. This schema describes the motion depicted in Fig. 4.1. The PHYSOB constraint describes the state of the ball at some instant in time, and the ACT constraints describe a piece of the ball's history.

particular motion to the description of possible motions explained in the next section.

In FROB the Action Sequence descriptions are embedded in a constraint language (see Steele & Sussman, [1978] for an overview, & Forbus [1981b] for a description of the particular language used). Each element of an Action Sequence is a constraint object, and they are connected together in a way such that partial information can be provided in whatever order is convenient. Local processes make deductions whenever possible, and can signal if an inconsistency is discovered.

The constraint descriptions used in FROB's Action Sequence include equations describing projectile motion to compute numerical values if numerical descriptions of the state parameters are obtained. The use of quantitative parameters in the qualitative description of motion makes possible a different kind of simulation from the usual incremental time simulations used in physics. When numbers are provided, an Action Sequence can be produced by generating a description of the next motion from the last known state of motion. The time to generate the description, as well as the complexity of the result, depends on the qualitative complexity of the motion rather than some fixed increment of time used to evolve a set of state parameters. FROB's simulation capability was used as a way of generating motion descriptions for qualitative analysis.

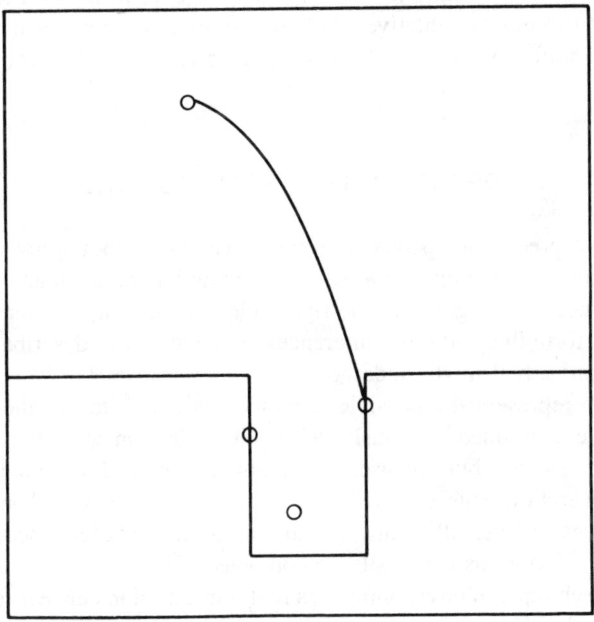

```
CONTRADICTION DISCOVERED CONCERNING (>>(A2 YSUM1 ENERGY F1)
WHOSE VALUE 8.888888896 DEPENDS ON
THE NEW VALUE 2.111111112 COMPUTED BY (RULE-3 . G0892) DEPENDS ON
1 ( >> Y   S1) = -4.0 from USER
BOTH VALUES SHARE THESE ASSUMPTIONS-
2 ( >> (CHECKED-VALUE COR-CHECK S3) (C-O-R  S3) ) = 0.5 from USER
3 ( >> Y- COMPONENT VELOCITY S5) = 0.0 from USER
4 ( >> Y S5) = 7.0 from USER
5 ( >> X S5) = -4.0 from USER
6 ( >> Y S3) = -3.0 from USER
7 ( >> X S1) = -2.0 from USER
8 ( >> X S3) = 2.0 from USER
CHOOSE ONE TO RETRACT BY CALLING ANSWER WITH ITS NUMBER
;BKPT CONTRADICTION-HANDLER
```

FIG. 4.4. An inconsistent description of motion. This motion is impossible because the ball could not get as high as it does after the second collision unless it had gone higher on the first. If it had gone higher after the first, the second collision would not even have happened. To discover that this description is inconsistent FROB requires a specific velocity at the highest point and a specific value for the elasticity of the ball as well as the coordinates of the collision points.

A proposed motion can be analyzed by building an Action Sequence for it, letting the knowledge of the equations of motion attached to the resulting constraint network look for inconsistencies and fill in consequences of what is known. FROB's dependence on quantitative parameters in the Action Sequence is a drawback. For example, FROB can detect that the situation in Fig. 3.4 is inconsistent only after being given some final height for the ball and a value for the elasticity. People can argue that this proposed motion is impossible with simpler arguments that require less information. To deal with this, FROB could be extended with a more qualitative set of analysis methods. One such rule for the Bouncing Ball domain would be "A ball cannot increase its energy from one act to the next."

4. DESCRIBING POSSIBLE MOTIONS

There are some predictions people can make even when they know very little about a situation. For example, if a ball is bouncing leftwards on an infinite flat plane, it will never start going to the right unless something interferes with it. People can perform this and other inferences by the ability to describe the set of possible motions a ball might undergo.

One way to represent the possible motions of a ball is to use the idea of a qualitative state mentioned previously. Simulation rules can be written that operate on qualitative states, but because of the ambiguity in the description they may predict that several motions are possible from some state. There are only a small number of places and a small number of motions possible at each place, so all the possible kinds of motions can easily be computed. This process is called *envisioning*. The technique of envisioning was first introduced in deKleer, (1975) for answering simple questions about a scene directly and as a planning device for algebraic solutions to physics problems. In FROB the result of envisioning is called the *Sequence Graph,* which uses the Space Graph for its spatial framework (see Fig. 4.5). The Sequence Graph is more complicated because it deals with a truly two dimensional domain and includes the effects of dissipative forces. Like deKleer's envisioner it is used to answer simple questions directly, but is also used to assimilate global constraints on motion.

The place vocabulary of the Space Graph is chosen to keep the Sequence Graph simple yet precise. Each different surface and border of the diagram must be a place, but there are many possible ways to carve up free space. A non-overlapping decomposition is used so that any quantitative state will map to a unique qualitative state. The considerations that were imposed on the Space Graph by its role as a framework for the Sequence Graph are:

1. The motion description must be kept small. This means that unnecessary distinctions should be avoided.
2. The branching factor (the number of motions possible after some state)

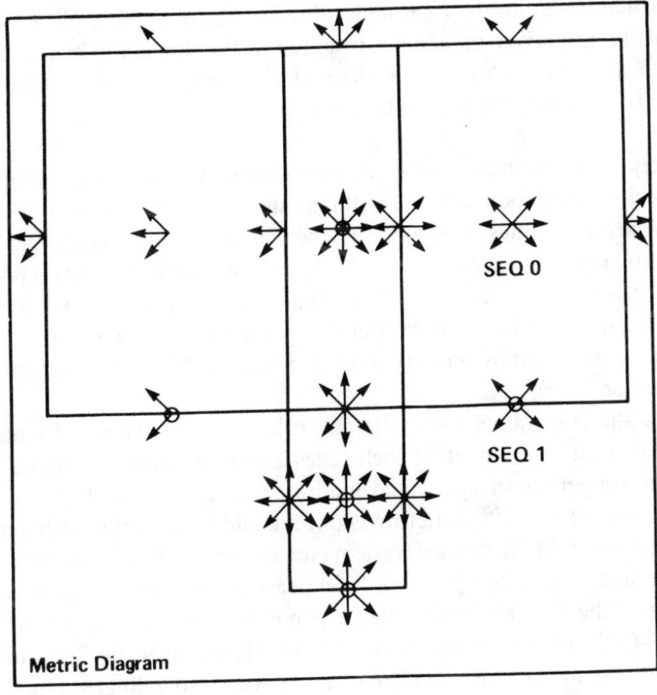


```
— >> (what-is ( >> root sequence-graph phob))
(    ROOT SEQUENCE-GRAPH PHOB) = SEQ0
NIL
—>>(pseq seq0)
 THIS IS THE START NODE OF THE GRAPH FOR G2860
SEQ0
(FLY SREGION3 (LEFT DOWN))
 CAN BE REACHED BY (SEQ12)
 NEXT CAN BE (SEQ1 SEQ2)
SEQ0
—>>(pseq .seq1)
SEQ1
(COLLIDE SEGMENT9 (LEFT DOWN))
 CAN BE REACHED BY (SEQ0)
 NEXT CAN BE (SEQ3 SEQ4)
SEQ1
```

FIG. 4.5. A Sequence Graph. The arrows represent the direction of a qualitative state at the place the arrow is drawn. Circles represent states without well defined directions. The possible temporal orderings of the states are not depicted.

must be kept small. One way of achieving this is to have only a single place be reached when travelling in a particular direction from another place.

3. Thanks to gravity the simplest motion of the domain is bouncing up and down over a horizontal surface. To keep the description of this motion simple, cut space by vertical and horizontal lines.

The Sequence Graph consists of all motions possible under the assumed initial condition. Knowing more about a ball than its state of motion at some time can restrict these possibilities. Energy limits the height a ball can reach, and knowing that a ball is perfectly elastic or completely inelastic excludes certain results of a collision. Assumptions about whether a ball must or may not reach a particular place or qualitative state can restrict the possibilities as well. The Sequence Graph can be modified by pruning states to reflect this information about the ball and its motion.

Each of the constraints above directly rules out some states of motion. The full consequences of eliminating such states are determined by methods that rely on specific properties of space and motion. It might appear that because this problem is concerned with belief revision, it could be solved by using a domain independent Truth Maintainence System (see Doyle, 1978; McAllester, 1980). A qualitative state would be "justified" if at least one predecessor state is possible and if one of the possible states after it is possible (unless it is a terminal state such as STOP). This does not work. The problem is that the Sequence Graph description contains a large number of cycles (corresponding to repetitive motion), making the computation of well founded support intolerably difficult. Instead the following facts of motion are used in pruning the Sequence Graph:

1. Only qualitative states that can be reached by some path of possible qualitative states from the initial one are themselves possible.
2. All motion occurs on a continuous path in space. Although implicit in (1) explicit use of this fact is advantageous because there are fewer places than qualitative states.
3. Unless a ball is perfectly elastic, it must either stop or leave the diagram.
4. A ball travelling in either the space above a surface with horizontal extent or between two surfaces with vertical extent in a particular direction can do so only if it either leaves the place going in that direction, changes direction, or stops within the place after moving in that direction.

Condition four is required to exclude situations whose qualitative description matches that of Zeno's paradox. An example is a ball bouncing on a horizontal surface travelling leftward, but never reaching the left border of the region it is in and never stopping.

Computations which use these facts are applied to the Sequence Graph to determine the consequences of the assumptions. Dependency information is

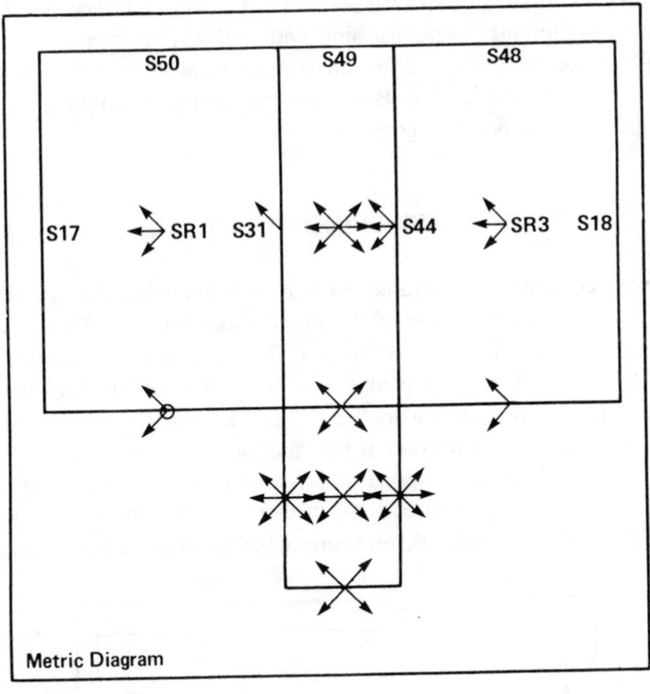


```
—»(why-not seq37)
 (CONTINUE SEGMENT17 (LEFT)) IS UNATTAINABLE BECAUSE
 (CANNOT-REACH SEGMENT17)
SEQ37
—»(why-not seq35)
 (CONTINUE SEGMENT50 (LEFT UP)) IS UNATTAINABLE BECAUSE
 (ENERGY)
SEQ35
—»(why-not seq77)
 (CONTINUE SEGMENT18 (RIGHT)) IS UNATTAINABLE BECAUSE
 (REQUIRED-STATES (SEQ22))
SEQ77
—»(pseq seq22)

SEQ22
 (PASS SEGMENT31 (LEFT UP))
  CAN BE REACHED BY (SEQ15)
  NEXT CAN BE (SEQ30
SEQ22
```

FIG. 4.6. Effects of assumptions on the Sequence Graph. Making assumptions about the physical properties of the ball or global properties of motion can reduce the ambiguity inherent in the Sequence Graph. Note the difference between this description and Fig. 4.5.

stored so that the effects of specific assumptions may be traced (see Fig. 4.6). Conflicting assumptions, overconstraint, and conflicts between a description of the actual motion (as specified by an Action Sequence) and its constrained possibilities are detected by FROB and the underlying assumptions are offered up for inspection and possible correction.

5. ANSWERING QUESTIONS

Many of the questions that could be asked by the Bouncing Ball domain can be answered by direct examination of the descriptions built by FROB. These include the first two questions in section 1.1. The three levels of motion description in FROB (the Action Sequence, the Sequence Graph, and the path of qualitative states corresponding to the Action Sequence) allow some kind of answer to be given even with partial information.

The more complicated questions about summarizing motion and collisions (questions 3 and 4 on p. 64) can be answered with additional computation. Summarizing motion includes determining whether or not a ball is trapped in a

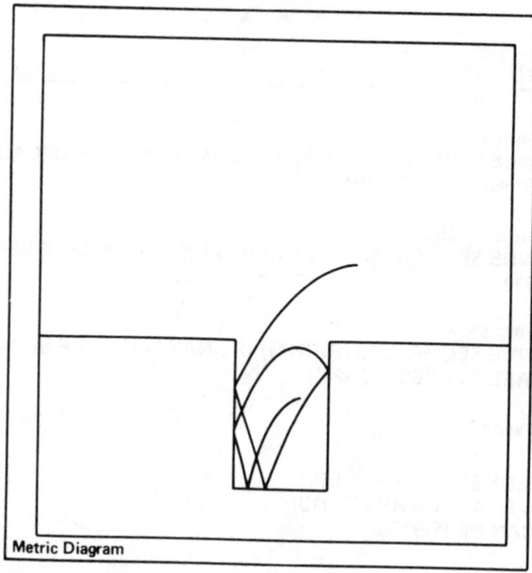


```
—>> (motion-summary-for b1)

  FOR G0364
  THE BALL WILL EVENTUALLY STOP
  IT IS TRAPPED INSIDE (WELLO)
  AND WILL STOP FLYING AT ONE OF (SEGMENT11)
NIL
```

FIG. 4.7. Summarizing motion.

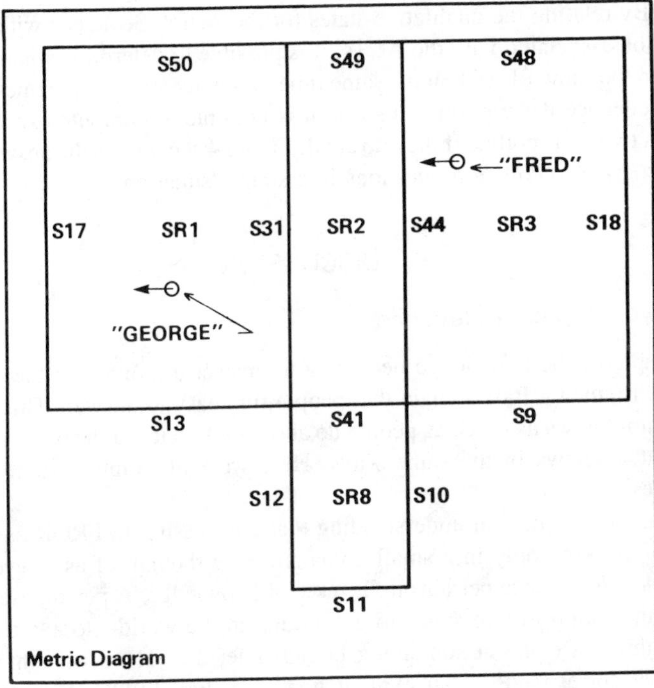


```
—>>(collide? fred george)
(POSSIBLE AT SEGMENT50 SEGMENT17 SEGMENT13 SREGION)
—>>(cannot-be-at  fred segment31)
(SEGMENT 31)
 UPDATING ASSUMPTIONS FOR (>>INITIAL-STATE FRED)
 CHECKING PATH OF MOTION AGAINST ASSUMPT IONS
—>>(collide? fred george)
NO
—>>(what-is (>> state initial-state fred)
(    STATE INITIAL-STATE FRED) = (FLY (SREGION3) (LEFT))
NIL
—>>(what-is (>> state initial-state george))
(>> STATE INITIAL-STATE GEORGE) = (FLY (SREGION) (LEFT))
NIL
```

FIG. 4.8. Collision problems.

well (see Fig. 4.7), which can be done by examining a Sequence Graph for the last state in an Action Sequence to see if it is possible to be moving outside the places that comprise the well. The places where a ball can stop or leave the diagram are known, and so the possibilities for its final disposition can be described.

Having several levels of detail allows collision questions to be answered more easily. Often a collision between two balls can be ruled out because the two balls are never in the same PLACE, as determined by examining their Sequence

Graphs. By relating the qualitative states for the Action Sequence with the time information associated with the ACTs, it is possible to determine whether or not a ball is in the same PLACE at the same time. With quantitative parameters in the Action Sequence description of motion it is possible to compute exactly where and when two balls collide if they do at all. Figure 4.8 contains the answers given by the program to collision questions in a simple situation.

6. DISCUSSION

6.1 Psychological Relevance

FROB captures the knowledge necessary to answer a number of the questions about the Bouncing Ball domain that people find easy to answer. This does not imply that it knows as much as people do about motion through space, nor that it uses what it knows in the same ways. Here we will examine some of these differences.

Two aspects of human understanding that are missing in FROB as a consequence of working only in a small domain can be thought of as *relevance* and *significance*. Relevance pertains to the uses of knowledge. A person uses knowledge about motion in free space to get around in the world—to avoid a falling rock, to throw a stone at something bothersome, etc. There is nothing inside FROB that corresponds to an explicit goal or value. FROB is an "it" only because in English it is convenient to characterize something that has processes and state as an entity.

By significance, I mean the ability to relate a piece of knowledge to other things you know. There is no interpretation of the tokens used in FROB's representations other than the processes that directly manipulate them, nor are they part of a larger corpus of knowledge. This makes FROB inflexible. For example, a person would understand that the only impact on his knowledge of halving the value of the gravitational constant would be that the value used in the equations of motion must be changed accordingly. He would understand that if gravity varied in magnitude with time the equations of motion would become more complex and if the sign varied as well his qualitative rules of motion would require revision.

Even within its intended domain, there are several differences between what FROB does and what people appear to do. First of all, people are far more flexible about the ways they divide space. In the well picture, for example, the chunks of space are people usually describe are "inside the well" (SregionO and its borders) and "outside the well" (Sregional, Sregion2, Sregion3, and their borders). If necessary, they can make finer distinctions, such as which side of the well something is on (Sregionl or Sregion3). One way that FROB could be modified to exhibit this behavior would be to compute a tree of places, with the current Space Graph corresponding to the most detailed level of the tree. A set of rules about what level of the tree to use for envisioning and other computations would be needed as well as methods to compare descriptions at different levels. Relaxing the restriction of a single qualitative description of space will almost certainly be necessary for more complex domains. This makes the existence of an underlying quantitative representation even more important, to serve as a communication device between different qualitative descriptions.

The answers people give when asked to describe what motions are possible in some situation do not look much like a natural language version of the Sequence Graph. Part of the lack of correspondence is due to the differences in place vocabulary described earlier, but not all. The descriptions people give often ignore certain of the possible motions. If pressed they can determine whether or not one of these unconsidered possibilities can indeed occur. There are several possible explanations for this phenomena. They might be performing envisionment, but pruning the results when communicating since it is very tedious to express a graph structure with many cycles as a string. They might instead be choosing only one alternative when using a set of qualitative simulation rules, and have the ability to backward chain using these rules when asked if some state that did not appear in their description can occur.

Another interesting question concerns how people actually assimilate qualitative assumptions about motion. In FROB a complicated process prunes the Sequence Graph and leaves behind a trace of why certain states cannot occur. A person may just perform the envisioning over again and stop when a state that is explicitly ruled out is reached. The states which in FROB would be pruned as a consequence of the new assumptions would then never be generated. In pure form this would not solve the problem of the Qualitative Zeno's Paradox, so some pruning would still be required. Careful protocols (and perhaps timing studies) of people deciding why or why not a state of motion is possible could shed light on the matter.

6.2 New Directions

Although the results of programs like FROB may be encouraging, there is still much to be understood about people's fluency in dealing with the physical world. Part of the progress can come from building programs like FROB, which reason about domains that form a separable part of physics (such as motion through space, sliding on a surface, etc.), by identifying a place vocabulary and a definition of qualitative state adequate for solving some set of problems. However, there are at least three areas which lie outside this approach and must be incorporated into it if we are eventually to succeed in creating a theory of common sense reasoning about physics.

The first area concerns the way qualitative knowledge is used, the *style* of reasoning performed. In FROB the use of qualitative knowledge centers around envisioning: the PLACE vocabulary was chosen to make it easy to perform, and creating and manipulating Sequence Graphs provides the means to answer questions that require qualitative knowledge. Much of the theory of the domain physics is encoded in the qualitative simulation rules and in the programs that prune the envisionment. Deductions based on the envisionment implicitly use the assumption that the simulation rules are complete and have been run to completion when ruling states in or out. Although envisioning is an important technique, I believe the burden of building a complete description of possible states is too onerous outside very small domains, and is too restrictive a style to capture all of the ways people use qualitative physical knowledge.

The envisionment for a complicated situation will be large because the PLACE description of the situation will be large. As discussed earlier, this could be ameliorated by greater flexibility in the PLACE vocabulary and especially by making it hierarchical. This leaves us with the issue of deciding what level of description to use in a problem (which is interesting on its own merits). A more serious complication arises if collisions between moving objects are explicitly represented. Because there is no information about time other than the orderings of the qualitative states a collision is possible after each state in the graph. This causes an explosive increase in the connectivity of the graph. A similar problem in more complex domains occurs when two processes or objects are acting in concert to produce an effect. An example is boiling water by passing steam through pipes in the container. To capture all possible states in this situation requires considering all possible time orderings for events, such as running out of water and shutting down the steam. Certainly some questions about these situations would require that much work, but surely not all. Still another complication ensues if analyzing a machine with controls. Consider for example a steam plant, which may have several hundred valves that could be adjusted at any time. There is no way to predict such an event with the physics of the plant, nor would explicitly representing the set of all the effects of all such possible events be attractive.

Even when envisioning is possible, it is not clear that people do it. Consider for example the situation in Fig. 4.9 which contains a lever with a pin in its path. When asked if the tip of the lever can get to point A (or B or C), the answer people give is no. The reasons they give are different in each case. For A the reason is that the pin stops the lever from moving. For B and C however, the reason is that the rigidity of the lever means it cannot bend, stretch, grow, or shrink to reach these points. The simplest envisioning system imaginable would only be able to say that these states are not considered possible. A more subtle one (as in FROB) would perform the envisioning without the pin, and prune the part of the path made impossible by the pin while keeping track of the reason for its rejection. But to remove the premise of rigidity would cause the number of possible motions to grow quite large. A simpler way to solve such a problem is to consider the ways the proposed state might come about. In this situation the only ways of getting the tip to B are by moving the pivot point or shrinking or bending the lever. These three prospects are easily eliminated by the assumptions that the pivot is fixed and the lever rigid, and so it can be concluded that the tip cannot be at B.

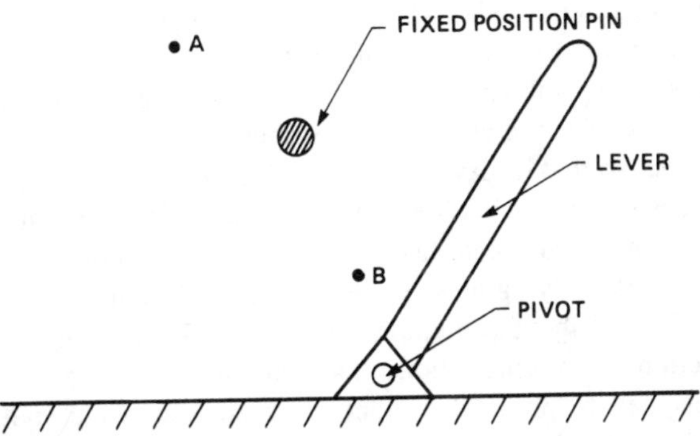

FIG. 4.9. Questions of excluded states. The pivot is in a fixed position and the lever is rigid. Consider whether or not the tip of the lever can reach A, B, and C in turn. The answers people give to these questions are the same that a system relying only on envisionment would give, but their reasons are quite different.

This example illustrates what can be done if qualitative knowledge is encoded more flexibly than in simulation rules. Questions about possible states can concern past states as well to infer possible causes, and in both cases simple deductions could often yield results. For example, a prerequisite for an object to get from one place to another is the existence of a path between the two places—no path, no motion. The same properties of physical theories that make envisioning possible, such as making influences explicit and few in number and allowing them to operate only through explicit connections,[4] make the number of theories that can link possible states small as well. This limited forward deduction is perhaps one of a number of "styles" of reasoning that should be explored.

Let us consider an abstract example to illustrate the other two areas I think are important for future work in this field. Imagine an object or a collection of objects for which we have a qualitative state description based on some theory about how they work. For the particular state they are in we know the possible states they might be in next, and perhaps if we have more detailed quantitative data we can actually calculate which of these possible states will occur. If we were to continue to project the possibilities for each possible state we would be performing envisioning. But these two possibilities do not exhaust our options. One thing we might do is make assumptions about the situation, based on past experience, that could lead to some of the alternatives being ruled out. We might

[4]In "Non-Naive" physics these properties are reflected in the unification of different influences into the notion of force and in the bias against action at a distance.

also consider what different things we would see depending on which state actually occurred, and just wait to find out what happens.

Both options remove us from the world of "armchair physics" in which our investigations so often reside. The main reason common sense physics is so interesting is that it is useful in helping us to get around in the world. If we are reasoning in order to deal with the world, we want to be able to make predictions quickly when possible. We want to reason about how some state of affairs could have come about so that it may be duplicated if desirable, or avoided if not. We need techniques to see if what we know about a situation is consistent with our physics for we can be mistaken, lied to, or ignorant. Current practice in Artificial Intelligence makes studying these kinds of issues difficult. A program is usually told all it will be told about a situation in one initial description and is not allowed to propose actions or execute actions that would provide more information. They are often designed to provide a quantitative answer in the style of a student solving a physics problem. These restrictions on the design of programs can be valuable simplifications of an already complex task, but if we maintain them too long our efforts may well become distorted.

Using experience probably has two roles in common sense physics. It is sensible to assume that the description of objects we begin with when applying our theories about the world are fairly far from the idealizations of the physics. Experience with the world could guide the process of choosing the right physics and mapping from the given objects and relations to the idealizations. Another role for experience is the source of default assumptions. Few people viewing the lever (see Fig. 4.9) would volunteer that it would not reach B because the friction in the pivot was so high that the lever could not move at all, yet this could be the case. This aspect of physical reasoning skates close to the deep and turgid waters of learning and does not look simple.

Physical objects can be seen and touched, and while not all of the terms in our theories about them are perceptable (such as density), their effects certainly are. To discover if our theory about a situation is correct we are often goaded into performing actions upon the world. Few people, for example, would claim to fully understand an unfamiliar mechnical gadget just by looking at it; they push and poke its parts to see how it moves, and often modify their theories about it accordingly. A theory of common sense physical reasoning should include theories of what to observe and how to experiment within a situation. It should be able to deduce what the observable consequences of alternate theories concerning a situation are and deduce what sort of manipulations can be made to gain required information.

REFERENCES

Bundy, A. *MECHO: Year one*. Research Report No. 22, Department of Artificial Intelligence, Edinburgh, 1976.

de Kleer, J. *Qualitative and quantitative knowledge in classical mechanics*. Technical Report 352, MIT AI Lab, Cambridge, Mass., 1975.

de Kleer, J. *Causal and teleological reasoning in circuit recognition*. MIT AI-TR-529, Cambridge, Mass., Sept. 1979.

Doyle, J. *Truth maintenance systems for problem solving*. MIT AI Lab Technical Report 419, Cambridge, Mass., Sept. 1978.

Forbus, K. *A study of qualitative and geometric knowledge in reasoning about motion*. TR-615, MIT AI Lab, Cambridge, Mass., Feb. 1981. (a)

Forbus, K. *A Conlan Primer*. BBN Technical Report, 1981. (b)

Funt, B. V. *WHISPER:A computer implementation using analogues in reasoning*. Unpublished doctoral dissertation, University of British Columbia, 1976.

Hayes, P. J. The naive physics manifesto. In D. Michie (Ed.), *Expert Systems in the Micro-Electronic Age,* Edinburgh University press, May 1979. (a)

Hayes, P. J. *Naive physics 1—ontology for liquids*. Memo, Centre pour les etudes Semantiques et Cognitives, Geneva, 1979. (b)

Hinton, G. Some demonstrations of the effects of structural descriptions in mental imagery. *Cognitive Science,* Vol. 3, No. 3, July–September 1979.

Kosslyn, S. & Schwartz, S. P. A simulation of visual imagery. *Cognitive Science,* Vol. 1, No. 3, July 1977.

Marr, D. *Artificial intelligence—a personal view*. Memo No. 355, MIT AI Lab, Cambridge, Mass., March 1976.

McAllester, D. *An outlook on truth maintenance*. MIT AI Lab Memo 551, Cambridge, Mass., August 1980.

McDermott, J., & Larkin, J. *Re-representing textbook physics problems*. Presented at the 2nd National Conference of the Canadian Society for Computational Studies of Intelligence, Toronto 1978.

Novak, G. *Computer understanding of physics problems stated in natural language*. Technical Report NL-30, Computer Science Department, The University of Texas at Austin, 1976.

Steele, G., & Sussman, G. *Constraints*. Memo No. 502, MIT AI Lab, Cambridge, Mass., November 1978.

Waltz, D., & Boggess, L. Visual analog representations for natural language understanding. Presented at *IJCAI-79,* Tokyo, Japan, August 1979.

5 The Role of Problem Representation in Physics

Jill H. Larkin
Carnegie-Mellon University

Inasmuch as people are good at predicting the outcome of physical interactions in the world around them, why are they so bad at physics, even the branch of physics (mechanics) that deals with the interaction of everyday objects? I argue here that the process of mentally simulating events so as to predict their outcome, a facility possessed by most people for common contexts, is extended and refined in a skilled scientist to become a sharp and crucial intuition that can be used in solving difficult, complex or extraordinary problems. Novices, lacking this extended intuition, find such problems difficult.

More specifically, many differences in the problem-solving performance of experts and novices can be related to use of different problem representations. Novices use what I call a *naive* problem representation; it is composed of objects that exist in the real world (blocks, pulleys, springs) and developed through operators that correspond to developments that occur in real time. Such a representation is a runnable model of the real problem situation. Experts, in addition to this naive representation, are able to construct what I call a *physical* representation that contains fictitious, imagined entities such as forces and momenta. A representation involving these entities is developed by operators corresponding to laws of physics. Thus the expert has a second mental model of a problem situation, a model with particularly powerful attributes.

This chapter develops these ideas and uses the proposed expert-novice difference in representation to explain recent experimental results comparing expert and novice performance. The final section briefly addresses how problem representations are treated in textbooks, and why students may have difficulty learning to construct expert representations.

I. PROBLEM REPRESENTATIONS

Naive Representation

The process of predicting the motion of objects in a familiar (although idealized) domain has been studied and formalized by de Kleer (1975, 1977). He calls the process "envisionment," and it can be well illustrated through a discussion of the following problem (de Kleer, 1975).

A small block slides from rest along the indicated frictionless surface (see Fig. 5.1. Will the block reach the point marked X? De Kleer presents the following hypothetical "protocol" analyzing the problem which corresponds to an envisionment constructed by his simulation program, NEWTON. The block will start to slide down the curved surface without falling off or changing direction. After reaching the bottom it starts going up. It still will not fall off but it may start sliding back. If the block ever reaches the straight section it will not fall off there, but it may change the direction of its movement.

As shown in Fig. 5.2 the envisionment of a problem consists of a tree, with a top node corresponding to where the particle starts, with subsequent nodes produced by operators that predict the immediately subsequent motion of a particle from its current motion, and branches produced wherever two subsequent motions are possible (e.g., the block might continue along its path, or it might slide back down).

The central features of envisionment as discussed by de Kleer are the following:

1. The entities in problem representation are objects familiar in everyday life and appearing directly in the problem. In Fig. 5.2 the entities include falling and sliding; envisionments for problems involving explicit interaction as well as motion would involve familiar objects (blocks, hills) and familiar interactions (e.g., touching, near).

2. The envisionment tree is developed by unidirectional operators that develop new information consistent with the passing of time. This is why the envisionment is a tree rather than a graph; there is no possibility of upward branching backwards in time. This feature also implies that for each piece of new information there's only one source; there is no possibility for a single piece of information to be obtained redundantly from two other nodes.

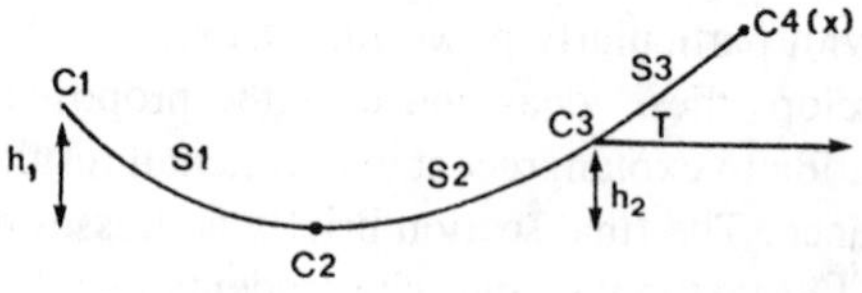

FIG. 5.1. A block sliding on a smooth curved path (de Kleer, 1975).

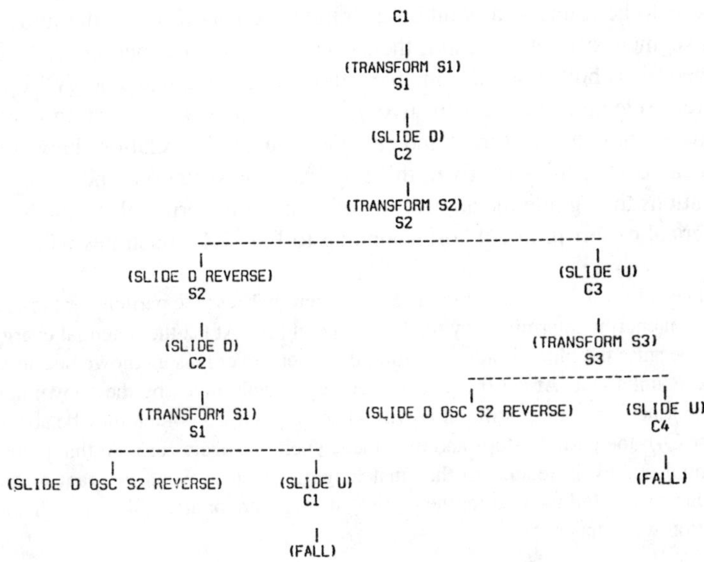

FIG. 5.2. Envisionment given by de Kleer for the problem of the sliding block.

As de Kleer points out, envisionments would seem to be central to some aspects of problem-solving. Primarily they enable a solver to answer directly simple questions such as whether the block in Fig. 5.1 will reach the bottom.

For clarity in what follows I shall substitute the term *naive representation* for envisionment. A naive representation is an internal representation of the problem that contains direct representations of the familiar, visible entities mentioned in the problem, and that simulates the interaction of these entities through operators that predict subsequent events on the basis of former events, following the usual direction of time flow. This naive representation contrasts with what I shall call a *physical representation.* As discussed in the following pages, a physical representation involves entities (e.g., forces, momenta) that are not familiar but have meaning only in the context of formal physics. Both naive and physical representations are distinct from a *mathematical* representation, a set of equations reflecting physical principles applied to the problem.

Physical Representation

In de Kleer's (1975, 1977) NEWTON system, the naive representation guides directly the selection and application of quantitative physical principles. This is done by means by heuristic rules, acting on the naive representation, that are stored with the various principles. For example, when NEWTON tries to apply kinematic relations to the sliding block problem, it encounters a rule stating that, if speed is to be found at a point on a straight segment (S3) but the initial speed on that segment cannot be found, then kinematic rules are inappropriate. NEWTON then tries another set of principles (those associated with energy). I propose a different selection mechanism involving a *physical* representation containing fictitious entities such as forces and energies. Qualitative relations between these entities can be "seen" directly in this physical representation, and these qualitative relations then guide the application of quantitative principles. The following hypothetical expert protocol corresponding to Fig. 5.1, illustrates what I mean:

> The energy at C1 consists of kinetic energy, zero because the particle is at rest, and potential energy determined by the known height h_1. At C2 the potential energy is zero, because the block is at the bottom; the kinetic energy is unknown because the speed is unknown. At C3 the potential energy is determined by the known height h_2; the kinetic energy is still unknown. At some point C5 (which may be above or below C4), the particle stops and the kinetic energy is again zero. At that point the potential energy is related to the final height, which is what we want to know (because it will tell us whether the particle stops before or after C4). Thus the basic equation we want is
>
> $$\text{energy at C1} = \text{energy at C5}$$
>
> or
>
> $$0 + mgh_1 = 0 + mg(h_2 + X/\sin T)$$
>
> where X is the distance the block travels after point C3, and may be larger or smaller than S3.

In Table 5.1, as in subsequent tables summarizing physical representations, the top line indicates the entities in the representations (here kinetic and potential energies) and the bottom line has mathematical expressions for these entities in terms of known and desired quantities. I do not think that expert solvers immediately make use of these expressions, although they are ultimately used in constructing a mathematical representation. Their presence is intended to specify

TABLE 5.1
Physical Representation (in Terms of Energies) for the Sliding Block Problem

Energies					
At C1		At C3		At C5	
Kinetic	Potential	Kinetic	Potential	Kinetic	Potential
0	mgh_1	unknown	mgh_2	0	mgh_2 + X/sin T

how entities in the physical representation are related to known and desired quantities.

An appropriate physical representation guides the writing of mathematical relations as illustrated by the preceding example. In contrast an inappropriate physical relation quickly reveals itself, allowing the solver to try something else. For example, a force-acceleration representation for the sliding block problem might be developed in the following way:

> At point C1 the block is at rest. As the block moves along S1, it is acted on by a force directed roughly downward along the path, and so its speed increases. However, because we don't know the shape of the path, we can't find the value for this force, and there is no way to determine how the block's speed will change.

Table 5.2 compares the main features of naive and physical problem representations. Both are built by taking information from the problem and using rules of inference to create new information. Both seem to involve entities that might readily be imaged, perhaps with the aid of a diagram. The naive representation is a direct simulation of events involving real (imagable) objects. It is less clear that the physical representation must always be imagable, but it is worthy of comment that most physical representations seem to have this feature. Even very abstract physical phenomena (e.g., energy states of an atom, conservation of quantum properties in the interaction of elementary particles) have corresponding imagable representations (energy levels, Feynman diagrams) used in solving related problems. In both naive and physical representations the inferencing rules are qualitative, and not tied directly to equations. The differences in the representations are in the kind of entities involved (familiar objects or abstractly defined physics entities) and in the rules of inference used to generate new information (operators developing new information in the timed sequence of a simulation, or operators producing new information in any order in a time independent representation).

TABLE 5.2
Comparison of Naive and Physical Representations

Naive Representations (Envisionments)	*Physical Representations*
Problem representations with qualitative inferencing rules	
Imagable entities	
"Familiar" entities	Physical entities
Simulation inferencing (follows time flow)	Constraint inferencing
Distant from physics principles	Closely tied to physics principles
Tree structure, single inference sources	Graph structure, redundant inferences sources
Diffused properties of entities	Localized properties of entities

The physical representation (unlike the naive representation) does not explicitly include time. For example, the representation in Table 5.1 would be the same whether the particle moved right to left or left to right or oscillated between C1 and the stopping point C5. The slots in the representation can be filled in any order either quantitatively (with the algebraic expressions in Table 5.1) or qualitatively by being marked as *known* (determined by known quantities) *desired* (knowledge of this quantity would provide information about the desired quantity), or *unknown* (not determined by any combination of known or desired quantities).

The physical representation of a problem is closely tied to the instantiation of the quantitative physics principles describing the problem. The energy representation in Table 5.1 is closely tied to the principle that the change in energy of a system is equal to the work done on it. This close relationship makes the physical representation a means of planning a final quantitative solution because if all the slots in a physical representation can be filled, then all the corresponding parts of an equation can be written. Viewed in this way, the time independent nature of the physical representation corresponds to the fact that physical principles are constraint relations that can be used to make inferences in any direction, independent of time flow.

Finally, the entities in physical representation have *localized* attributes, that is, one doesn't learn any more about the entity by considering the context in which it appears. This is not the case for entities in naive representations. For example, an attribute of a toboggan in a naive representation might well be that it goes down hills. However, if it does not go down a hill, the fault may be that something is wrong with the toboggan (it's improperly waxed, or full of splinters); but the fault may also be outside the toboggan (the snow is wet). Thus an attribute of the toboggan (it goes down hills) can be violated by changes not in the toboggan, but in its environment. I think this is never the case with physical entities. Nothing in the environment of a force can change any of the attributes of the force. This property of physical representations, that attributes of entities are localized to that entity and not diffused throughout the environment, is identical to the principle of "no function in structure" introduced by de Kleer and Brown (1981) as a disideratum for models of complex systems.

To illustrate the use of a physical representation, consider the following problem.

> What constant horizontal force F must be applied to the large cart in Fig. 5.3 (of mass M) so that the smaller carts (masses m_1 and m_2) do not move relative to the large cart? Neglect friction.

The following excerpt from a typical novice protocol for this problem illustrates the difficulty untrained individuals have in constructing even a naive representation for this problem.

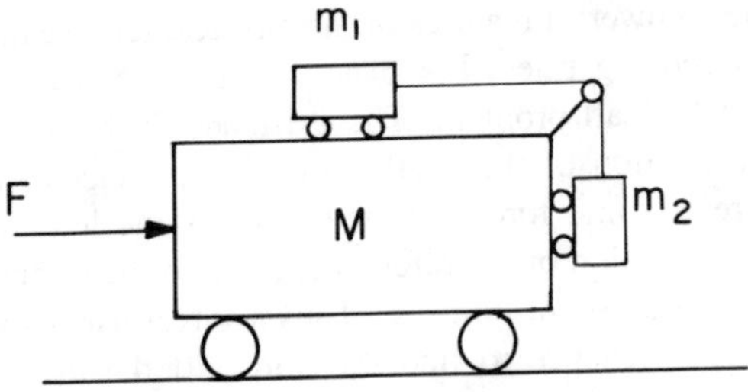

FIG. 5.3. Three carts.

> Well, I'm right now trying to reason why it isn't going to move.
> I mean I can see, if you accelerated it at a certain speed,
> the wind would push on m_1 so m_2 wouldn't fall.
> (later)
> Once I visualize it, I can probably get started.
> But I don't see how this is going to work.

This subject, like most other novices, never did succeed either in understanding what was going on in the problem or in solving it. In contrast, consider the following excerpt from the protocol of an expert subject solving the same problem using a physical representation involving reference frames and pseudo-forces.

> Well, with a uniformly accelerating reference frame, all right?
> So that there is a pseudo-force on m_1 to the left
> That is just equivalent—
> Just necessary to balance out the weight of m_2.

This subject proceeded immediately to write an equation equating the pseudo-force on m_1 and the tension force due to the weight of m_2 and then to solve the problem. This subject and all the other expert subjects looked at this problem not as a confusing collection of carts and ropes and pulleys, but as an abstracted object (of mass m_1) at rest at an accelerated reference frame (of the large cart), and therefore acted on by a pseudo-force to the left as well as the obvious tension force to the right. [The so-called pseudo-force in physics is that "force" that you feel snapping your head back in the accelerated reference frame of a car starting quickly from a stoplight. It is not a true force due to another object, but a fictitious force experienced because the frame of reference (e.g., the car) is accelerating.] The fact that the object is at rest means that these two forces must be equal in magnitude. Thus the *physical* representation used by the skilled subjects to solve this problem seems profoundly different in content from *naive* representation used by the novice subjects (or the envisionments used by NEWTON).

One of the most powerful features of the physical representation is the redundancy of the inferencing rules. For example, Table 5.6a shows one physical representation for the cart problem. The existence of the tension force and the fact that the acceleration of the small cart is zero (relative to the large cart) implies that there is some force directed towards the left. This force is also implied by the acceleration of the reference frame to the right, and therefore the existence of a leftward pseudo-force $\mathcal{F}$. Thus a solver using such an inferencing scheme has a double chance to find this force. If the pseudo-force rule was forgotten, the existence of this force might still be inferred (and the pseudo-force rule remembered) due to the redundant inferencing rule.

Schemas for Producing Physical Representations

How are physical problem representations, like those discussed earlier, constructed? The following paragraphs give examples of two plausible schemas for constructing physical representations in mechanics. For each the inferencing rules have been divided into *construction* rules that act on the original (naive) problem representation to produce entities in the physical representation, and *extension* rules that act on an existing physical representation to add new entities within that representation.

Forces Schema

This schema corresponds to the physical principle that the total force on a system (along a particular direction) is equal to the system's mass times its acceleration (along that direction). The schema applies to the following situations.

1. A system that has zero acceleration (along a particular direction) and is acted on by two forces (parallel to that direction) that have equal magnitudes and opposite directions.
2. A system that has a nonzero acceleration (in a particular direction) and is acted on either by one force in that direction, or by two opposite forces, the one with larger magnitude being along the acceleration.

Construction Rules. These rules correspond to force laws that allow inference of the direction and magnitude of a force from the characteristics of the object exerting it. For example, on an object of mass m, a force law states that the earth exerts a downward force of magnitude mg, where g is a known constant. The remainder of the construction rules correspond to what are called *kinematic* principles, that relate the acceleration of a system to other descriptions (e.g., velocity, distance travelled) of its motion.

Extension Rules. There are two complementary rules: If the acceleration is zero, and one force is known, then there is another force of equal magnitude and opposite direction. If there are two forces of equal magnitude and opposite direction, then the acceleration is zero. (For simplicity these rules are stated in terms of just two forces. All can be generalized by letting each force equal the sum of all the forces in that direction.)

Work-Energy Schema

This schema corresponds to the physical principle that the total energy of a system changes by an amount equal to the work done on it.

Construction Rules. These rules correspond to principles describing the various kinds of energy a system (or component of a system may have). For example, the kinetic energy of a particle is determined by its mass m and speed v, and is quantitatively equal to $\frac{1}{2} mv^2$. An additional rule relates the work done on a system to the "non-conservative" forces on the system and to the path it travels.

Extension Rules. Consider the initial energy of a system, its final energy, and the work done on it in the relevant interval. If any two of these are known, then the third can be found.

Example

As illustration of the application of these schemas, consider the problems stated in Table 5.3, and the corresponding physical representations summarized in Table 5.4. Problem 1 concerns a block. In a physical representation involving forces, the block is acted on by two forces having magnitudes $F_1 = mg \sin \theta$ and $F_2 = \mu \ mg \cos \theta$. It has an acceleration which can be shown to be $v^2/2l$. Using energies, the physical representation of the same problem involves an initial energy $E_1 = mgl \sin \theta$ of the block at the top of the ramp, a final energy $E_2 = \frac{1}{2} mv^2$ of the block at the bottom of the ramp, and a work $W = \mu mg \cos \theta \, l$ done on the block during the intervening time. The physical representations of problem 4 are analogous.

TABLE 5.3
Two Easy Problems

Problem 1.	A body of mass m starts from rest down a plane of length l inclined at an angle θ with the horizontal. If the coefficient of friction is μ, what is the body's speed as it reaches the bottom of the plane?
Problem 4.	What is the minimum stopping distance for a car traveling along a flat horizontal road, with initial speed v_0, if the coefficient of friction between tire and road is μ?

TABLE 5.4
Schema Slots and Fillers for Problems in Table 5.3. Numbers Indicate the Order Expert Subjects Filled the Slots

(a) Force Representation

	Problem 1			*Problem 4*	
	F_1	F_2	a	F_1	a
	$mg \sin\theta$	$\mu mg \cos\theta$	$v^2/2l$	μmg	$v^2/2l$
S1:	1	2	3	1	2
S2:	2	1	3		
S3:	1	2	3	1	2
S5:	2	1	3	1	2
S6:	1	2	3		
S7:	1	2	3		
S8:	1	2	3	1	2
S11:	1	2	3	1	2

(b) Work-Energy Representation

	Problem 1			Problem 4		
	E_1	E_2	W	E_1	E_2	W
	$mg/ \sin\theta$	$\frac{1}{2}mv^2$	$\mu mg \cos\theta/$	$\frac{1}{2}mv^2$	0	$\mu g/$
S2:				2	.	1
S4:	3	2	1	2	.	1
S6:				.	1	2
S7:				.	1	2
S9:	2	3	1	1	.	2
S10:	2	3	1	1	.	2

II. EMPIRICAL STUDIES

The remainder of this chapter discussed empirical studies relevant to how physical representations function in problem solving and how expert-novice differences in problem-solving performance can be explained by saying that experts are much better able to construct and use physical representations.

The Order of Principles Applied in Easy Problems

In solutions to very easy problems, the use of a physical representation is mainly visible in the order in which principles are applied. Consider the two problems in Table 5.3. Physical representations can be constructed for these problems using either forces or energies.

Table 5.4 shows physical representations for these problems constructed using either the force or work-energy schemas. Using the force schema, the slots are the acceleration and the constant force(s) exerted on the objects of interest (in problem 1 a component of the gravitational force and a frictional force, in problem 4 just a frictional force). Underneath the label for each slot is the value filling this slot in that problem (e.g., mg sin θ for the gravitational force component in problem 1). In the representation constructed using the work-energy schema, the slots are an initial energy, a final energy, and an intervening work.

Eleven expert and 11 novice subjects completed solutions to these problems while thinking aloud to provide a description of their work. The novice subjects were students at the University of California, Berkeley, who had completed about 8 weeks of their first university-level physics course (an introductory physics course for students in physics and engineering). The expert subjects were professors and advanced graduate students in physics at Berkeley, who had taught an elementary mechanics course within 2 years.

For the two problems in Table 5.3, seven of the novices and ten of the experts provided solutions that could be interpreted. (Two other papers (Larkin, 1981; Larkin, McDermott, Simon, & Simon, 1980) provide details of this study.)

If the expert subjects are using the schemas summarized in Table 5.4, one would expect the expressions corresponding to slot entries to appear as intermediate results in the problem solution. Thus one would expect in a force solution problem 1 some statement that

$$mg \sin \theta$$

is the relevant component of the gravitational force. In contrast a solution violating this expectation might include

$$F_g = mg$$

connected to other information by

$$F_g = (ma + f)/\sin \theta.$$

In Table 5.4 a number (1, 2, or 3) indicates that the subject referenced by the number at the left used as an intermediate result the schema-slot entry listed above. The value of the number is the order in which these results were stated. Clearly intermediate results generally to correspond to schema-slot entries. Also, known schema slots are generally filled before those related to desired quantities. Thus the result reported elsewhere (Larkin, 1981; Larkin, McDermott, Simon, & Simon, 1980; Simon & Simon, 1978) that experts tend to work forward, to "develop knowledge" is reinterpreted here by saying that experts fill slots in a schema to make a physical representation, starting with slots related to known quantities.

In contrast, novice solutions to the same two problems do not show an order corresponding to filling slots in a force or energy schema. Instead their solutions are consistent with the hypothesis that novices solve the problem using not a physical representation but a naive representation which enables them to comprehend the real-world situation, but which provides little guidance in selecting principles for application. Without such guidance, novices are forced to fall back on a primitive means-ends strategy the mathematical equations representing physics principles. As reported extensively elsewhere (Larkin, McDermott, Simon, & Simon, 1980; Simon & Simon, 1978), novices do use a means–ends strategy involving writing an equation, assessing differences between this equation and an equation that would provide the desired answer, and then taking steps to eliminate this difference. Specifically, novices first write an equation involving the desired quantity (speed v in problem 1, distance l in problem 4). They then assess the resulting equation for any quantities that are unknown and therefore can not appear in the final expression. This cues access of a new equation that contains this undesired quantity and therefore allows substitution for it.

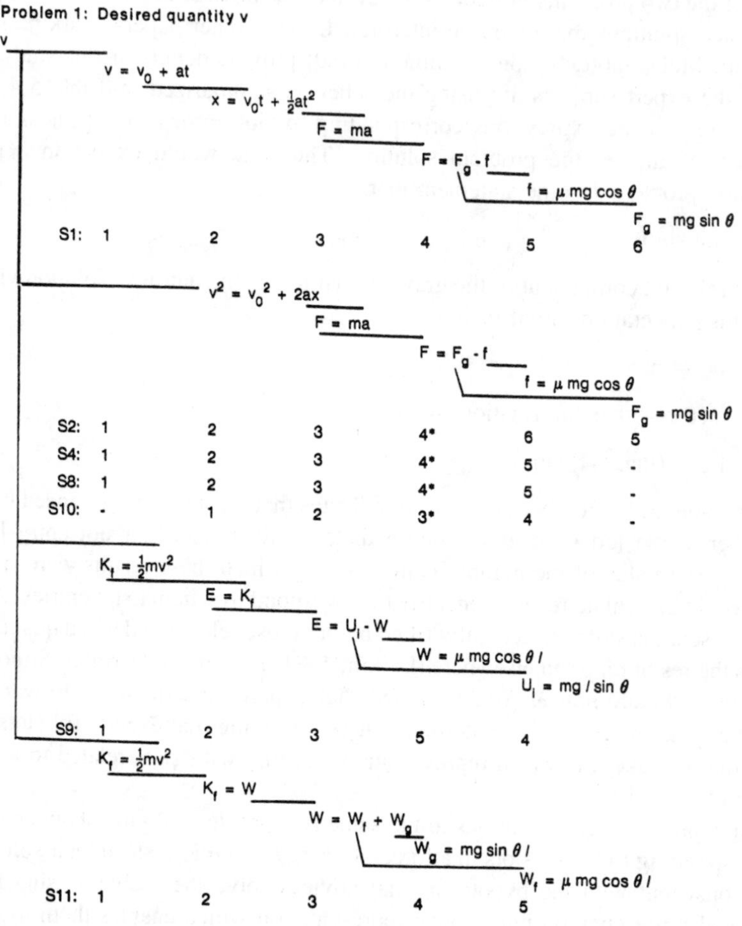

FIG. 5.4. Tree of relations generated by a means-ends strategy for problems in Table 5.3. Numbers indicate the order in which novice subjects accessed these equations.

Figure 5.4 shows principles connected by lines indicating the order in which this means–ends strategy selects these principles for application. The structure is a tree, with an equation cuing the access of one equation (or more than one alternative equations) each containing a quantity that was unknown in the preceding equation. The numbers underneath each branch of the tree describe the order of principles selected by the novice subjects. In general, their work can be accounted for quite well by the algebraic means–ends strategy reflected by the tree.

Combination of Schemas in Harder Problems

What happens when experts and novice subjects solve harder problems, for example, those in Table 5.5?

The same subjects who solved the easier problems (Table 5.3) also solved those in Table 5.5. A total of 11 (out of 11) novice subjects and 8 (out of 11)

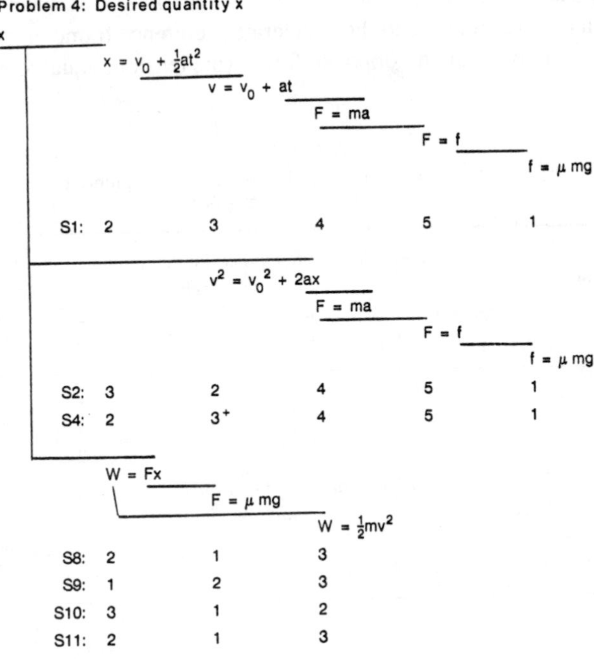

* Used incorrect version of principle (see Larkin, 1981).

+ Accessed both $v^2 = v_0^2 + 2ax$ and $v = v_0 + at$.

FIG. 5.4. *(continued)*

TABLE 5.5
Two Hard Problems

Problem 3.	What constant horizontal force F must be applied to the large cart (of mass M) so that the smaller carts (masses M_1 and M_2) do not move relative to the large cart? Neglect friction.
Problem 5.	A particle of mass m is suspended from a frictionless pivot at the end of a string of unknown length, and is set whirling in a horizontal circular path in a plane which is a distance H below the pivot point. Find the period of revolution of the particle in its orbit.

expert subjects produced interpretable solutions to these problems. (Only the initial sections of the novice protocols were considered.)

One explanation of why these problems are difficult is that their physical representations require coordination of more than one of the schemas described earlier. Considering first problem 3, Table 5.6 shows the two alternate physical representations used by the expert subjects to solve this problem. Part (a) shows a physical representation constructed by applying the force schema to the following two aspects of the cart problem. Schema 1 involves cart 1 which is at rest (acceleration a_1 zero) relative to the accelerated reference frame of the large cart. This is because two equal and opposite forces (the tension, equal to m_2g, and the

TABLE 5.6
Schema Slots and the Order Expert Subjects Filled Them
For Problem 3 in Table 5.5

(a) Accelerated Reference Frame

	Schema 1			*Schema 2*		
Slots	F_I	F_2	a_I	F_I	a	m
Fillers	$\mathcal{F} = m_I a$	$T = m_2 g$	0	F	a	$M + m_I + m_2$
S2	4	5	·	2	1	3
S5	2	1	·	3	5	4
S9	4	5	·	1	2	3

(b) Inertial Reference Frame

	Schema 1		*Schema 2*		
Slots:	F_I	a	F_I	a	m
Fillers:	$m_2 g$	a^a	F	a^a	$M + m_I + m_2$
S3	2	1	4	·	3
S4	1	2	3	5	4
S6	1	2	3	5	4
S7	1	2	4	3	5
S8	2	1	3	4	5

[a]These accelerations equal.

pseudo-force $\mathcal{F}$ due to the acceleration a of the reference frame) are balanced. Schema 2 focuses on the system of all three carts, and relates the total force on this system (just the applied force F) to the acceleration a and the total mass $\mathcal{M} = M + m_1 + m_2$ of this system. Thus the total horizontal applied force F is equal to the total mass $\mathcal{M}$ of the system times acceleration a. Table 5.6b shows an alternate physical representation for the problem in which cart 1 is viewed as having an acceleration a relative to the inertial reference frame of the ground, an acceleration caused by the tension force T which is equal to m_2g. The other part of this physical representation is identical to that in part (a).

As in Table 5.4, Table 5.6 shows the slots and instantiations associated with each of these schemas, and the order in which these schema elements were mentioned by each of the expert subjects. As one would expect if these schemas are guiding experts' work, in all cases the work associated with one schema is completed before work associated with another is begun.

The situation for problem 5 is similar. The coordinated force schemas used to solve this problem are shown in Table 5.7. (T is the tension force of the string; θ is the angle between the string and the vertical; R is the radius of the circular path; τ is the period of the motion.) The two relations at the right do not come from any schema I currently recognize—one is simply a relation among quantities describing circular motion, the other an application of a tigonometric definition. As the order-numbers below the schemas indicate, expert subjects do seem to use these schemas. Furthermore, they generally complete the related force schemas before proceeding to the extra kinematic and trigonometric relations.

Turning to novice performance on the same two difficult problems, if novice solvers work with a mathematical representation, then their solutions should begin with expressions involving the desired quantities. For difficult problems,

TABLE 5.7
Schema Slots and the Order Expert Subjects Filled Them for Problem 5 in Table 5.5

	Horizontal		*Vertical*			*Kinematics*	*Trigonometry*
	F_1	a	F_1	F_2	a		
	$T \sin \theta$	v^2/R	$T \cos \theta$	mg	0	$v = 2\pi R/\tau$	$H = R \tan \theta$
S2:	1	2	5	6	·	3	4
S3:	3	4	1	2	·	6	5
S4:	3	4	1	2	·	5	6
S5:	3	4	1	2	·	5	6
S6:	3	4	1	2	·	5	6
S7:	3	4	1	2	·	6	5
S8:	3	5	1	2	·	6	4
S9:	2	1	3	4	·	5	6

their solutions should end when they can no longer think of any relations to substitute. This result is most striking in the novice performance in problem 5. Ten out of 11 subjects began their work with a relation involving the desired quantity, τ the period of revolution. (No expert subject did so.) Only two novice subjects completed the solution, and they did so with a completely means–ends dictated order.

In problem 3 the situation is somewhat different. The only equation containing the desired quantity is F = ma applied to the composite system of all three carts. Apparently novice subjects do not readily see this application, as none of them began with this equation.

Blocked from their usual means–ends approach, novice subjects were apparently driven to try to use a physical representation. The result is shown in Table 5.8. The representation is a single force schema applied to cart 1, which is at rest with acceleration zero, and is acted on by a tension force equal to m_2g. As indicated by the presence of order-numbers in Table 5.6, most subjects completed that much of the representation. They then knew that an additional left-directed force F_1 had to exist to keep the cart 1 at rest, and many expressed puzzlement over what it could be. However, as indicated in Table 5.6, most completed this final schema slot by inserting (incorreclty) the most salient force, the desired force F.

Schema Selection in a Very Hard Problem

The problems considered in the preceding discussion involve the use of multiple schemas to construct a physical representation, and are sufficiently difficult that most novice solvers could not complete them. However, these problems are still

TABLE 5.8
Schema Elements Used by Novice Solvers of Problem 3 in Table 5.5

	F_1 F	F_2 $T = m_2g$	a 0
S1:	2	1	.
S2:	.	.	.
S3:	2	1	.
S4:	.	.	.
S5:	.	.	.
S6:	2	1	.
S7:	2	1	.
S8:	.	1	.
S9:	.	1	.
S10:	.	1	.
S11:	.	1	.

straightforward for expert subjects, who quite immediately selected and applied the appropriate schemas. What is the situation if we turn to even more difficult problems, problems where even the selection and application of an appropriate schemas is difficult? For example, consider the following problem:

> A loop of flexible chain, of total weight w, rests on a smooth right circular cone of base radius r and height h. The chain rests in a horizontal circle on the cone, which has a vertical axis. What is the tension is the chain?

Six expert subjects, advanced graduate students or faculty in the Physics Department of the University of California, Berkeley, attempted to solve this problem. One subject became thoroughly confused and his data was not analyzed.

The main features seen in the five analyzed protocols are illustrated by the excerpt from a sample protocol shown in Table 5.9. After reading the problem and constructing a naive representation for it, This subject initially tries to construct a physical representation involving forces on a small element of the chain. This attempt is based on two decisions: the decision to use forces, and the decision to focus on a small element of the chain. Apparently these decisions were made quite rapidly as they are reflected by no statements in the protocol.

Table 5.10 shows why the subject ultimately abandons this representation attempt. He knows the element of chain is at rest and thus expects the physical representation to show forces balanced in both directions. Although, because of the curvature of the cone, the tension force actually has a small component directed toward the left, the subject assumes that the tension force is perpendicular to the plane of the paper. Thus he can not find any force balancing the horizontal component of the force S' due to the surface of the cone. As he realizes this, there is a long pause in the protocol during which he apparently selects another possible schema for constructing a physical representation.

As indicated in the labels for the protocol in Table 5.9 each attempt is based on a decision about the kind of physical schema to use (forces, virtual works) and about the aspect of the problem (element of chain, whole chain, half of chain) to be considered. In all cases but the last he fails to complete the physical representation, abandons the effort, and selects an alternative type of physical representation. With the fourth attempt, in which he applies a force schema to half of the chain (Table 5.9), he is finally successful in achieving a physical representation in which the various inferences involving schema slots are consistent. That is the horizontal rightward force due to the cone surface is balanced by the two leftward tension forces on the ends of the chain, thus accounting for the zero acceleration of the chain (Table 5.10). He then proceeds immediately to write corresponding equations that lead to a correct solution.

All five protocols were analyzed by considering just those statements made before the subject wrote his first equation, presumably statements corresponding

TABLE 5.9
Protocol of an Expert Subject Solving the Cone Problem

Naive Representation
[reads problem]
So I draw a right angle, or a triangle, such that the bottom is *r* and the side is *h*. And the chain is resting at some point. I'll just draw a cross section of it.
Force Representation of Small Element of Chain
The tension . . . um is acting perpendicular to the plain of the paper.
Let me think about that a minute. Well let me think about that a minute.
Tension is always acting in the same direction as the direction of the . . .
Yeah, it has to be perpendicular to the plane of the paper.
I'll think about it. I'll draw a dot there.
And then there will be another force on the chain, which will be perpendicular to the edge of the cone. Which will be something. And the upward component is something.
Let's call that something S. Will also be equal to mg.
Because, because, the chain isn't moving up or down.
So the other component is going to be . . . something else . . . something else.
[long pause]
Virtual Work Representation of Whole Chain
I'm starting now to think sort of of virtual work.
But that's not going to get me anywhere, because . . .
[qualitative statements omitted]
[long pause]
Force Representation of Small Arc of Chain
All right, well look.
If I look down on the cone from the top, I get a circle.
And the tension at any point there is pulling in opposite directions.
And if I look at a short arc of that . . .
[qualitative statements omitted]
Um . . . the problem is that in any infinitesimal cross section of the chain, the two tension forces almost perpendicular, not parallel.
Force Representation of Half Chain
Well, but if I cut the circle in half, I can say that the total tension acting on one half of the chain in one direction is 2T.
So there's a force acting in that direction which is 2T.
Meanwhile the force acting in the other direction, which is a component of S, is going to be . . . I'd have to integrate.
[applies this chunk to begin generating equations.]

---

to the construction of physical representations. These statements were subdivided into sections, each corresponding to a single attempt to build a physical representation, specifically to a decision about a type of representation (forces or works) and an aspect of the problem to be considered.

Each protocol contains one or more attempts at physical representations, with the last attempt followed by a corresponding mathematical representation that leads to a correct solution. Two different patterns were seen in the attempted physical representations. Two subjects immediately selected the one representation (virtual work applied to the whole cone) that in fact leads to the most direct

TABLE 5.10
Physical Representations of the Cone Problem Described by the Protocol in Table 5.9

Element of Chain					
Vertical Forces			*Horizontal Forces*		
F_1	F_2	a	F_1	F_2	a
component S′	mg	0	??	component S′	0
			Half Chain		
			Horizontal Forces		
			F_1	F_2	a
			2T	integrated component S′	0

solution. This selection was accompanied by a statement like "I know how to do this one. It's virtual work." After completing the slots of the physical-representation schema, these two subjects proceeded immediately to a corresponding correct mathematical solution. Apparently for these subjects this problem was *not* difficult, because they immediately knew what physical representation it involved. The remaining three subjects each considered two or more possible physical representations elaborating each very much as illustrated in Table 5.9. Only the last representation was accompanied by equations.

In summary then, expert subjects confronted with a difficult problem selected a physical representation through successive attempts. Although the mechanism for initially selecting a schema for such a representation is not clear, it seems to be rather quick and uncritical. Then considerable effort is expended to develop or fill the slots in that representation. These slots are filled through redundant inferencing paths. For example, in the first part of the protocol in Table 5.9 the subject infers that there must be a force directed to the left (because the chain-element is at rest), but is unable to infer a value for that force. If such inconsistencies arise, the representation schema is abandoned and another selected and tried. Only when a schema is successfully instantiated to form a complete consistent representation is it accepted and translated into a mathematical representation.

III. POSSIBILITIES FOR INSTRUCTION

The experimental results summarized in the preceding section suggest that physical representations are used by expert subjects. Easy problems are solved through filling slots in a single schema for a physical representation; harder problems require coordination of two or more schemas, and very difficult problems are attacked by successive attempts to validate schemas, with computation occurring only when a completed schema can guide it. In contrast, novice solutions do not show these features and are often incorrect.

Thus it should be possible to improve success in problem solving by training students to represent problems using physical-representation schemas, and the adequacy of a textbook should be reflected by the extent to which it fosters use of such schemas.

The Effect of Teaching Physical Representation

In one experiment, the effect of directly teaching the use of representation schemas was assessed in the following way.

Beginning physics students were taught to apply individually seven principles describing DC circuits. After this initial instruction, a randomly selected half of the students received additional training on physical representations whereas the remaining students received training in systematically applying these principles to generate equations, and in algebraically combining these equations to obtain the desired results. After training, each student attempted to solve three problems requiring the joint application of several of the individual principles he had studied. Further details of this study are given in an earlier paper (Larkin, 1977).

The ten subjects were volunteers enrolled in the second quarter of a three-quarter, calculus-based physics course for students interested in biology and medicine. They were prepared to study DC circuits, but had no exposure to this area before the experiment. The seven principles used in the experiment included the equivalents of Kirchoff's laws, principles describing resistors and emf sources ($V = RI$, $V = \mathscr{E}$), and a few definitions. To learn the individual principles, all subjects used a programmed booklet, and worked unsupervised for about 3 to 6 hours. During the first part of each experimental session each subject demonstrated the ability to apply each principle correctly to generate an equation. If the subject made errors or seemed uncertain, additional explanation and practice were provided.

Five randomly selected subjects saw diagrams illustrating two ways of constructing physical representations of DC circuits using the analogy between electric currents and fluid flow, and the analogy between potential and height. This instruction was intended to enable the students to do some of the things experts do in thinking about simple circuits—visualize how the current combines and separates in the wires; relate the potential changes in various parts of the circuits. The remaining five subjects spent an equivalent amount of time cataloguing principles by grouping together principles containing the same quantity; and studying an algebraic strategy for systematically relating the various currents in the problem, then the potential drops, and finally the currents to the potential drops.

Each test problem required use of several of the seven principles, sometimes to more than one aspect of the problem. While working on the problems, each subject had available a chart summarizing the seven principles. Subjects talked aloud as they worked, and errors were identified and explained without indicating what should correctly be done. A problem was considered "solved" if the subject produced a correct solution within a time limit of 15 or 20 minutes.

The number of problems solved by these two groups was strikingly and significantly different $P < .05$ using a small-sample version of the Mann-Whitney test. Of the subjects receiving experimental training, three solved all three problems, and two solved two problems. Of the remaining subjects (receiving the control training), four of the five subjects solved no more than one problem. (The fifth subject solved all three problems.)

Physical Representations in a Textbook

The preceding experiment directly manipulated the teaching of physical representations. To conclude the discussion on instructional possibilities, I describe briefly a preliminary study of one subject learning from an existing physics textbook. She was asked to study a section describing accelerated motion along a straight line in a widely used physics text (Halliday & Resnick, 1966) pp. 38–44, and to work the problems at the end of the chapter marked as corresponding to these sections. She talked aloud as she studied and worked the problems for a total of 3 hours. Relevant to the central thurst of this chapter, that the ability to construct physical representations is central to skill in problem solving, several features of her protocol, particularly in the first hour that involved reading the text, are very striking.

Her work while studying these sections was divided into the categories listed in Table 5.11. I searched for, but was unable to find, any statements reflecting development of qualitative inferencing, links that might be used in building the physical representation. Specifically, I looked for any qualitative interpretations of the central physical relations presented in the chapter. For example, the equation presented in the chapter as

$$x = x_0 + v_0t + \frac{1}{2} at^2$$

can be written as

$$x - x_0 = v_0t + \frac{1}{2} at^2$$

TABLE 5.11
Times for Various Tasks While Reading a Physics Text

Task	Time
Reading and comprehending prose text.	16 min
Doing algebra.	11 min
Studying and comprehending graphs.	26 min

TABLE 5.12
Table of Kinematics Relations Given in Halliday and Resnick (1966)

Equation	*Contains* x	v_x	a_x	t
$v_x = v_{0x} + at$	X	√	√	√
$x = x_0 + \frac{1}{2}(v_{x0} + v_x)t$	√	√	X	√
$x = x_0 + \frac{1}{2}at^2$	√	X	√	√
$v_x^2 = v_{x0}^2 + 2a(x \cdot x_0)$	√	√	√	X

and interpreted by a sentence like: The distance travelled by a particle moving with constant acceleration is equal to the initial velocity times the time, plus or minus an extra term reflecting the fact that it is accelerating or deaccelerating. No such statements were found.

This subject spent an enormous amount of time trying to understand the graphical presentations in the text. Most of this time (about 15 min) was spent on the initial set of graphs describing nonuniform acceleration. These graphs are indeed very complex and the subject's protocol revealed serious misunderstandings. Furthermore, although in two of the problems making graphs are suggested, the subject was never able to use any graphical techniques to help her in solving problems.

The section of text most relevant to the problems solved, and the only section used by the subject as she solved the problems, is that presented in Table 5.12. The striking feature about this section is its emphasis on a mathematical equation-based representation.

In summary, it doesn't seem surprising that students who have studied a text similar to that discussed in the preceding pages tend not to construct or to use physical representations. In this case the physical representation discussed (graphs) was both confusing and not relevant to the problems. The material most relevant to the problems was in completely mathematical form. The subject herself made no interpretations of the equations that might have been used in making physical representations.

IV. SUMMARY

Most individuals can mentally represent a simple physical situation sufficiently well that they can make simple inferences about what will happen next. I have described here an analog to this ability to construct *naive* representations, an ability which begins to account for how skilled individuals reason qualitatively or intuitively about complex situations. This *physical representation* in contrast to naive representations, has the following features:

- The entities are technical, with meaning only in physics.
- The inferencing rules are qualitative.
- The inferencing rules are time-independent and redundant.
- The representation is closely associated with fundamental principles of physics.
- Properties of the entities are localized to those entities.

This representation was illustrated by preliminary versions of rules for creating and extending two kinds of physical representations (force and work-energy).

Empirical studies relevant to this conceptualization of expertise include the order in which experts and novices access principles in solving simple problems, and the extent and nature of the qualitative discussion preceding any quantitiative work on a more difficult problem. In the easy problems, experts seemed to use principles in an order dictated by the schemas they were completing, whereas novices either followed an order based on a mathematical or were unable to do the problem. In more difficult cases, experts seemed to assess whether a schema could be completed without contradictions before doing any quantitative work. Once this was ascertained, then the quantitative work proceeded uneventfully.

Finally I have suggested how work is beginning to elucidate how physical representations might function in instruction. One primitive study obtained dramatic results by training subjects essentially to use physical representations. Yet study of a popular textbook, and of one subject studying that text, suggests that information relevant to such representation is sparce and hard to apply to problems.

ACKNOWLEDGMENT

This work was supported by NIE-NSF grant number 1-55862, by NSF grant number 1-55035 and by the Defense Advanced Research Projects Agency (DOD), ARPA Order No. 3597, monitored by the Air Force Avionics Laboratory under Contract F33615-78-C-1151.

REFERENCES

de Kleer, J. *Qualitative and quantitative knowledge in classical mechanics*. Master's thesis, MIT, December 1975.

de Kleer, J. Multiple representations of knowledge in a mechanics problem solver. *International Joint Conference on Artificial Intelligence*, 1977, *5*, 299–304.

de Kleer, J., & Brown, J. S. Mental Models of Physical Mechanisms and their Acquisition. In J. Anderson (Ed.), *Cognitive skills and their acquisition*. Hillsdale, N.J.: Lawrence Erlbaum Assoc., 1981.

Halliday, D., & Resnick, R. *Physics, second edition*. New York: Wiley, 1966.

Larkin, J. H. *Problem Solving in Physics* (Tech. Rep.). Group in Science and Mathematics Education, University of California, Berkeley, 1977.

Larkin, J. H. Enriching formal knowledge: A model for learning to solve problems in physics. In J. R. Anderson (Ed.), *Cognitive skills and their acquisition*. Hillsdale, N.J.: Lawrence Erlbaum Associates, 1981.

Larkin, J. H., McDermott, J., Simon, D. P., & Simon, H. A. Models of competence in solving physics problems. *Cognitive Science*, 1980, *4*, 317–345.

Simon, D. P., & Simon, H. A. Individual differences in solving physics problems. In R. Siegler (Ed.), *Children's thinking: What develops?* Hillsdale, N.J.: Lawrence Erlbaum Associates, 1978.

6 Flowing Waters or Teeming Crowds: Mental Models of Electricity

Dedre Gentner
Bolt Beranek and Newman

Donald R. Gentner
University of California, San Diego

> *Question:* When you plug in a lamp and it lights up, how does it happen?
> *Subject Delta:* . . . basically there is a pool of electricity that plug-in buys for you . . . the electricity goes into the cord for the appliance, for the lamp and flows up to—*flows*—I think of it as flowing because of the negative to positive images I have, and also because . . . a cord is a narrow contained entity like a river.

Analogical comparisons with simple or familiar systems occur often in people's descriptions of complex systems, sometimes as explicit analogical models, and sometimes as implicit analogies, in which the person seems to borrow structure from the base domain without noticing it. Phrases like "current being routed along a conductor," or "stopping the flow" of electricity are examples.

In this paper we want to explore the conceptual role of analogy. When people discuss electricity (and other complex phenomena) in analogical terms, are they thinking in terms of analogies, or merely borrowing language from one domain as a convenient way of talking about another domain? If analogies are to be taken seriously as part of the apparatus used in scientific reasoning, it must be shown that they have real conceptual effects.

There are two lines of observational evidence (aside from the protocol cited) for the proposition that analogies can have genuine effects on a person's conception of a domain. First, analogies are often used in teaching, as in the following introduction to electricity (Koff, 1961).

> The idea that electricity flows as water does is a good analogy. Picture the wires as pipes carrying water (electrons). Your wall plug is a high-pressure source which you can tap simply by inserting a plug. . . . A valve (switch) is used to start or stop flow.

Thus, educators appear to believe that students can import conceptual relations and operations from one domain to another.

A more direct line of evidence is that working scientists report that they use analogy in theory development. The great astronomer Johannes Kepler wrote (quoted in Polya, 1973): "And I cherish more than anything else the Analogies, my most trustworthy masters. They know all the secrets of Nature, and they ought to be least neglected in Geometry [p. 12]." The Nobel Prize lecture of nuclear physicist Sheldon Glashow (1980) makes constant reference to the analogies used in developing the theory of the unified weak and electromagnetic interactions:

> I was lead to the group SU(2) × U(1) by analogy with the approximate isospin-hypercharge group which characterizes strong interactions. . . .
> Part of the motivation for introducing a fourth quark was based on our mistaken notions of hadron spectroscopy. But we also wished to enforce an analogy between the weak leptonic current and the weak hadronic current. . . .

These kinds of remarks are strongly suggestive of the conceptual reality of generative analogy. But people's understanding of their own mental processes is not always correct. It could be that, despite these introspections, the underlying thought processes proceed independently of analogy and that analogies merely provide a convenient terminology for the results of the process. This hypothesis, the Surface Terminology hypothesis, contrasts with the Generative Analogy hypothesis that analogies are used in generating inferences.

Our goal is to test the Generative Analogy hypothesis: that conceptual inferences in the target follow predictably from the use of a given base domain as an analogical model. To confirm this hypothesis, it must be shown that the inferences people make in a topic domain vary according to the analogies they use. Further, it must be shown that these effects cannot be attributed to shallow lexical associations; e.g., it is not enough to show that the person who speaks of electricity as "flowing" also uses related terms such as "capacity" or "pressure." Such usage could result from a generative analogy, but it could also occur under the Surface Terminology hypothesis.

The plan of this paper is to (1) set forth a theoretical framework for analogical processing, called structure-mapping; (2) use this framework to explore the analogies people use in the domain of electronic circuitry, based on evidence from introductory texts and from interviews; (3) present two experimental studies that test the Generative Analogy hypothesis; and finally, (4) discuss the implications of our findings for a general treatment of analogy in science.

A STRUCTURE-MAPPING THEORY OF ANALOGICAL THINKING

Just what type of information does an analogy convey? The prevailing psychological view rejects the notion that analogies are merely weak similarity statements, maintaining instead that analogy can be characterized more precisely (Miller, 1979; Ortony, 1979; Rumelhart & Abrahamson, 1973; Sternberg, 1977; Tourangeau & Sternberg, 1981; Verbrugge & McCarrell, 1977). We argue in this section that analogies select certain aspects of existing knowledge, and that this selected knowledge can be structurally characterized.

An analogy such as

1. The hydrogen atom is like the solar system.

clearly does not convey that *all* of one's knowledge about the solar system should be attributed to the atom. The inheritance of characteristics is only partial. This might suggest that an analogy is a kind of weak similarity statement, conveying that only some of the characteristics of the solar system apply to the hydrogen atom. But this characterization fails to capture the distinction between literal similarity and analogical relatedness. A comparable literal similarity statement is

2. There's a system in the Andromeda nebula that's like our solar system.

The literal similarity statement (2) conveys that the target object (The Andromeda system) is composed of a star and planets much like those of our solar system, and further, that those objects are arranged in similar spatial relationships and have roughly the same kind of orbital motion, attractive forces, relative masses, etc. as our system.

Like the literal comparison, the analogy (statement 1) conveys considerable overlap between the relative spatial locations, relative motions, internal forces, and relative masses of atom and solar system; but it does *not* convey that the objects in the two domains are similar. One could argue with the literal statement (2) by saying "But the star in the Andromeda system isn't yellow and hot." if the star happened to be a white dwarf. To argue with the analogical statement (1) by saying "But the nucleus of the atom isn't yellow and hot." would be to miss the point. The analogy, in short, conveys overlap in relations among objects, but no particular overlap in the characteristics of the objects themselves. The literal similarity statement conveys overlap both in relations among the objects and in the attributes of the individual objects.[1]

---

[1]An adequate discussion of literal similarity within this framework would require including a negative dependency on the number of *nonshared* features as well as the positive dependency on the number of shared features (Tversky, 1977). However, for our purposes, the key point is that, in

The analogical models used in science can be characterized as structure-mappings between complex systems. Such an analogy conveys that like relational systems hold within two different domains. The predicates of the base domain (the known domain)—particularly the relations that hold among the objects—can be applied in the target domain (the domain of inquiry). Thus, a structure-mapping analogy asserts that identical operations and relationships hold among nonidentical things. The relational structure is preserved, but not the objects.

In such a structure-mapping, both domains are viewed as systems of objects[2] and predicates. Among the predicates, we must distinguish between object attributes and relationships. In a propositional representation, the distinction can be made explicit in the predicate structure: *Attributes* are predicates taking one argument, and *relations* are predicates taking two or more arguments. For example, COLLIDE (x,y) is a relation, whereas RED (x) is an attribute. We will use a schema-theoretic representation of knowledge as a propositional network of nodes and predicates (cf. Miller, 1979; Rumelhart, 1979; Rumelhart & Norman, 1975; Rumelhart & Ortony, 1977; Schank & Abelson, 1977). The nodes represent concepts treated as wholes and the predicates express propositions about the nodes. The predicates may convey dynamic process information, constraint relations, and other kinds of knowledge (e.g. de Kleer & Sussman, 1978; Forbus, 1982; Rieger & Grinberg, 1977). Figure 6.1 shows the structure-mapping conveyed by the atom/solar system analogy. Starting with the known base domain of the solar system, the object nodes of the base domain (the sun and planets) are mapped onto object nodes (the nucleus and electrons) of the atom. Given this correspondence of nodes, the analogy conveys that the relationships that hold between the nodes in the solar system also hold between the nodes of the atom: for example, that there is a force attracting the peripheral objects to the central object; that the peripheral objects revolve around the central object; that the central object is more massive than the peripheral objects; and so on.

Structure-Mapping: Interpretation Rules

Assume that the hearer has a particular propositional representation of a known domain B (the *base* domain) in terms of object nodes $b_1, b_2, \ldots, b_n$ and predicates such as A, R, R′. Assume also a (perhaps less specified) representa-

analogy, a structural distinction must be made between different types of predicates. In Tversky's valuable characterization of literal similarity, the relation-attribute distinction is not utilized; all predicates are considered together, as "features." This suggests that literal similarity (at least in the initial stages of study) does not require as elaborate a computational semantics as metaphor and analogy.

[2]The "objects" in terms of which a person conceptualizes a system need not be concrete tangible objects; they may be simply relatively coherent, separable component parts of a complex object, or they may be idealized or even fictional objects. Moreover, often a target system can be parsed in

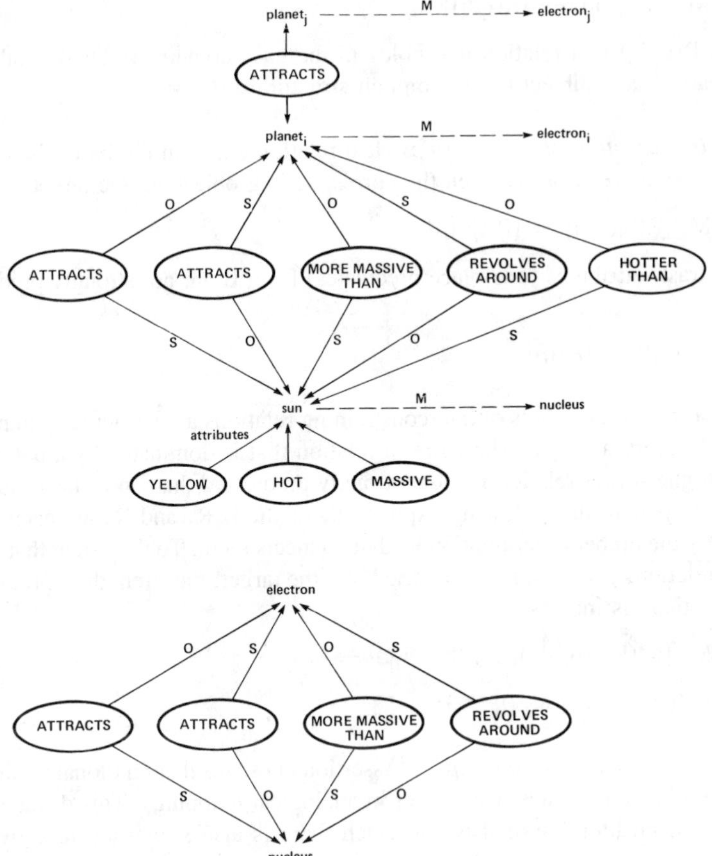

FIG. 6.1. Representations of knowledge about the solar system and the hydrogen atom, showing partial identity in the relational structure between the two domains.

tion of the domain of inquiry (the *target* domain) in terms of at least some object nodes $t_1, t_2, \ldots, t_m$. Then a structure-mapping analogy maps the nodes of B into the nodes of T:

$$M: b_i \rightarrow t_i$$

The hearer derives analogical predications by applying predicates valid in the base domain B to the target domain T, using the node substitutions dictated by the mapping:

---

various ways by different individuals, or even by the same individual for different purposes. [See Greeno, Vesonder & Majetic (this volume) and Larkin (this volume).] The important point is, once the objects are determined they will be treated as objects in the mapping.

$$M: [R(b_i,b_j)] \rightarrow [R(t_i,t_j)]$$

where $R(b_i,b_j)$ is a relation that holds in the base domain B. These analogical predications are subject to two implicit structural rules:

1. *Preservation of relationships.* If a relation exists in the base, then predicate the same relation between the corresponding objects in the target:

$$M: [R(b_i, b_j)] \rightarrow [R(t_i, t_j)]$$

In contrast, attributes (one-place predicates) from B are not strongly predicated in T:

$$[A(b_i)] \not\rightarrow [A(t_i)]$$

2. *Systematicity.* Sets of interconstraining relations are particularly important in explanatory analogy. Therefore, a relation that is dominated by a potentially valid higher-order relation is more strongly predicated than an isolated relation. For example, in the following expression, relations R_1 and R_2 are each dominated by the higher order relation R' that connects them. To the extent that any of these relations can be validly imported into the target, the strength of predication of the others is increased.

$$M: [R'(R_1\ (b_i,\ b_j),\ R_2\ (b_k,\ b_1))] \rightarrow$$

$$[R'(R_1\ (t_i,\ t_j),\ R_2\ (t_k,\ t_1))]$$

Preservation of Relationships. Assertion (1) states that relational predicates, and not object attributes, carry over in analogical mappings. This differentiates analogy from literal similarity, in which there is also strong attribute overlap. This follows from the central assertion that analogical mappings convey that identical propositional systems apply in two domains with dissimilar objects. For example, in the solar system model of the atom, the ATTRACTS relation and the REVOLVES AROUND relation between planet and sun are carried across to apply between electron and nucleus, whereas the separable *attributes* of the base objects, such as the color or temperature of the sun, are left behind. Mass provides a good illustration: The *relation* ''MORE MASSIVE THAN'' between sun's mass and planet's mass carries over, but not the absolute mass of the sun. We do not expect the nucleus to have a mass of 10^{30} kilograms, any more than we expect it to have a temperature of 25,000,000°F.

Systematicity. Assertion (2) states that predicates are more likely to be imported into the target if they belong to a system of coherent, mutually constraining relationships, the others of which map into the target. These interconnections among predicates are explicitly structurally represented by higher-order relations between those predicates (e.g., Smith, in preparation). One common higher-order relation is CAUSE; for example, CAUSE (R_1, R_2) expresses a causal chain between the lower-order relations R_1 and R_2. Focusing on such causal chains can make an analogical matcher more powerful (Winston, 1981).

Figure 6.2 shows the set of systematically interconnected relations in the Rutherford model, a highly systematic analogy. Notice that the lower-order relations—DISTANCE (sun, planet), REVOLVES AROUND (planet, sun), etc.—form a connected system, together with the abstract relationship ATTRACTIVE FORCE (sun, planet). The relation MORE MASSIVE THAN (sun, planet) belongs to this system. In combination with other higher-order relations, it determines which object will revolve around the other. This is why MORE MASSIVE THAN is preserved while HOTTER THAN is not, even though the two relations are, by themselves, parallel comparisons. HOTTER THAN does not participate in this systematic set of interrelated predicates. Thus, to the extent that people recognize (however vaguely) that gravitational forces play a central role in the analogy they will tend to import MORE MASSIVE THAN, but not HOTTER THAN, into the target.

The systematicity rule aims to capture the intuition that explanatory analogies are about systems of interconnected relations. Sometimes these systems can be mathematically formalized. Some of the interrelations within this solar system are described in this equation:[3]

$$F_{grav} = Gmm'/R^2 \quad (1)$$

This equation embodies a set of simultaneous constraints on the parameters of the objects, where m is the mass of the sun, m′ is the mass of the planet, G is the gravitational constant, and F_{grav} is the gravitational force. For example, if F_{grav} decreases while the masses are constant, then the distance R between the sun and the planet must increase. Equation (1) summarizing the interrelations in the base maps into a corresponding target equation:

$$F_{elec} = -qq'/R^2 \quad (2)$$

---

[3]Mathematical models represent an extreme of systematicity. The set of mappable relations is strongly constrained, and the rules for concatenating relationships are well-specified. Once we choose a given mathematical system—say, a ring or a group—as base, we know thereby which combinatorial rules and which higher-order relations apply in the base. This clarifies the process of deriving new predictions to test in the target. We know, for example, that if the base relations are addition (R_1) and multiplication (R_2) in a field (e.g., the real numbers) then we can expect distributivity to hold: $c(a+b) = ca + cb$, or

$$R_2\ [(c,\ R_1\ (a,b))] = R_1\ [R_2\ (c,a),\ R_2\ (c,b)]$$

A mathematical model predicts a small number of relations which are well-specified enough and systematic enough to be concatenated into long chains of prediction.

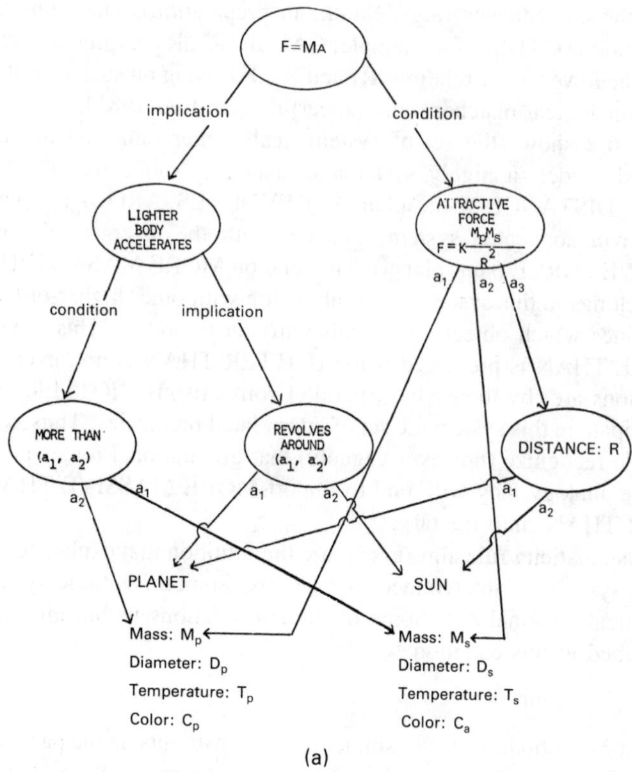

FIG. 6.2. More detailed representation of knowledge about (a) the solar system and (b) the atom, showing partial identity in the higher-order relational structures between the two domains.

where q is the charge on the proton, q′ the charge on the electron, R the distance between the two objects, and F_{elec} is the electromagnetic force.[4]

All these analogical predications are attempted predications, to use Ortony's (1979) term; they must be checked against the person's existing knowledge of the target domain. But the structural bias for relationality and systematicity provides an implicit guide to which predications to check.

[4]Notice that the analogy shown in Fig. 6.2 actually involves two different systems of mappings that do not completely overlap. Each system is dominated by a different higher-order relation. Although the *object* mappings are the same in both cases, the *attribute* mappings are different. (Recall that object attributes, like objects themselves, can be mapped onto arbitrarily *different* elements of the target, according to the structure-mapping theory; only the resulting *relations* need be preserved.)

The first system of mappings is dominated by the attractive force relation

$$(F = G\, m_1\, m_2 / R^2).$$

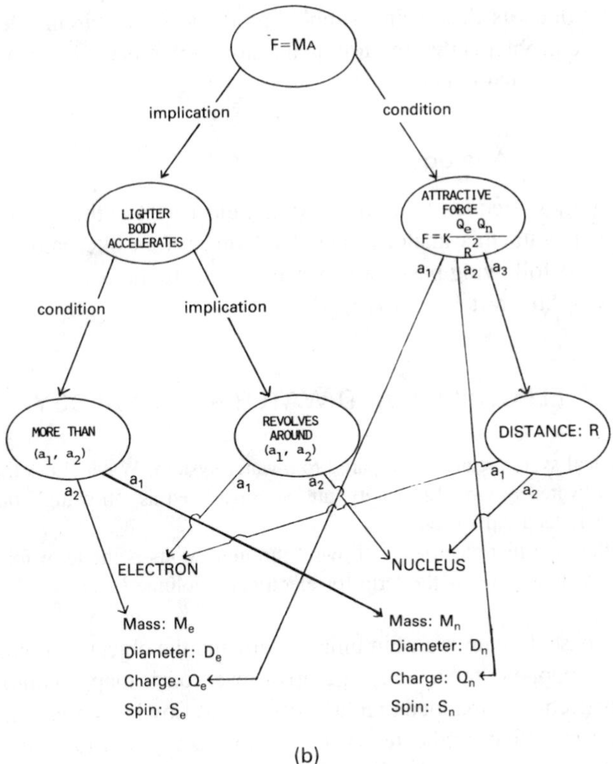

FIG. 6.2. (*continued*)

TWO ANALOGIES FOR ELECTRICITY

The domain of simple electricity is ideal for investigating the role of analogy. It is a familiar phenomenon; everyone in our society knows at least a little about it. Further, it is tractable: We can define ideal correct understanding. Yet because its mechanisms are essentially invisible, electricity is often explained by analogy. Moreover, because no single analogy has all the correct properties, we can compare different analogies for the same target domain. Finally, a great advan-

---

In this system, the *mass* of objects in the solar system is mapped onto the *charge* of objects in the atom. This system includes the higher-order relation that attractive force decreases with distance.

The other system is dominated by the inertial relation (F = ma); in this system, the *mass* of objects in the solar system maps into the *mass* of objects in the atom. This system includes the inference (expressed as a higher-order relation in Fig. 6.2) that the less massive object moves more than the more massive object.

tage of electronics is that, using simple combinations of circuit elements, it is easy to devise problems that require quantitative inferences that cannot be mimicked by mere lexical connections.

The Water-Flow Analogy

The analogy most frequently used to explain electricity is the water-flow analogy. We begin with this analogy, and later discuss an alternative analogy for electricity. The following passage is part of the instructions for a miniature lamp kit (Illinois Hobbycraft Inc., 1976).

ELECTRICITY AND WATER—AN ANALOGY

> An electrical system can be compared to a water system. Water flows through the pipes of a water system. Electricity can be considered as "flowing" through the wires of an electrical system.
> Wire is the pipe that electricity "flows" through. Volts is the term for electrical pressure. Milliamperes is the term for electrical "volume."

Here the base domain is a plumbing system and the object mappings are that a water pipe is mapped onto a wire, a pump or reservoir is mapped onto a battery, a narrow constriction is mapped onto a resistor, and flowing water is mapped onto electric current. What predicates is this analogy supposed to convey? Not that electricity shares object attributes with water, such as being wet, transparent, or cold to the touch. This analogy is meant to convey a system of relationships that can be imported from hydraulics to electricity. In the next passages we discuss this relational structure, first for hydraulics and then for electricity. This will serve both to explicate the analogy and to provide some insight into electricity for readers who are unfamiliar with the domain. Then we compare the hydraulic analogy with another common analogy for electricity, the moving-crowd model.

Simple Hydraulics. We begin with a reservoir with an outlet at its base. The *pressure* of the water at the outlet is proportional to the height of water in the reservoir. (See Fig. 6.6, following.) The *rate of flow* through any point in the system is the amount of water that passes that point per unit time. Pressure and flow rate are clearly distinguishable: Rate of flow is *how much* water is flowing, while pressure is the *force* per unit area exerted by the water. Yet there is a strong relation between pressure and flow: The rate of flow through a section is proportional to the *pressure difference* through that section. This means that the greater the height of water in the reservoir, the greater the flow rate, all else being equal.

A *constriction* in the pipe leads to a drop in pressure. Water pressure, which is high when the water leaves the reservoir, drops across the constriction. Constrictions also affect flow rate: The greater the constriction in a section, the flow rate through that system. Figure 6.3b shows the relations among flow rate, pressure and degree of constriction for a hydraulics system.

The Analogy with Electricity. An electrical circuit is analogous to the plumbing system just described. Table 6.1 shows the object correspondences, as well as some of the predicates that are imported from base to target. Notice that the predicates that are shared are relational predicates: for example, that increasing voltage causes an increase in current.

The first insight derivable from the analogy is the distinction between the flowrate and pressure, which maps onto an analogous distinction between current

SIMPLE CIRCUIT

α
Voltage Across
Current Through
Resistance of
Battery
Wire 1
Electricity
Resistor
Wire 2
Connected to
Connected to
Connected to
Connected to

WATER SYSTEM

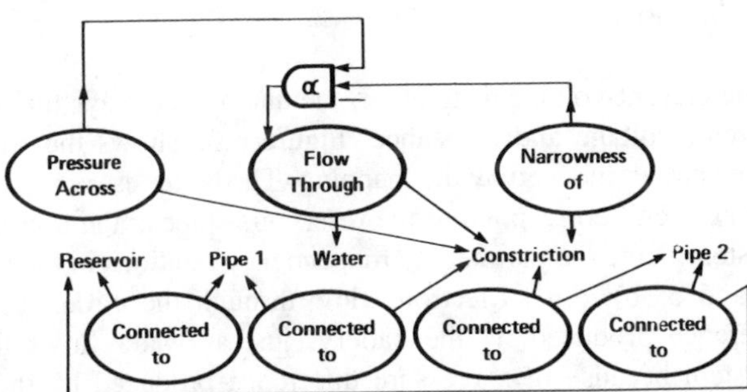

FIG. 6.3. Representation of knowledge about (a) simple electric circuits and (b) simple hydraulic systems, showing overlap in relational structures. The relation stands for a higher-order qualitative division relation: The output (e.g., current) varies monotonically with the positive input (e.g., voltage) and negative—monotonically with the negative input (e.g., resistance).

TABLE 6.1
Mappings Between Water Flow and Electricity

Base-Hydraulic System	*Target–Circuit*
Object Mappings:	
pipe	wire
pump	battery
narrow pipe	resistor
Property Mappings:	
PRESSURE of water	VOLTAGE
NARROWNESS of pipe	RESISTANCE
FLOW RATE of water	CURRENT (FLOW RATE of electricity)
Relations Imported:	
CONNECT (pipe, pump, narrow pipe)	CONNECT (wire, battery, resistor)
INCREASE WITH (flow rate, pressure)	INCREASE WITH (current, voltage)
DECREASE WITH (flow rate, narrowness)	DECREASE WITH (current, resistance)

(the number of electrons passing a given point per sec) and voltage (the pressure difference through which the current moves). This aspect of the analogy is important because novices in electricity often fail to differentiate current and voltage; they seem to merge the two of them into a kind of generalized-strength notion. For example, one subject, defining voltage, says:

> . . . Volts is . . . the strength of the current available to you in an outlet. And I don't know if it means there are more of those little electrons running around or if they're moving faster; . . . .

Besides the current-voltage distinction, the analogy conveys the interrelation between current, voltage and resistance. Figure 6.3a shows the structural description of the circuit induced by the mapping. The batteries, wire, and resistors of an electrical circuit correspond to the reservoirs, pipes, and constriction of a plumbing system. Note the parallel interdependency relations in the two systems (Figs. 6.3a and 6.3b): e.g., Electrons flow through the circuit because of a voltage difference produced by the battery, just as water flows through the plumbing system because of a pressure difference produced by the reservoir. Thus, the analogy conveys the dependency relations that constitute Ohm's Law, $V = IR$. Of course, naive users of the analogy may derive only simpler proportional relations such as ''More force, more flow'' and ''More drag, less flow.'' These qualitative-proportion relationships (see Forbus, 1982) may be phenomenological primitives, in the sense discussed by diSessa (this volume).

The Moving-Crowd Model

Besides the hydraulics model, the most frequent spontaneous analogy for electricity is the moving-crowd analogy. In this analogy, electric current is seen as masses of objects racing through passageways, as in these passages from interviews:

> (1) You can always trick the little devils to go around or through. . . Because they have to do that. I mean, they are driven to seek out the opposite pole. In between their getting to their destination, you can trick them into going into different sorts of configurations, to make them work for you. . . .

> (2) If you increase resistance in the circuit, the current slows down. Now that's like a highway, cars on a highway where . . . as you close down a lane . . . the cars move slower through that narrow point.

The moving-crowd model can provide most of the relations required to understand electrical circuits. In this model current corresponds to the number of entities that pass a point per unit time. Voltage corresponds to how powerfully they push. Like the water analogy, the moving-crowd model establishes a distinction between current and voltage. Further, the moving-crowd model allows a superior treatment of resistors. In this model we can think of a resistor as analogous to a barrier containing a narrow gate. This "gate" conception of resistors is helpful in predicting how combinations of resistors will behave, as we describe in the following section. However, it is hard to find a useful realization of batteries in this model.

EXPERIMENTS ON ANALOGIES FOR ELECTRICITY

Rationale and Overview

The language used in the protocols suggests that people base their understanding of electronics at least in part on knowledge imported from well-known base domains. But are these true generative analogies or merely surface terminology? In order to verify that the use of a particular model leads to predictable inferences in the target domain, we performed two studies of analogical models in electronics. In Experiment 1, we elicited subjects' models of electronics and asked whether their models predict the types of inferences they make. In Experiment 2, we taught subjects different analogical models of electronics and compared their subsequent patterns of inference.

The Four Combinatorial Problems

We wished to test deep indirect inferences that could not be mimicked by surface associations. At the same time, we needed to keep our problems simple enough for novices to attempt. The solution was to ask about different combinations of simple components. There were four basic combination circuits, namely the four circuits generated by series and parallel combinations of pairs of batteries or resistors, as shown in Fig. 6.4. For example, we asked how the current in a simple circuit with one battery and resistor compares with that in a circuit with two resistors in series, or with two batteries in parallel.

The chief difficulty in these combination problems is differentiating between serial and parallel combinations. The serial combinations are straightforward: More batteries lead to more current and more resistors to less current. This accords with the first level of novice insight: the "More force, more flow/more

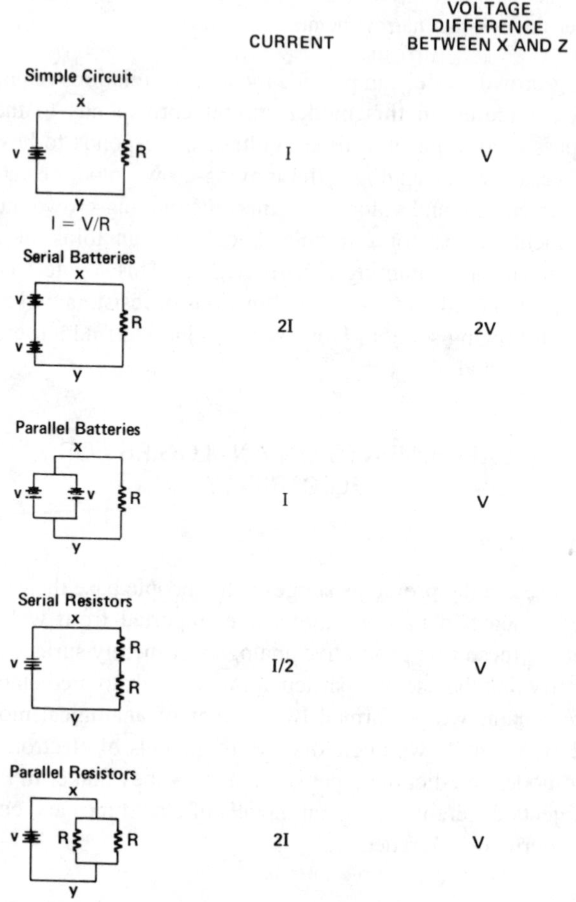

FIG. 6.4. Current and voltage for the four combination circuits: serial and parallel pairs of batteries or resistors. A simple battery-resistor circuit is shown at top.

drag, less flow.'' model, in which current goes up with the number of batteries and goes down with the number of resistors. But the parallel combinations do not fit this naive model: As Fig. 6.4 shows, parallel batteries give the *same* current as a single battery, and parallel resistors lead to *more* current than a single resistor (always assuming identical batteries and resistors).

Combinations of Batteries. To gain some intuition for these combinations, we return briefly to the water domain for a review of serial and parallel reservoirs. Consider what happens when two reservoirs are connected in series, one on top of the other. Because the pressure produced by the reservoirs is determined by the height of the water and the height has doubled, two reservoirs in series produce *twice* the original pressure, and thus *twice* the original flow rate. This conforms to the intuition that doubling the number of sources doubles the flow rate. However, if two reservoirs are connected in parallel, at the same level, the height of the water will be the same as with the single reservoir. Because pressure depends on *height,* not on total amount of water, the pressure and flow rate will be the same as that of the original one-reservoir system (although the capacity and longevity of the system will be greater).

Figure 6.5 shows the higher-order relationships comparing flow rate given parallel or serial reservoirs with flow rate in the simple one-reservoir system. The same higher-order relationships hold in the domain of electricity: The current in a circuit with two serial batteries is greater than current with a single battery. Current given two parallel batteries is equal to that given a single battery.

Combinations of Resistors. These combinations are understood most easily through the moving-crowd model, in which resistors can be thought of as gates. In the serial case, all the moving objects must pass through two gates, one after the other, so the rate of flow should be lower than for just one gate. In the parallel case, the flow splits and moves through two side-by-side gates. Since each gate passes the usual flow, the overall flow rate should be twice the rate for a single gate. Applying these relationships in the domain of electricity,[5] we conclude that serial resistors lead to less current than a single resistor; whereas parallel resistors lead to more current.

---

[5]In combinations of resistors, the key principle is that the voltage changes significantly only when current encounters a resistance. When the circuit contains two identical resistors in a row, the total voltage drop gets divided between the two resistors. Thus the voltage drop across each resistor is only half as great. As the current is proportional to the voltage drop, the current through each resistor is only half the original current. By conservation of charge, this reduced current is constant throughout the system. When the resistors are connected in parallel, each resistor has the full voltage drop across it. Therefore, current passes through each of the resistors at the original rate. This means that in the parts of the circuit where the two currents are united (before and after the resistors) the total current will thus be twice the current given one resistor.

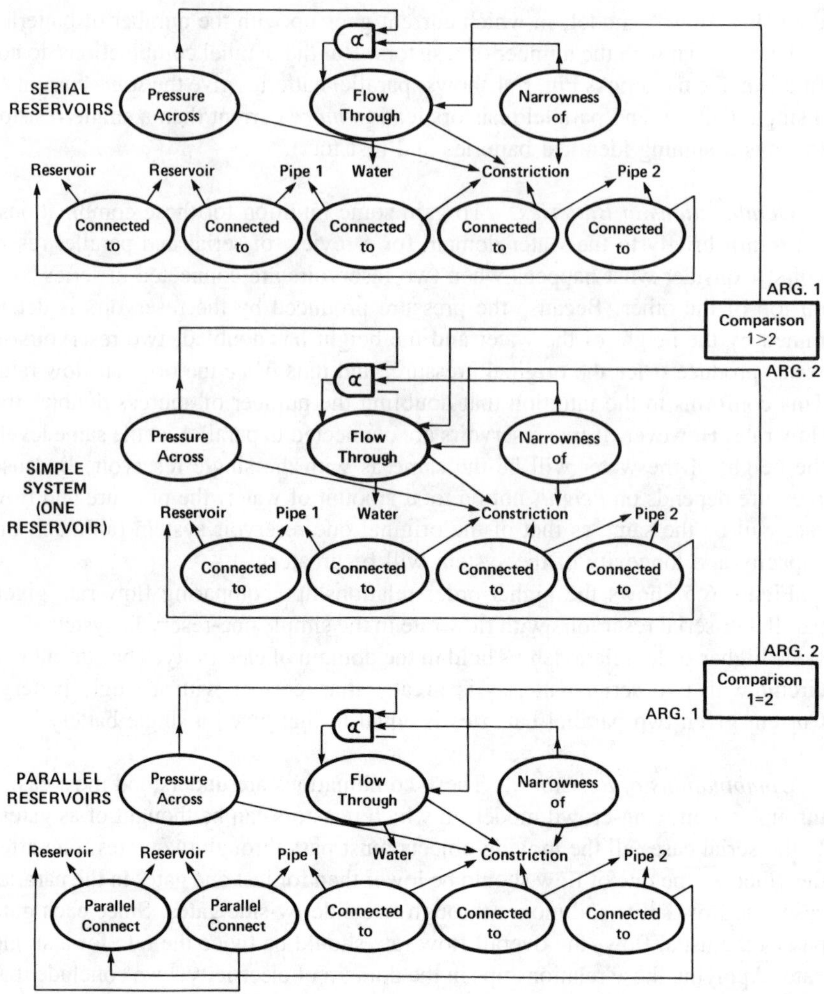

FIG. 6.5. Representation of knowledge in the hydraulic domain, showing higher-order comparison relations between rate of water flow in systems with parallel reservoirs and systems with serial reservoirs as compared with simple one-reservoir systems.

Predicted Differences in Patterns of Inference

The flowing-water and moving-crowd models should lead to different patterns of performance on the four combination circuits. Both models can yield the first-stage "More force, more flow/more drag, less flow" law. Where the models should differ is in the ease with which further distinctions can be perceived. Subjects with the flowing-water model should be more likely to see the difference between the two kinds of battery combinations. Subjects with the moving-crowd model should be more likely to see the difference between the two kinds of resistor combinations.

Flowing-fluid Model. Subjects who use the flowing-fluid model should do well on the battery questions. This is because, as described earlier, serial and parallel reservoirs combine in the same manner as serial and parallel batteries; thus already-familiar combinational distinctions can be imported from the water domain. However, subjects with the fluid flow model should do less well on resistor combinations. In the hydraulic model resistors are viewed as impediments. This often leads people to adopt the ''More drag, less flow'' view. Here, people focus on the idea that in both parallel and serial configurations the water is subjected to *two* obstacles rather than one. They conclude that two resistors lead to less current, regardless of the configuration.

Moving-crowd Model. For subjects with the moving-crowd model, the pattern should be quite different. In this model, configurations of batteries should be relatively difficult to differentiate, since it is hard to think of good analogs for batteries with the correct serial-parallel behavior. In contrast, resistors should be better understood, because they can be seen as gates. This should lead to better differentiation between the parallel and serial configurations, as described earlier. Subjects using this model should correctly respond that parallel resistors give more current than a single resistor; and serial resistors, less current.

The following protocol excerpt illustrates the superiority of the moving-crowd model for understanding parallel resistors. The subject began with the flowing-fluid model and incorrectly predicted less current in a parallel-resistor circuit:

> We started off as one pipe, but then we split into two. . . . We have a different current in the split-off section, and then we bring it back together. That's a whole different thing. That just functions as one big pipe of some obscure description. So you should not get as much current.

The experimenter then suggested that the subject try using a moving-crowd analogy. With this model, the subject rapidly derived the correct answer of *more* current for parallel resistors:

> Again I have all these people coming along here. I have this big area here where people are milling around. . . . I can model the two gate system by just putting the two gates right into the arena just like that. . . . There are two gates instead of one which seems to imply that twice as many people can get through. So that seems to imply that the resistance would be half as great as if there were only one gate for all those people.

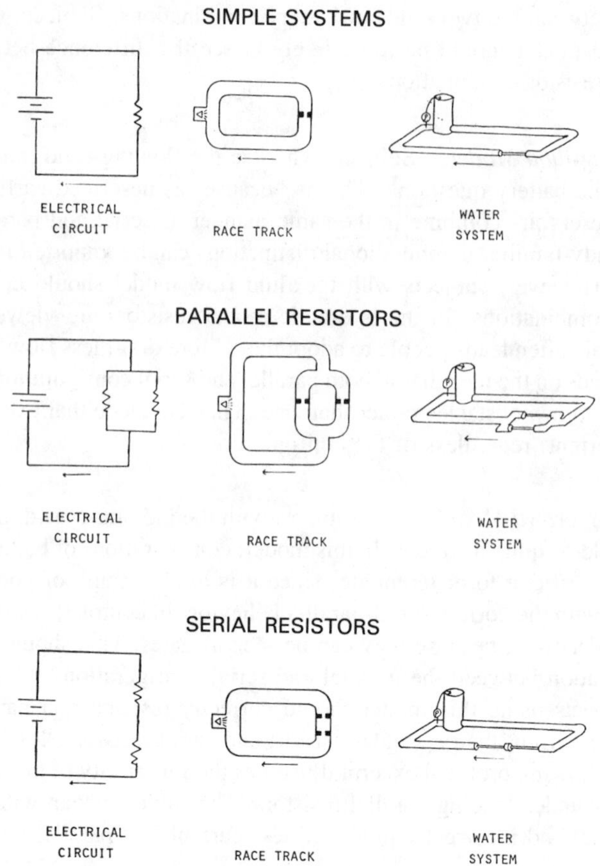

FIG. 6.6. Diagrams of electrical circuits, moving-crowd tracks and hydraulic systems, showing analogous systems for simple circuits, parallel-resistors circuits and serial-resistors circuits.

Figure 6.6 shows drawings of the analogs in the two systems, similar to those drawn by the subject. (Drawings of simple and serial-resistor systems are shown for comparison.)

These two sections of protocol suggest that models do affect inferences. The subject who drew incorrect conclusions using the water analogy later drew correct inferences using the moving-crowd analogy. The following study tests this pattern on a larger scale. If these models are truly generative analogies, we should find that the fluid-flow people do better with batteries than resistors, and the moving-crowd people do better with resistors than with batteries.

EXPERIMENT 1

Subjects

The subjects were 36 high school and college students, screened to be fairly naive about physical science. They were paid for their participation. Only subjects who used the same model throughout the study, as determined from their questionnaire responses, are included in the results discussed below. Also, among subjects who used a fluid-flow model, only those who correctly answered two later questions about the behavior of water systems were included. There were seven subjects who consistently used fluid flow models and eight subjects who consistently used moving-object models. The responses of subjects who were inconsistent in their use of models were analyzed separately and are not reported here.

Method

Qualitative Circuit Comparisons. Subjects were given booklets containing a series of questions and allowed to work at their own pace. The first page showed a simple circuit with a battery and a resistor, like the simple circuit in Fig. 6.4. Succeeding pages showed the four series-and-parallel combination circuits (see Fig. 6.4). They were asked to circle whether the current (and voltage) in each of the combination circuits would be greater than, equal to, or less than that of the simple battery-resistor circuit.

Questions About Models. After the subjects gave their answers for all four combination circuits, they were asked on a separate page to describe the way they thought about electricity, in their own words. On the next page, they were given a more specific choice: For each of the four circuit problems, they were asked to circle whether they had thought about flowing fluid, moving objects, or some other view of electricity while working on the problem. On the final page of the booklet they were asked questions about the behavior of reservoirs in the water domain.

Results

Figure 6.7 shows the results for subjects who reported using either the flowing-fluid analogy or the moving-crowd analogy consistently, on all four problems.

The patterns of inference are different depending on which model the subject had. As predicted, people who used the flowing-fluid model performed better on batteries than on resistors. The reverse is true for the moving-crowd people: they performed better with resistors, particularly in parallel, than with batteries. A

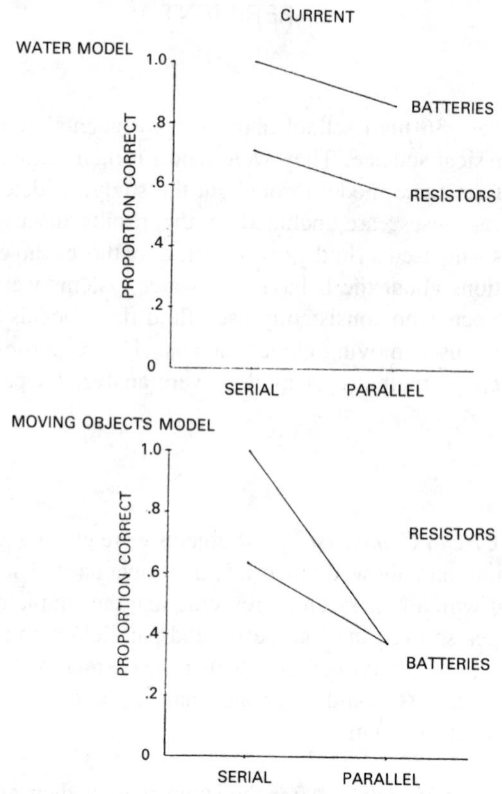

FIG. 6.7. Results of Experiment 1: Proportions correct, for subjects with either a water-flow model or a moving-crowd model of electricity, on serial and parallel problems for batteries and resistors.

Model X Component X Topology 2 X 2 X 2 analysis of variance was performed on the proportions of correct answers. Here Model refers to whether the subject was using a flowing-fluid or moving-crowd model of electricity; Component refers to whether the combination was of batteries or resistors; and Topology refers to whether the problem involved a serial or parallel configuration. As predicted, the interaction between Model and Component was significant; $F(1,13) = 4.53$; $p < .05$. No other effects were significant.

Conclusions

The results of the study indicate that use of different analogies leads to systematic differences in the patterns of inferences in the target domain. Subjects with the flowing fluid model did better with batteries, while moving objects subjects did better with resistors. These combinatorial differences cannot be attributed to shallow verbal associations. These analogies seem to be truly generative for our subjects; structural relations from the base domain are reflected in inferences in the target domain.

EXPERIMENT 2

In this study we taught subjects about electricity, varying the base domain used in the explanation. We then compared their responses to a series of questions about the target domain. Three different models of electronic circuitry were used. The first two models were versions of the hydraulic model, with fluid flow mapping onto current, pumps or reservoirs mapping onto batteries, pipes onto wires, and narrow pipes onto resistors. The two versions of this model varied according to what maps onto the battery: either a pump (Model P) or a reservoir (Model R). The third model was a moving-crowd model (Model M). In this model, current was seen as a moving crowd of mice and voltage was the forward pressure or pushiness of the mice.

The basic method was to present different groups of subjects with different models of electronics and then observe their responses to circuit problems. As in Experiment 1, the dependent measure is not merely percent correct but the pattern of responses. Each model should cause particular incorrect inferences as well as particular correct inferences. We also presented problems in the base domains. It seemed possible that subjects might have misconceptions in the base domains (such as hydraulics); in this case the knowledge available for importing into the target would deviate from the ideal knowledge.

Predicted Results

In the two hydraulics models, reservoirs (R) or pumps (P) are sources of pressure (voltage), which results in a flow of liquid (current) depending on the narrowness of the pipes (resistance). In the moving-crowd model, M, the forward pressure on the crowd (voltage), is generated by a loudspeaker shouting encouragement. This pressure creates a certain number of mice past a point per unit time (current) depending on the narrowness of the gates (resistance). Table 6.2 shows the correspondence among the three models.

Our major predictions were

1. that the moving-crowd model (M) would lead to better understanding of resistors, particularly the effects of parallel resistors on current, than the hydraulics models.

2. that the reservoir model (R) would lead to better understanding of combinations of batteries than either the moving-crowd model (M) or the pump model (P). With reservoirs, the correct inferences for series versus parallel can be derived by keeping track of the resulting height of water, as discussed earlier.

TABLE 6.2
Comparison of Water Flow, Moving Crowd, and Electricity Domains

Water Flow Models (R,P)	*Moving Crowd Model (M)*	*Electrical Circuit*
	Object Mappings	
hydraulic system	race course	circuit
water	mice	electricity or electrons
pipe	wide corridor	wire
pump or reservoir	loudspeaker	battery
constriction in pipe	gate in barrier	resistor
	Attribute Mappings	
PRESSURE OF water	PRESSURE OF mice	VOLTAGE
NARROWNESS OF pipe	NARROWNESS OF gate	RESISTANCE
FLOW OF pipe	PASSAGE RATE OF mice	CURRENT
	Relations between Objects that Hold in All Domains	
pump CONNECTED TO pipe	loudspeaker CONNECTED TO corridor	battery CONNECTED TO wire
pipe CONNECTED TO constriction	corridor CONNECTED TO gate	wire CONNECTED TO resistor
	Higher-order Relations that Hold in All Domains	
(FLOW OF water) *INCREASES WITH* (PRESSURE ACROSS constriction)	(PASSAGE RATE OF mice) *INCREASES WITH* (PRESSURE ACROSS gate)	(CURRENT) *INCREASES WITH* (VOLTAGE ACROSS resistor)
(FLOW OF water) *DECREASES WITH* (NARROWNESS OF constriction)	(PASSAGE RATE OF mice) *DECREASES WITH* (NARROWNESS OF gate)	(CURRENT) *DECREASES WITH* (RESISTANCE)
[SUM OF (FLOW INTO point)] *EQUALS* [SUM OF (FLOW OUT OF point)]	[SUM OF (PASSAGE RATE INTO POINT)] *EQUALS* [SUM OF (PASSAGE RATE OUT OF point)]	[SUM OF (CURRENT INTO point)] *EQUALS* [SUM OF (CURRENT OUT OF point)]
	Relations that Do Not Hold in All Domains	
RATIO OF (cross-section WIDTHS OF pipe and constrictions) is typically 100:1	*RATIO OF* (WIDTHS OF corridor and gate) is typically 10:1	*RATIO OF* (RESISTANCES OF resistor and wire) is typically 1,000,000:1

Neither the pump analog nor the loudspeaker analog has as clear a combination pattern.

Method

Subjects. Eighteen people participated, all either advanced high school or beginning college students from the Boston area. Subjects had little or no previous knowledge of electronics. They were paid for their participation. Due to experimenter's error, there were seven subjects in the M group, six in the P group and five in the R group.

Procedure. After filling out a questionnaire concerning their general backgrounds, subjects were divided into three groups, each receiving different models. The procedure was as follows:

1. *Model-teaching.* Subjects were given a brief introduction to electricity consisting of Ohm's Law (I=V/R) together with an explanation of one of the three models.
2. *Simple test.* All three groups were given an identical set of five simple circuit problems to calculate. In each case the circuit was a simple battery-plus resistor circuit, and subjects solved for current, voltage or resistance by applying Ohm's Law. We required that subjects solve at least four problems correctly to be included in the study.
3. *Qualitative comparisons.* Subjects were next shown diagrams of the four complex circuits (SB, PB, SR, and PR, as shown in Fig. 6.4) along with a diagram of a simple battery-resistor circuits. For each such complex circuit, we asked subjects to compare current and voltage at several points in the circuit with that of the corresponding point in a simple circuit; e.g., they were asked whether current just before the resistors in a parallel-resistor circuit is *greater than, equal to* or *less than* the corresponding current in a simple circuit.
4. *Quantitative scaling.* Each subject received each of the four kinds of complex circuits (SB, SR, PB or PR) and filled out a series of scales indicating current and voltage at the same test points as in task (3).
5. *Drawing base given target analog.* Each subject received, for each of the four complex circuits, a sheet containing a simple base version of the standard simple system (analog of battery plus resistor); and a circuit drawing of one of the four complex circuits (SB, SR, PB or PR). They were told to draw the *base* version of the complex circuit shown.
6. *Base qualitative questions.* To test knowledge of the base system, subjects were given a picture of one of the four complex systems in the base, and answered qualitative questions about pressure and flow rate in the base system. Each sheet showed a simple system (the analog of battery plus resistor) plus a complex system (the analog of SB, SR, PB or PR). The subjects made judgments at the same points as in tasks (3) and (4).
7. *Thought questions.* Subjects were asked to write out answers to questions such as "What will happen if there is no resistor in the circuit?"; and "Do electrons go faster, slower or the same speed through the resistor as through the wire?"

Results: Prediction 1

Results supported the first prediction, that the moving-crowd model (M) would lead to better performance on parallel-resistor problems than the water models (P and R).

TABLE 6.3
Results of Experiment 2:
Performance on Problems Involving
Current with Parallel Resistors

	M	*P*	*R*
Qualitative Comparisons[a]	.93	.58	.70
Quantitative Scaling[b]	.71	.50	.40

[a]Proportions of responses that current in parallel-resistor circuit is greater than or equal to current in simple one-resistor circuit.

[b]Proportions of responses that current in parallel-resistor circuit is greater than current in simple circuit.

Qualitative Comparisons. In the M group, 93% of the subjects answered that current given two parallel resistors would be greater than or equal to current given a single resistor, as compared with .63 for the combined P and R groups. This difference between the M group and the P and R groups combined was significant by a X^2 test ($p < .05$). Table 6.3 shows the results for current given parallel resistors both for the qualitative comparisons task and for the quantitative scaling task.

The pattern of M-superiority on parallel-resistor problems also obtained for voltage. The proportions of questions in which subjects (correctly) answered that the voltage in a circuit with two parallel resistors is equal to the voltage in the simple circuit with one resistor were, for the M group, .86; for the P group, .42; and for the R group, .50. Again, the M group is significantly different from the combined P and R groups by a X^2 test ($p < .025$); M differs from P significantly as well (Fisher test, $p < .05$).

Quantitative Scaling. The differences, though nonsignificant, were in the predicted direction, as shown in Table 6.3. The proportions of times subjects answered that current in a parallel-resistor circuit would exceed current given a single resistor were .71 for M, .50 for P, and .40 for R. For voltage, the proportions of times subjects answered that voltage in a parallel-resistor circuit equals that in a simple circuit were .86 for M, .83 for P and .60 for R.

Results: Prediction 2

Our second prediction, that the R group would be superior to the M and P groups on parallel-batteries problems, was not supported.

Qualitative Comparisons. The proportions of times subjects correctly answered that the voltage given parallel batteries is equal to the voltage given a single battery were .40 for the R group, .64 for the M group, and .33 for the P group. None of these differences was statistically significant.

For serial-battery problems, we expected less difference between the groups. This is because the correct answer—that voltage is greater in a circuit with two batteries in serial than with just one battery—is derivable from several different models, even from the naive "More force, more flow" view. The results are that the proportion of correct responses was .60 for R and .50 for P; for the M group, it was .57 (no significant differences).

Quantitative Scaling. Again we failed to find clear evidence that the R group understood parallel-battery problems better than the P group. The proportions of correct answers (that voltage is the same for PB as for a simple circuit) were .2 for R and .33 for P. The R group did perform better on the serial battery problems: .8 of the R answers indicated more voltage with serial batteries, whereas only .33 of the P answers did so. None of these differences is significant. (This lack of significance may seem surprising; however, we had only one data point per subject.) Rather surprisingly, the M group, with .86 correct, was significantly better than the other two groups on parallel batteries ($p < .025$, X^2).

Other Results in the Qualitative Comparison and Quantitative Scaling Tasks

There were two other significant differences. First, in the qualitative comparisons task, the P group was superior to the R group for current in a serial-resistor circuit. The proportion of times subjects correctly answered that current is lower with two serial resistors than with a single resistor was .58 for P and .10 for R ($p < .05$). There were no other significant differences on the qualitative comparison task.

The other remaining significant result is that, in the quantitative scaling problems, the R group performed better (at .40 correct) than the M group (0 correct) or P group (0 correct) on answering that current is constant everywhere in a purely serial circuit (such as SB or SR). The difference between R and P is significant ($p < .05$) as well as the difference between R and M ($p < .025$). This issue of constant steady-state current flow seems quite difficult for subjects, as discussed next.

Subjects' Knowledge of the Base. We were puzzled by the failure of Prediction 2: the finding that the R group did not excel at combinations of batteries, in spite of the seeming transparency of the corresponding combinations in the reservoir domain. One possible explanation is that, contrary to our intuitions, our subjects did not understand serial and parallel reservoirs any better than they understood serial and parallel pumps or loudspeakers. To check this possibility, we examined the subjects' answers in the base domains.

The results of the Base Qualitative Comparisons task revealed that subjects indeed failed to grasp the distinction between parallel and serial pressure sources in the base domains. Scores on the qualitative comparison problems concerning rate of flow of water or animals (analogous to current) were .35 for R, .42 for P and .32 for M. It is not surprising, then, that the R subjects failed to make correct inferences in the target domain of electricity.

Subsequent interviews have borne out the suspicion that even college-educated people fail to understand the way water behaves. They have difficulties not only with series versus parallel combinations of reservoirs or pumps, but also with the notion of steady-state flow. Current is seen not as a steady flow, constant throughout the system, but rather as a progression: Flow is strong and rapid at the source and gradually weakens as it goes through the pipes, with a drastic cut-back as it goes through the constriction. Moreover, people often fail to make the distinction between flow rate and related physical variables. Many people seem to have a *generalized strength-attribute* which is a composite of velocity, pressure, force of water, and rate of flow. This strength is thought to be very high at the outset, just after the reservoir, to diminish as the water travels around the water system, and to decrease sharply at the constriction.

Similar misconceptions show up in electronics. People in interviews do appear to have a kind of composite strength attribute that is interchangeably referred to as current, voltage, velocity of the electrons, power, pressure, or force of the electrons. This strength attribute fails to obey steady-state: It decreases as the stuff flows around the circuit, with the sharpest diminution occurring at the resistor.

The subjects' misconceptions in electronics are strikingly analogous to those in hydraulics. Therefore, subjects' failure to import veridical differentiations from the base domain does not constitute evidence against the Generative Analogies hypothesis. Even a fully generative, rigorous structure-mapping process cannot produce correct distinctions in the target domain unless subjects have grasped these differentiations in the base domain. Our investigations bring home the point that an analogy is only useful to the extent that the desired relational structure is present in the person's representation of the base domain.

DISCUSSION

It is an appealing notion that analogies function as tools of thought (Clement, 1981; Darden, 1980; Dreistadt, 1968; Hesse, 1966; Hoffman, 1980; Jones, in preparation; Oppenheimer, 1955). In this research we have sought to bring psychological evidence to bear on this claim.

We first noted that we find analogical references in people's spontaneous discussions of natural phenomena; for example, when a person discusses electric current in terms of traffic or in terms of flow of water. Our protocols suggest that people use analogies to help structure unfamiliar domains. The pervasiveness and generative quality of people's analogical language suggests that the analogies are used in thinking (Lakoff & Johnson, 1980; Quinn, 1981; Reddy, 1979; Schon, 1979). But to make this conclusion it must be demonstrated that the thinking truly depends on the analogy: that the analogy is more than a convenient vocabulary in which to discuss the results of independent inferential processes.

Evidence for the conceptual role of analogy comes from the introspections of creative scientists. The journals and self-descriptions of scientists from Johannes Kepler (1969; see also Koestler, 1963) to Sheldon Glashow (1980) seem to lean heavily on analogical comparisons in discovering scientific laws. Glashow's account of his use of generative analogies in nuclear physics was quoted earlier. Kepler's journals show several signs of generative analogy use. First, he makes reference to the analogy in stating his theory. Second, he appears to derive further insights from the analogy over time. Finally, as quoted earlier in this chapter, Kepler himself states that he uses analogy to further his thinking. The tempting conclusion is that, for scientists like Kepler and Glashow, analogies are genuine conceptual tools.

However, self-reports concerning psychological processes are not conclusive evidence, as Nisbett and Wilson (1977) have argued. In this research we tested the Generative Analogy hypothesis that analogy is an important source of insight by asking whether truly different inferences in a given target domain are engendered by different analogies. We chose as our target domain simple electricity, partly because it has the right degree of familiarity, and partly because there are two good, readily available base domains—flowing water and moving crowds—that support different inferences in the target domain.

To test this hypothesis, we needed to find problems for which the inferences required in the target could not be mimicked by verbal patterns, but would reflect structural relations imported from these different base domains. We chose the four combinatorial problems described earlier: serial and parallel combinations of resistors and batteries. These problems are simple enough to be posed even to a novice, yet are nontransparent enough that they require some sustained thought. We predicted that the parallel-serial distinction for batteries should be clearer using flowing fluid as the base. This is because the pressure difference between serial and parallel reservoirs can be understood in terms of height of fluid, a relatively accessible distinction. Therefore, use of the water system as a base domain should improve understanding of batteries. In contrast, the parallel-serial distinction for resistors should be more obvious using the moving-crowd base domain. In the moving-crowd model, resistors can be thought of as gates (inferior passages) rather than as obstructions. Subjects who use that model should see that parallel resistors, analogous to gates side by side, will allow more flow than a single resistor. The opportunity is there to find effects of thinking in different analogical models.

In Experiment 1, we divided subjects according to which analogy they reported using for electricity and compared their inferences about the current in our four combination problems. We found, as predicted, that subjects using the water model (given that they understood the way water behaves) differentiated batteries more correctly than resistors, and that subjects who used the moving-crowd model were more accurate for resistors than for batteries. These results support the generative analogies claim of a true conceptual role for analogical models. The pattern of inferences a subject made in the target domain did indeed match the pattern that should have been imported from the base domain.

Experiment 1 provided evidence for the Generative Analogies hypothesis for people's preexisting spontaneous analogies. Experiment 2 examined the effects of analogical models that were taught to subjects. In Experiment 2, we taught people to use one of three models and compared their subsequent patterns of inference. If people's inferential patterns varied according to the model they were taught, this would provide a second line of evidence for analogical reasoning. We found some of the predicted effects in Experiment 2. Subjects who were taught the moving-crowd analogy could differentiate parallel versus serial resistor configurations more accurately than subjects who had learned either of the water models. However, we did not find the predicted differences in ability to differentiate the two types of battery combinations.

We suspect that there are two main reasons that the results of Experiment 2 were weaker than those of Experiment 1. The first problem was that we did not screen people for knowledge of the water domain in Experiment 2. In many cases, people simply did not understand that serial reservoirs and parallel reservoirs yield different pressure in the domain of water. Because we had information concerning subjects' knowledge of the respective base domains, we were able to demonstrate that in many cases the failure of the analogical inference was due to the lack of the corresponding inference in the original base domain.

The phenomenon of mapping erroneous knowledge may be fairly widespread. Several independent researchers have reported that mental representations of physical phenomena—even among college populations—often contain profound errors. Yet, although these initial models may be fragmentary, inaccurate, and even internally inconsistent, nonetheless they strongly affect a person's construal of new information in the domain (Brown & Burton, 1975; Brown, Collins & Harris, 1978; Chi, Feltovich, & Glaser, 1981; Clement, 1981, this volume; diSessa, this volume; Eylon & Reif, 1979; Gentner, 1980, 1982; Hayes, 1978; Hollan, Williams & Stevens, this volume; Larkin, this volume; McCloskey, this volume; Miyake, 1981; Sayeki, 1981; Stevens & Collins, 1980; Stevens, Collins & Goldin, 1979; Wiser & Carey, this volume). Our research, and that of other investigators, suggests that these domain models, whether correct or incorrect, are carried over in analogical inferencing in other domains (Collins & Gentner, in preparation; Darden, 1980; Gentner, 1979; Johnson-Laird, 1980; Riley, 1981; VanLehn & Brown, 1980; Winston, 1978, 1980, 1981; Wiser & Carey, this volume).

Aside from the subjects' lack of insight in the base domain, the second problem with Experiment 2 is that the teaching sessions may have been inadequate to convince all the subjects to use the models. People simply read a one-page description of the model that they were to learn, and then began answering questions. Accepting a new model often requires considerable time and practice. The problem of convincing subjects to use a particular model did not exist in Experiment 1; subjects were sorted according to the model they reported using a priori. This possible pattern of conservatism in use of new models accords with that found in experimental studies of analogical transfer by Gick and Holyoak (1980), and Schustack and Anderson (1979). Both these studies found that, although subjects are demonstrably able to import relational structure from one domain to another, they often fail to notice and use a potential analogy. We suspect that one reason subjects may be slow to begin using a new analogy for an area is that they normally enter a study with existing models of the domain.

However, although Experiment 1 produced stronger results than Experiment 2, the results of the two experiments taken together provide clear evidence for the Generative Analogies hypothesis. People who think of electricity as though it were water import significant physical relationships from the domain of flowing fluids when they reason about electricity; and similarly for people who think of electricity in terms of crowds of moving objects. Generative analogies can indeed serve as inferential frameworks.

ACKNOWLEDGMENT

This research was supported by the Department of the Navy, Office of Naval Research under Contract No. N00014-79-0338.

We would like to thank Allan Collins and Al Stevens, who collaborated on the development of these ideas, and Susan Carey, Ken Forbus, David Rumelhart, Billy Salter and Ed Smith for helpful comments on earlier versions of this paper. We also thank Molly Brewer, Judith Block, Phil Kohn, Brenda Starr and Ben Teitelbaum for their help with the research and Cindy Hunt for preparing the manuscript.

REFERENCES

Brown, J. S., & Burton, R. R. Multiple representations of knowledge for tutorial reasoning. In D. G. Bobrow & A. Collins (Eds.), *Representation and understanding*. New York: Academic Press, 1975.

Brown, J. S., Collins, A., & Harris, G. Artificial intelligence and learning strategies. In H. F. O'Neil (Ed.), *Learning strategies*. New York: Academic Press, 1978.

Chi, M. T. H., Feltovich, P. J., & Glaser, R. Categorization and representation of physics problems by experts and novices. *Cognitive Science*, 1981, *5*, 121–152.

Clement, J. Analogy generation in scientific problem solving. *Proceedings of the Third Annual Meeting of the Cognitive Science Society*, Berkeley, California, August 1981.

Collins, A. M., & Gentner, D. Constructing runnable mental models, in preparation.

Darden, L. Theory construction in genetics. In T. Nicklles (Ed.) *Scientific discovery: Case studies*. D. Reidel Publishing Co., 1980, pp. 151–170.

de Kleer, J., & Sussman, G. J. *Propagation of constraints applied to circuit synthesis*. Artificial Intelligence Laboratory, AIM-485, Cambridge, Mass.: M.I.T., 1978.

Dreistadt, R. An analysis of the use of analogies and metaphors in science. *The Journal of Psychology*, 1968, *68*, 97–116.

Eylon, B., & Reif, F. *Effects of internal knowledge organization on task performance*. Paper presented at the meeting of the American Educational Research Association, April 1979.

Forbus, K. D. *Qualitative process theory*. A.I.M. 664, Artificial Intelligence Laboratory, M.I.T., February 1982.

Gentner, D. *The structure of analogical models in science*. Technical Report No. 4451, Bolt Beranek and Newman, July 1980.

Gentner, D. Are scientific analogies metaphors? In D. S. Miall (Ed.), *Metaphor: Problems and perspectives*, Brighton, Sussex, England: Harvester Press Ltd., 1982.

Gick, M. L., & Holyoak, K. J. Analogical problem solving. *Cognitive Psychology*, 1980, *12*, 306–355.

Glashow, S. L. Toward a unified theory: Threads in a tapestry. Nobel prize lecture; Stockholm, December 1979. Reprinted in *Science*, 1980, *210*, 1319–1323.

Hayes, P. J. *The naive physics manifesto*. Unpublished manuscript, University of Essex, Colchester, May 1978.

Hesse, M. B. *Models and analogies in science*. Notre Dame, Indiana: University of Notre Dame Press, 1966.

Hoffman, R. R. Metaphor in science. In R. P. Honeck & R. R. Hoffman (Eds.), *The psycholinguistics of figurative language*. Hillsdale, N.J.: Lawrence Erlbaum Associates, 1980.

Johnson-Laird, P. N. Mental models in cognitive science. *Cognitive Science*, 1980, *4*, 71–115.

Jones, R. S. *Physics as metaphor*. In preparation.

Kepler, J. *Epitome of Copernical astronomy*, Books IV and V, Volume 1. New York: Kraus Reprint Company, 1969.

Koff, R. M. *How does it work?* New York: Doubleday, 1961.

Koestler, A. *The sleepwalkers*. New York: The Universal Library, Grosset & Dunlap, 1963.

Lakoff, G., & Johnson, M. *Metaphors we live by*. Chicago, Ill.: University of Chicago Press, 1980.

Miller, G. A. Images and models: Similes and metaphors. In A. Ortony (Ed.), *Metaphor and thought*. Cambridge, England: Cambridge University Press, 1979, 202–250.

Miyake, N. The effect of conceptual point of view on understanding. *The Quarterly Newsletter of the Laboratory of Comparative Human Cognition*, 1981, *3*, 54–56.

Oppenheimer, R. *Analogy in science*. Paper presented at the 63rd Annual Meeting of the American Psychological Association, San Francisco, Calif., September 1955.

Nisbett, R. E., & Wilson, T. D. Telling more than we know: Verbal reports on mental processes. *Psychological Review*, *84*, 1977, 231–259.

Ortony, A. The role of similarity in similes and metaphors. In A. Ortony (Ed.), *Metaphor and thought*. Cambridge, England: Cambridge University Press, 1979, 186–201.

Polya, G. *Mathematics and plausible reasoning*, Volume 1. Princeton, N.J.: Princeton University Press, 1973.

Quinn, N. Marriage is a do-it-yourself project: The organization of marital goals. *Proceedings of the Third Annual Conference of the Cognitive Science Society*, Berkeley, Calif., August 1981, pp. 31–40.

Reddy, M. J. The conduit metaphor: A case of frame conflict in our language about language. In A. Ortony (Ed.), *Metaphor and thought*. Cambridge, England: Cambridge University Press, 1979.

Rieger, C., & Grinberg, M. The declarative representation and procedural simulation of causality in physical mechanisms. *Proceedings of the Fifth International Joint Conference on Artificial Intelligence*, 1977, 250–255.

Riley, M. S. *Representations and the acquisition of problem-solving skill in basic electricity/electronics*. Paper presented at the Computer-based Instructional Systems and Simulation meeting, Carnegie-Mellon University, January 1981.

Rumelhart, D. E. Some problems with the notion of literal meaning. In A. Ortony (Ed.), *Metaphor and thought*. Cambridge, England: Cambridge University Press, 1979.

Rumelhart, D. E., & Abrahamson, A. A. A model for analogical reasoning. *Cognitive psychology*, 1973, *5*, 1–28.

Rumelhart, D. E., & Norman, D. A. The active structural network. In D. A. Norman, D. E. Rumelhart & the LNR Research Group, *Explorations in Cognition*. San Francisco: W. H. Freeman & Co., 1975.

Rumelhart, D. E., & Ortony, A. Representation of knowledge. In R. C. Anderson, R. J. Spiro, & W. E. Montague (Eds.), *Schooling and the acquisition of knowledge*. Hillsdale, N.J.: Lawrence Erlbaum Associates, 1977.

Sayeki, Y. "Body analogy" and the cognition of rotated figures. *Quarterly Newsletter of the Laboratory of Comparative Human Cognition*, 1981, *3*, 36–40.

Schank, R., & Abelson, R. *Scripts, plans, goals, and understanding*. Hillsdale, N.J.: Lawrence Erlbaum Associates, 1977.

Schon, D. A. Generative metaphor: A perspective on problem-setting in social policy. In A. Ortony (Ed.), *Metaphor and thought*. Cambridge, England: Cambridge University Press, 1979.

Schustack, M. W., & Anderson, J. R. Effects of analogy to prior knowledge on memory for new information. *Journal of Verbal Learning and Verbal Behavior*, 1979, *18*, 565–583.

Smith, B. C. *Computational reflection*. Doctoral dissertation, Electrical Engineering and Computer Science. M.I.T., in preparation.

Sternberg, R. J. Component processes in analogical reasoning. *Psychological review*, 1977, *84*, 353–378.

Stevens, A., & Collins, A. Multiple conceptual models of a complex system. In R. E. Snow, P. Federico, & W. E. Montague (Eds.), *Aptitude, learning, and instruction*, Vol. 2. Hillsdale, N.J.: Lawrence Erlbaum Associates, 1980.

Stevens, A., Collins, A., & Goldin, S. E. Misconceptions in students' understanding. *Journal of Man-Machine Studies*, 1979, *11*, 145–156.

Tourangeau, R., & Sternberg, R. J. Aptness in metaphor. *Cognitive Psychology*, 1981, *13*, 27–55.

Tversky, A. Features of similarity. *Psychological Review*, 1977, *84*, 327–352.

VanLehn, K., & Brown, J. S. Planning nets: A representation for formalizing analogies and semantic models of procedural skills. In R. E. Snow, P. A. Federico, & W. E. Montague (Eds.), *Aptitude, learning and instruction*, Vol. 2. Hillsdale, N.J.: Lawrence Erlbaum Associates, 1980.

Verbrugge, R. R., & McCarrell, N. S. Metaphoric comprehension: Studies in reminding and resembling. *Cognitive psychology*, 1977, *9*, 494–533.

Winston, P. H. Learning by creating and justifying transfer frames. *Artificial Intelligence*, 1978, *10*, 147–172.

Winston, P. H. Learning and reasoning by analogy. *CACM*, 1980, *23*, no. 12.

Winston, P. H. *Learning new principles from precedents and exercises: The details*. AIM 632, Artificial Intelligence Laboratory, M.I.T., November 1981.

7 Human Reasoning About a Simple Physical System

Michael D. Williams
Xerox Palo Alto Research Center

James D. Hollan
Navy Personnel Research and Development Center

Albert L. Stevens
Bolt Beranek and Newman

I. INTRODUCTION

What are people doing when they use a mental model? As psychologists, we are attempting to understand how people learn and reason about physical systems. We are trying to describe in detail the event of human reasoning. We believe that such a description is necessary to guide the development of theories of human reasoning and of formalisms intended to capture the salient aspects of the way people reason about physical mechanisms. This chapter is exploratory and descriptive. We derive a definition of mental models from a set of distinctions made by de Kleer and Brown (de Kleer, 1979; de Kleer & Brown, 1981) and then employ it to examine protocols taken as a subject answers questions about a heat exchanger. Our concern is primarily with the descriptive and predictive power of the models we evolve based on this definition. Do they predict the subject's errors, the deductions he makes, and the objects and parameters he refers to? Although we formulate a detailed model, which accounts for a substantial portion of our subject's reasoning behavior, we do not intend this model to be the primary content of our exploration. We use modeling as a discipline to help us pull apart the structure of the subject's reasoning.

We begin with an example of the phenomenology characteristic of mental-model reasoning. Next, we provide a characterization of what we mean by the term mental model and a set of rules we have used to constrain our model construction. We then use these notions to analyze and describe several mental models our subject invents, modifies, and uses in attempting to understand the mechanism of a heat exchanger. Finally, we critique our analysis, showing where it fails to account for the protocol, where we feel uncomfortable with it, and what we think are necessary extensions.

II. AN EXAMPLE OF THE PHENOMENOLOGY

Initially the subject was presented with a description of a heat exchanger along with a simple diagram identifying the important parameters (see Fig. 7.1). The description was as follows:

> The function of a heat exchanger is to cool down a hot fluid. This fluid might be water or oil, used to lubricate and cool a machine. The heat is removed by a cold fluid, usually river or sea water. The parameters of importance to heat exchanger operation are the rate of flow of the hot fluid (f_1), the inlet and outlet temperatures of the hot fluid (T_1 and T_2), the flow of the cold fluid (f_2), and the inlet and outlet temperatures of the cold fluid (T_3 and T_4).

The subject was then asked to think out loud while answering a series of questions about the values of the parameters and about the qualitative effects of parameter changes. The questions proceeded from queries about relative parameter values, through implications and justifications for increases and decreases of those values, to deductions about potential causes for various parameter fluctuations. A list of the questions is presented in Appendix A. In order to answer these questions, the subject was forced to do considerable reasoning about the functioning of a heat exchanger. The following protocol segment is an example:

E: What would happen to T_4 if T_1 were to increase?
S: T_4 would increase also. Ah., that probably contradicts that earlier model, ah, ... I guess my first thought was that if T_1 is hotter then that's pumping more heat into the whole system. . . .
E: Into the whole heat exchanger?

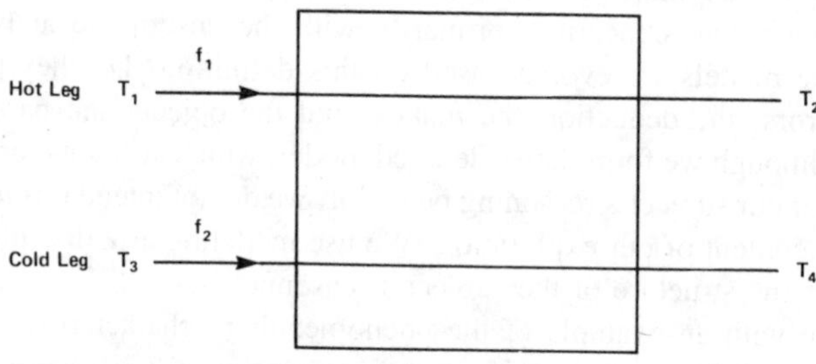

FIG. 7.1. Heat exchanger. T_i denotes the temperature of the fluid at the point labeled.

S: Yeah, and that the primary, the primary outlet for heat, and the intended outlet for heat is T_4 is the water out. Ah, and so there would be more heat coming out of T_4. It would heat up. If the incoming oil were hotter and the outgoing water would be hotter, ahh, because there would be more heat coming from the oil. More heat would be transferring from the oil to the water.

In this protocol segment, notice that the subject makes explicit reference to parameters such as temperatures, decomposes the heat exchanger mechanism into subparts, and uses local qualitiative inferences such as "if T_1 were hotter then that's pumping more heat into the whole system." It is features such as these that we regard as typical of reasoning with mental models and for which we are attempting to give a precise description.

III. DEFINING MENTAL MODEL

One question that must be addressed by any serious effort to be explicit about what one means by "mental model" is how reasoning with mental models differs from other forms of human reasoning. Although we are not ready to present a set of necessary and sufficient conditions for mental-model reasoning, we do want to provide more than the ostensive definitions generated by pointing to various protocol segments. In this section we develop the ideas that seem fundamental to our conception of mental models: that they are composed of autonomous objects with an associated topology, that they are "runnable" by means of local qualitative inferences, and that they can be decomposed.

Central to this conception of mental models is the notion of autonomous objects. An autonomous object is a mental object with an explicit representation of state, an explicit representation of its topological connections to other objects, and a set of internal parameters. Associated with each autonomous object is a set of rules which modify its parameters and thus specify its behavior.

A mental model is a collection of "connected" autonomous objects. Running a mental model corresponds to modifying the parameters of the model by propagating information using the internal rules and specified topology. Running a mental model can also occur when autonomous objects change state. For us the definition of state is distinct from the current parameter values of an object. A state change consists of the replacement of one set of behavior rules with another. For example, a transistor model would replace one set of rules with another when going from its operating region into saturation (de Kleer, 1979). A heat exchanger is a simple passive device (at least over the range of questions we are asking our subject) and does not exhibit any state changes. In spite of this apparent simplicity, we shall see that learning and reasoning about a heat exchanger can be an enormously complex activity.

We see mental models as fulfilling an important role in human reasoning. They serve to qualitatively model the effects of changes in a system. In order to accomplish this the mental model itself must contain an interpreter of sufficient power to interpret the rules and propagate parameter values between locally connected objects. When used as part of the complete reasoning system, other processes must be able to construct the mental model, to initialize it, to manipulate parameters, and to observe and record the sequence of changes within the model.

The notion of an autonomous object is our attempt to capture the salient characteristics of everyday reasoning about objects. Autonomous objects are mental objects that have definite boundaries. The behavior of autonomous objects (defined as changes in parameter values) is governed strictly by internal rules reacting to internal parameter changes and to highly constrained external provocation. The internal operations (rules) by which objects achieve their input/output characteristics across object boundaries are not directly introspectable (nor meaningful). This results in the object having a certain opacity. According to this view, one cannot ask how any given behavior occurs but can only observe the object's overt behavior.

Autonomous objects, as we conceive of them, have explicit parameter value information. For example, a region of fluid, which serves as an object in one of the models we develop, might have a parameter such as temperature. In the qualitative calculus we describe below, the temperature parameter can take on one of four values (increasing, decreasing, constant, or indeterminate). The propagation of changes in parameter values provides the sense of "running" that seems so omnipresent in reasoning about physical systems.

Inherent in our notion of autonomous objects is an explicit representation of the connectedness of the objects. Objects interact with a limited number of other connected objects by passing changes in parameter values through what we call ports. Thus, a mental model of a heat exchanger might include an object to represent a heat transfer mechanism and several objects representing fluid regions. Certain of the fluid region objects would be connected to the heat exchanger object and only those could pass information about, for example, fluid change. We suspect that the number of ports per autonomous object commonly used in any given mental model is severely limited (say to 3 or 4). This limitation may be an important factor in determining the character of mental models that people create.

Autonomous objects are further constrained by containing a limited calculus. In this chapter, we represent the calculus alternately by lists of qualitative reasoning rules or by simple qualitative constraint networks. We do not feel committed to either of these forms of representation as the correct form for the calculus. Any local computational mechanism running over a limited set of parameters would do. One can even envision people "remembering" the specific behavior of each parameter value configuration. What we are committed to is the notion that the output of this calculus is primarily qualitative.

Though autonomous objects are normally opaque, they can, at times, be decomposed. This decomposition results in a new mental model, itself composed of autonomous objects of a given topology, which can be used to produce explanations of the behavior of the initial higher level object. We refer to this decomposition process as embedding. An embedded model can be used to infer the behavior of an object in conditions that are not specified by the higher level model's input/output behaviors (which, perhaps, have been forgotten), to determine how the object carries out its behaviors, or to elaborate on why the object behaves as it does.

The notion of autonomous objects is a strong constraint on the construction of a reasoning system. For example, production-rule based reasoning systems allow arbitrary communication between productions. Any production can write information into a global memory that can then be inspected by all other productions. Autonomous objects define an explicit locality and topology over which communications can take place.

Our notion of an autonomous object evolves from an attempt to capture everyday intuitions about real world objects. Those intuitions include the idea that an object carries its mechanisms for responding to the world entirely internally, that objects respond to limited sets of external conditions, and that these external conditions can frequently be attributed to changes in internal parameters of other objects (thus yielding a topology). Reasoning within the limits of what we have defined as autonomous objects and mental models may work well for humans (particularily with designed artifacts) because of the nearly decomposable nature of much of the world (as described by Simon, 1969).

What we are referring to as autonomous objects, de Kleer and Brown (1981) have called device models. Our notion of a mental model can be mapped onto their definition of a device topology. We restrict their notion by imposing the constraint that autonomous objects can have at most a small number of ports (we use four) and we elaborate it by allowing embedding. Currently we avoid discussion of issues about the management of assumptions in reasoning systems that has served as the focus of much of Brown and de Kleer's research.

Another major question that often comes up when talking about mental models is "Why do people use mental models?" We think mental models assist human reasoning in a variety of ways. They can be used as inference engines to predict the behavior of physical systems. They can also be used to produce explanations or justifications. In addition, they can serve as mnemonic devices to facilitate remembering. In the work we report here, we focus on the use of mental models to produce explanations and justifications.

IV. AN ANALYSIS OF A PROTOCOL

In this section, we examine in some detail the protocol of a person attempting to understand and explain how a heat exchanger works. The primary tool for this analysis is the development of a series of models based on our characterization of mental-model reasoning. Major elements of these models have been simulated in a Smalltalk program called QM which was developed to permit ready construction of such systems. We do not claim the models represent a theory of reasoning nor the simulations a test of a theory. Rather, the models are employed as tools to help us structure our description of the subject's behavior and the simulation system allows us to implement the models and test their internal consistency.

The analysis of the protocol illustrates the interaction of mental models with other kinds of reasoning, the use of multiple models, the errors and inconsistencies in the subject's models, and the techniques he uses to fashion a reasoning network for solving problems about heat exchangers. The analysis we have done provides what we think is a plausible account of the subject's attempts to understand and describe how a heat exchanger works.

Figure 7.2 depicts a collection of eight production rules that are sufficient to handle the range of heat exchanger behavior we are covering. One can envision these as a set of rules defining the behavior of an isolated autonomous object which serves as a degenerate case of a mental model. The parameters of this object are the temperatures and flows of the hot and cold fluid inlets and outlets. For example, the rule $dT_1 \Rightarrow dT_2$, expresses the notion that any change in the inlet temperature, T_1, causes a corresponding change in the outlet temperature T_2. The rule $df_2 \text{-}\!\Rightarrow dT_4$ states that any change in f_2 causes a change in the opposite direction in T_4. Thus, an increase in the cold fluid flow results in a decrease in the temperature of the cold fluid outlet. These rules express the "compiled-in" knowledge that an expert in steam power generation might have about the overt behavior of a heat exchanger. However, these rules are not

$dT_1 \Rightarrow dT_2$
$dT_1 \Rightarrow dT_4$
$df_1 \Rightarrow dT_2$
$df_1 \Rightarrow dT_4$
$dT_3 \Rightarrow dT_2$
$dT_3 \Rightarrow dT_4$
$df_2 - \Rightarrow dT_2$
$df_2 - \Rightarrow dT_4$

FIG. 7.2. "Compiled" model of heat exchanger. The symbol $\Rightarrow$ means that any change in the parameter on the left causes a change in the same direction as the parameter on the right. Thus the rule $dT_1 \Rightarrow dT_2$ says that an increase in T_1 causes an increase in T_2 and a decrease in T_1 causes a decrease in T_2. The symbol $-\Rightarrow$ means that a change in the parameter on the left causes a change in the opposite direction in the parameter on the right. Thus the rule $df_2 -\Rightarrow dT_2$ says that an increase in f_2 causes a decrease in T_2 and a decrease in f_2 causes an increase in T_2.

sufficient by themselves to represent the deeper understandings of the underlying mechanisms of a heat exchanger. We contend it is these underlying mechanisms which a novice must acquire in order to be able to construct, justify, understand, and remember these rules.

We present our analysis by describing three models of the heat exchanger derived from our formulation of mental models and use these models to characterize the subject's protocol.

(Model 1) Temperature Division

One of the initial models the subject appears to use is a "container model." From the subject's protocol we get the following description of the model: "This basic model [is] that more heat is being pumped into the system and the ways that heat comes out are by the oil out and by the water out." This container model of the heat exchanger has obvious roots in experiential knowledge and brings with it a set of knowledge that can be applied to make predictions about the behavior of the heat exchanger. This model is diagrammed in Fig. 7.3. It consists of four autonomous objects and three ports. Though we have given some parameters different subscripts, three of the objects, the input and output connections to the container are the same. They have the same parameters and rule set. We call them portals to distinguish them from ports. (A port is the mental connection between the autonomous objects in the mental model; a portal is the physical connection between the physical heat exchanger and other physical objects.) The rule dT< = >dQ states that a change in temperature (T) results in an equivalent change in the total heat (Q) of the fluid in that connection and that a change in total heat results in a corresponding change in temperature. This rule says that the parameters representing heat and temperature covary in a portal. The rule df ⇒ dHx(out) means that an increase in the flow implies an increase in the heat flow out of the portal. The internal calculus of the "container" consists of a three rule set, dHx(in)=>dQ, dQ = >dHx(out$_1$), and dQ = >dHx(out$_2$). Ports map heat flow parameter values onto one another.

The following protocol segments illustrate the subject's use of this model.

(1) E: What would happen to T_4 if T_1 were to increase? . . . (section omitted where experimenter requests S to think out loud)
S: If T_1 is hotter, then that's pumping more heat into the whole system. . .

(2) E: Let's say I were to increase the flow of the hot fluid, what would happen to T_2?
(section omitted where experimenter repeats question)
S: Okay, increase t_1, then that's going to increase T_2.
E: Okay.
S: Because you're pumping more heat into the system.

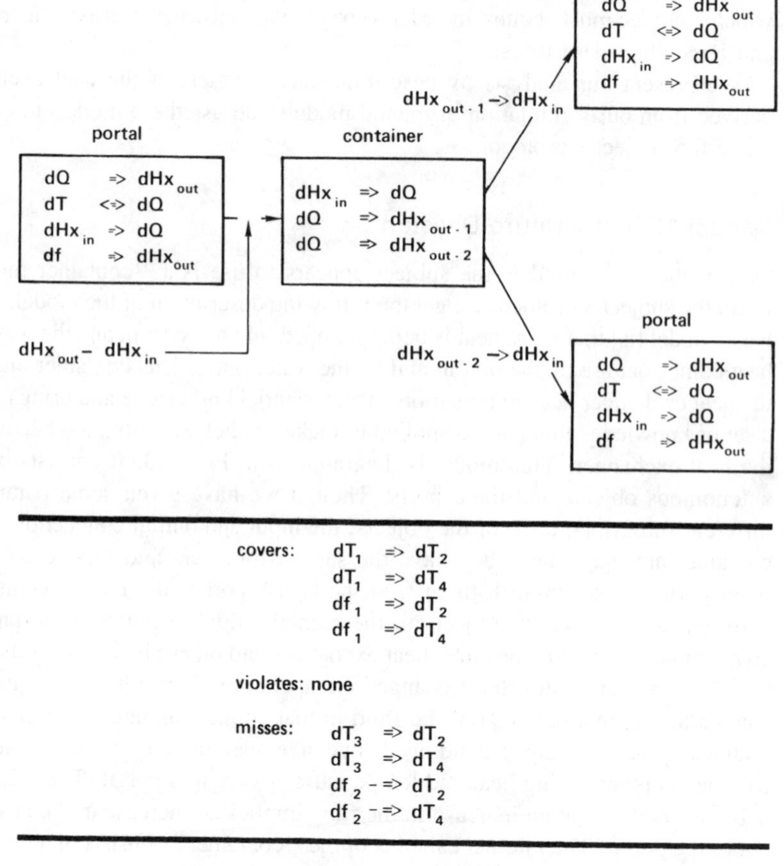

FIG. 7.3. The container model (Model 1).

(3) E: What happens to T_4 [when T_1 increases], does it increase or decrease or stay the same?
S: Well, I would guess that it increases, ah, again with this basic model that more heat is being pumped into the system and the ways that heat comes out are by the oil out and the water out, so I think that they would both increase.

People commonly confound the notions of stored heat, heat flow, and temperature in verbal descriptions of their reasoning.

We believe this occurs primarily because they use the terms heat and temperature indiscriminately in all three roles. This confounding occurs even though they often have a relatively deep understanding of many of the differences.[1] This heat/temperature confounding is accounted for in our model by the configuration of rules in the portals. For example, these heat/temperature confounding rules permit the claim that the heat flow in has increased to be made relatively directly from positing that the temperature of the fluid flowing into the heat exchanger is increasing. The container primarily serves to split the incoming ''stuff'' and distribute it to the outputs.

This model permits four of the eight possible inferences specified in our original compiled model of the heat exchanger. The inferences permitted by this model do not violate any of the eight possible inferences but four of the inferences are not addressed.

There are two fundamental problems with this model: it covers few useful predictions and includes only the most superficial notion of mechanism. This results in a model that produces answers but no good explanations. Furthermore, there is little to distinguish it from any other form of reasoning and there is only the weakest sense of structure. The important distinctions between mental models and other forms of reasoning arise when one considers larger collections of autonomous objects in more complex topologies.

(Model 2) A Constant Heat Flow Model

The second model the subject appears to use supplements the first model. Whereas the first model is used to produce an answer to an initial question, the second model is used to justify that answer. In this model, there are seven objects, six of which we refer to as fluid regions. The other object is the heat exchanger itself (or at least, an agency for the heat exchanger). Because the rule lists tend to get cumbersome, we have used constraint networks to produce the behavior of the fluid regions and the heat transfer mechanism. These are shown in Fig. 7.4 and the model of the entire heat exchanger is represented in Fig. 7.5. Each fluid region has parameters, T (for temperature), F (for flow), Q (for total heat energy), dHx (for heat flow in or out of the region), M (for mass), and dt (for time). Each fluid region has ports to adjacent fluid regions. Two of the fluid regions, those ''inside'' the heat exchanger, have ports to and from the heat transfer mechanism.

We do not wish to talk about the constraint network internal to the fluid regions at length. They are used to propagate qualitative parameter values. Thus if F increases, dt must decrease because M is fixed. The ''diode-like'' element in

[1]Subjects also seem to be uncertain about the ideas of specific heat and heat of vaporization.

a. **Fluid Region Constraint Net**

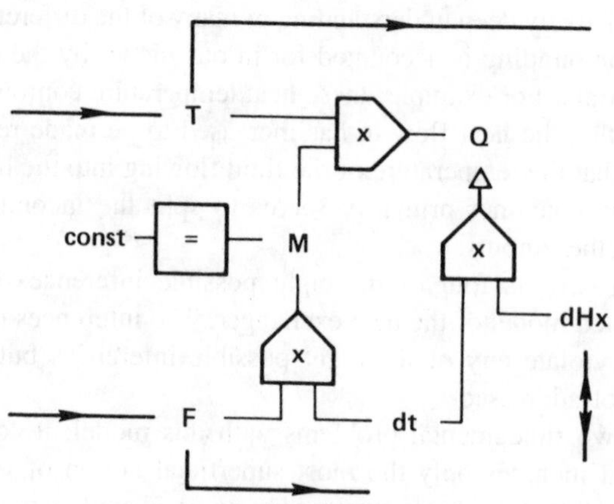

b. **Heat Transfer Mechanism Net**

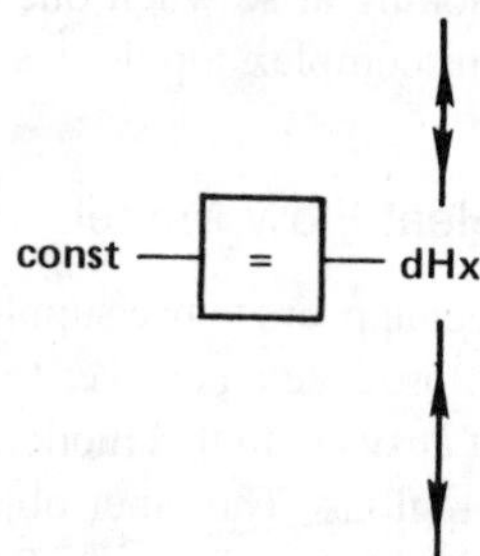

FIG. 7.4. Fluid region constraint network. These qualitative constraint networks summarize a set of rules. For example, the network relating T, M & Q says that the product of T and M equals Q. The network relating M and const says that M = const. Thus, since M remains fixed, if T increases, Q increases and if T decreases, Q decreases.

the connection from the dt-dHx rule to Q is used to constrain the direction of propagation. There are three distinct dt-dHx qualitative multiplication rules depending on the direction of the prevailing flow of heat from the region (dHx >, <, or = to 0).[2] Again, our interest is not in the particular internal calculus of the autonomous objects. As far as we are concerned the subject could just as well recall the behavior of a fluid region to a change in temperature as infer it.

---

[2]This action reintroduces the notion of state into our model. In this case, however, state does not change during running. Thus we avoid dealing dynamically with assumptions of state.

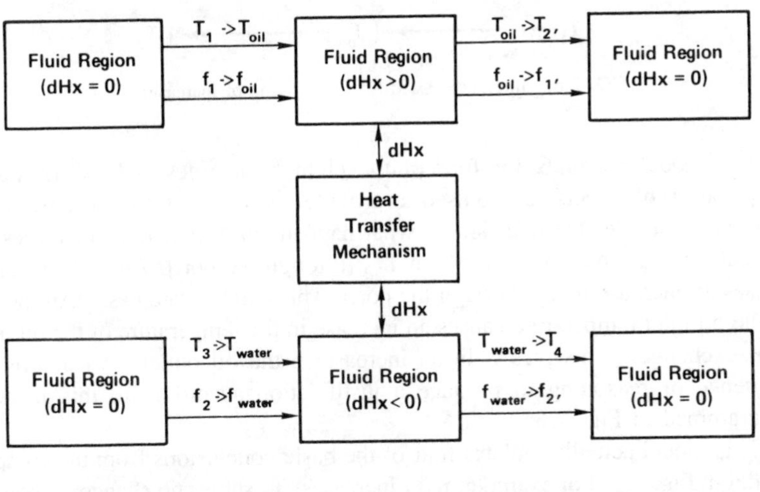

covers: $dT_1 \Rightarrow dT_2$
$dT_3 \Rightarrow dT_4$
$df_1 \Rightarrow dT_2$
$df_2 \text{-}\Rightarrow dT_4$

violates: $dT_1 \Rightarrow dT_4$
$dT_3 \Rightarrow dT_2$
$df_1 \Rightarrow dT_4$
$df_2 \text{-}\Rightarrow dT_2$

FIG. 7.5. Constant heat flow model (Model 2).

In this model, the calculus for the heat transfer mechanism constrains the heat flow from the oil to the water to be constant and independent of other parameters in the model.

The following protocol segment illustrates the subject's use of this model:

E: What would happen to T_2 if T_1 were to increase?
S: If T_1 were to increase, then I think T_2 would increase also.
E: Okay. Why do you think that is?
S: Well I guess the first cut is that the heat exchanger is going to drain off a fixed amount of heat from the, from this liquid
(segment omitted where E and S agree to refer to the hot leg fluid as "oil" and the cold leg fluid as "water")
S: Ah, first model was that there would be a fixed amount of heat and it would be drained off of the oil as it went through and similarly, if T_1 were hotter, then T_2 would also be hotter.

$\uparrow T_1 \longrightarrow \uparrow T_{oil} \longrightarrow \uparrow T_2$

FIG. 7.6. Inferences Used for Justification of Increasing T_2.

The model accounts for four of the eight basic rules and by tracing the propagation of effects can be used to provide justifications for these rules. For example, consider the question of what happens to T_2 when T_1 increases. An increase in T_1 causes an increase in T_{oil} [through the port]. An increase in T_{oil} causes an increase in T_2 [through the port]. This can be stated as: "An increase in the oil inlet temperature causes an increase in the temperature of the oil in the heat exchanger. This results in an increase in the oil outlet temperature." A sequence of reasoning to produce a justification according to this model is diagrammed in Fig. 7.6.

This model actually violates four of the basic conclusions from the compiled model in Fig. 7.2. For example, if T_1 increases, T_4 shows no change. A constant heat flow precludes any propagation of the effect of an increase in hot-leg temperature.

The subject makes explicit reference to this faulty model and some of its erroneous inferences in the protocol segment immediately following that above (we repeat the subject's last statement for continuity):

> S: . . . Ah, first model was that there would be a fixed amount of heat and it would be drained off of the oil as it went through and similarly, if T_1 were hotter, then the T_2 would also be hotter.
> E. Okay
> S: That model would probably predict that there would be a fixed difference between T_1 and T_2.

With the introduction of another question the subject is able to both detect the flaw in his model and to introduce a modification which yields a third model.

(Model 3) Dependent Heat Flow Model

Model 3, depicted in Fig. 7.8, is the same as Model 2 except that it is developed in an attempt to account for the fact that the heat flow of the heat exchanger is proportional to the difference between the temperatures of the hot and cold fluids. This modification is expressed by a modification to the constraint network of the heat transfer mechanism which makes the heat flow (dHx) sensitive to T_{oil} and T_{water} and by the addition of two ports from fluid regions to the heat transfer mechanism. The new constraint network is depicted in Fig. 7.7.

In this segment, the subject who has just inferred that a decrease in T_3 causes a decrease in T_4, is attempting to justify why that occurs.

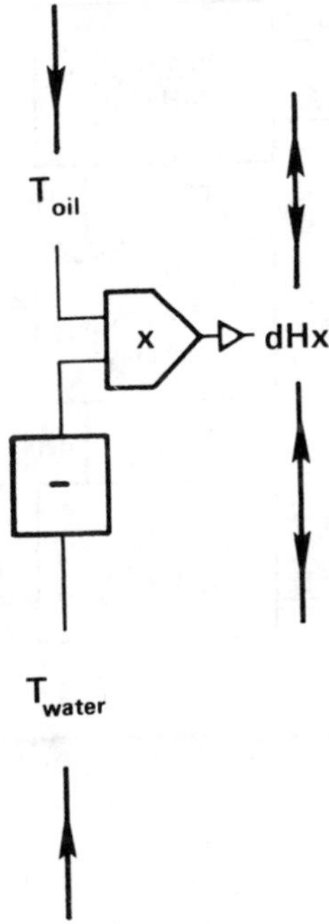

FIG. 7.7. Model 3 constraint network.

S: . . . I mean that's really not obvious to me. I think it would certainly, I guess I think it would certainly lower T_2, that is, it would remove more heat from the oil. Ah I feel fairly confident about that. . . .

This modification permits Model 3 to provide answers and justifications to an additional four of the basic conclusions with no violations. It also introduces the potential for serious ambiguities. For example, unless some special provision is taken for multiple inference paths, increasing inlet temperatures result in arguments for both increasing and decreasing outlet temperatures.

A More Detailed Analysis

In addition to simply looking at the protocol for statements by the subject describing the models he uses, we have begun developing a more formal and rigorous analysis technique to examine the sufficiency of the models we have presented. The analysis so far is based on categorized events from the first 15 minutes of the subject's protocol. The events we use were of three types: correct inferences, incorrect inferences, and boggles. We define a boggle as an event in

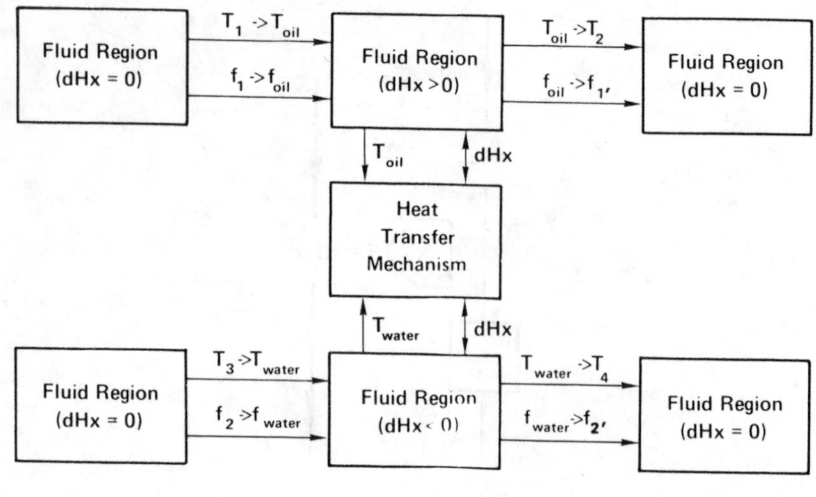

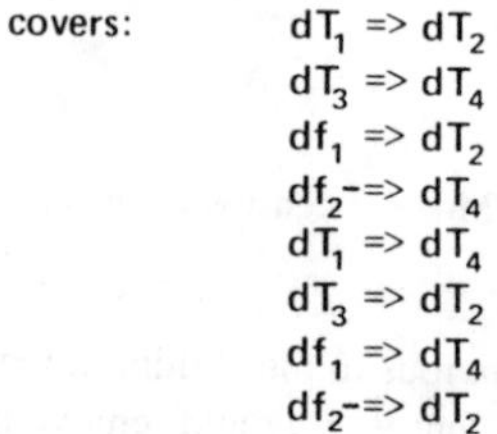

FIG. 7.8. Dependent heat flow model (Model 3).

which the subject makes an inference and then questions its accuracy. Our goal at this stage of the work is to define a set of mental models that can account for these events.

To illustrate the analysis, consider how model 3 would be used to infer what happens to T_4 if T_3 decreases. A diagram for the inference paths resulting from decreasing T_3 is shown in Fig. 7.9. Dotted lines are placed around the inferences occurring in each object. The critical point to notice is that two inference paths result in contradicting arguments for the value of T_4. One suggests an increase, the other a decrease. This is the ambiguity to which we were referring earlier.

Consider what happens when T_3 decreases. T_3 decreasing implies T_{water} decreases and that in turn implies that T_4 decreases. This is a perfectly good answer. However, T_{water} decreasing also implies that T_{out} in the heat transfer mechanism decreases. T_{out} decreasing implies that more heat should flow from the oil and into the water. This increased heat flow implies that Q_{water} should

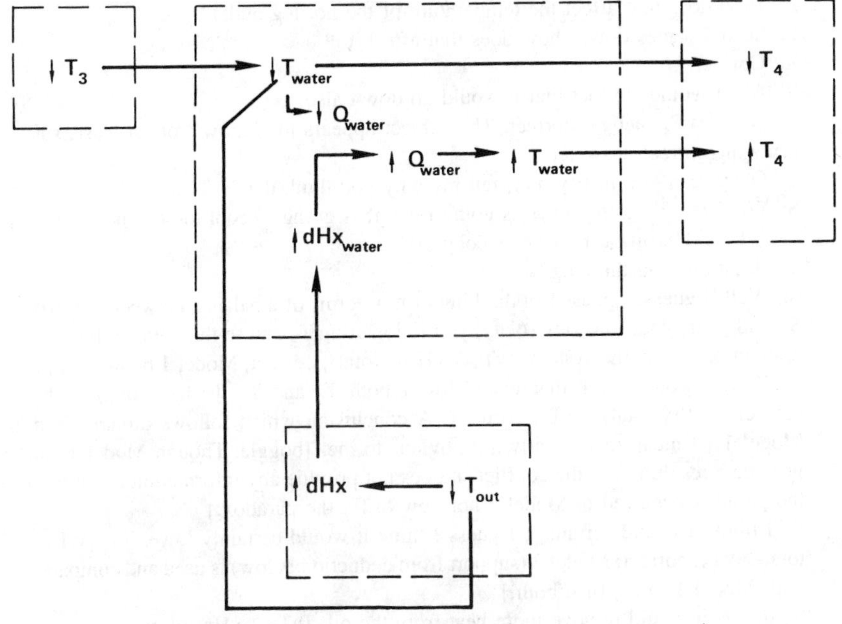

FIG. 7.9. Inference path diagram for decreasing T_3.

increase, which implies that T_{water} should increase, and finally results in the conclusion that T_4 should increase! A contradiction has been generated since the model can provide arguments that T_4 both increases and decreases.

This inconsistency is a flaw in the reasoning possible with this model. We did not intend nor plan this flaw. At the time we constructed this model we were attempting to model the correct reasoning about a heat exchanger using our self imposed restrictions about autonomous objects, ports, etc. Initially, we were frustrated by this "bug" in our model. Then we examined the subject's protocol in more detail and were surprised to find that he made precisely the same mistake.

This clash can be resolved by appealing to a slightly modified version of Model 1. This modified version permits T_3 to be considered a heat source of the same status as T_1. If T_3 decreases then the total heat input decreases. The decrease in total heat implies a decrease in both T_2 and T_4. Thus, this modified Model 1 can resolve the conflicting arguments of Model 3 by claiming that T_4 will decrease.[3] Now let us look at S1's protocol when asked what happens to T_4 when T_3 decreases:

[3]This modified Model 1 has serious flaws in it. In particular, consider what happens when f2 changes.

E: How does that affect the temperature of the hot leg outlet?
S: So if T_3 goes down, how does that affect T_4?
E: Correct.
S: Ah, I would suspect that it would go down also.
[vT_3->vT_4, hedge, correct; The subject appears to "know" or, at least, suspects the correct answer.]
E: Okay, can you justify that, tell my why you think that?
S: Well, ah, T_3 going down is going to ahh, is going to cool the oil more. ahh,
[vT_3 ->Hx(oil,out), correct, boggle][4]
E: What are you thinking?
S: Well, I guess, I guess I'm thinking of it in terms of a balance between the two,
S: and your, your lowering, okay, you're lowering T_3 and so that reduces the total amount of heat in the system. [vT_3->vH(hx total), correct; Model 1 being set up.] And so, I would think that would lower both T_2 and T_4. [vH(hx total)->vT_2, correct; vH(hx total)->vT_4, correct] [A conclusion which follows directly from Model 1.] I mean that's really not obvious to me. [boggle; Though Model 1 can provide a resolution to the conflict, it does not provide any information about why the paradox occurred in Model 3 nor how to fix the paradox.]
S: I think it would certainly, I guess I think it would certainly lower T_2, [vH(hx total->vT_2, correct; Model 3 (support from deduction below) is used and compared with Model 1 to confirm both.]
S: that is it would remove more heat from the oil. [vT_2->vHx(oil,out), correct?; From Model 3.]
S: Ah, I feel fairly confident about that. And as to whether that would end up lowering T_4, I don't know. My guess is that it would. [vH(hx total)->vT_4, correct, hedge]

Although the subject is willing to guess that T_4 decreases, the unresolved paradox from Model 3 and his inability to find a reason to defeat the deduction path which claims T_4 increases leave him uncertain. The annotations in brackets in the above protocol segment are representative of those we coded. For every correct inference, incorrect inference or boggle, we notated the protocol. We then used the collection of models to see if they predicted these events. With the models described earlier, we are able to account for 30 of 33 correct inferences, 5 of 7 incorrect inferences, and 7 of 7 boggles. In addition, there are 2 functional arguments and 18 miscellaneous events that we do not account for.

This protocol segment illustrates another interesting observation. The subject did not simply progress through the series of models we have described, but rather played off against each other and compared them to arrive at an inference. This is discussed in more detail in the following section.

---

[4]As in any protocol, the subject only articulates a fragment of the processing activity. He appears to have jumped to a crucial deduction from the middle of an inference path through Model 3. Here we believe the boggle results from a conflict between the initial answer and the alternative deduction path available from Model 3 diagrammed in Figure 8 above. Note that the conflict is with a deduction which follows from what the subject has said, not directly with the statement he has just made.

Dealing with Conflicting Inference Paths

We have identified five basic ways for dealing with the conflicting inference paths observed above. (1) A subject could understand the abstract notion in qualitative models. (2) He could have an experiential notion of how to cope with it in the sense that, for example, one can have a notion of dampening. (3) He could essentially ignore it by using the first value inferred for a parameter. (4) He could avoid the bug completely by following a "one-pass" heuristic. Thus, rather than propagating the implications of a parameter change to all the objects with appropriate ports, a single propagation path is followed. This traversal would, of course, have to be guided. But, one can imagine a simple heuristic, based on the input parameter given and the output parameter queried, which would generate a simple path from one to the other and in effect prune out cycles and alternative inference paths. (5) A fifth method is to appeal to an alternate model to resolve ambiguities. For example, in the aforementioned protocol, Model 1 provides the "correct" answer but without benefit of a justification. The path in Model 3 which gives the same answer is used as the justification.

The subject seems to consider the paradoxes discovered in his model to be true paradoxes. We take this as evidence that he is not aware of the first two methods mentioned for coping with conflicting inferences. The protocol above gives us some evidence to support the assertion that he is using the fifth method, although the final hedged answer still shows some degree of uncertainty. We believe that justifications produced with little apparent awareness of uncertainty or ambiguity, which this subject also produces on occasion, would be evidence in support of the use of methods 3 and 4.

Reasoning Outside the Scope of Mental Models

There is an array of activities present in the subject's protocol which fall outside of what we term mental-model reasoning. These include not only the invention, set up, and debugging of the mental models, but also the management of multiple models, the use of experiential knowledge, and the use of other forms of reasoning such as constraint arguments.

Constraints and Limiting Cases. Here we present a protocol segment in which the subject seems to make use of high-level constraint arguments and of limiting cases. In the following protocol segment, the subject has just been asked "What happens to T_2 and T_4 if we decrease the flow of oil?" The subject first uses Model 1 to generate an answer to a query concerning what will happen to the outlet temperatures (T_2 and T_4) if the oil flow decreases. Then, as he is producing an explanation, he seems to apply arguments which use the model but draw important constraints from outside the model.

S: If the flow decreases, there's less oil coming in, ah, then T_2 should go down. There's a heat exchanger that's more efficient. Ahh, it's roughly, thinking about the global argument again, it's roughly removing the same amount of heat, and since there's less heat coming in, ahh, then it's going to do a better job, that is, the temperature, T_2 will go down. . . . So if you reduce the amount of oil coming in and it's at the same temperature, then ahh, it's going to be in the heat exchanger longer and ahh, therefore, it's going to come out colder.

E: Okay.

S: That's using a model that says if you left the oil is there, ah, all day, you know, for a very, very long time, it would end up, it would end up being the same temperature as the water. That is, it would, it would end up being, T_2 would end up being equal to T_3. So if, as you move in that direction, then, ahh, you get closer to that so T_2 would be reduced.

The calculus of the models we have proposed is not prepared to handle notions of limit such as "T_2 would end up being equal to T_3." The idea of monotonicity the subject introduces to account for a smooth transition of T as time increases also seems outside of the scope of the calculus we have suggested. One can imagine such an inference might be made by observing for successive applications of a decreasing dt that each application results in a decrease in Q and thus a decrease in T. However, we have made no provision for the tools necessary to model this type of activity.

The Use of Multiple Mental Models. The subject often appeared to use more than one mental model to answer questions. He shifted models when one would provide an answer but no justification or when a bug or ambiguity occurred in the model he was using. One thing that surprised us about his use of multiple models was the extent to which he seemed to switch between models in the midst of a single chain of reasoning. It was as though a dialectic had been formed to serve as a basis for reasoning. We consider the use of multiple models to be one of the crucial features of human reasoning.

Experiential Knowledge. One additional observation we have made in our analysis of the protocol concerns the way the subject uses experiential knowledge. Much as a scientist or engineer might develop an analytic model of a physical system by observing the effects of various parameter manipulations, our subject frequently seems to use experiential knowledge as a data source to test his developing models.

In the heat exchanger protocol, the most obvious example arises from the subject's use of knowledge about "stuff in containers." He assumes that heat can be thought of as a type of stuff and that different parts of the heat exchanger act as containers for the heat. This mapping brings with it powerful knowledge about conservation of stuff which enables the subject to derive, test, and justify the mental models he develops. For example, when asked the relationship of T_1

to T_3, the subject answers that T_1 is greater than T_3 and justifies the answer by arguing that "the heat's going to transfer from this pipe, the top pipe down to the lower pipe, so T_1 would be hotter."

Similar justifications appear throughout the protocol and in protocols we have collected about other domains. In one of these, we asked a subject the set of questions that de Kleer and Brown (this volume) describe. The subject, when asked what happens to the frequency of a buzzer as the weight of the clapper is increased, made use of experiential knowledge from a related domain.

> S: . . . I immediately have a picture of a gamelon or something else where you have a bunch of bells, and the big ones are high frequency, I mean low frequency and the tiny ones are high frequency. . . .

This is not a new point. In work by Stevens, Collins & Goldin (1979) analyzing students' understanding of meteorological principles, it was found that the errors students made could often be traced to underlying experiential knowledge that they used in developing their meteorological models. One common example involved the application of knowledge about sponges, and the associated ideas of pressure and moisture, to reasoning about air masses. Students often predicted that air masses absorb moisture when they expanded and expel it when pressure increased.

The types of protocols we have collected probably foster this interaction of experiential knowledge with a developing mental model. We placed subjects in a situation where the only data they have to validate their newly developed mental model is the answers the experimenter is willing to supply (and those are few) and experiential knowledge. On the other hand, this is characteristic of many learning situations.

Summary of the Protocol

The earlier sections attempt a detailed characterization of the "mental models" employed by a subject while constructing an understanding of the operation of a simple heat exchanger. In this section, we provide an overall description of the protocol.

In the protocol the subject appears to invent a series of three mental models. Each model is progressively more powerful. The subject's initial reasoning can be captured by a simple container model (Model 1). When asked for a justification for one of the answers that can be generated but not justified by this model, the subject introduces a more elaborate model which presumes a complex topology of fluid regions and a heat transfer mechanism with constant heat flow (Model 2). After the discovery of a bug in this new model, the subject modifies the heat transfer mechanism to account for heat flow being dependent on the temperature differential between the hot and cold fluid regions (Model 3). It is important to note that each succeeding model either makes more predictions than the preceding one or provides correct predictions where the prior model made erroneous ones.

We assume that the subject starts with a set of basic heuristics for creating mental models. These heuristics may evolve out of the subject's experiential knowledge. They include the notion of what an autonomous object is, what the permissible interactions among objects might be, and a means of employing the internal calculus of the objects. The subject appears to be driven by our questions to produce models that are locally successful. When he is unable to answer a question or determines that an answer a model produces is incorrect, in that it violates experiential knowledge or is inconsistent with a higher order model, he seeks to revise the calculus of the model or to construct a new model.

Although an advanced model generated by our subject is capable of producing the correct inferences and justifications for the set of questions we asked, it only produces those answers nonparadoxically if one understands how to deal with conflicting inferences in qualitative reasoning. This subject does not appear to understand that notion and is left with a model containing paradoxes. He attempts to resolve these inconsistencies by appealing to a prior model. The resulting dialectic between these two models provides more power than either model alone. In effect, the subject appears to take two incomplete and inaccurate models and merge them into a successful reasoning device. This ability to use inaccurate and often incomplete models is an important characteristic of human reasoning.

V. A CRITIQUE

Our ultimate goal is to be able to provide a computational account of how mental models are used in human reasoning about physical systems. We view this study as an initial exploration of a particular characterization of mental models involving autonomous objects. We recognize many of the limitations of the formalism we have chosen. Much of what others may wish to call mental models falls outside of the expressiveness of our formalism.

In keeping with this exploratory nature, we comment briefly on some of the problems we see in our formulation of mental models. There are a variety of problems with our present account. First, it is quite difficult to distinguish in any evidential sense the theoretical ideas that we put forth (objects, runability, etc.) from the particular models we use to account for the subject's protocol. We are much more committed to these underlying ideas than we are to the particular models we have presented. Yet we don't know of any technique to explore or test the basic concepts independent of particular models.

Another problem is that, although we have explicitly formulated sets of rules or qualitative constraint networks to comprise the internal calculus of our objects and have specified the means of propagation of information between objects (by ports), we have been particularly silent about a considerable portion of the interpretive and control processes. How are the objects setup and initialized? How does the running of one model provide information for another model? How are inconsistencies and paradoxes recognized? We are only beginning to explore these processes using QM, the qualitative model simulation facility we have built. We hope that experimentation within QM may yield some hints about the nature of these processes.

As mentioned earlier, we have difficulty handling the ideas of limit and monotonicity within our qualitative calculus. Currently notions of limits, monotonicity, inequality and crude equality, iteration and induction, among others have been cut out of our characterization of a mental model. Forbus (1981) presents one technique for introducing inequalities into qualitative simulations.

We have had considerable trouble dealing with the concept of time in our models. The partitioning of the fluid regions in Models 2 and 3 serves the function, in part, of imposing time intervals or sequencing in the models. Also the way that intervals (labeled "dt" in our diagrams) interact with dHx and Q seems awkward.

We also do not have a clear definition for the concept of experiential knowledge. One conception of experiential knowledge that might fit well with our conception of mental models is to view it as fragments of mental models previously known and used. Thus, the experiential knowledge that "hot objects radiate heat" might simply be an expression of a piece of calculus from an earlier mental model of a radiator and heat sink. Such a fragment of a model could be retrieved and incorporated into other models to provide a simple means of repair.

Even though the individual models we have constructed strike us as being plausible, we are hard pressed to provide evidence from the protocol which assures us that one model is substantively better than many others we might have constructed to cover the same inferences. Furthermore, we seem to catch ourselves using many internal criteria to select between one characterization of an autonomous object and another or between one object topology and another. This is part of the reason we have been so careful to declare our lack of commitment to the particular models we have put forth.

Though we argue that we have a plausible story for the need and use of multiple models of a single system we have no convincing proof. This results from the difficulty of determining when one topology of objects is distinct from another and from the problem, mentioned earlier, of not being able to specify a direct mapping from the data (the protocol) onto specific inferences from a given model. These difficulties strike us as particularily bothersome because of the importance we would like to attribute to the conjecture that people can use several defective models to construct powerful inference engines for reasoning about physical systems.

Because of the domain we chose, we encountered mental models of a quite limited topology. The restricted structure of the simple heat exchanger may have also enhanced the uncertainty we felt about the topologies of each of our models.

This structural simplicity, no doubt, restricted the opportunity to observe the embedding and decomposition which is of considerable import to our view of mental models. The mental models we would expect a subject to use in reasoning about a more complex system such as an automobile engine would likely enhance the importance of the topology and provide more opportunity to observe the embedding of models.

One final difficulty with this effort is our avoidance of the subject of the management of assumptions. To simplify our problem we purposefully chose a mechanism for which we would not have to manipulate assumptions of state. In spite of this, we encountered numerous problems with default assumptions of parameter values during our computer modeling effort with QM. For the sake of expediency we have not detailed those difficulties here. However, we are now coming to the conclusion, put forth by de Kleer, Brown, and others, that a theory for the management of assumptions is one of the central problems in understanding human reasoning.

VI. CONCLUSIONS

This chapter takes a set of distinctions from recent theoretical research on qualitative reasoning (de Kleer, 1979, and de Kleer & Brown, 1981), and examines what percentage of a specific, albeit small, piece of human reasoning and learning behavior they could capture. The subject's protocol was used to guide the construction of a set of device topologies (which we refer to as mental models) for various aspects of the operation of a simple heat exchanger. As anticipated by de Kleer and Brown, the device topologies were fraught with limitations. The subject's protocol provides explicit examples of the inherent difficulties with such a reasoning technique. The mental models used by our subject frequently produced partial answers, or incorrect answers, or even contradictory answers. Nonetheless, this subject was able to correct many of these problems by the efficient management of a dialectic between models and by appealing to experiential knowledge.

Rather than being dismayed by this verification of the limitations of mental models and qualitative reasoning we are encouraged by our models' descriptive power. The mental models we describe both seem plausible and can be manipulated to produce a substantial percentage of our subject's inferences (both correct and incorrect) and even some of the uncertainties he expressed.

We are excited by the numerous problems that the models bring into focus. Further analysis of the extensive use of multiple models and their blending to fill gaps and repair or circumvent flaws may well be a criticially important area for exploration. The apparent ease with which one flawed model was identified by our subject as bugged and then repaired by an appeal to experiential knowledge may point to one of the primary strengths of reasoning with mental models.

APPENDIX I: QUESTIONS

Which temperature is hotter, T_1 or T_3?

What would happen to T_2 if T_1 were to increase? Why?

What would happen to T_4 if T_1 were to increase? Why?

What would happen to T_4 if T_3 were to decrease? Why?

What happens to T_2 if f_1 increases? Why?

What happens to T_4 if f_2 decreases? Why?

What happens to T_4 if f_1 decreases? Why?

Let us say T_2 increased. What might be the cause of this? Why? How could you tell if you could only look at temperature parameters (no fluid flows)?

Let us say T_4 decreased what might be the cause of this? Why? How could you tell if you could only look at temperature parameters (no fluid flows)?

ACKNOWLEDGMENT

We would like to express our appreciation to ONR for supporting the Mental Models Conference and to UCSD for hosting the conference. The views expressed in this chapter are those of the authors and should not be interpreted as representing the official policies of any government agency.

REFERENCES

de Kleer, J. *Causal and teleological reasoning in circuit recognition.* MIT AI-TR-529, 1979.

de Kleer, J., & Brown, J. Mental models of physical systems and their acquisition. In J. R. Anderson (Ed.), *Cognitive skills and their acquisition,* Hillsdale, N.J., Lawrence Erlbaum Assoc., 1981.

Forbus, K. *Qualitative reasoning about physical processes.* Proceedings of IJCAI, August 1981.

Simon, H. *The sciences of the artificial.* MIT Press, 1969.

Stevens, A., Collins, A., & Goldin, S. Misconceptions in students' understanding. *International Journal of Man-Machine Studies,* 1979, *11,* 145–156.

8 Assumptions and Ambiguities in Mechanistic Mental Models

Johan de Kleer
John Seely Brown
Xerox Palo Alto Research Center

INTRODUCTION

Our long-range goal is to develop a model of how one acquires an understanding of mechanistic devices such as physical machines, electronic and hydraulic devices, or reactors. We focus on two aspects of this problem. First, we lay out a framework for investigating the structure of people's mental models of physical devices, which we call *mechanistic mental models*. This involves developing a precise notion of a qualitative simulation and the kinds of "work" one expects it to do. The concept of qualitative simulation derives from the common intuition of "simulating the machine in the mind's eye." One of the goals of this chapter is to put this common intuition on a more solid theoretical base.

Although one would intuitively expect qualitative simulations to be simpler than quantitative simulations of a given device, they turn out to be equally complex, but in a different way. Their complexities are not readily apparent from protocols of subjects reasoning about a mechanistic device, a fact that we account for in the latter part of the chapter. These complexities arise, in part, from the fact that devices may appear nondeterministic and underconstrained when the quantities and forces involved in their makeup are viewed solely from a qualitative perspective. Therefore, if the qualitative simulation of the device is to behave deterministically, additional knowledge and reasoning must be used to further constrain or disambiguate these "apparent" ambiguities. Thus, the second aspect of this research investigates the kinds of ambiguities that arise when a device is analyzed qualitatively, and explores the various techniques and knowledge sources that can be used to circumvent or resolve them.

It is surprisingly difficult to construct mental models of a device, if these models are to be capable of predicting the consequences of events that have not already been considered during the creation of the model. Thus, the process for constructing a good mental model involves a different kind of problem-solving than the process for "running" the resultant mental model; a distinction that we find crucial to understanding how people use mental models. In fact, simply clarifying the differences between the work involved in constructing a qualitative simulation—a process we call *envisioning*—and the work involved in simulating the result of this construction—a process we call *running*[1]—turn out to have both theoretical and practical ramifications.

The first two sections of the chapter provide an outline of a theory of qualitative simulation. The last section explores some of the psychological implications of this theory. We discuss several kinds of learning and illustrate how people might learn "ideal" models by making successive refinements to their non-robust, initial models, making explicit the hidden assumptions in them. We also discuss two ways to use nonideal models to explain how something works: first, to provide a framework for embedding models within models and, second, to sequence a collection of models that converge on an ideal understanding of the device.

QUALITATIVE SIMULATIONS

A Basis for Mechanistic Mental Methods

Complex devices, such as machines, are built from combinations of simpler devices (components). Let us assume we know the behaviors of the components, as well as the way in which they are connected to form the composite device. The behaviors of the components are described qualitatively, with the quantities of importance to the operation of the device described by qualitative values such as "going up" or "going down," "high," or "low." The qualitative simulation presents the interesting events in the functioning of the machine in their causal order. Figure 8.1 illustrates a conventional door-buzzer (for the moment we will ignore the push button that activates the buzzer) which we will use as one of our main examples throughout the chapter. The buzzer is a simple device, but one complex enough to explore ideas of qualitative simulation (see de Kleer & Brown, 1981, for a more detailed description). The buzzer's qualitative simulation might be expressed as: *The clapper-switch of the buzzer closes, which causes the coil to conduct a current, thereby generating an electromagnetic field which in turn pulls the clapper arm away from the switch contact, thereby opening the switch, which shuts off the magnetic field, allowing the clapper arm to return to its closed position, which then starts the whole process over again.*[2]

[1]In some of our earlier papers we referred to this process as *envisionment*.

[2]The repetitive opening and closing of the switch (i.e., its vibration) produces an audible sound.

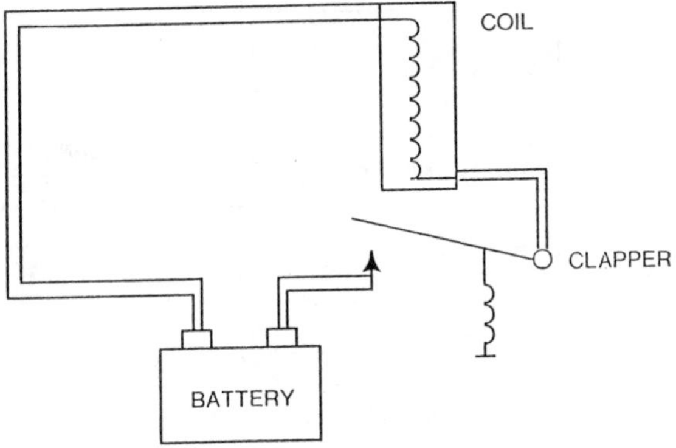

FIG. 8.1. Buzzer.

Qualitative simulation does not account for all of the kinds of qualitative reasoning that are possible about the device. In particular, it does not account for those aspects of a component's behavior which are "noncausal" or more "constraint-like." A complete qualitative *analysis* would consist of more parts. The first, of which we just gave an example, identifies the path of causal action in the device's functioning, and a second identifies the support which enables the causal action path to exist. However, in this chapter we are primarily concerned with qualitative *simulation*, which only concerns the first. For example, a qualitative simulation of the steam plant illustrated in Fig. 8.2 might be: "*The heat input to the steam generator causes the production of steam which is carried through the pipe to the turbines causing the turbines to turn. . .*" Although this simulation details the causal action of the plant, it does not make the inference that the water is conserved in the system because no single component loses water. These more constraint-like arguments, although they are qualitative, are part of the support structure[3] for the causal action, and thus not discussed here.

The simplicity of the qualitative simulation as expressed in the preceding two examples is deceptive. Qualitative simulation encompasses a variety of ideas which need to be carefully differentiated. For example, we must distinguish simulation as a process from the results of that process. A simulation process operates on a representation describing the device, producing another representation that describes how the device functions. One source of confusion is that this latter representation can likewise be "interpreted" or simulated, but doing so

[3]Roughly speaking, the biasing network of a transistor is another example of a support structure because it *enables* the transistor to amplify but does not itself play a active role in the amplification. However, this kind of support seems to be a different kind of support than the one mentioned in the steam plant. This suggests that the action-support distinction may turn out to be independent from the cause-constraint distinction although action more commonly requires causal reasoning while support more commonly requires constraint-like reasoning.

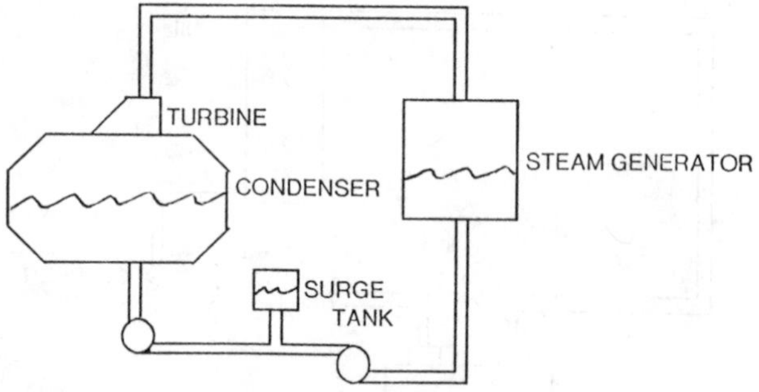

FIG. 8.2. Steam plant.

will produce very little more than what is already explicitly represented in the functional representation produced by the first kind of simulation.[4]

We need to distinguish four related notions which form the basic distinctions for a theory of qualitative reasoning. The most basic, *device topology,* is a representation of the structure of the device (i.e., its physical organization). For example, the steam plant consists of a steam generator, turbine, condenser, their connecting pipes, etc. The second, *envisioning,* is an inference process which, given the device's structure, determines its function. The third, *causal model,* describes the functioning of the device (i.e., a description of how the device's behavior results from its constituent components which is stated in terms of how the components causally interact). The last is the *running* of the causal model to produce a specific behavior for the device, by giving a chain of events each causally related to the previous one. Thus, both the structure and functioning of a device are represented by some knowledge representation scheme (device topology and causal model, respectively), with the former being the input to the envisioning process and the latter being its output, which, in turn, is then used in the running. The two examples of qualitative simulation presented earlier are ambiguous as to whether they refer to the envisioning, the causal model, or the running.

Determining the functioning of a device solely from its structure, i.e., envisioning, often requires some very subtle reasoning. The task, in essence, is to figure out how the device works given only its structure, and the knowledge of some basic principles. Structure describes the physical organization of the device, namely its constituent components and how they are connected, but it does not describe how the components function in the particular device. (That is one of the end results that the envisioning process is trying to discover.) The "behaviors" of each component are described in a manner that is independent of the

[4]Note that this latter kind of simulation is just one of the kinds of inference mechanisms that can use or "interpret" the functional representation. Others can inspect it in order to answer such questions as "Could x cause y to happen?"

particular context in which the component is embedded (i.e., context-free). These behaviors form a component model (or schema) which characterizes all the potential behaviors of the component, and the envisioning process instantiates a specific behavior for each component from these models. These component models are the basic principles which the envisioning process draws upon to derive the functioning from the structure.

We will discuss these component models in detail in the following section, but a simple example from the steam plant will help clarify the point for this discussion. The specific behavior of the pipe connecting the boiler and turbine might be that the contents flow from right to left. This certainly is an inadequate component model for the pipe throughout the entire model as the contents flow from left to right in the pipes from the condenser to the boiler. A possible component model for the pipe, overall, is "the contents will flow from the high-pressure end to the low-pressure end; and if these pressures are the same, nothing will flow." This component model for pipes works for every pipe in the steam plant. To determine the functioning of the overall device, each component's model must be examined and an individual, specific behavior instantiated for it. Thus, the functioning of the entire device is determined, in part, by "gluing together" the specific behaviors of all of its components. The problem for envisioning is determining for each component which behavior is actually manifested given all the possible behaviors its model characterizes.

What makes the problem-solving effort involved in the structure-to-function inference process difficult is that the behavior of the overall device is constrained, not only by local interactions of its component behaviors, but also by global interactions. Therefore, in principle, the behavior models of the components which are specified qualitatively may not provide enough information to identify the correct functioning of the device. For example, if values are described qualitatively, fine-grained distinctions cannot be made, such as, whether one force is stronger than another. Thus, in the case of the buzzer, the envisioning may not be able to determine whether the force of the magnetic field is stronger than the restoring force of the spring. Which of the forces is the greater may, in fact, be crucial to the functioning of the device. Also, because the primitives used for constructing simulations are the component models, they are, by definition, local and hence cannot reference or utilize aspects of global behaviors. For example, the buzzer makes noise because it oscillates, but oscillation is a property of the combination of the models of the components on the feedback path, not of any one in particular.

In order to describe how the resultant behavior derives from the behaviors of the constituents, first, each important event in the overall behavior must be causally related to preceding events. Then, each causal relationship must be explained by some fragment of the component model of one of its components. The first example we gave, describing Fig. 8.1, is, at best, an abridged description of the buzzer's function. It causally relates each event to the preceding one, but fails to state any rationale for these causal connections. Because it is impossible to tell, a priori, whether the component models lead to unique behavior, the problem-solver must entertain the possibility that the structural evidence is underconstraining. Therefore the envisioning must take into account the possibility that one structure may lead to multiple possible functionings among which the envisioning cannot, in principle, distinguish.

The problem-solving methods for envisioning that we have investigated are based on the two techniques of relaxation and propagation. (In this brief discussion of the methods, we will ignore the added complexity introduced by the possibility of nonunique outcomes; both methods can be extended to deal with it.) The method under consideration in this chapter is that of propagation, because relaxation, even qualitative relaxation,[5] has the disadvantage of failing to identify the causal relationships (and thus also the mechanisms producing them) of the device's behavior. To solve by propagation, one starts with a single, noncausally produced event (e.g., an input or a state in disequilibrium), then examines the nearby components to determine what events resulted, and repeats the procedure indefinitely. This technique has the advantage of automatically constructing the causal relationships between events, and at the same time identifying the mechanisms of the causal relationships. However, because its method is to proceed locally, without referencing global effects, it often produces multiple behaviors, only one of which is possible.

''Running'' the resulting causal model is closest to the original psychological intuition of ''simulating the machine in the mind's eye.'' By running the model, one, in essence, does a straight-forward simulation of the machine; the running itself does not have to determine or ''prove'' the causal or temporal ordering of events, as the envisioning process already has done so, and encoded the information in the causal model which serves as the input data for the running process.

The simplicity and elegance of the running process is the result of the complex problem-solving (i.e., envisioning) that constructed it. Our intuition that ''simulation in the mind's eye'' is simple is manifested by this running process. However, that sense of simplicity is deceptive, for the running is not possible without the more complex problem-solving which preceded it, removing all the ambiguities about how the machine *might* function.

Understandably, the problems that arise in constructing causal models and the mechanisms that suffice in solving these problems become important for cognitive psychology and artificial intelligence. For psychology, it is important because they provide a framework for analyzing the ''competency'' involved in determining how a novel machine functions. Inasmuch as envisioning is restricted to being based solely on structural evidence, it becomes an interesting

---

[5]Qualitative relaxation begins by assigning all possible qualitative values to all the interacting quantities and then repeatedly applies all the local component models to restrict the values for each quantity it references.

inference strategy in its own right for artificial intelligence applications, especially given the desire for artificial intelligence systems to be robust, i.e., to be able to deal with novel situations. The resulting models are more likely to be void of any implicit assumptions or built-in presuppositions based on how the device was intended to behave.

Let us now consider the major ingredients of the envisioning process.

Device Topology and Class-Wide Assumptions

We have developed a language of primitives for expressing and defining the structure of a machine. A machine consists of constituents. Some of these constituents represent parts which themselves can be viewed as smaller machines (e.g., resistors, valves, boilers). Other constituents represent connections (e.g., pipes, wires, cables) through which the parts communicate by transmitting information. These connections can be thought of as conduits through which ''stuff'' flows, its flow captured by conduit laws, which are explained later. We call the representation of the machine in these terms its *device topology*.

As illustrated in Fig. 8.3, the parts of the buzzer are the spring-loaded clapper with an attached switch, the coil, and the battery. The conduits of the buzzer are three wires and a magnetic field. The clapper is connected electrically between the battery and the coil, and the ''stuff'' that flows in these wires is electrical charge. The clapper is also connected to a magnetic field, a very different kind of conduit than wire.

Assumptions are embodied in the identification of the important constituents of the machine, in their models, and in the physics of the conduits. Some of these assumptions are idiosyncratic to a particular constituent or device, but others apply to a wide class of devices. For example, the above buzzer explanation ignores any currents the magnetic field of the coil might induce; this assumption

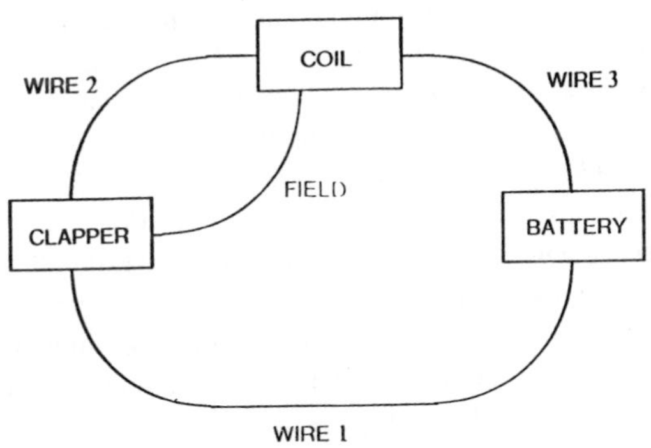

FIG. 8.3. Device topology of the buzzer.

is valid for most electro-mechanical devices. Similarly, for most electro-mechanical devices, one can assume that electrical charges (or current) flows instantaneously in the wires. We call such assumptions *class-wide assumptions*. They form a kind of universal resolution for the "microscope" being used to study the physical model.

We use this microscope to view behavior, focusing only on certain aspects of the behavior and then only to a certain level of precision. Because we use the same microscope to view the behaviors of all the devices of a certain class (e.g., elctro-mechanical), it makes the same basic assumptions for each. Although, depending on one's philosophical position, it may be possible to employ an assumption-free microscope, certainly the microscope used for qualitative modeling is not. We introduce the notion of class-wide assumptions to distinguish them from assumptions that apply to only one particular device; the latter, though, plays a major role later in this paper.

Conduit Laws

The conduits contain stuff (e.g., water, oil, steam, electrons, etc.) which mediates the interactions between components. (See Williams, Hollan, & Stevens, this volume for a discussion of "stuff.") The physics of these conduits explains how this stuff communicates information. The stuff can be modeled as a set of identical objects, each of which obeys a rigidly defined set of rules. For example, in the lemming metaphor (Gentner & Gentner, this volume) for current flow, the running lemmings represent flowing current and the battery supplies the noise (impetus) to urge the lemmings to move. These mythical objects, though not necessarily representative of actual objects, serve to give a causal account of the transfer of *information* in the connections. In this chapter we will not concern ourselves with accounting for this transfer, and will instead rely solely on its existence so that we can speak simply of conduits transferring information between components.

The brevity of the discussion here belies the importance of the qualitative physics of stuff in conduits. The choice of the physics for the conduits has enormous influence on the models for the components; they too are subject to the same physics, being processors and manipulators of the stuff in the conduits. In this chapter we utilize an oversimplified account of stuff. To prevent later confusion, however, we must make two important observations. First, although in the functioning of the machine all the conduits contain stuff, all of which may be flowing, at any given time only *some* of that stuff contributes to the causal action. And second, the communication of information within a conduit does not necessarily mean that stuff is flowing in it. For example, the introduction of a quantity of water in one end of a pipe will almost instantaneously increase the pressure at the far end of the pipe even though it might be a very long time (if ever) before the quantity of water moves to the far end of the pipe.

We assume that the behavior of the objects in the conduits can be summarized as a collection of attributes (e.g., pressure, velocity, current, voltage, volume). These attributes are a collective description of the objects in the conduits. When a conduit connects two components, both components have direct access to the values of the attributes in the conduit. Each component is modeled by rules that monitor the attribute values in some of the conduits connected to it and, which can change the state of the component accordingly, thereby affecting other conduits connected to it. These behavioral rules form the essence of a component model.

Component Models

In order to explore the ramifications of these ideas, a formalism for rules comprising a component model must be developed. The formalism will provide a common language for expressing the model of a component. Also, the existence of a formalism should remove any potential ambiguities about the component models and make it easier to study the simulation and problem-solving processes which use them. A component model characterizes all the potential behaviors that the component can manifest. It does not, however, specify which ports or conduits connected to them are the inputs, and which are the outputs; very often that can only be determined in the broader context of how a particular component is used in the overall device.[6]

A component's behavior is typically divided into a number of distinct regions or states within which its behavior is relatively simple. For example, a switch has two states, "on," and "off," each of which specifies radically different, but simple, behaviors. The behavior of each state is described by a definition part and a transition part; the definition part describes how the attributes of the connecting conduits interrelate, and the transition part describes how attribute values of the connecting conduits can change the state of behavior of the component.

The transition part is a collection of conditions on attribute values along with their resulting effect on the state of the component. The definition part is a collection of qualitative equations on attribute values which define what it means to be in that state. This definition part can be used to determine the consequences of a component being in a given state. If the envisioning process knows a component is in a particular state, it can use the definition part to infer the new values of attributes in some of its connecting conduits and thus to determine the component's behavior. The definition part can also be used as a criterial test to determine whether a component is in that state. This is done by determining

[6]Determining which conduit(s) is (are) actually functioning as the input may seem obvious but for n-conduit devices (where $n > 2$), such as transistors such determination can be problematic without recourse to a global analysis of the overall device.

whether the definition attribute equations of a hypothetical state hold in the particular behavioral context. (The utility of this second use though, will not become evident until assumptions are introduced.)

The general form of a component model is as follows:

```
‹component› : ‹state1›:
                 ‹definition-part›,
                 ‹transition-part›.
              ‹state2›:
                 ‹definition-part›,
                 ‹transition-part›.
              . . .
```

The definition part is a sequence of "‹attribute› ⇐ ‹value›" or "‹attribute› ⇔ ‹attribute›." (For more complex examples, this simple definition of the attribute equation would have to be extended, but it suffices for this chapter.) The transition part is a sequence of "IF ‹attribute-test› CAUSES: ‹transition›." Note that the only attributes a model may reference are those of the conduits attached to the component and the only state that may be referenced is the component's own.

In this example, fields are described by the single attribute of field strength (indicated by an "F") and wires are described by the single attribute of current flow (indicated by an "I"). Figure 8.4 diagrams the attributes corresponding to the conduits of Fig. 8.3. One possible set of specific models for the buzzer is:

```
CLAPPER : OPEN:
                 I1 ⇐ 0, I2 ⇐ 0
                 IF F1 = 0 CAUSES: clapper will become CLOSED.
          CLOSED:
                 I1 ⇐ 1, 12 ⇐ 1
                 If F1 = 1 CAUSES: clapper will become OPEN.
COIL : ON:
             F1 ⇐ 1
             IF I2 = 0 CAUSES: coil will become OFF
             IF I3 = 0 CAUSES: coil will become OFF.
       OFF:
             F1 ⇐ 0
             IF I2 = 1 CAUSES: coil will become ON
             IF I3 = 1 CAUSES: coil will become ON.
BATTERY: I1 ⇔ I3.
```

(Model 1)

Note that we also introduce the idea of qualitative time. The statements "will become" do not make quantitative discriminations. If two component models were simultaneously to cause state transitions, the simulator, by itself, would not

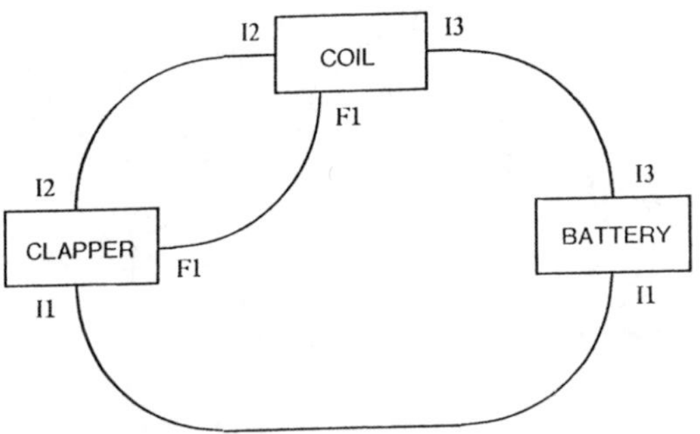

FIG. 8.4. Attribute topology of the buzzer.

be able to determine which necessarily happens first. Additional information or additional inference machinery would be required, as will be discussed later.

Causal Model

These models can now be used by the envisioning process to determine the behavior of the buzzer and construct its causal model. The envisioning problem-solving process consists of a propagation phase followed by a filtering phase (which is discussed later). The first phase of envisioning is very much like a simulation, albeit a very specialized one. Intuitively, this first phase consists simply of starting with particular values for the conduit attributes, and then, using the component models repetitively, deducing the changes in other conduit attributes and component states. This view, however, does not illustrate the power of envisioning as it suggests the result is simply a historical trace of attribute values over time.

Each application of a component model derives value(s) for unknown attribute values from known ones. This relationship between antecedents and consequences establishes a primitive causal connection between causes (antecedents) and effects (consequences). Thus, envisioning is simply a kind of composition process that glues together primitive causal connections by attaching the effects of one primitive to the causes of another. The particular attribute values become secondary, bringing the rules and their relationships (i.e., the causality) to the forefront. This is best illustrated by the diagram shown in Fig. 8.5. Because the causal model identifies which attributes cause component behavior and which attributes are caused by component rules, it distinguishes the inputs and outputs of each component.[7]

[7]Again, note that for more complex components, determining the inputs and outputs can be problematic. For example, it is not necessarily true that the conduit that is first ‘‘activated’’ is the component's input, especially if the overall device has feedback paths.

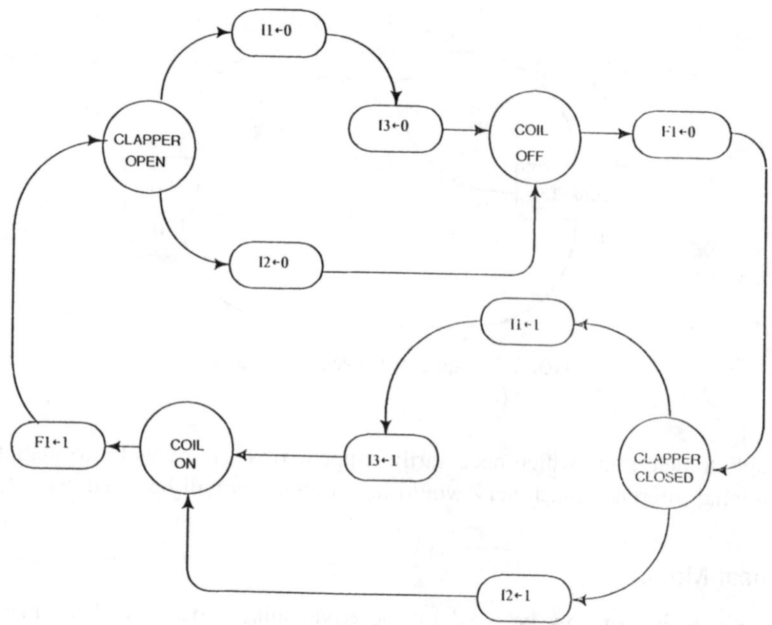

FIG.8.5. Causation in the buzzer.

Each node in the diagram represents a component model applied to some particular attribute values. Each edge in the diagram represents the results of a piece of one component's model affecting some component state or conduit attribute. Consequently, the result of the envisioning is an explicit representation of the causality inherent in the device's function.

Each edge in Fig. 8.5 corresponds to the application of only a piece of a component model. For example, the edge from COIL ON to F1 ⇐ 1 corresponds to the piece of the component model:

COIL: ON:
  F1 ⇐ 1

The essential character of envisioning is that it converts one kind of description into another, primitive structural pieces into behavioral ones. The causal model of Fig. 8.5 is much more than a simple dependency graph of effects and causes— it also identifies the structural mechanism which connects each effect to its causes. Thus Fig. 8.5 represents the connection between the buzzer's structure and its function.

The necessity of establishing, a principled connection between structure and function was one of the motivations for the choice of the model syntax introduced in the previous section. Consider another model for the buzzer, one which does not obey our syntax:

```
CLAPPER : OPEN:
              coil will become ON.
          CLOSED:
              coil will become OFF.

COIL : ON:
          clapper will become OPEN.
       OFF:
          clapper will become CLOSED.
                                                  (Model 2)
```

This model, with its clapper and coil component models, produces the same state transition behavior as that indicated in Fig. 8.5. However, it provides little useful information on how its functioning relates to the structure, let alone on how it could be derived from the structure. For example, it cannot explain the means by which the clapper affects the coil. Syntax alone, however, is insufficient to gain all the important properties we want a causal model to possess.

Most devices (unlike the buzzer) have interesting external inputs. For example, an engine typically has a throttle, which serves as an external input to the machine. Different input values can cause different behaviors, and thus different causal paths. These different causal "stories" will often show marked similarity, as the behaviors were produced by the same structure. We consider all stories produced by the different values of inputs to be all part of the causal model. This causal model usually consists of only a small set of stories because most of the input values produce duplicate causal paths with only the attribute values varying. For example, between the minimum throttle setting at which the engine runs and the maximum throttle setting at which it disintegrates, the causality of an engine does not change.

Constraints on the Formulation of Causal Models

In order for a simulation of a fixed resolution to be the most useful or "valid," thus maximizing the work realizable by the simulation, the simulation must satisfy constraints beyond those imposed by the formalism for component models. Both establishing and satisfying these constraints turns out to be a far more complex and subtle issue than it first appears. However, the cost of not satisfying them would be great because running the causal model produced by the envisioning process for any previously untested case would be unreliable. Ideally a simulation should be *consistent, corresponding,* and *robust*.

A *consistent* causal model is free of internal contradictions: No two component models may specify different values for the same attribute for any single composite state of the device. Consistency can be defined analogously for component models.[8]

The *correspondence* constraint specifies that the causal model must be faithful to the behavior of the actual device under examination. The resolution established by the class-wide assumptions defines an abstraction map from the actual physical object to the structure upon which the envisioning operates. The actual physical structure is, so to speak, operated on by nature producing some behavior. The representation of the structure is operated on by the envisioning to produce a description of the device's behavior. Another description of the device's behavior is gotten by describing the observed behavior. For a causal model to be *corresponding,* these two behaviors, one derived through an envisioning and the other derived through observing the actual system, must be the same.

Correspondence is not quite enough to establish robustness. For example, if the device experiences unusual operating conditions the causal model may no longer correspond. Unusual operating conditions can result from unexpected inputs or from unexpected failures in the components. For a causal model to be *robust* it also must be useful in unusual situations. In particular, we would like the envisioning to produce a causal model that satisfies the correspondence constraint even when the device's structure is perturbed. For example, suppose we had a machine consisting of four parts, one of which was faulted; *robustness* stipulates that by substituting the faulty component model for the correct one (i.e., the perturbation), the causal model produced for the overall device must represent the behavior of the actual faulted system. The main way to achieve the robustness of the causal model is to have the component models, themselves, be robust.[9]

Unfortunately, it is very difficult to tell whether the component models used in the envisioning are robust or not. To help solve this difficulty we introduce esthetic principles which can be used to identify particular sources of nonrobustness and which can also provide guidance in the choice and construction (i.e., learning) of component models. Our central esthetic is the no-function-in-struc-

---

[8]Actually, a rigorous definition for a component model being consistent is beyond the scope of this chapter. First, in order for the definition of consistency to have any force, we need to add a restriction that there be only one model for each component. Without this restriction, any set of rules specifying the behavior of a component could be consistent by just segregating them into different models for the same component. Second, one has to carefully decide what aspects of the "outside world" can or need to be considered. For example, if a model has an internal contradiction in an unrealizable state is it consistent? Similarly, if syntactically different attributes asserted in a state definition become dependent as a consequence of the physics of the environment (e.g., voltage and current) and through that dependency their values become contradictory, is the model, by itself, consistent?

[9]We assume that the envisioning process itself is error-free and complete (i.e., that it makes all possible deductions).

ture principle. This principle states that the rules for specifying the behavior of any constituent part of the overall device can in no way refer, even implicitly, to how the overall device functions. Thus every part of the same type must be modeled in the same way. One consequence of this principle is that component models may only reference attributes of adjoining conduits (i.e., a locality principle). For example, the component model for the battery (see Fig. 8.3) may only reference information in WIRE1 and WIRE3; it may not reference the internal state of the coil or clapper. Localness, however, does not guarantee that the no-function-in-structure principle holds. The clapper-switch model (Model 1) presented earlier violates this principle (as we see in the next section) in that it presumes itself connected in a loop with the battery.

Motivations and Consequences of the Constraints[10]

These three constraints, consistency, correspondence, and robustness, are important for nearly all applications of qualitative simulations. Consistency, for example, is crucial, because without it the causal model may not be able to predict any behavior at all for the device. Having consistent component models enables the envisioning to attribute any discovered contradictions to some assumption it made while locally propagating behaviors of components. As we discuss later, the ability to make and then later retract assumptions is the crux of envisioning.

Robustness is the most subtle constraint and is also the most difficult to satisfy. In order to appreciate its importance, consider the operator of a nuclear power-plant that has just suffered a serious casualty where he cannot physically go and safely observe its internal state. Indeed, he must use his own mental model of the reactor's functioning in order to hypothesize and test what state the system is actually in, given the available (often scanty) external evidence. If his mental, causal model is predicated on some implicit assumption that holds for the correct functioning of the reactor, but not for the particular faulted reactor, then as he "runs" his model under his current hypothesis, its behavior need not (and probably will not) correspond to the behavior of the faulted reactor. This will lead him either to reject a correct hypothesis or accept an incorrect one. If his model is sufficiently nonrobust, it can become so nonrepresentative of the actual faulted reactor that the faulted reactor becomes cognitively "impenetrable" to the operator.

In order to illustrate these constraints, consider the previous buzzer model which has been artificially perturbed through the seemingly innocuous addition of a button which acts as a switch to turn the buzzer on and off (see Fig. 8.6).

---

[10]This section is rather technical and may be skipped on initial reading.

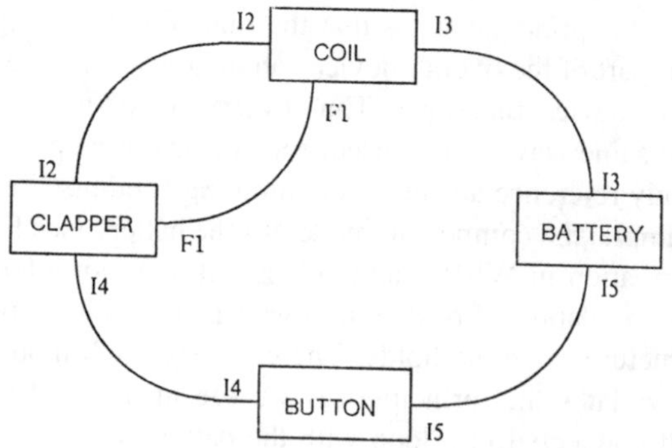

FIG. 8.6. Attribute topology of the buzzer with button.

```
SWITCH : OPEN:
            I4 ⇐ 0, I5 ⇐ 0
            IF BUTTON = PUSHED
               CAUSES: switch will become CLOSED.
         CLOSED:
            I4 ⇐ 1, I5 ⇐ 1
            IF BUTTON = RELEASED
               CAUSES: switch will become OPEN
                                                        (Model 3)
```

Although the causal model produced by the original model set (Model 1) was consistent and corresponding, this new model set (Model 1 amended with Model 3) is neither. To see this, we must use the definition parts both imperatively (as specifying what consequences follow from being in a particular state) and criterially (as a test to determine whether a component is in a particular state). Consider the case where the switch is closed. Used imperatively, the definition part of the switch model indicates that current flows. Using the definition parts of the clapper states criterially (from Model 1), the clapper cannot be in state open as that state predicts no current flow and therefore the clapper must be closed. Thus the model set predicts that if the switch is closed the clapper is always open, which is contrary to the observed facts. To avoid this difficulty, a better switch model would be:

```
SWITCH : OPEN:
            14 ⇐ 0, 15 ⇐ 0
            IF BUTTON = PUSHED
               CAUSES: switch will become CLOSED.
         CLOSED:
            14 <=> I5
            IF BUTTON = RELEASED
               CAUSES: switch will become OPEN.
                                                        (Model 4)
```

In Model 4, the rules for the closed state are now satisfactory, but problems remain with the open state. Imperatively, the definition part of the switch model says no current can flow in the wires connected to it. Using the definition parts of the clapper states criterially (from Model 1), the clapper therefore cannot be closed and must be open. Thus the model set predicts that if the switch is open, the clapper is open, which is still contrary to the observed facts. Furthermore, the coil model (from Model 1) says that if there is no current the coil must (or will) be off and thus the clapper will close. This next state is inconsistent because the clapper says the current is flowing and the switch says it is not. No modification of the switch model will resolve these violations of consistency and correspondence. The problem lies with the lack of robustness in the clapper.

A similar example can be used to illustrate the need for robustness in handling casualties or troubleshooting devices. The troubleshooter, in order to identify a faulty component, must be able to correctly hypothesize the consequences of perturbations in the component models of the device. Let us use the buzzer model as an extreme example, and suppose that the troubleshooter wanted to hypothesize the consequences of a dead battery:

$$\text{BATTERY} : I1 \Leftarrow 0, I3 \Leftarrow 0. \qquad \text{(Model 5)}$$

As with the button model above, when this model is used by the envisioning, the envisioning generates an internal contradiction implying that it cannot be used to predict any behavior for the buzzer, let alone to compare the hypothetical behavior with the observed symptoms. The nonrobust model, Model 1 amended with Model 4, presumes the correct functioning of the faulty part (the battery) in one of its neighbors (the clapper-switch). Usually, this results in making the perturbed simulation nonrepresentative of the actual facts, but sometimes, as is the case here, the perturbed simulation is simply inconsistent. Also, in actuality a dead battery is typified by a closed clapper-switch with no current flowing through it—a direct contradiction with the component model itself. The model for the clapper stated current would flow if it was closed, whereas in actual fact it should state that current would flow if there was current available to flow.

In this chapter we do not discuss the procedure by which the faulty component might be identified. The form of robustness we have defined merely insures that, for any faulty component (with a known model), envisioning can construct a corresponding causal model. A far stronger form of robustness is that this causal model be identifiable from studying the differences between the device's actual and correct behaviors. The identification process imputes unexpected behaviors to possible causes, and the causal model produced by the envisioning provides the groundwork for this because it can also be used to relate effects to causes. This is discussed further in the section on troubleshooting.

Robustness is far more likely to be a problem for a mechanistic mental model than for a numerical simulation tool (e.g., SPICE [Nagel & Pederson, 1973]). In a simulation tool the component models provided by the tool designer are apt to be "context free" as he does not know what composite devices will be constructed from his components and thus cannot embed implicit assumptions into the component models about how the composite device functions. Also, the bottom-up analysis style of a designer using a simulation tool makes it easier for him to maintain a clean separation between structure and function in his own model. However, in the cognitive science arena, we are more interested in the *synthesis* process, the kind that one is likely to go through in an attempt to construct an understanding of an already-designed artifact. Here, a person is much more likely to let his partial understanding of how the device functions impact the way he thinks about (i.e., models) the particular components.

Much of the discussion has proceeded as if a person has *a* model of a device, when in fact he usually continually improves his understanding or model of a system by changing the component models, altering the device topology, and inventing new physics for the objects in the conduits. But improvement (or learning) needs to be driven by tests or "critics"; the consistency, correspondence and robustness constraints intend to provide the basis for such criticism.

AMBIGUITIES, ASSUMPTIONS AND MECHANISMS

Origin of Ambiguities

The apparent simplicity in the movement from structure to function for the buzzer example (Fig. 8.3 to Fig. 8.5) is somewhat misleading. In this example, every step in the simulation was uniquely predicted by the preceding ones and thus the causal mechanism was trivial to construct. This is not a usual case—usually one event can cause many others and it is extremely difficult to identify which of the possibilities will actually happen. A more robust model of the buzzer has several such ambiguities. For example, there is no way we can tell from the structural description of Fig. 8.3 whether the magnetic field is necessarily strong enough to lift the clapper against the restoring force of the spring. This is a particularly easy ambiguity to resolve if we assume the purpose of the buzzer is to make a noise. In particular, if the magnetic force is insufficient to overcome the restoring force it will never be able to lift the clapper and hence never make a noise.

To illustrate the ambiguity of whether the field has sufficient strength, let us consider a slightly more accurate model for the clapper:

```
CLAPPER : OPEN:
              I1 ⇐ 0, I2 ⇐ 0
              IF F1 < spring-force CAUSES:
                 CLAPPER will become CLOSED.
          CLOSED:
              I1 ⇐ 1, I2 ⇐ 1
              IF F1 > spring-force CAUSES: CLAPPER will become
          OPEN.
```

(Model 6[11])

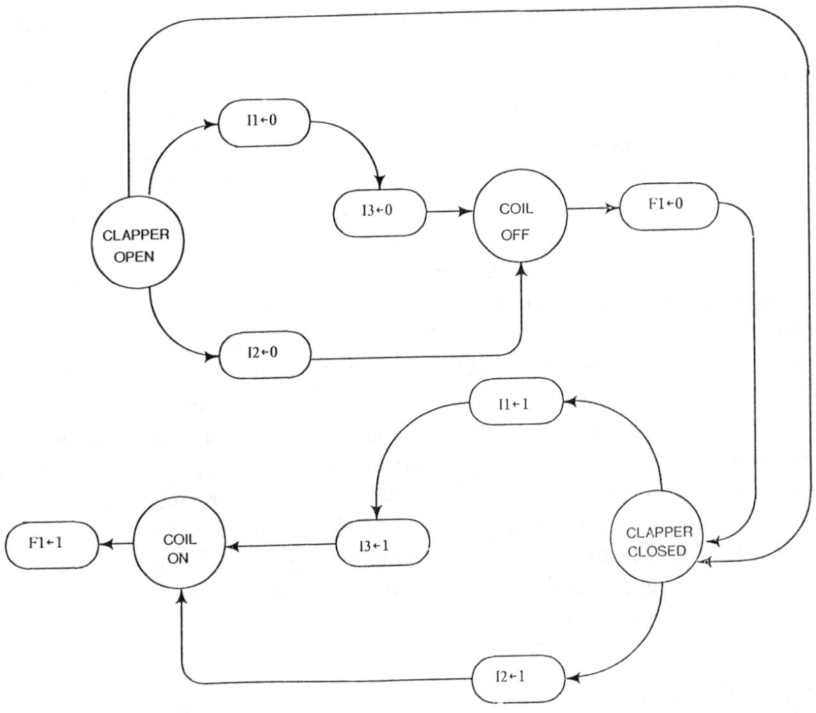

FIG. 8.7. A noiseless causal model.

With the information provided in Model 1 amended with that of Model 6 there is no way to tell whether the buzzer will make a noise (i.e., vibrate). At best we can come up with two possible functionings for the buzzer, that it will be silent, or that it will make noise. Neither alternative can be chosen, though, without violating the no-function-in-structure principle (by referencing the buzzer's overall function to see if it makes noise).

Thus the result of an envisioning can be a collection of different causal models, each with its own underlying assumptions. In the case under consideration, two causal models are produced. The first one assumes the field can overcome the spring and is illustrated by Fig. 8.5, and the second, illustrated by Fig. 8.7, assumes it cannot. The two causal models show marked similarity. Because Fig. 8.7 is so similar to Fig. 8.5, we could just collapse the two by annotating two of the edges as being dependent on an assumption. Such a simple merging is usually not possible because the causal models under different sets of assumptions will not usually be so similar to each other. In order to determine the correct functioning of the device, the correct set of assumptions must be selected.

[11]Because this model is oversimplified, we could have used purely syntactic techniques to resolve the ambiguities discussed in this section.

In general, ambiguities originate from the fact that the information available to the qualitative analysis underdetermines or partially characterizes the actual behavior of the overall device. There are three reasons for this underdetermination. The first and most obvious is that the quantities referenced by the component models are qualitative and thus fine-grained distinctions cannot be made between the attribute values or component states. This is the origin of the ambiguity illustrated between Fig. 8.5 and 8.7. Second, because the implicit time progression in the simulation is qualitative, it is not always possible to determine the actual ordering of events. And the third reason, not directly related to the qualitative nature of the models, comes from the limitations on the kinds of information captured by the models. Because envisioning is trying to identify a global flow of action by gluing together local cause-effect rules of the component models, a component model encodes only those aspects of the component's behavior that can be used in such a fashion. However, our understanding of a given component often involves knowledge that is not (or, perhaps, cannot be) encoded in such mechanistic rules. For example, in modeling the internal operation of a pump we know from the laws of physics that fluid is conserved in passing through the pump. But, because this piece of knowledge is a *constraint* and cannot be represented by any cause-effect rule, it can lead to a given component model being underdetermined.

Origin of Assumptions

In the previous buzzer example, because of the qualitative nature of the attribute values, the envisioning process cannot determine whether the spring is stronger than the magnetic field. In this impasse, it is forced to consider two hypothetical situations: one in which it *assumes* the spring is stronger than the magnetic field (Fig. 8.5) and one in which it *assumes* the spring is weaker than the field (Fig. 8.7).

Inasmuch as qualitative analysis is inherently ambiguous, any algorithm that implements it will, in general, not be able to discover a unique causal description for the device's functioning. Because envisioning presumes that there is a unique description, the consequences of these ambiguities are manifested as impasses during the envisioning process. These impasses occur when it cannot evaluate a condition in a transition part to determine whether a transition occurs or invoke an attribute equation in a definition part to determine the value of an unknown attribute. In order to proceed around impasses, the envisioning must introduce assumptions about the truth or falsity of conditions or about the values of unknown attributes.

The buzzer example illustrates an impasse that arises from being unable to determine whether a transition condition holds. In this impasse the envisioner introduces an assumption that the condition "F1 > spring force" is true, and then proceeds to analyze the new resulting state. Of course, the resulting causal model will then contain two accounts of the device's functioning: one in which the transition takes place and one in which it does not.

The second kind of impasse results when the envisioning stops because it cannot discover all of the necessary attribute values to use an attribute equation of a definition part imperatively, thus leaving some attributes unknown. This type of impasse does not occur with our buzzer model. Although this type is far more difficult to deal with, there are some heuristic strategies to circumvent such impasses. The basic one is to choose attributes and their values that will allow the envisioning to continue tracing an unbroken path of possible causal action. The choice of attribute must be one at the "boundary" between where conduit attributes are known and unknown, such that the assumed attribute values will combine with other known attributes to lead to the discovery of new values. In this way the assumption will never break the tracing of the potential causal path, because the assumption, itself, will never be the sole cause for an effect.

The difficulty with the above assumption-introduction strategy is that, even after the unknown attributes have been selected, the envisioner still needs to choose a value for it. One must appeal to some other source of knowledge. The analysis of complex devices can be decomposed into two relatively independent parts. The first concerns itself with what the attribute values are when the machine is "at rest" (i.e., at equilibrium) and the second with how disturbances from that equilibrium propagate through the device. Envisioning is the most useful for this latter type of analysis inasmuch as it provides a causal account of how the disturbance propagates through the device. Because the analysis is concerned with disturbances from equilibrium originating from some localized signal it can be fairly reliably assumed that those disturbances which have been discovered causally dominate those which have not. The strategy is, until proven otherwise, to *temporarily assume* that unknown attributes have negligible value. This is best illustrated by an example.

The flow rate of water through a constricted pipe is proportional to the difference in pressure between the ends of the pipe. The envisioner may discover that the pressure rises at one end of the pipe but may be unable to determine the change in flow through it because the pressure change at the other end is unknown. In this case, the impasse can be resolved by assuming the pressure change at the other end of the pipe is negligible. The attribute equation for the pipe can then be applied to determine the flow through the pipe. Note that the pressure change at the far end of the pipe has not yet been discovered and thus is not propagated, the impasse is circumvented by proceeding *as if* it were negligible compared to currently known values. This pressure change remains to be discovered, perhaps as a consequence of making the assumption in the first place.

Some impasses also result purely from the fact that the envisioning process itself proceeds locally. These impasses appear indistinguishable from those discussed, but unlike assumptions which arise from the inherent ambiguity of

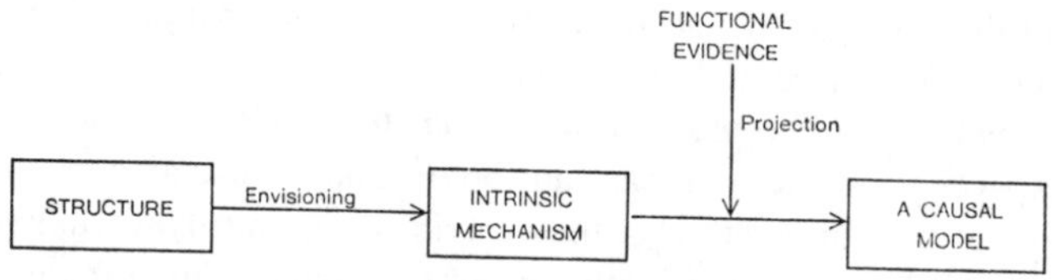

FIG. 8.8. Intrinsic mechanism.

qualitative analysis, these assumptions are often resolved by the conclusion of the analysis. Locality in the envisioner leads to both kinds of assumptions, and both can be resolved. For assumptions which originate from unevaluable transition conditions, the envisioner may discover better values for the attributes and hence directly determine whether the condition holds. It may also be discovered that the new state is inherently contradictory in which case the condition cannot hold. Assumptions of the second type can only be resolved indirectly. The assumption that some unknown attribute is negligible may lead to an immediate contradiction. In such cases, the alternate causal path which provided the contradictory value assigns a value to the unknown attribute so the impasse does not recur as a result of the contradiction.

The introduction of assumptions forces some redefinition of consistency, correspondence and robustness. But because their redefinitions will not alter the basic concepts of these constraints, we do not discuss them.

The Intrinsic Mechanism

In general, external evidence is required to resolve the ambiguities by either verifying or rejecting the various assumptions created by the envisioning process. This external information is functional (behavioral) in nature, thereby requiring an additional kind of problem-solving in order to use it to resolve the assumptions. As we have discussed in the case of the buzzer, the external evidence that is needed is that "the buzzer makes noise." Before expanding this point, we need to introduce the notion of an *intrinsic mechanism* of a device as being a description of all the potential causal models of the device that are produced by the envisioning.[12] The intrinsic mechanism represents the essential character of the device's operation. The external evidence then selects the one causal model of the intrinsic mechanism under which the machine actually operates. This selection process is called *projection* (see Fig. 8.8).

[12]Issues concerning whether a device has a unique intrinsic mechanism, whether it depends on the resolution of the analysis, or whether it simply depends on the calculus as opposed to the resolution, need not concern us here but will be discussed in a later paper.

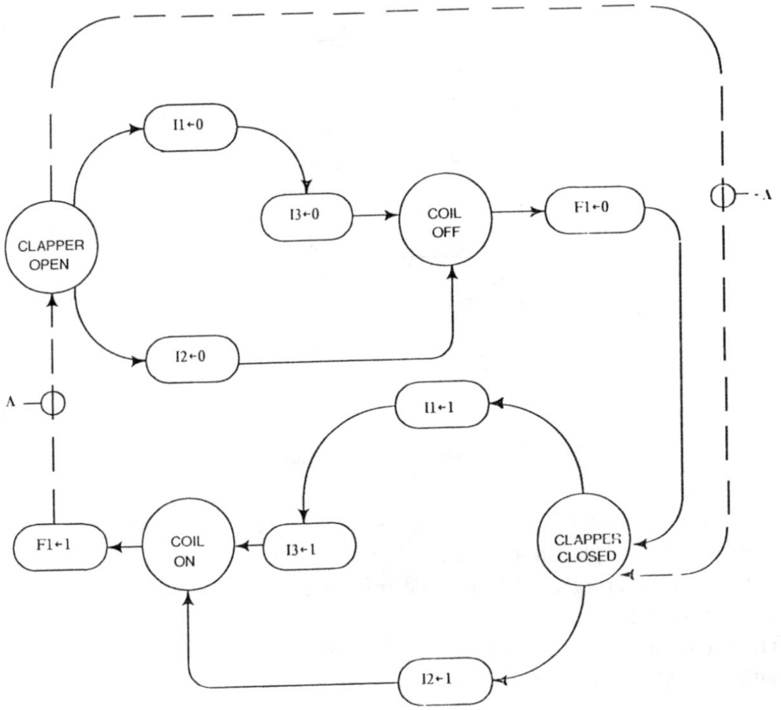

FIG. 8.9. Intrinsic mechanism for buzzer.

We represent the intrinsic mechanism as a structure that has each causal model maximally collapsed upon the others. Figure 8.9 is a simple example which diagrams the intrinsic mechanism for the buzzer consisting of the causal models of Figs. 8.5 and 8.7. The dashed lines indicate that an assumption must be introduced whose validity will determine whether this edge is in force or not. This representation is similar in some ways to Rieger and Grinberg's (1977, 1978) and encompasses all possible behaviors of the machine.

An example of a more complex intrinsic mechanism is that of a Schmitt Trigger (Fig. 8.10). (The electrical models used to analyze it are not presented here [see de Kleer, 1979].) Of importance is how an intrinsic mechanism (see Fig. 8.11) with multiple competing assumptions might be represented. The Schmitt Trigger's intrinsic mechanism contains three interdependent assumptions: to include P1, to include P2, and to include P3. Of the six apparent possibilities only four are realizable: both P1 and P2, both P1 and P3, P2 alone, and P1 alone. The intrinsic mechanism illustrated in Fig. 8.11 thus encodes four different causal models for the circuit. Any electrical engineer would know that assumptions P1 and P3 select the correct causal model, but only because he

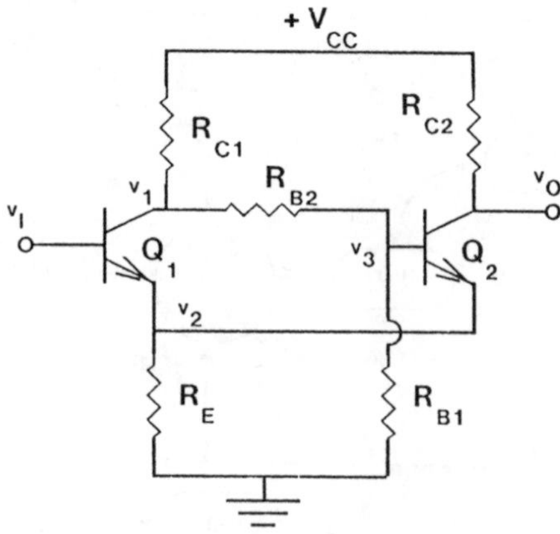

FIG. 8.10. Schematic of Schmitt Trigger.

knows what the Schmitt Trigger is supposed to do. The three other causal models are possible, but implausible in normal circuits. However, were the engineer to design a Schmitt Trigger, or to troubleshoot one, he would have to be aware of the other possibilities.

The projection of external evidence on intrinsic mechanisms can be difficult because the external evidence may be given in entirely different terms from those describing intrinsic mechanisms. The external evidence may be "it makes noise," "it oscillates," "it has a snapping action," or "it latches." The intrinsic mechanism may be more of the form "the spring causes the clapper to close" or "the rising voltage triggers the monostable." This functional evidence varies with how closely it is related to the representational primitives of the intrinsic mechanism. At one end of the scale, the functional evidence makes specific reference to branch points (e.g., whether or not the magnetic field lifts the clapper), whereas at the other end of the scale it refers to aspects of the intrinsic mechanism's operation (e.g., "it oscillates" or "it makes noise"). The closer the kind of evidence is to the branch points of the intrinsic mechanism, the easier the problem-solving will be in projecting it and thereby selecting the actual functioning of the correctly working device.

The subject of the projection problem-solving is the translation of the functional evidence into a vocabularly that is directly related to the intrinsic mechanism. This requires the invention and development of a technical vocabulary of mechanism and function. One simple projection is to have a special kind of simulator which constantly monitors the progress of the simulation and explicitly rejects any collections of assumptions which already manifest behavior inconsistent with the functional evidence. In this way projection can be done very efficiently.

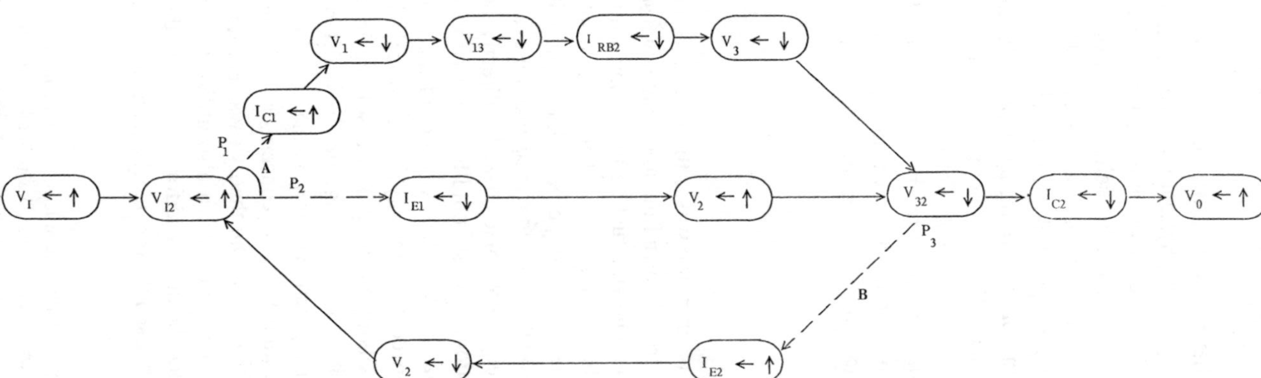

FIG. 8.11. Intrinsic mechanism for Schmitt Trigger. A voltage between two nodes is indicated by two subscrpts: V_{12} represents the voltage from node *I* to 2. The current is labeled as "*I*" with a subscript indicating the component, or in the case of transistors with a terminal label and a transistor number. Thus I_{C1} represents the current in the collector of transistor Q_1.

IMPLICATIONS OF THE THEORY

In the previous sections we have detailed a partial theory of qualitative simulation, a technique for reasoning about physical machines. Although the conceptual distinctions we have introduced have emerged primarily from building various kinds of qualitative simulations, we believe that many of these distinctions may be useful for investigating human performance.[13] In this section we will discuss some of the potential psychological implications of the theory by indicating how it could account for some of the apparent phenomena produced by people reasoning about machines. We have not performed any experiments per se, and thus most of the following accounts are speculative. However, by presenting some of these accounts we hope to show the power that a theoretical account can provide, to further clarify our own notions of mechanistic mental models for the reader, and to provide conjectures for future investigation and experiment.

Troubleshooting

The task of troubleshooting is, in many ways, the inverse of envisioning. The troubleshooter needs to move from known function to unknown structure, whereas the envisioning moves from known structure to unknown function. If a fault has in some way perturbed the structure of the device, the troubleshooter, even though he may have complete access to the behavior of the faulted device, no longer has total information about its structure (because, for example, a fault that opened a diode's junction might not, of course, be directly observable). The troubleshooter asks the question, ''What could have caused this (symptomatic) overall behavior?'' rather than, ''What behavior do all these local component behaviors produce when connected in this way?'' This troubleshooting process, like that of envisioning, entails extensive problem solving in order to resolve ambiguities. For the troubleshooter, the ambiguities lie in determining which of the many possible causes for a given symptom is the actual one.

A great deal of troubleshooting expertise concerns associating patterns, often generalized, of symptoms with causes. Our theory says very little about this. On the other hand, the troubleshooter must often also utilize his understanding of device functioning to determine the fault, and for this task our theory has more to say. The distinction between the intrinsic mechanism and the correct causal

---

[13]Indeed, many of the simulations we built were at least guided by intuitions about how we, the authors, reasoned about complex systems. Nevertheless, the main motivation for our doing this work was to better understand the subtleties of qualitative simulations; it was not to build a theory grounded on psychological data.

model suggests a possible solution to the long-standing issue of why people find some faults so much harder to troubleshoot than others. The difficulty of a fault is determined by how much effort needs to be expended to locate it. For many faults this difficulty is directly related to how much the perturbation in structure (i.e., the fault) perturbs the function. Before this statement can have any predictive value, however, there needs to be a way to measure how much the fault perturbs function, i.e., a metric on the causal model (function) space.[14] In general this is difficult to do, but the intrinsic mechanism view provides at least a language for discussing the degree of perturbation. In particular, three cases can be discerned for characterizing how much a fault has perturbed the correct functioning of the device.

The first and simplest case is where the function of the perturbed device is basically unchanged, meaning that the "perturbed" causal model is identical to the one of the correctly working device. Two examples containing such an occurrence would be an amplifier that wasn't producing its expected output power rating and an engine with a partially clogged fuel line whose rate of revolution was lower than expected. In all cases where the functioning remains unchanged, the original causal model can be consulted to identify which components could cause the changed outputs. Accordingly, finding this kind of fault should be relatively straightforward.

In the second case, the function of the perturbed device violates the correct causal model, but is still contained in the intrinsic mechanism. In this situation the troubleshooter can apply a two-phase strategy: first do a differential diagnosis on the intrinsic mechanism, and second, consult the resulting perturbed causal model to identify which components could cause the changed outputs as in the previous case. An example of this might occur in a high-gain amplifier. High-gain amplifiers are susceptible to undesirable positive-feedback, and designers choose particular component values to avoid it. Positive feedback, although it is part of the *intrinsic* mechanism, is not a part of the intended causal model. Thus, if the device exhibits the symptom of positive feedback, this two-phase strategy, being used as a heuristic, will localize the fault.

The last case is conjectured to be the most difficult. Here, the fault so perturbs the function that the function is not even part of the intrinsic mechanism. In this case, unless the symptom is of some known type, the troubleshooter faces a prohibitively explosive combinatorial number of searches, hypothesizing each fault and envisioning its consequences. Even worse, the envisioning process cannot utilize external evidence such as teleology and design because the faulted device will not necessarily manifest the intended teleology.

[14]If the fault produces recognizable symptoms, the fault is often easy to locate independent of what it does to the function. For example, the causes for catastrophic faults where smoke or fire comes out of the machine is often easily identifiable structurally.

Three Kinds of Learning

We can distinguish three forms of learning in which one might engage while acquiring an understanding of a new machine. The first kind of learning involves establishing a connection between the structure of the device and its function. The second involves making the structure-function connection more robust by making implicit assumptions explicit. And, the third type of learning is the "caching," or the storing, of the results of the projection problem-solving on the intrinsic mechanism.

A learner trying to acquire a deep understanding of a particular device will be likely to employ all three types of learning. Early in the learning process he is either given or infers some collection of component models, and from these primitives he synthesizes, via the envisioning process, a connection between the structure and function of the device. Synthesizing this connection is also known as "constructing a mechanistic mental model of the device."[15] Being preliminary, his mental model invariably includes many implicit assumptions, which may or may not be correct. As the learning progresses, he identifies and makes explicit these assumptions. His progress is motivated by discovering violations to the consistency, correspondence and robustness constraints. He might notice the latter of the three by encountering situations where his mental model fails to explain the behavior of the system (as when the system is experiencing a given fault or casualty), or by examining the consequences of hypothetical modifications to his model and thus finding that it becomes self-contradictory. Every time such violations happen the learner has the chance to identify an underlying or implicit assumption in one of his component models. Thus the impetus for this second type of learning is to increase the robustness of his mental model by making its *implicit* assumptions *explicit*. But, as we saw in the case of the buzzer, this evolution invariably creates new ambiguities for the envisioning process which then must get resolved by the *explicit* use of external functional evidence, which entails a third kind of learning.

---

[15]This view of a mental model as establishing a principled connection between the structure of the device and its causal model helps us better understand the subtleties of using a simulator in computer-based training and educational systems. In particular, what has often been ignored in the design of training simulators is that a student using a simulator, even one that animates the state changes that a device goes through, must still construct his own causal model for these state transitions from his underlying component models. Thus he must do several tasks simultaneously: infer or refine the component models, if he doesn't already have satisfactory ones; select the appropriate parts of each; and then connect these parts so as to capture the causality of the system. In other words, he must, metaphorically speaking, parse the surface structure events as portrayed by the training simulator into a deep structure causal model of the device. Without knowing the ingredients of causal model and without knowing, at least, a hypothetical process for constructing it, the designer will have difficulty determining how to animate the simulator (or augment it with a "coach") so to facilitate and disambiguate the student's understanding of causal *process*. See the STEAMER and SOPHIE projects for examples of the use of training simulators (Williams, Hollan, & Stevens, 1981) and (Brown, Burton, & de Kleer, 1982).

As the primitives or component models of a device get stripped of their implicit assumptions about the functioning of the overall device, the problem-solving work performed by projection increases. The third form of learning concerns a technique for preserving this "work" so that it can be called upon only when needed and otherwide remains transparent. In essence, one can cache the results of projection (namely problem-solving) by recording what aspects of the component models were actually used in the device's correct causal model. From this knowledge he can synthesize new idiosyncratic component models which make explicit just those aspects, thereby eliminating the genesis of any ambiguities. Using only these idiosyncratic primitives, he can then "re-envision" the machine extremely efficiently. But what makes these models different from the nonrobust versions with which the learner started out? The difference is that now these idiosyncratic models can be linked with their embedded assumptions, which act as caveats, whereas the nonrobust models did not articulate their assumptions. If these caveats are violated, then the learner invokes the original models. For a somewhat artificial example, let us revisit the buzzer. Were we to start the envisioning process on this device using the more robust, second set of component models, we would discover two possible causal models, one with the buzzer oscillating and the other with the clapper always closed. By using the external evidence that the buzzer always makes a noise (when properly working), we would know which of these two models was in force. We could then safely use a highly simplified model of the clapper switch (as in Model 1) and efficiently re-envision the buzzer. In general, a particular device uses only a small subset of a component's rules when the overall device is functioning correctly, and the learner can identify this small subset (once he has identified the correct causal mechanism) and mold it into a simpler, but idiosyncratic, component model along with the appropriate functional caveats.[16]

One of the consequences of these three kinds of learning is that the phenomenological accounts of expert's and novice's behavior are not likely to *appear* very different for any one task. The novice unwittingly embeds assumptions about how the device is intended to function in his component models. He holds these assumptions implicitly, meaning that he cannot articulate them. The expert's explanations of how the device works uses models much like the novice's in that they contain implicit assumptions; the difference, of course, is that the expert can recover the assumptions, as well as the more robust component models when needed. This ability to recover these assumptions stems, in part, from having explicitly reasoned through and resolved the ambiguities.

---

[16]A variant of this form of learning involves augmenting the technical functional vocabulary so as to facilitate the projection actually reasoned through for the case at hand. This technical vocabulary is useful for any device which instantiates this mechanism, not just the particular device under study. For a related discussion, see diSessa (this volume) on the growth of phenomenological primitives.

Explanations

The above discussion concerning this third kind of learning suggests that non-robust component models can be used in another important role, that of explanation. In particular, it is important to realize that the explainer often purposely violates the no-function-in-structure principle. In explaining how a device works, one wants to construct a *sequence* of explanations, commencing with one built around component models that have the not-easily-understood aspects of the device's functioning implicitly embedded in them. That is, it is often pedagogically expedient to let an "explanation" presuppose part of what it is trying to explain. By using highly simplified primitives (component models), the correct causal model or running process can be more easily communicated. Furthermore, from the learner's perspective, the simply constructed, but correct causal model can serve as a cognitive framework for organizing forthcoming refinements derived from models with fewer implicit assumptions (and thus fewer violations to the no-function-in-structure principle).

Thus, an "ideal" explanatory sequence would start with a set of component models that enabled the envisioning process to produce an intrinsic mechanism identical to that of the desired causal model (meaning the qualitative simulation would encounter no ambiguities). Further explanations would then refine these component models, so that none of them contained implicit assumptions. The resulting sequence of "explanations" would eventually lead the learner to converge on an intrinsic mechanism built around robust component models, where each new element of the sequence articulated an implicit assumption, produced and resolved a new ambiguity, and grew a new link in a path (or set of links) in the intrinsic mechanism representation. Note that all such refinements necessarily would produce only additions to the initial causal model; no radical reformulation of its organization would ever be necessary, which is why choosing models that produce the correct causal model can serve as such a powerful backbone for an explanation sequence. Of course, depending on the device, the correct causal model might be too complex to easily grasp. This suggests changing the resolution of the models and using hierarchical or embedded component models, a topic to be discussed in the multiple models section.

Impediments to Learning

A learner's impediment to his own robust understanding is his tacit application of external evidence to the choice of component models or to the envisioning process itself. By knowing that the buzzer actually makes noise, a learner may have started with a component model for the clapper in which the magnetic field was always strong enough to lift the clapper. The resulting mental model would be useless for predicting the cause of a faulty behavior (stemming, in reality,

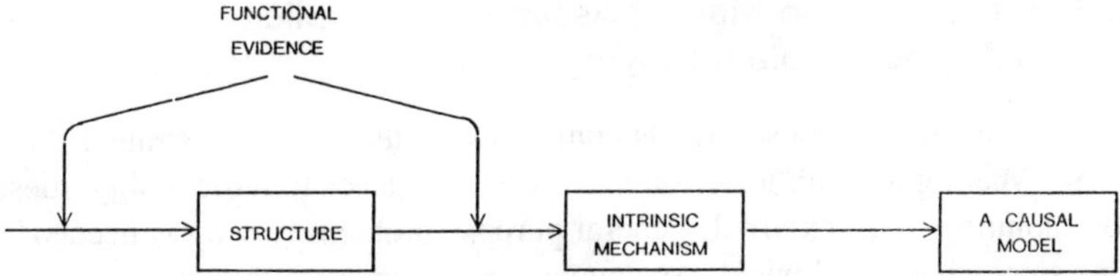

FIG. 8.12. Nonrobust understanding.

from a weak battery), because it would predict that the clapper would rise regardless of how weak the battery was.

Figure 8.12 represents some of the ways external evidence can be implicitly (and undesirably) projected onto the choice of structure and the envisioning process. For any given device, the learner implicitly projects functional evidence onto the structure, thereby producing hidden assumptions in the component models. For robustness, the learner should project the evidence explicitly onto the intrinsic mechanism, and thereby resolve the explicit assumptions. The goal of the learning process is acquiring a more robust understanding, as illustrated in Fig. 8.8.

The Limits of Learning

The learning process is open-ended: A learner can never be sure that he has identified every implicit assumption. A practice in physics is to identify and group the implicit assumptions for some large class of machines and then presume them for every device in the class. These class-wide assumptions provide an elegant way of being reasonably sure that, except for a certain known set of assumptions, the no-function-in-structure principle has not been violated.

Although there is no definitive test of whether important implicit assumptions remain unidentified, one thing is certain about a set of component models for which all implicit assumptions have been eliminated: Every possible behavior of a real machine with the same structure must be consistent with one of the ambiguities produced by the envisioning using that model set. For example, the earlier buzzer analysis contained an ambiguity about whether the clapper would rise. It is possible to design two different buzzers with the same structure as shown in Fig. 8.3 one of which is silent and one of which buzzes. It would be very desirable that the converse hold; that is, every possible ambiguity predicted by the envisioning be manifested by some actual machine with the same structure. The extent to which this latter condition holds determines how informative the intrinsic mechanism is, especially for the purposes of how it is used in troubleshooting.

The Conflict Between Making Assumptions Explicit and Simplifying Problem Solving

The desire for more robust models conflicts with the desire for simpler problem solving. Making the implicit assumptions explicit leads to more ambiguities, for whose solution more external, general purpose problem solving is needed. This seems somewhat paradoxical: As one gets more exposure to devices, and hence has component models with fewer hidden assumptions, understanding the next new device becomes harder, rather than easier. That is, the more experience one has understanding devices, the harder it is to construct an understanding of another device which is built out of the same components. A mitigating factor is that, as the learner's familiarity with the domain and machine increases, he will develop a more powerful technical vocabulary describing functional notions, which in turn will make his projection problem-solving simpler. Indeed, electrical engineers have an extensive vocabulary, one sufficiently powerful that often just by knowing that a device satisfies one functional predicate (e.g., the Schmitt Trigger involves hysteresis), the engineer can disambiguate all potential interpretations of how it works.

Multiple Models

In reasoning about a particular physical device, a human appears to use multiple models for the same constituent component. Williams, Hollan and Stevens (this volume) present protocols of a subject using multiple models for a heat exchanger. The phenomenology of using multiple models can arise from diverse sources and often what appears as multiple models may be instead the result of a single envisioning model. Multiple models is a very amorphous subject and one to which we cannot do justice in this brief discussion. We hope that this discussion raises some interesting distinctions for further progress in this area. An important presupposition we make in this section is that the subject's model is, to some extent, derived from studying the device and not solely from being told about the device's operation.

The task of discovering which component models the subject is using is a difficult one. It requires working backwards from the subject's explanations, his "simulations in the mind's eye." Recall, however, that running processes is relatively simple, as the causal models upon which they are based encode most of the necessary problem-solving work. This means that the facets of the component models actually reported or "seen" in the running are likely to be only a small fragment of the model which the envisioning used to construct the causal model originally. This means that the subject might manifest having two different models for a component. Although phenomenologically these two models might be different, they are just different facets of the same more complete (underlying) model. A strategy is needed to uncover when the phenomenological accounts stem from a single model or multiple models.

One potential strategy for probing the underlying models is to query the subject about the ambiguities produced when the models abstracted from his running process (by the experimenter) are used in envisioning. The aim of this strategy is to force the learner to articulate the ambiguities and problem-solving episodes that were involved in his constructing the running, but which were not evident in the running process, itself. Another strategy is to ask the subject to analyze different devices built from the same primitive components.

The difference in the way models are manifested in the envisioning and in the running can make it appear as if there are multiple models when, in fact, one is just a derivative of the other. It is important to note that the simpler model might actually contradict the model from which it is derived, because the simpler model may not incorporate boundary conditions automatically presumed in the running. However, this simpler model will not contradict its "parent" model if it incorporates the assumptions underlying the correct causal model.

The more interesting cases occur when multiple models are used in envisioning (as opposed to when they appear to be used in the running). As we saw in the earlier section on learning, the learner's component models evolve as he better understands the given device. Thus, there is the possibility that the subject learned during the envisioning process, and consequently revised one of his component models. A subject's protocol might then reveal two models: the model before his learning episode and the new model constructed as its result. The final running need not refer to the earlier model, but the protocol might indicate some reasoning based on the earlier one. The learning episode that occurred, separating the two models, was probably precipitated by violations of the consistency or correspondence constraints (e.g., a disagreement with some known aspect of the device's global behavior).

A component model is simply a description of the input-output behavior of the particular component. The model's rules make no reference to *how* the component achieves this input-output behavior. For example, the model of the clapper does not explain the mechanism by which the field moves the clapper. However, one can, recursively, view a component as a composite device. Each component in turn consists of internal subcomponents and subconduits. These subconstituents also have models, which we call the *embedded* models of the original component. The input-output behavior of a component is explained by these embedded models. In the example of the clapper, the embedded models may describe the flow of information in magnetic fields and the effects of magnetic forces on materials. Were a more detailed analysis required during the envisioning process, it might be necessary to reference such embedded models. The situation is analogous for conduits: a conduit may be modeled by its own device topology which explains how the conduit transmits information.

Embedding leads to different kinds of multiple models. The simplest is the original model and its expansion through the inclusion of its embedded submodels. Usually, however, only one of the embedded submodels is needed to resolve a particular difficulty in the envisioning. Thus, there may exist multiple models of the component, each expanded through an embedded model that explains the component's behavior for a given situation. These differing models may manifest themselves for different states of the same component or for different occurrences of the same component type in the device. These different models often appear to contradict each other, as different expansions of the same model may predict different behaviors. But this contradiction is in appearance only, because each expansion is made under some specific assumption and it is those *assumptions* that are contradictory, not the models.

What may at first appear to be multiple models may be the result of different kinds of inferences on the same consistent component model. However, people certainly use multiple models in problem solving in ways not accounted for earlier. For example, if the multiple models do not contradict each other predicting the same results, or noninterfering results (e.g., results on different conduits), then they may be considered as one single consistent model for the purposes of our theory. However, differences in the ''style'' (e.g., constraint vs. mechanistic) of component models may motivate considering two consistent models as distinct (see Stevens & Collins, 1980). The consistency constraint explicitly rules out multiple contradictory models, even though the latter can be, of course, extremely useful in learning new devices and components, because they form a dialectic which the learner can use to form new models. Often multiple contradictory models arise through consideration of different embedded models. Their boundary conditions, however, can be overgeneralized so that the different expanded models actually do contradict each other. Unfortunately, our theory has no mechanism to handle or to profit from this situation; nor does it say anything about multiple device topologies.

Multiple component models, of course, lead to multiple device models (causal models). But these causal models are multiple only because one of the device's constituent components has multiple models. The multiple causal models do, however, identify the consequences of the different component models and therefore can play a important role in a dialectic process by revealing some of the entailments of the different choices for component models.

Methodological Considerations

The processes discussed in this chapter are not meant to be a complete or accurate account of how people acquire an understanding about physical mechanisms. Rather, the primary purpose of this research is to identify some of the underlying knowledge states and interpretive processes for those states that a constructive theory of mechanistic models must eventually account for. In addition, the resulting technical distinctions and corresponding vocabulary help extend an ontology that the empirical psychologist can use for perceiving and describing subtleties in a subject's behavior.

There is much evidence that suggests that the major mode humans use to "understand" a complex device involves recognizing structural patterns in the device whose functionality is already understood. Although it may have been relatively simple for us to build an "understander" based on pattern recognition of structural schemata, it would have deflected us from our goal of understanding how a subject can construct a mechanistic mental model as opposed to understanding how he recognizes the instantiation of one. Although recognition rules or structural schemata may speed the discovery process, their origin must be accounted for and their limitations understood.[17]

In order to construct a learning theory having generality or validity, we need to follow some methodological constraints (or principles). If we need to add a new rule every time we encounter a machine we can't recognize, our learning theory would be of little use. We must impose some a priori constraints on the nature of our rules. For example, a preferable set of rules would be one that was guaranteed to recognize all members of a specific class without needing to add any more rules. Another preferable set would be one which only needed rules added under a very specific set of conditions and then, only need a limited number. We choose to employ the meta-theoretic constraint of using no recognition rules, and, instead, demand that the theory be able to construct its own recognition schemata. Of course, the necessity for some external evidence (perhaps provided by the structural recognition rules) is inevitable, but by taking this approach we develop a deeper understanding of the capabilities of qualitative simulation and of the kinds of information external evidence must provide.

ACKNOWLEDGMENTS

We would like to thank Allan Collins and Bob Lindsay for their tremendous help with this paper. Various discussions with Mike Williams and Kurt VanLehn clarified many of the ideas. We also wish to thank Jackie Keane for drawing the figures. Rachel Rutherford and Eric Larson helped edit early drafts.

[17]In an earlier paper (Brown, Collins, & Harris, 1978) we explored the notion of augmenting device-recognition schemata with explicit information about the consequences of generic faults in the component models or plan fragments. The work reported on in this paper, grew, in part, out of our realization of the inherent brittleness of understanding devices and faults with such recognition schemes, although for a fixed class of devices that recognition scheme has its merits.

REFERENCES

Brown, J. S., Collins, A., & Harris, G. Artificial intelligence and learning strategies. In H. O'Neil (Ed.), *Learning strategies,* N.Y.: Academic Press, 1978.

Brown, J. S., Burton, R. R., & de Kleer, J. Pedagogical, natural language and knowledge engineering techniques in SOPHIE I, II, and III. In S. Derek & J. S. Brown (Eds.), *Intelligent tutoring systems,* N.Y.: Academic Press, 1982.

de Kleer, J. *Causal and teleological reasoning in circuit recognition.* Artificial Intelligence Laboratory, Technical Report-529, Cambridge, Mass.: M.I.T., 1979.

de Kleer, J., & Brown, J. S. Mental models of physical mechanisms and their acquisition. In J. R. Anderson (Ed.), *Cognitive skills and their acquisition,* Hillsdale, N.J.: Lawrence Erlbaum Associates, 1981.

Nagel, L. W., & Pederson, D. O. Simulation program with integrated circuit emphasis. *Proc. of the 16th Midwest Symposium Circuit Theory,* Waterloo, Canada, April 1973.

Rieger, C., & Grinberg, M. The declarative representation and procedural simulation of causality in physical mechanisms. *Proc. of the Fifth International Joint Conference on Artificial Intelligence,* 1977, 250–255.

Rieger, C., & Grinberg, M. A system for cause-effect representation and simulation in computer aided design. *Proc. of the IFIP Working Conference on Artificial Intelligence and Pattern Recognition in Computer-Aided Design,* North Holland, 1978.

Stevens, A. L., & Collins, A. Multiple conceptual models of a complex system. In R. Snow, P. Federico, & W. Montague (Eds.), *Aptitude, learning and instruction, Vol. 2,* Hillsdale, N.J.: Lawrence Erlbaum Associates, 1980.

Williams, M., Hollan, J., & Stevens, A. An overview of STEAMER: An advanced computer assisted instructional system for propulsion engineering. *Behavior Research Methods and Instrumentation,* 1981, *13*(2), 85–90.

9 Understanding Micronesian Navigation

Edwin Hutchins
Navy Personnel Research and Development Center

For more than a thousand years long distance noninstrumental navigation has been practiced over large areas of Polynesia, Micronesia, and perhaps in parts of Melanesia. In Polynesia, the traditional techniques atrophied and were ultimately lost in the wake of contact with colonial powers. Only the Micronesians have maintained their traditional skills and in the past decade they have been the well-spring of navigation knowledge for a renaissance of traditional voyaging throughout the Pacific basin(Finney, 1979; Lewis, 1976, 1978).

Without recourse to mechanical or electrical or even magnetic [1] devices the navigators of the Central Caroline Islands of Micronesia routinely embark on oceanic voyages that take them several days out of the sight of land. Their technique seems at first glance to be inadequate for the job demanded , yet it consistently passes what Lewis (1972) has called "the stern test of landfall." Of the thousands of voyages made in the memory of living navigators only a few have ended with the loss of a canoe. Western researchers travelling with these people have found that at any time during the voyage the navigators can accurately indicate the bearings of the port of departure, the goal island, and other islands off to the side of the course steered even though all of these may be over

[1]The utility of a magnetic compass is not lost on the navigators of the Caroline Islands. Most canoes now carry magnetic compasses, but they are used only for secondary orientation purposes when the stars are not visible. Even when they are used, readings are not taken in degrees. The navigator simply identifies a point on the compass rose with the star course he wants to follow and uses the compass as a reference when the stars are not available. Some of the older navigators complain that the use of the compass by younger navigators is robbing them of the skills of maintaining orientation by reference to the direction of the swells (cf. Gladwin, 1970 and Lewis, 1972).

the horizon out of the sight of the navigator. These navigators are also able to tack upwind to an unseen target keeping mental track of its changing bearing, something that is simply impossible for a Western navigator without instruments.

The central issue of this chapter is how these Micronesian navigators accomplish these things. I offer a description of how their conception of the voyage permits them to do things that are impossible for a Western navigator, stripped of his instruments. But the description of how their mental models structure their performance of this difficult task is only part of the story of cognitive structure and task performance in this domain. An equally interesting cognitive task, which is logically prior to our description of the Micronesian mental models is the researcher's task of coming to understand what the Micronesian navigator is doing. There is a real methodological bind here due to the fact that we as researchers use our culture's notion of motion both to navigate ourselves and to understand how others navigate. The enterprise is clearly fraught with opportunities to misinterpret observations and bias descriptions.

In order to weave the methodological and substantive strands together in a coherent whole, the chapter is composed of four sections: The opening section presents the basic "facts" of Micronesian navigation as they appear in the literature. The second section describes some attempts to infer the nature of the navigators' reasoning while doing the task. This section also points to a number of apparent anomalies in the previous accounts which result from the imposition of aspects of our own system of navigation onto the Micronesian case. The third section presents an account of the mental model of a voyage employed by Micronesian navigators that resolves the apparent anomalies, agrees with the ethnographic record, and is capable of doing the observed task. In the final section I discuss some of the methodological and substantive implications of the preceding sections.

CAROLINE ISLAND NAVIGATION

In the neighborhood of the Caroline Islands, less than two tenths of one percent of the surface of the Earth is land. It is a vast expanse of water dotted with about two dozen atolls and low islands. Experienced navigators in these waters routinely sail their outrigger canoes as many as 150 miles between islands.[2] The knowledge required to make these voyages is not held by all, but is the domain of a small number of experts.[3]

The world of the navigator, however, contains more than a set of tiny islands on an undifferentiated expanse of ocean. Deep below, the presence of submerged reefs changes the apparent color of the water. The surface of the sea undulates

---

[2]Longer voyages of up to 450 miles were once made on a regular basis, and are becoming more frequent now as part of a revival of navigator's skills.

[3]See Gladwin (1970) for a discussion of the sociology of navigational knowledge.

with swells born in distant weather systems, and the interaction of the swells with islands produces distinctive swell patterns in the vicinity of land. Above the sea surface are the winds and weather patterns that govern the fate of sailors. Sea birds abound, especially in the vicinity of land. Finally, at night, there are the stars. Here in the central Pacific, away from pollution and light sources on the ground which make the atmosphere opaque, the stars shine brightly in incredible numbers. All of these elements in the navigator's world are sources of information. The whole system of knowledge used by a master navigator is well beyond the scope of this chapter. Here, we treat only a portion of the navigators' use of celestial cues.

The most complete description of this system comes from the work of Thomas Gladwin who worked with the navigators of Puluwat atoll (see Fig. 9.1). Gladwin divides the pragmatics of Puluwat navigation into 3 parts (1970:147). First one must set out in a direction such that, knowing the conditions to be expected en route, one will arrive in the vicinity of the island of destination. Second, while on the way to this island the canoe must be held steady on its course and a running estimate maintained of its position. Finally, when the craft is near its goal there should be available techniques for locating the destination island and heading toward it.

One of the most widespread notions employed in Pacific noninstrumental navigation is the concept of "star path." From the point of view of the earth, the positions of the stars relative to each other are fixed. As the earth rotates about its axis the stars appear to move across the sky from east to west. As the earth moves through its orbit about the sun, the stars that can be seen at night (that is, from the side of the earth away from the sun) change. But from any fixed location on the earth, any given star always rises from the same point on the eastern horizon and always sets into the same point in the western horizon regardless of season[4]. A star path, also known as a linear constellation (Aveni, 1981), is a set of stars which all "follow the same path" (Gladwin, 1970). That is, they all rise in succession from the same point in the eastern horizon, describe the same arc across the sky, and set into the same point in the western horizon. Star paths are typically composed of from six to ten stars fairly evenly spaced across the heavens (Lewis, 1972). Thus, when one star in the linear constellation has risen too far above the horizon to serve as an indication of direction, another will soon take its place. In this way, each star path describes two directions on the horizon, one in the east and one in the west, which are visible regardless of season or time of night as long as the skies are clear.

It is known that star paths have long been used to define the courses between islands in many parts of Oceania (Lewis, 1972). The navigators of the Caroline Islands have combined 14 named star paths with the position of Polaris to form a

---

[4]Movement to the north or south does change the azimuth of the rising and setting positions of any star. Within the range of the Caroline Island navigator, however, the effects of such movements are small; on the order of three degrees or less.

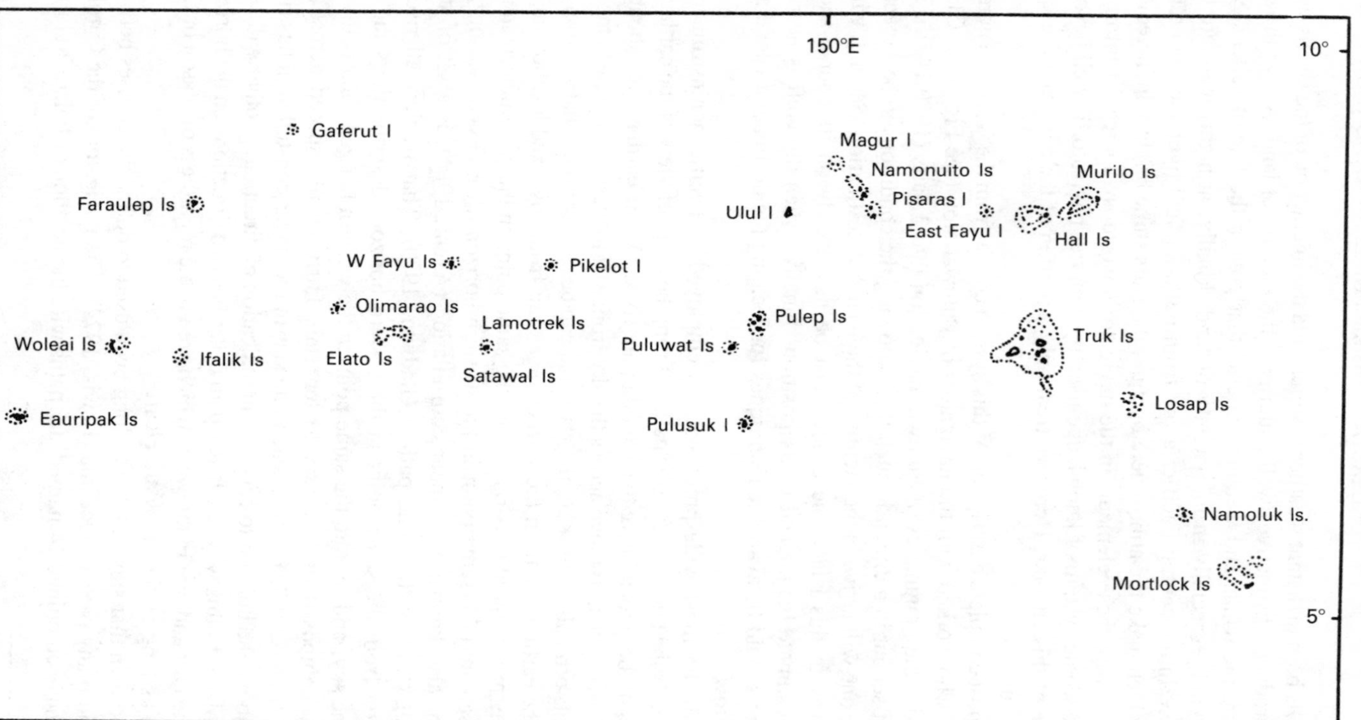

FIG. 9.1. Caroline Islands.

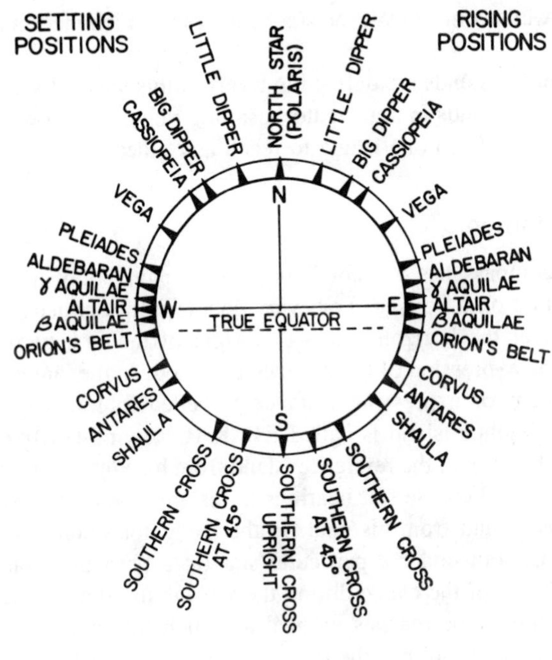

FIG. 9.2. Schematic representation of Caroline Island star compass (after Goodenough, 1953).

sidereal compass that defines 32 directions around the circle of the horizon. Figure 9.2 shows a schematic representation of the Caroline Island sidereal compass. As can be seen, most of the recognized star bearings are named for major stars whose paths intersect the horizon at those points. Those which are not so named are the true north bearing which is named for Polaris (the North Star) which from the Caroline Islands is always about eight degrees above the northern horizon and three bearings in the south which are defined by orientations of the Southern Cross above the horizon.

The inclusion of other stars that travel the same path guarantees that as long as the weather is clear the complete compass is available to the navigator no matter what time of year he is sailing. In fact, a practiced navigator can construct the whole compass mentally from a glimpse of only one or two stars near the horizon. This ability is crucial to the navigator's performance because the star bearings which concern him during a voyage may not be those which he can readily see. The star compass is an abstraction which can be oriented as a whole by determining the orientation of any part. During the day, the orientation of the star compass can be maintained by observing the star bearings from which the major ocean swells come and/or the star bearings at which the sun and moon rise and set.

Courses among islands are defined in terms of this abstract sidereal compass. For every pair of islands in a navigator's sailing range, he knows the star under which he must sail from one island to reach any other.

Distance Judgments

The sidereal compass has a second function in navigation: the expression of distance travelled on a voyage. For every course from one island to another, a third island (over the horizon and out of sight of the first two) is taken as a reference for the expression of the distance travelled. In the language of Puluwat atoll, this system of expressing distance travelled in terms of the changing bearing of a reference island is called ETAK (Gladwin, 1970). The navigator knows the star bearing of the reference island from his voyage origin. Because he knows all interisland course star bearings in his area, he also knows the bearing of the reference island from his goal. In the navigator's conception, this reference island starts out under a particular star (at a particular star bearing) and moves back abeam of the canoe during the voyage through a succession of star bearings until the canoe reaches its goal at which time the reference island is under the point which defines the course from the goal island to the reference island. The changing star bearing of the reference island during the voyage is shown in Fig. 9.3. The movement of the reference island under the sucession of star bearings divides the voyage conceptually into a set of segments called the ETAKs of the voyage. Each voyage has a known number of ETAK segments defined by the passage of the reference island under the star bearings.

A fundamental conception in Caroline Island navigation is that when underway on course between islands, the canoe is stationary and the islands move by the canoe. This is, of course, unlike our notion of what happens in a voyage. A passage from Gladwin (1970) captures the scene:

> Picture yourself on a Puluwat canoe at night. The weather is clear, the stars are out, but no land is in sight. The canoe is a familiar little world. Men sit about, talk, perhaps move around a little within their microcosm. On either side of the canoe, water streams past, a line of turbulence and bubbles merging into a wake and disappearing into the darkness. Overhead there are stars, immovable, immutable. They swing in their paths across and out of the sky but invariably come up again in the same places. You may travel for days on the canoe, but the stars will not go away or change their positions aside from their nightly trajectories from horizon to horizon. Hours go by, miles of water have flowed past. Yet the canoe is still underneath and the stars are still above. Back along the wake however, the island you left falls farther and farther behind, while the one toward which you are heading is hopefully drawing closer. You can see neither of them, but you know this is happening. You know too that there are islands on either side of you, some

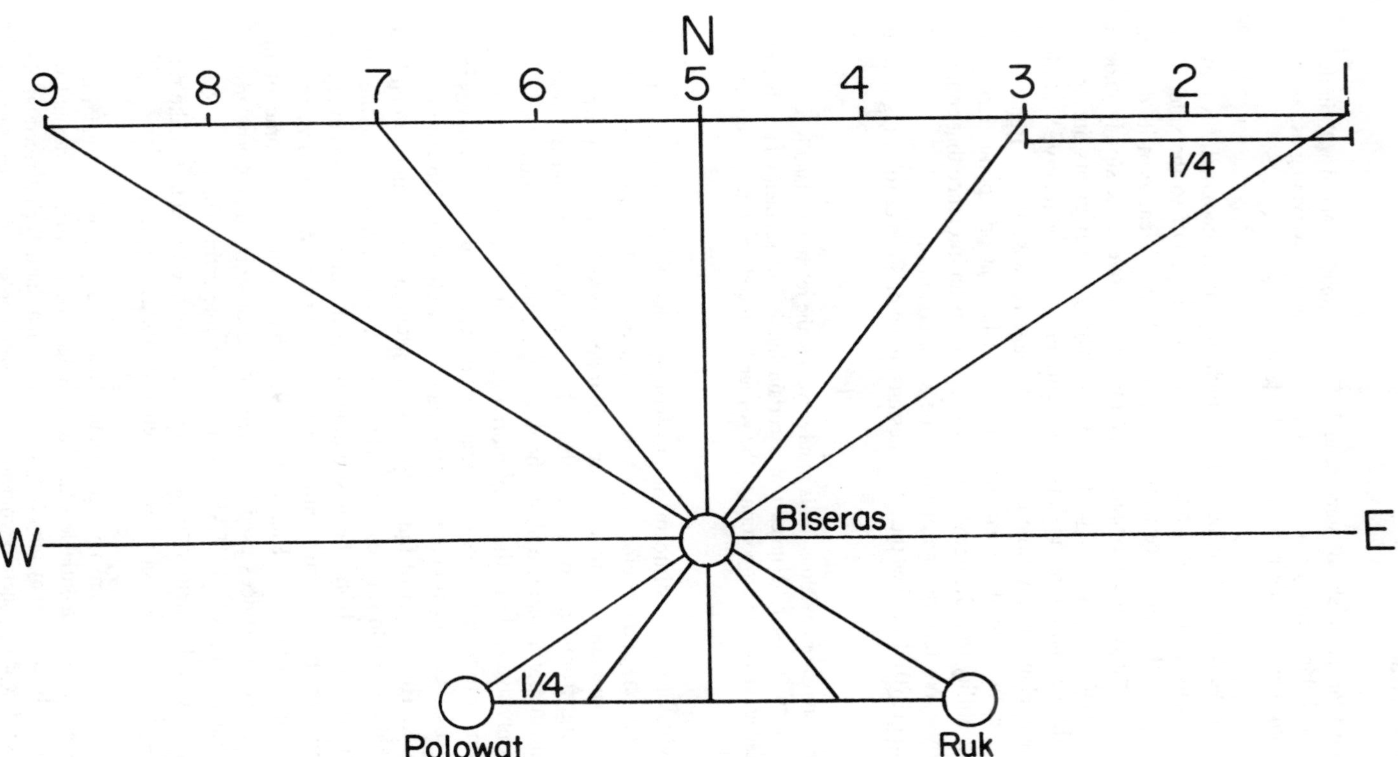

FIG. 9.3. The changing bearing of the reference island (after Sarfert, 1911). The line between Polowat (Puluwat) and Ruk (Truk) represents the course to be steered, Biseras is the reference island. The numerals at the top of the diagram indicate star bearing directions through which the reference island is imagined to pass. At the beginning of the voyage the reference island is under bearing 1 and at the end of the voyage it is under bearing 9.

near, some far, some ahead, some behind. The ones that are ahead will, in due course, fall behind. Everything passes by the little canoe—everything except the stars by night and the sun in the day [p. 182].

Here we have a conceptualization in which the known geography is moving past the navigator, his canoe, and the stars in the sky. Off to the side of the course steered is the reference island. It cannot be seen because of its distance over the horizon, yet the navigator imagines it to move back slowly under a sequence of star points on the horizon. Observations of navigators during voyages have shown that the navigators can accurately judge the relative bearing of the reference island at any time during the voyage (Lewis, 1972). Because the navigator has not actually *seen* the reference island at any point during the voyage, his ability to indicate where it lies represents an inference that could not be made by a Western navigator under the same conditions.

Gladwin (1970) describes the Micronesian navigator's use of this judgment as follows:

When the navigator envisions in his mind's eye that the reference island is passing under a particular star he notes that a certain number of segments have been completed and a certain proportion of the voyage has therefore been accomplished [p. 184].

The navigator uses this information to estimate when he will be in the vicinity of his destination, and therefore when he should start looking for signs of land. Because land based birds venture as far as 20 miles to sea, seeing them arrive at a fishing ground from land, or seeing them depart a fishing ground for land can give information at a distance about the direction in which land lies. This information is only available in the early morning, and at dusk, when the birds are moving from or to their island. A navigator who arrives at what he believes to be the vicinity of his destination at midday is therefore well advised to drop sail and wait for dusk. The danger of failing to make an accurate judgment of when land is near is that one could sail near land when no signs were available and then sail past and be far away from the destination when homing signs are available.

The nature of this system requires that the navigator commit to memory a large body of information. Riesenberg (1972) has documented some of the elaborate mnemonic devices used by navigators to organize their knowledge of geography, star courses and ETAK segments. An interesting finding of Riesenberg's work is that the memorized systems of knowledge frequently make reference to islands which do not exist. Riesenberg (1972) explains:

In a few instances, when unknown geographical features were mentioned and when enough courses from identifiable islands to them have been given, an attempt has been made to locate them by projecting the courses on a chart. The intersections of the projected courses generally coincide poorly with known bathemetric features [p. 20].

The role of these phantom islands is an issue described in a later section.

Tacking

Tacking up wind when out of sight of the goal is the navigator's most difficult task. A navigator will be forced to tack when the wind is coming from a direction such that the canoe cannot sail directly to its target. Because these canoes are normally not sailed closer than about 72 degrees from the direction of the true wind, anytime the wind is coming from nearer the goal than 72 degrees on either side, the navigator will face a tacking situation. Tacking is a set of maneuvers in which the canoe sails as close to the wind as is possible and makes a zig-zag course in order to reach its goal. The problem for the navigator is to know when to begin the next tack of his voyage. This can be quite critical, because errors in the judgment of the length of tacks can accumulate such that the goal island never comes within sighting range. In the direct voyage situation, as long as the course is correct, errors in the estimation of distance are not critical, because the goal island will eventually come into view.

Of tacking Gladwin (1970) says:

> The moving island construct provides the *totality* of the navigational guidance when tacking, whereas ETAK, when it is used, deals only with one of several aspects of the navigator's task, distance estimation. By the same token, since the moving island is only a logical construct and thus does not contribute any factual support for the navigator's decisions, tacking over long distance with only the moving island for guidance necessarily places the greatest demands of any routine navigational exercise upon the judgment and skill of the navigator [p. 189].

I have reproduced a diagram of tacking from Gladwin (1970) in Fig. 9.4. He provides the following commentary on the navigator's task:

> His guidance comes from the ''movement'' of the destination island ''B,'' which is more or less on his beam. In just the same way as an ETAK reference island, ''B'' is moving south as long as the canoe is moving north (although ETAK itself is disregarded during tacking). In doing so it passes under navigation stars. The number of stars it will be allowed to slide beneath is a decision for the navigator. The more stars, the longer the tack and the fewer changes in direction to be made. It must be kept in mind that all this time the island ''B'' is out of sight and will remain so until near the end of the voyage. Its position must be construed solely from the navigator's knowledge of where it should be in both distance and bearing and how much progress the canoe has made on its heading through the water [pp. 190–192].

This description provides some useful constraints on the navigator's actions, but leaves a number of important questions unanswered. How does the navigator know when it is an appropriate time to come about? If the navigator is basing his decision to tack on his estimation of the distance he has travelled on a particular

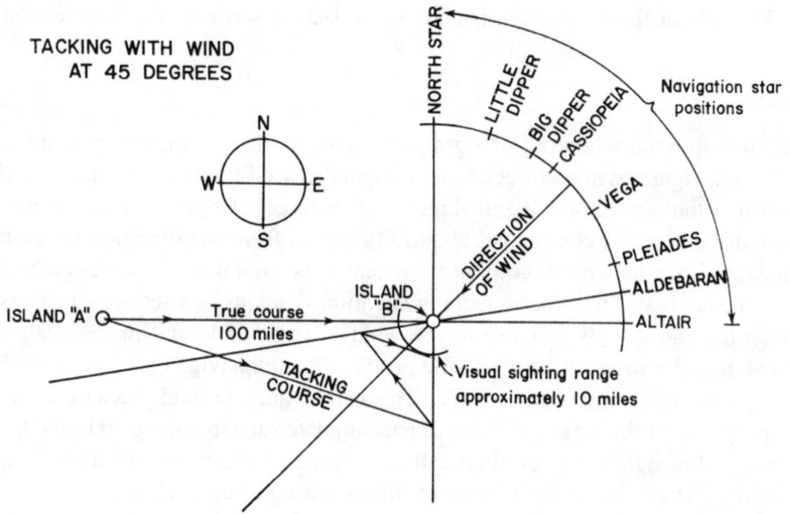

FIG. 9.4. Tacking upwind (after Gladwin, 1970).

tack, how does he come to know what distance is appropriate for a given tack? In what units is the distance expressed? If it is expressed in ETAK-like units based on the movement of the goal island under star points, we notice that the unit defined by any two stars changes with each tack, getting shorter each time. How does the navigator know how much shorter a segment should be on each successive tack? (See Fig. 9.4).

SOME ANOMALOUS INTERPRETATIONS

The history of attempts to understand how the Micronesian navigators accomplish their feats reads like a detective story in which we know who did it, but not how it was done. Each of several researchers have provided us with useful clues, and in their attempts to fit the pieces together meaningfully, supplied a few red herrings as well. Inasmuch as these navigators are still practicing their art, one may well wonder why the researchers don't just ask the navigators how they do it. Researchers do ask, but it is not that simple. As is the case with any truly expert performance in any culture, the experts themselves are often unable to specify just what it is they do while they are performing. Doing the task and explaining what one is doing require quite different ways of thinking. In addition, when the bounds of culture and language are crossed, one is never entirely sure what question the expert thought he was asked or what he intended his answer to mean.

There is little dispute about the nature of course-keeping with the sidereal compass. The earliest accounts of the star compass go back to at least 1722

(Schück, 1882), and its use seems relatively easy to observe and document. The most detailed description of the star compass of the Caroline Islands was provided by Goodenough in 1953. This is the star compass shown in Fig. 9.2 of the preceeding section. Although this is, as far as we know, a completely accurate depiction of the stars used by the Caroline Island navigators and gives the first complete tabulation of the azimuths (true bearings on the horizon) and names of the star points, it contains a potentially misleading distortion that was probably incorporated to make the compass concept more accessible to readers from our culture. Goodenough has drawn the compass as a circular compass rose, the way compasses are traditionally represented in our culture. The original records of *native* depictions of the star compass, however, are all box shaped. Figure 9.5 shows such an early description of a Caroline Island star compass.

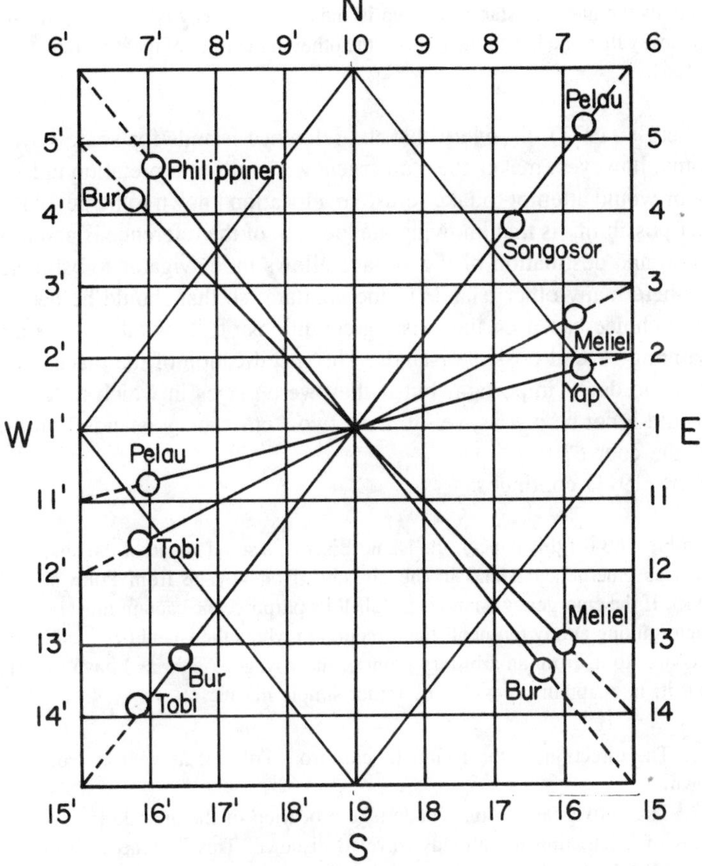

FIG. 9.5. Traditional box-shaped star compass. Note that the compass/chart does not depict the relative positions of the islands, but only the relative directions between selected pairs of islands.

To date there have been two attempts to explain just how the Caroline Island navigators use the concept of ETAK to keep track of their progress on a voyage. The first description of the use of the ETAK system appeared in a paper by E. Sarfert of Leipzig in 1911 and the second is Gladwin's (1970) description in *East is a Big Bird*. Sarfert's (1911) description is rich and compact and bears careful consideration:

> In an arbitrary voyage between two determined islands, the native captains have still a third island in mind, besides the starting point and goal of the trip. For the voyage between every pair of islands this is a specific island. As of now I will refer to this island simply as ''emergency island'', (*notinsel* in the original German) corresponding to the purpose that it serves as a last place to flee to in case of extenuating circumstances that make it impossible to reach either the starting point or goal of the trip. This island is placed off to the side of the course. In rare situations the natives established two islands as emergency islands, specifically in such a way that one lies to the left and the other to the right of the direction of travel [p. 134].

Riesenberg's (1972) discovery that the reference islands for some voyages are phantoms, however, makes the ''emergency island'' interpretation unlikely. No navigator would attempt to take refuse in a location known to be devoid of land. Another possibility is that knowing the location of the reference island as well as the origin and destination of the voyage allows the navigator to estimate accurately where many other islands in the area are, so that should he need to take refuge, a choice based on the existing conditions of the wind and sea might be made among several possible islands. The specification of the placement of the islands is no doubt important, but if they were places in which to take refuge, why would it not be just as well to have two ''emergency islands'' on the same side of the course?

Sarfert (1911) continues:

> In Fig. 9.3 (of this paper), the island Biseras, a small island of the Onona atoll, serves as emergency island in the already given voyage from Polowat to Ruk (Truk). If the emergency island is to fulfill its purpose, the captain must be capable of determining at any moment, the direction in which the island lies, and therefore the course to it, from an arbitrary point of the voyage. As far as I have experience about it, he (captain) does this by rather simple means:
>
> 1. The direction of the island Biseras from Polowat as well as from Ruk is known.
>
> 2. The native captain may undertake a bearing of the area during the trip by means of calculating the already-traveled distance. This is done with the aid of experience, knowledge of the normal duration of the voyage and with the help of an estimate of the speed that the canoe travels through the water. This last means, the so-called dead-reckoning, was also in general used by us for the same purpose before the introduction of the log at the end of the 16th century.

3. To determine the bearing of the emergency island from the vantage point of the canoe, the observation must necessarily be done such that, as Fig. 9.3 clearly demonstrates, it describes the emergency island, Biseras, from the canoe as a visible movement on the horizon in the opposite direction of the voyage. This visible movement of the emergency island appears, with the interpretation of the horizon as a straight line, in direct relationship to the already-traversed distance. If the captain estimates, for example, the covered path as being a quarter of the total voyage length, then the emergency island must have completed likewise a quarter of its visible path along the horizon. If the total length of the visible path totals 8 (ETAK) lines, then after one quarter of the trip they would have reached, accordingly, the third line. By means of this simple calculation, the course to the emergency island is confirmed and the captain is capable of seeking it out [p. 135].

The major issue raised in Sarfert's proposed calculation technique involves the method used to express the proportion of the total voyage that has been completed. It is easy enough to imagine how the navigator might represent the fact that the "emergency island must have completed a quarter of its visible path along the horizon," although, it is doubtful that proportions like "one quarter" are involved. But how does the captain compute that he has covered some proportion of the total voyage length? Further, the expression of the movement of the emergency island in terms of a proportion of the number of ETAK segments will work only if the ETAK segments themselves are all nearly the same size. We return to this point shortly.

Gladwin's descriptive model, like Sarfert's relates the bearing of the ETAK reference island to the distance travelled. They differ, however, in that Sarfert believed the navigator computed the apparent bearing of the ETAK island so that he could take refuge there whereas Gladwin asserts that the navigator uses that apparent position as an expression of the proportion of the voyage completed. Gladwin (1970) states:

When the navigator envisions in his mind's eye that the reference island is passing under a particular star he notes that a certain number of segments have been completed and a certain proportion of the voyage has therefore been accomplished [184].

This is similar to Sarfert's proportional derivation model, but the subtle difference raises an interesting issue. What is the nature of the computation? Is it, as Sarfert maintains, that the navigator uses his estimate of the proportion of the voyage completed to establish the bearing of the reference island, or, as Gladwin maintains, that the navigator uses his estimate of the bearing of the reference island to establish the proportion of the voyage that has been accomplished? Clearly these concepts are closely related for the navigator.

In practice, not every interisland course is situated such that there is an island to the side of the course with the desired properties of an ETAK island. Gladwin (1970) notes:

> If the reference island is too close, it passes under many stars, dividing the journey into a lot of segments. Worse, the segments are of very unequal length. They start out rather long (''slow'') and then as the canoe passes close by, they become shorter (''fast'') as the reference island swings under one star after another, and then at the end they are long again, a confusing effect. A distant reference island has an opposite effect making the segments approximately equal, but so few in number that they do not divide the journey into components of a useful size [187].

The effect of having a close reference island is confusing because when a voyage is divided into segments of very different lengths, the estimation of the number of segments remaining is a poor measure of the distance remaining in the voyage. Gladwin described another situation, also noted by Sarfert, in which this same sort of confusion was bound to arise. In a discussion with the master navigator Ikuliman of the Warieng school [5], Gladwin (1970) discovered that for the voyage between Puluwat and Pulusuk atolls, a distance of about 30 miles, the Warieng school indicates two ETAK islands, one to the west of the course and nearby, the other to the east and quite distant.

> This case well illustrates one of the difficulties with the practice: when two reference islands are used in this way, the segments are almost certain to be markedly different in length. Ikuliman was not able to offer a good explanation for using two islands, insisting only that this is the way it is taught. When I pressed him further, he observed dryly that Puluwat and Pulusuk are so close together that a navigator does not really need to use ETAK at all in order to establish his position on this seaway, so in this case my question was irrelevant [188].

Another feature of the system in use that seems to give rise to the same sort of conceptual difficulty is that the first and last two segments of all voyages are about the same length, regardless of the positioning of the reference island relative to the course and regardless of the density of star points in the portion of the horizon that the reference island is imagined to be moving through. Gladwin (1970) states:

> Upon leaving an island, one enters upon the ''ETAK of sighting,'' a segment which lasts as long as the island remains in view, usually about ten miles. When the island has at last disappeared, one enters the ''ETAK of birds'' which extends out as far as the flights of birds which sleep ashore each night. This is about twenty miles from land, making the first two and therefore also the last two, segments each about ten miles long. Having four segments of the voyage absolute in length is logically incongruous (by our criteria) with the proportional derivation of the remainder of the ETAK divisions [188].

---

[5]There are two major schools of navigation in the Central Caroline Islands. Both schools use the same concepts, although there are differences among them in the choice of reference islands and in the details of the lore and language that distinguish navigators from others.

Again, the problem with this conception is that it interferes with the computation of the distance remaining in the voyage because it destroys the consistency of the ETAK segments as units of distance. Gladwin explored this inconsistency with his main informant, the navigator Hipour—who later sailed with Lewis to Saipan and back using the system described here (Lewis, 1972, 1976, 1978). Gladwin (1970) continues:

> When I tried to explore with Hipour how he resolved the discrepancy he simply replied that beyond the ETAK of birds he uses the reference island to establish distance. When I asked how he handled the problem of segments ending in different places, under the two methods, he said he did not see this as a problem. As with Ikuliman's answer to my 'problem' over the dual reference islands, this ended the discussion [189].

The major difficulty with Sarfert's model and all of the ''problems'' that Gladwin has raised with his navigator informants spring from the observation that ETAK segments are unsuitable units for the measurement of distance covered on a voyage. One interpretation of this state of affairs is that what we took to be a logical organizing principle in navigation may be a useful description in the abstract, but that in the exigencies of use, it is not strictly adhered to. Gladwin (1970) concludes:

> Although ETAK has for us much of the quality of a systematic organizing principle or even a logical construct, the Puluwat navigator does not let logical consistency or inconsistency, insofar as he is aware of them, interfere with practical utility [189].

There is, of course, another possible interpretation. That is that the apparent anomalies result from the unwarranted assumption that the ETAK segments *are* units of measurement. The notion that consistent units of measurement are necessary for accurate navigation is very deeply ingrained in our cultural tradition. So much so in fact, that it is hard for us to conceive of a system of navigation that does not rely on such units and a set of operations for manipulating them. Yet there is no evidence in the record that the ETAK segments perform that function, nor is there any evidence of any set of mental arithmetic operations that would permit a navigator to manipulate ETAK segments as though they were units of distance. Before moving to the description of a system in which ETAK segments are not treated as units of distance, one more intriguing anomaly needs to be discussed.

A Conceptual Blindspot

The following revealing incident occurred while Lewis was working with the master navigators Hipour of Puluwat and Beiong of Pulusuk. According to Lewis (1972):

> On one occasion I was trying to determine the identity of an island called Ngatik—there were no charts to be consulted of course—that lay somewhere south-west of Ponape. It had not been visited by Central Carolinian canoes for several generations but was an ETAK reference island for the Oroluk–Ponape voyage and as such, its star bearings from both these islands were known to Hipour. On his telling me what they were I drew a diagram to illustrate that Ngatik must necessarily lie where these ETAK bearings intersected (see Fig. 9.6). Hipour could not grasp this idea at all. His concept is the wholly dynamic one of moving islands [142].

This passage raises several important questions. Why did Lewis use the technique of drawing the intersecting bearings in order to determine the location of the island called Ngatik? Why did Lewis assume that posing the question the way he did would make sense to Hipour? Why did Hipour not grasp the idea of the intersecting bearings?

Let's consider the questions about Lewis first. The technique Lewis used is clearly an effective one for the solution of this particular problem, but it contains some very powerful assumptions about the relation of the problem solver to the space in which the problem is being solved. First it requires a global representation of the locations of the various pieces of land relative to each other. In addition, it requires a point of view on that space which we might call the "bird's eye" view. The problem solver does not (and cannot without an aircraft) actually assume this relation to the real world in which the problem is posed. But he does assume this relation to a chart or a diagram which is an abstract representation of the space. This strategy, then, involves at least creating an abstract representation of a space and then assuming an imaginary point of view relative to the abstract representation. We can guess that Lewis did this because it is for him a natural framework in which to pose questions and solve problems having to do with the relative locations of objects in a two dimensional space. Part of his

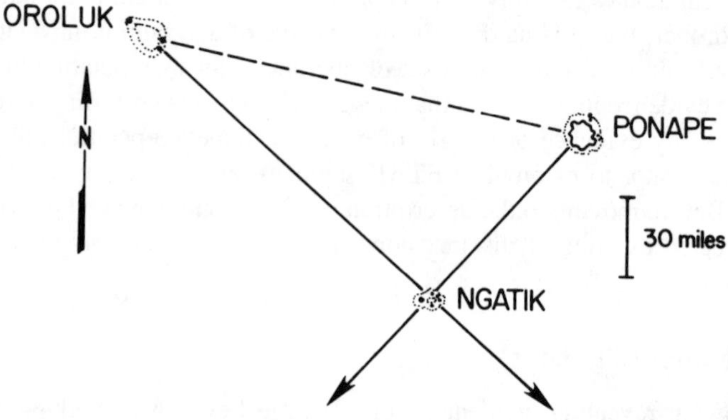

FIG. 9.6. Diagram of the sort drawn by Lewis to illustrate the location of Ngatik at the intersection of ETAK bearings.

training tells him that it is appropriate to use this strategy even when he is one of the objects in the relevant space. Posing the question this way also seems justified by the fact that these navigators are, and long have been, capable of creating chart-like representations of the islands among which they sail (Schück, 1882).

Western navigators make incessant use of this change in point of view. When the navigator takes a compass bearing on a landmark from the bridge of a boat he has a real point of view on a real space, but as soon as he leans over his chart, he is no longer conceptually on the boat, he is over the sea surface looking down on the position of his craft in a representation of the real local space. Novice navigators sometimes find this change of point of view disorienting especially if the orientation of their chart table does not happen to correspond to the orientations of objects in the world. We all face this same problem when in using a road map we have to decide whether to keep the northern edge or the edge toward our destination away from us. Regardless of problems of orientation, the change of point of view is manifest in the reconciliation of the map to the terrain.

Beiong was also puzzled by Lewis's (1972) assertion, and in reaching an understanding of it he provides us with an important insight into the operation of the conceptual system.

> He eventually suceeded in achieving the mental tour de force of visualizing himself sailing simultaneously from Oroluk to Ponape and from Ponape to Oroluk and picturing the ETAK bearings to Ngatik at the start of both voyages. In this way he managed to comprehend the diagram and confirmed that it showed the island's position correctly [143].

The nature of Beiong's understanding indicates that for the Caroline Island navigator, the star bearing of an island is not simply the orientation of a line in space, but the direction of a star point *from the position of the navigator*. In order to see that the star bearings would indeed intersect each other at the island, he had to imagine himself (in the role of navigator) to be at both ends of the voyage at once. This allowed him to visualize the star bearing from Oroluk to Ngatik radiating from a navigator at Oroluk and the star bearing from Ponape to Ngatik radiating from a navigator at Ponape. What Hipour probably imagined when Lewis asserted that the island lies where the bearings cross must have been something like the situation depicted in Fig. 9.7. Contrast this with what Lewis imagined he was asserting (Fig. 9.6). Hipour's consternation is now perhaps more understandable. The star bearings of the ETAK reference island are bearings which radiate out from the navigator. From his perspective they meet only at him. In his conception of the voyage in question the ETAK reference island begins under one of these bearings and ends under the other. That two relative bearings might meet anywhere other than at the navigator himself is literally inconceivable.

Because the Caroline Island navigator takes a real point of view on the real local space to determine the star bearings, it does not seem likely that the

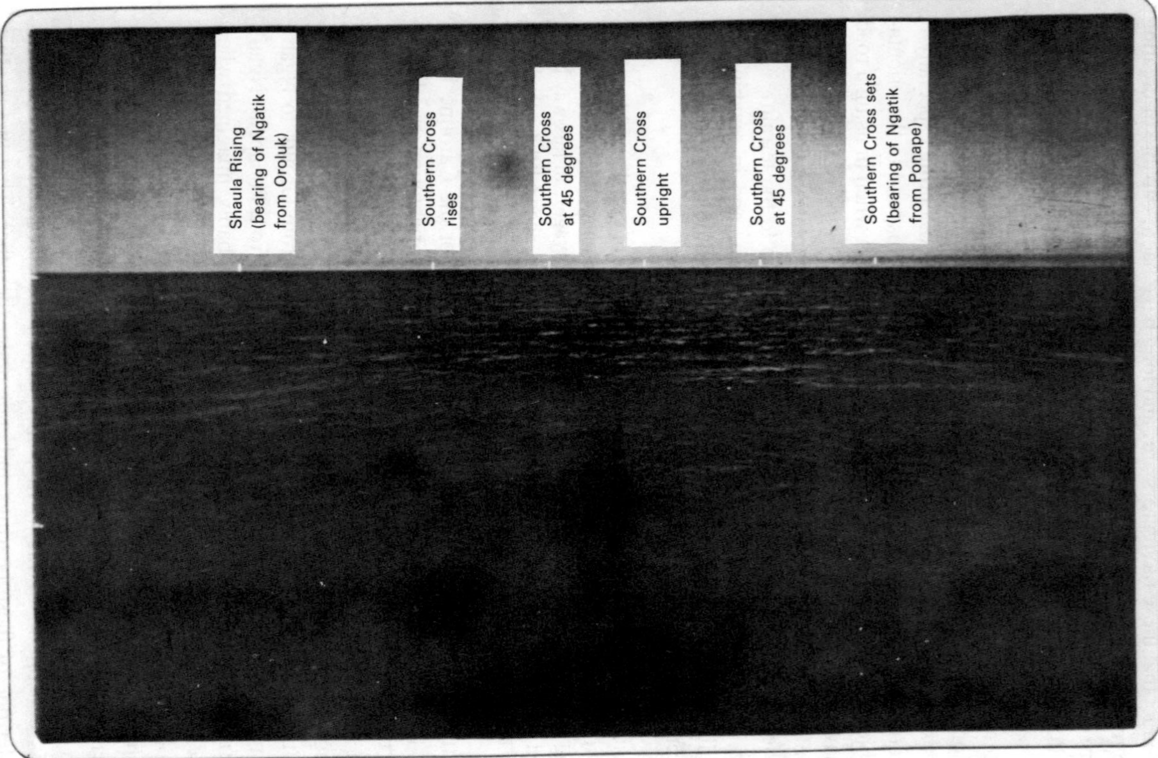

FIG. 9.7. What Hipour may have imagined. The star bearings radiate from the navigator himself. He ''sees'' them where the stars rise from or set into the horizon. To imagine the bearing of Ngatik from Oroluk (under Shaula rising), and the bearing of Ngatik from Ponape (under the Southern Cross setting), Hipour visualizes the horizon to the south-southeast. There he ''sees'' these two bearings and the others under which Ngatik would pass on a voyage between Oroluk and Ponape.

mapping of ETAK segments onto an abstract representation of the expanse of water between the islands is faithful to his conception. Gladwin's (1970) statement about the navigator noting that a "certain number of segments have been completed" and the diagrams that Lewis, Gladwin, and Sarfert use to represent the changing relative bearing of the ETAK reference island all contain the implicit assumptions (1) that the navigator uses some sort of "birds eye view" of the space he is in and (2) that he conceives of a voyage in terms of changes in the position of his canoe in a space upon which he has an unchanging point of view. These assumptions are true of the Western navigator's conception of a voyage, but they appear not to be true of the Caroline Island navigator's conception of a voyage. These assumptions are at odds with the verbal data (i.e., descriptions of islands moving relative to the navigator) and the behavioral data (i.e., consternation in the face of what ought to be a trivial inference).

It is tempting to criticize the Caroline Island navigators for maintaining an egocentric perspective on the voyage when the global perspective seems so much more powerful. But consider the following exercise: Go at dawn to a high place and point directly to the center of the rising sun. That defines a line. Return to that same high place at noon and point again to the center of the sun. That defines a second line. I assert that the sun is located in space where those two lines intersect. Think about it. In spite of the fact that the lines seem to be orthogonal to each other, it happens to be true. It is not intuitively obvious to us because our usual way of conceiving of the sun's location is not to conceive of its location at all. It is to think of its orientation relative to a frame defined by the horizons and the zenith on earth. The rotation of the earth is not experienced as a movement of the surface of the earth about its center, but as the movement of celestial bodies about the earth. From a point of view outside the solar system, however, the intersection of the lines is obvious and it is immediately apparent that the sun is in fact located where the lines cross (see Fig. 9.8).

Our everyday models of the sun's movement are exactly analogous to the navigator's conception of the location of the reference island. The choice of representations limits the sorts of inferences which make sense. Because we have all been exposed to the ideas of Copernicus, we can sit down and convince

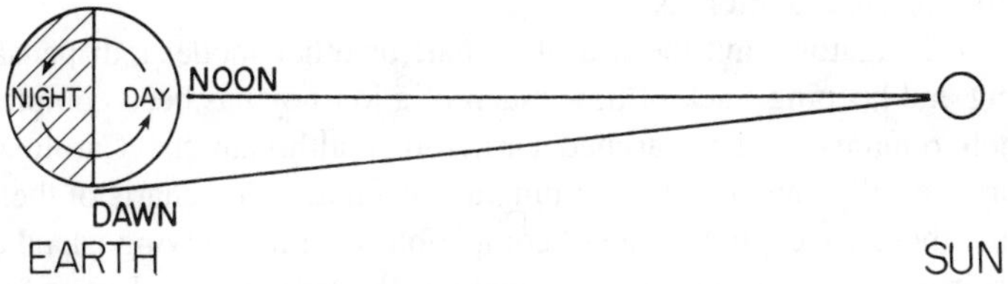

FIG. 9.8. The view from outside the solar system. The sun is located in space where the line defined by pointing to it at dawn intersects the line defined by pointing to it at noon.

ourselves that what we experience is an artifact of our being on the face of a spinning planet. That is, after all the "correct" way to conceive of it, but it is not necessarily the most useful way. Modern celestial navigation is deliberately pre-Copernican[6] precisely because a geocentric conception of the apparent movements of bodies on a rigid celestial sphere makes the requisite inferences about the apparent positions of celestial bodies much easier than a heliocentric conception. From a perspective outside the galaxy of course, the heliocentric conception itself is seen to be a fiction which gives an improved account of the relative movements of bodies within the solar system, but which is incapable of accounting for the motion of the solar system relative to the other stars in the universe. Such a "veridical" cosmology that describes the real movements of bodies through space, however, is irrelevant to any present day navigator's concerns.

The findings of this section place strong constraints on the candidate models of how the navigators use the ETAK system. Viable candidates must not rely on arbitrary units of distance, nor should they involve a birds-eye view of the navigator and his craft situated in some represented space.

AN ALTERNATIVE MODEL

We are now ready to consider what the Caroline Island navigator might gain by using the conception of the moving reference island. Gladwin was no doubt correct in claiming that the ETAK system is a way to express how much of a voyage has been completed and how much remains. In Gladwin's model the ETAK conception performs the recording function of a chart. According to Gladwin, the navigator, by means unknown, performs mental dead reckoning on the movement of his canoe and having determined where his canoe is along its track from island to island he then infers where the reference island must lie over the horizon. In that model, the ETAK concept and the use of the reference island are only ways to arrange the information at hand so that it can be remembered. This section shows how the ETAK conception does in a more elegant and direct way for the Caroline Island navigator just what a chart does for the Western navigator, that is, how it provides not only a framework for remembering, but a framework for computation as well.

Western navigators find the use of a chart or other model indispensable for expressing and keeping track of how much of a journey has been completed and how much remains. I have argued earlier that although the Caroline Island navigators are fully capable of imagining and even drawing charts of their island group, that these conceptions are not compatible with the moving island and star bearing conceptions they use while navigating. Remember that Hipour's problem

[6] See for example, Bowditch (1977, Vol. 1) or Maloney (1978) for discussions of the pre-Copernican fictions employed in modern celestial navigation.

was the difficulty of getting to a bird's eye point of view when he was thinking about star bearings. In addition, even though the necessary technology is available to them, we know that the navigators carry nothing like a chart with them on their voyages.

Consider the navigator's conception in its context of use. At the outset of any voyage, the navigator imagines that the reference island is off over the horizon ahead of him and to one side. It is for him under the point on the horizon marked by the rising or setting of a particular line of stars. During the course of the voyage, the reference island will move back along its track remaining out of sight of the navigator. As it does so, it will assume positions under a succession of star bearings until it lies under the star bearing which marks the course from the destination to the reference island. If the helmsman has kept a straight course, then the canoe will be at the destination when this happens. An important aspect of this imagined sweep of the reference island back along its track, out of sight of the navigator has been ignored by recent writers on Caroline navigation but was noticed by Sarfert (1911). Sarfert was struck by the fact that the navigators conceive of the horizon as being a straight line which lies parallel to the course of the canoe. For a Western navigator who normally conceives of the horizon as a circle around him, this is a puzzling observation. Why should these navigators make such a counterfactual assumption?

As Sarfert pointed out, if the navigator conceives of the horizon as a straight line, and he imagines the apparent movement of the reference island beyond it, then the horizon itself becomes a line parallel to the course steered on which the progress of the reference island from beginning bearing, through a set of intermediate bearings, and to final bearing is exactly proportional to the progress of the canoe from the island of departure across the sea between and to the goal island. That is, the imagined movement of the ETAK reference island just under the horizon is a complete model of the voyage which is visualizable (but not visible) from the natural point of view of the navigator in the canoe (see Fig. 9.9). It is a representation of the spatial extent of the voyage and one's progress along it that does not require either the construction of a map or a change of point of view. The straight line horizon conception is essential to the transformation of angular displacement into linear displacement.

The image of the ETAK reference island moving along just below the horizon can be quite naturally tied to the passage of time. Part of the knowledge that a navigator has about every voyage is the amount of time he can expect the trip to take under various conditions. Suppose that the navigator knows for a particular voyage that under good conditions, he will arrive at his goal after one day of sailing. If he leaves his island of departure at noon for instance (a common departure time) he can estimate that he will arrive at his destination about noon the following day. In terms of the movement of the reference island, that means that the island will move from under the beginning bearing to the position under the final bearing in one day. This image is shown in Fig. 9.10. Still assuming a

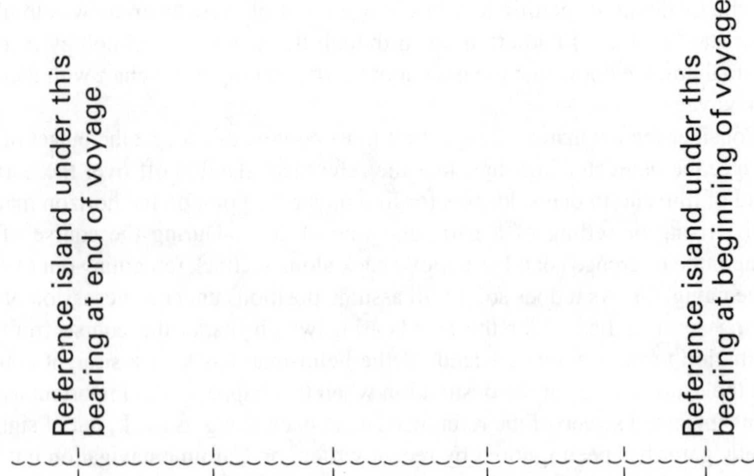

FIG. 9.9. The imagined movement of the ETAK reference island. Imagine that your are in a canoe moving from left to right. As you look out at the horizon to the side of the canoe, you see at your right (ahead of you) the star bearing under which the reference island lies at the outset of the voyage. As you travel, the ETAK reference island moves back along its apparent course beyond the horizon from right to left. At the end of the voyage it will be under its final star bearing, that is, the bearing from the goal island to the reference island.

normal rate, he can associate other times during the voyage with other bearings of the reference island as shown in Fig. 9.11. In so doing, he not only has a visual image that represents the extent of the voyage in space, he also has one that represents the voyage and its subparts in time as well. If the voyage was in fact sailed under the expected conditions, the task of determining where the reference island is positioned over the horizon at any point in time would be trivial. All the navigator need do is to determine what time of day it is and refer to the image of the reference island moving along under the horizon. By pointing to the position on the horizon that represents the present time of day, the navigator has pointed directly at the reference island. The imagery described is depicted in Fig. 9.12.

The assumption that ETAK segments are *units* of distance lead Gladwin (1970) to three related apparent inconsistencies. They are (1) the supposedly confusing effect of having ETAK segments be of different lengths, (2) the conflicting boundaries of ETAK segments defined by using more than one ETAK island at a time, and (3) the conflicting boundaries of ETAK segments at the beginning and end of a voyage caused by using the ETAK of birds and the ETAK of sighting in addition to the star bearing defined ETAK segments. Gladwin (1970) found these conceptions to be, "completely inconsistent with the theory as described above [p. 189]."

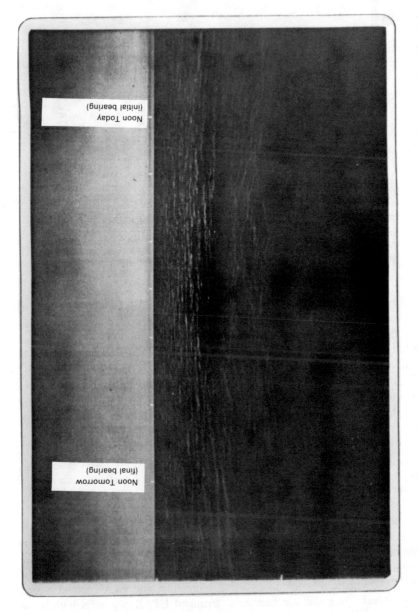

FIG. 9.10. Assumed time-bearing correspondences. Given an assumed rate, the time of departure and the expected time of arrival can be associated with the initial and final bearings of the ETAK reference island.

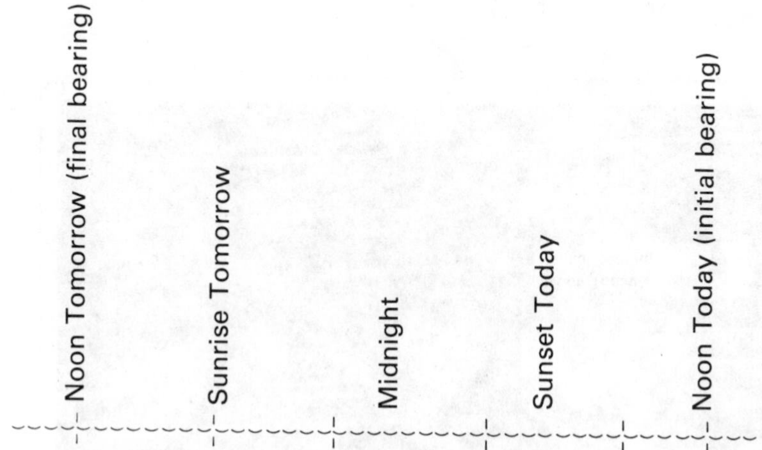

FIG. 9.11. Inferred time-bearing correspondences. Intermediate temporal landmarks can be associated with the intermediate bearings of the reference island. Notice that the temporal landmarks need not line up precisely with the established star point bearings.

In this model, there is no need to assume that the ETAK segments are units of distance. We dispense with the notion that they enter into a numerical computation of the proporation of the voyage completed or remaining. The inequality of their lengths is not an awkward conceptual problem, it simply means that on a typical voyage, the navigator will have more conceptual landmarks defined by star bearings in the middle of the voyage than at the ends. In fact, if we listen to the navigators, we find that they are not talking about the spatial duration (length) of the ETAK segments, but of their temporal duration. Gladwin (1970) states:

> They start out being rather long (''slow'') and then as the canoe passes close by, they become shorter (''fast'') as the reference island swings under one star after another, and then at the end they are long again, a confusing effect [p. 187].

The concern of the navigator is not how far he travels in a particular ETAK segment, but how long he will travel before asserting that the reference island has moved back under the next star bearing.

When the concept of the ETAK segment is freed from the notion of a unit of distance, the apparent problems of using more than one ETAK island at one time, or overlapping the star bearing determined ETAK segments with those determined by the range of birds and the range of sighting, disappear. Using one ETAK island to each side of a voyage gives the navigator more conceptual landmarks on his voyage. There is no reason for it to be a problem to the

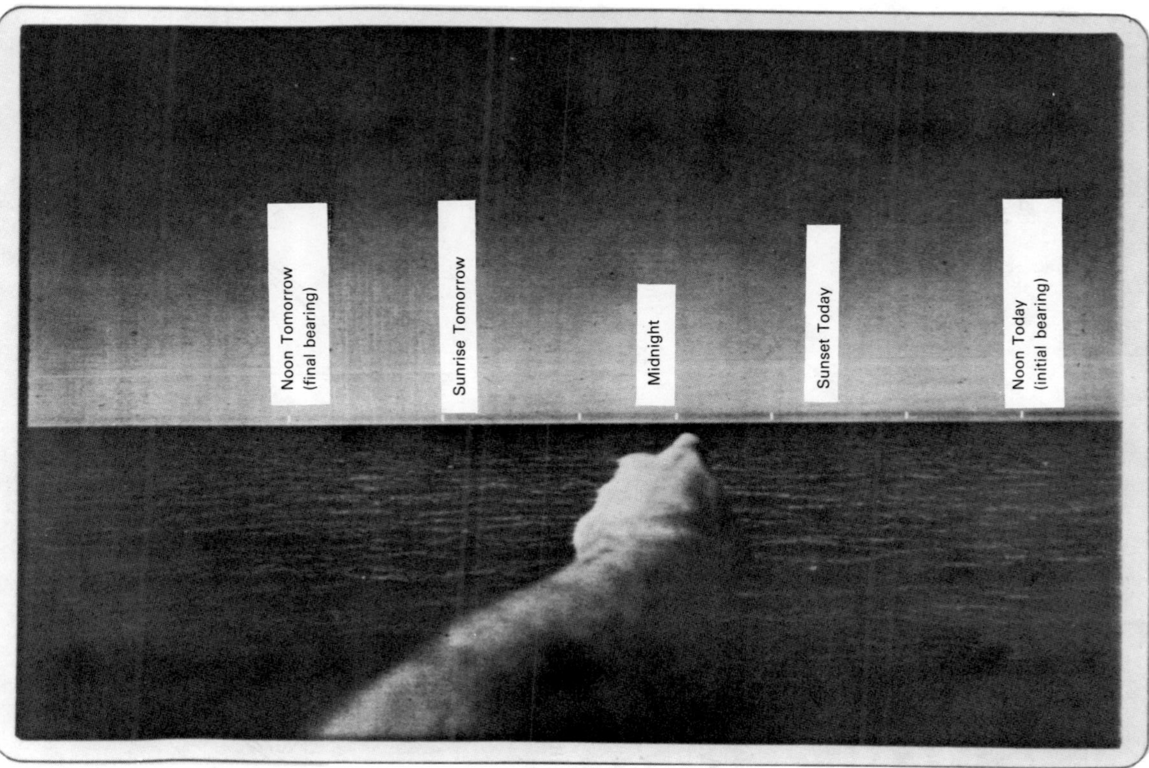

FIG. 9.12. Pointing at the ETAK reference island. The navigator points to the bearing of the ETAK reference island late in the evening of the first day of the voyage.

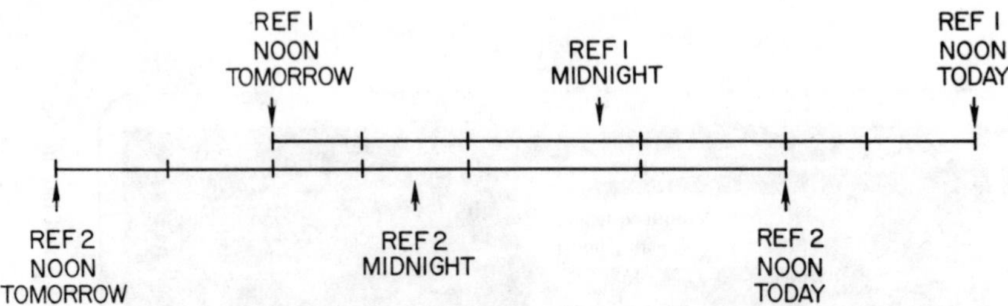

FIG. 9.13. Two reference islands on the same side of the course. This depicts the time-bearing correspondences for two reference islands mapped onto a single stretch of horizon. Note that where the segments overlap, they share star bearing points. This is confusing because two sets of temporal landmarks are mapped onto the same set of bearing points.

navigator. If two reference islands were on the same side of the voyage, however, the navigator would have two complete but non-coextensive sets of time-bearing correspondences superimposed on a single horizon and that probably would be a source of confusion (see Fig. 9.13). The confusion that Gladwin imagined with one reference island to each side does not arise because the ETAK segments are not mapped onto the course line, but onto the imagery on the horizon in front of the reference islands (see Fig. 9.14).

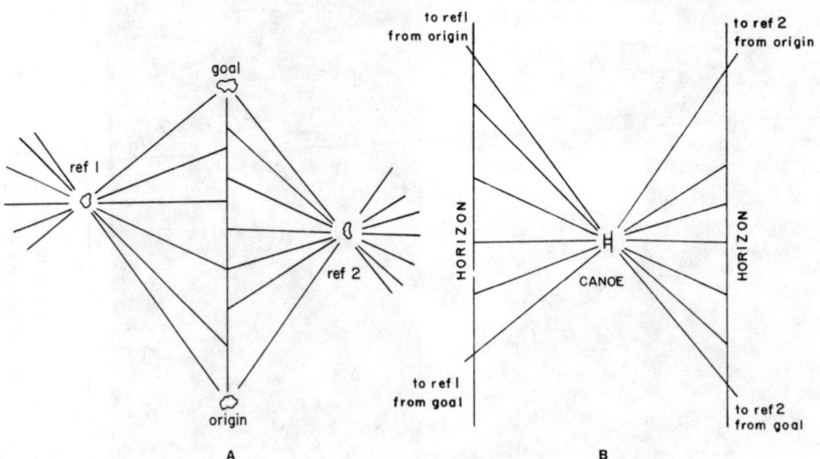

FIG. 9.14. One reference island on each side of the course. Figure 14a shows how confusion would indeed arise if the ETAK segments were mapped onto the course line rather than onto the horizon. Figure 14b shows the canoe between two straight horizons. The radiating grid of the star bearings intersects the horizons upon which the movements of the two reference islands are separately imagined.

The strategy of including the ETAK of sighting and the ETAK of birds is entirely consistent with the notion of the ETAK division as a conceptual landmark. The star bearing defined ETAK segments are conceptual landmarks derived in a particular way, and the ETAK of sighting is a conceptual landmark determined in another way. But once established, they function for the navigator in the same way. They do not enter into a numerical computation, but give the navigator a more direct representation of where he is, or rather where land is. In addition, because the star bearing ETAK segments are slow in coming near the beginning and end of the voyage, it may be helpful to the navigator to have these other conceptual landmarks at these points.

This conception and technique make the judgment of the location of land a trivial computation when conditions are favorable. Suppose, however, that the voyage must be made under conditions that differ from those expected at the outset of the voyage. How could the navigator update his image of the movement of the reference island to reflect what is happening to his rate of travel? The key to this problem lies in the judgment of rate and in the way that the judgment is expressed. Any experienced Western yachtsman can make fairly accurate judgments of his boat's speed through the water without the aid of instruments. By attending to the feel of the boat as it moves through the water, the accelerations developed as it moves over waves, the feel of the apparent wind, the appearance and sound of the wake (it sizzles at speeds in excess of about five knots), the response of the helm, and many other sensations, the small boat sailor can make judgments that he normally expresses as a number of units, usually knots. The knot is a good choice for the yachtsman, because as one nautical mile per hour, it is a convenient form for the sorts of subsequent numerical calculations he is likely to make. He might have expressed the rate as furlongs-per-fortnight or on a scale of how thrilling it is, but neither of these fits especially well with the useful subsequent calculations. The same must be true for the Caroline Island navigators. There is no doubt that they can make accurate judgments of rate, but expressing those judgments in terms of knots would not be advantageous at all because that unit is not compatible with any interesting computations on a visual image of the moving reference island.

Clearly what is wanted is an expression of the rate that bears a compatible relationship to the imagery. Consider the following hypothetical scheme. At some point in the voyage (and it could be any point including the very beginning) the rate of the canoe changes. The navigator reconstructs his image of the movement of the reference island with the time landmarks placed in accordance with the previous rate. If the change occurs at the very beginning of the voyage, the usual or default rate will be taken as the previous rate. Let the segment of the horizon from the present position of the reference island to any convenient future time landmark represent the previous rate (see Segment 1, Fig. 9.15). This represents the expected movement of the reference island at the previous rate during the period between the present time and the temporal landmark chosen.

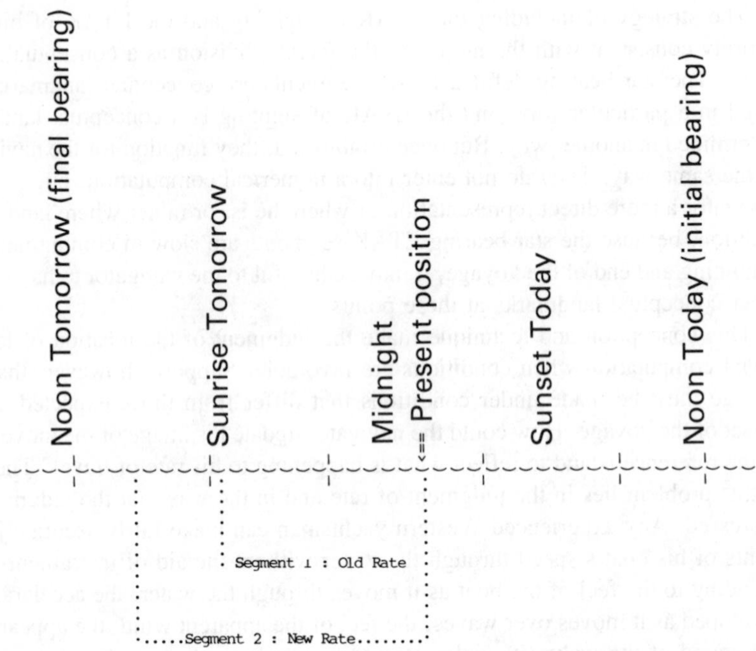

FIG. 9.15. Adjusting for a change in rate: step 1. Segment 1 represents the expected movement of the reference island over some future period of time given the previous rate. Segment 2 is constructed such that it is as much longer (or shorter) than segment 1 as the new rate is faster (or slower) than the previous rate. The canoe is moving from left to right, so the reference island is moving from right to left.

The problem is to determine the movement of the reference island during the same time period at the new rate. If the new rate is greater than the old rate, then the reference island will move further along the horizon in the same period, if the rate is less, the movement will be less. Using Segment 1 as a scale, imagine another segment (Segment 2, Fig. 9.15) starting at the present position of the reference island and extending in the direction of the apparent movement of the reference island which represents a judgment of the magnitude of the new rate relative to the old rate. Now simply move the time landmark from the end of Segment 1 to the end of Segment 2. Segment 2 now defines the new time scale for the new rate. The other time landmarks for subsequent portions of the voyage can be moved in accordance, as in Fig. 9.16 and a complete new set of expectations for the times at which the ETAK reference island will assume future positions is achieved. This procedure can of course be applied anytime there is a noticeable change in the rate of travel of the canoe through the water. Thus, the

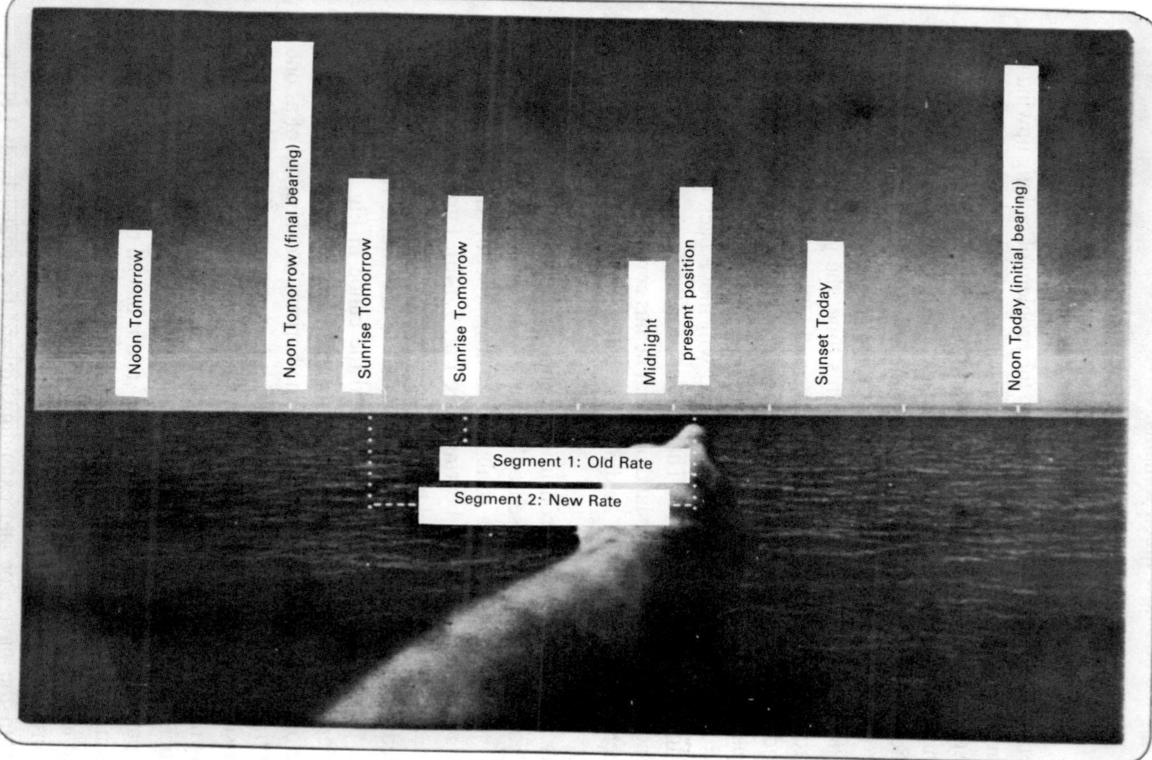

FIG. 9.16. Adjusting for a change in rate: step 2. Adjustment for change in rate is accomplished by moving the temporal landmark previously at the end of segment 1 to the end of segment 2. Adjustment is completed by relocating all temporal landmarks representing future times in accordance with the new scale. In this case, ''sunrise tomorrow'' is moved first to the end of segment 2. Then the ''midnight'' and ''noon tomorrow'' landmarks are moved to conform to the new scale defined by the new distance from the present time (late evening) to ''sunrise tomorrow.'' At the new, faster, rate, the goal will be reached sometime after sunrise tomorrow rather than at noon tomorrow.

navigator can always keep an updated set of time/bearing correspondences for the ETAK reference island which allows him to gauge how much of his voyage has been completed and how much remains.

Tacking

This same set of concepts provides a solution to the problem of tacking upwind to an unseen target. Gladwin (1970) tells us that when tacking is necessary, the navigator dispenses with the reference island and concentrates his attention on the goal island. When it becomes necessary to tack, the navigator can consult his imagery of the ETAK reference island to determine how long it would have taken him to reach his goal had he been able to continue to sail toward it (the time duration of the segment A in Fig. 9.17a). At this time, the goal island still lies under its original star bearing. As the canoe turns and settles onto its new course, the goal island, which was previously straight ahead of the canoe now lies ahead and off to one side of the canoe's course. Like an ETAK reference island, the goal island is out of sight, over the horizon and will move back under the star bearings off to one side of the canoe. The problem for the navigator in keeping track of the movement of the goal island now that he has come onto a new course is that he needs a set of temporal landmarks to calibrate the movement of the island.

There may be several ways of constructing such landmarks. In this section I present a hypothetical method, based on a simple geometric construction. This construction exploits the fact that a straight line forms a set of triangles when it intersects the radiating grid of star bearings (see Fig. 9.14b). Further, the set of triangles formed by any line parallel to the course of the canoe is congruent with the set formed by any other line which is parallel to the course (try moving a straight edge parallel to the course line toward the canoe in Fig. 9.14b). The ratios of the lengths of the segments is the same regardless of the distance of the line from the origin of the grid. As we know, the horizon is conceived of as one such straight line. The bearing to the goal island is an imaginary line from where the navigator sits across the canoe deck, across the outrigger, (because the canoe is sailing upwind and the outrigger is always kept to windward) and out to the horizon. Notice how the star bearings cross the outrigger. The outrigger lies in a line roughly parallel to the course of the canoe[7] and it has all the same attributes as the horizon as a frame for the imagery. The navigator can map the star bearings onto locations on the outrigger. If he could determine a set of temporal landmarks there too, he would have solved his problem. Imagine a bearing line emanating from the navigator and extending toward the goal island. Let the

[7]Being of shallow draft, these canoes make considerable leeway. The course made good, however, is near enough to the course steered that the differences do not effect the use of the outrigger as a frame for the imagery.

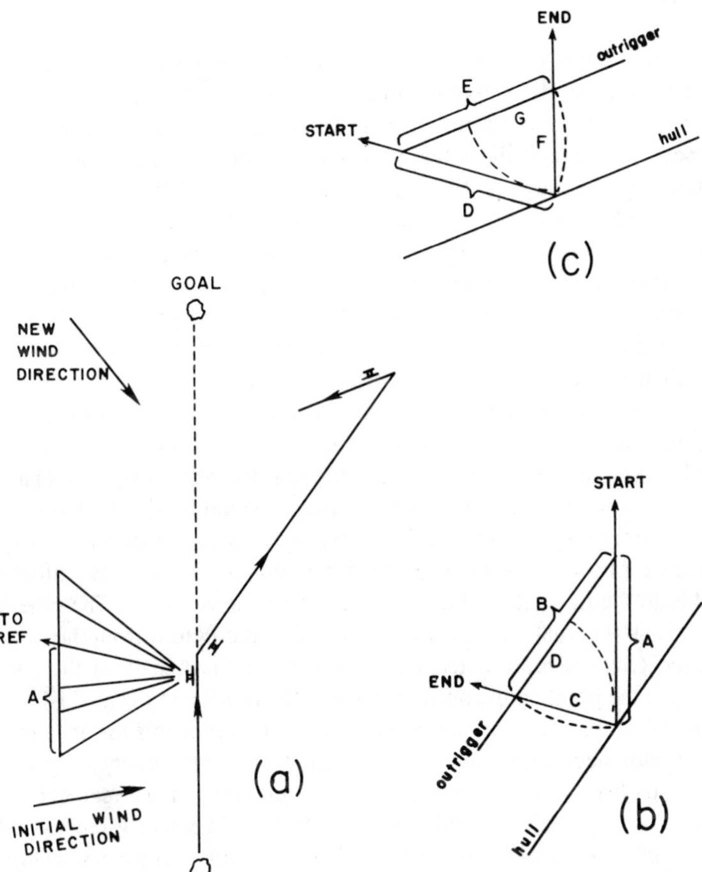

FIG. 9.17. Procedure for tacking upwind to an unseen target. (a) The navigator consults the horizon imagery to determine how much longer he would have sailed on his original course to reach his destination. That is the amount of time represented by the segment A which spans the horizon from the current bearing of the reference to its final bearing. Assume that is six hours. (b) The time established in the previous step is mapped onto the movement of the goal island as it will appear on the new course. This gives the navigator two time-bearing correspondences: 1) at present the goal island is still at its original bearing, and 2) at the time the canoe would have arrived at the goal on the original course (six hours hence) the goal island will be off in the direction of the point where segment A, mapped onto the outrigger as segment B, ends. At that time the goal island will be as far distant in direct sailing time as the length of segment C. That time can be determined by mapping segment C onto the outrigger as segment D and comparing its length with the length of segment B. In this case, if B represents 6 hours, then D (and therefore C) must be about 4 hours. (c) On each successive tack, the distance from the goal island is rescaled and mapped onto the triangle. In this case, knowing that the goal island will be about 4 hours distant at the beginning of the next tack allows the navigator to scale a new mapping for the movement of the goal island on the new tack.

distance from the navigator's seat to the point where that bearing line crosses the outrigger represent the length of time the canoe would have had to sail to reach the goal island (Segment A in Fig. 9.17b). If the canoe makes the same speed on its present course as it did when it was sailing directly toward the goal island, then when the amount of time represented by that distance has elapsed, the bearing of the goal island will have moved a like distance along the outrigger (Segment B in Fig. 9.17b). This gives the navigator two time/bearing correspondences. This is all he needs to construct a complete set of correspondences and to adjust those correspondences in accordance with any perceived difference between the present and previous rates. The navigator can then make a decision about when to tack on the basis of these correspondences.

The remaining problem is to derive a new set of correspondences for the course set on the next tack. Before coming onto the new tack, the navigator would like to know how long it would take to sail directly to the goal island from where he is when he tacks. If he knew this, he would be able to derive a new set of time/bearing correspondences by applying the same procedure he used to get the time/bearing correspondences for his previous course. That information is available to the navigator while he is on the previous course. The time it would take to reach the goal island if one could sail directly to it from the point where the canoe tacks is represented by the length of the line from the navigator's platform to the point on the outrigger where the bearing to the goal island crosses (Segment C in Fig. 9.17b). To find out how much time this distance represents, the navigator need only swing this segment onto the time/bearing correspondences established on the outrigger by the previous step (Segment D in Fig. 9.17b). The application of this result to the new geometry created when the canoe tacks is shown in Fig. 9.17c. Thus, a single simple procedure can be applied on each tack to determine the length of time to sail and the movement of the goal on the following tack.

The notion of mapping the geometry of the situation onto the structure of the canoe is more speculative than the horizon imagery, but there is additional supportive evidence in the widely noted practice of helmsmen maintaining course by keeping particular star bearings over particular structural members of the vessel (Lewis, 1964; Schück, 1882). The procedure for rate adjustment can be applied at each construction of the new course line, and whenever changes in conditions make it necessary. This construction means that the navigator always can determine both where the goal island is and how long it would take to sail to it if one could go directly there.

The model just presented is true to the ethnographic record, it is capable of doing the job, and it resolves the apparent anomalies produced by previous accounts. The question of how Micronesian navigators do what they do, however, is by no means resolved. This model contains features that can only be confirmed (or refuted) by further observation. The basic model of constructing the image of the movement of the reference island on the horizon is almost certainly correct. The mechanisms of rate adjustment and of mapping star bearings onto the outrigger in tacking are more speculative. There are, at present, no data bearing directly on these issues because the models entertained by previous researchers gave no indication that these phenomena existed. Until further field research is conducted, they remain hypotheses generated by a theory of the task.

DISCUSSION

The contrast between the Micronesian navigation techniques and the techniques employed by Western navigators is a reflection of more general differences in computational style. With the advent of literacy and of arithmetic operations as models of events in the world, our cultural tradition made a radical break with previous styles. The prototypical computation in our tradition is a digital arithmetic procedure. The relations of our computations to the world we wish to know about are mediated by analogue to digital (A/D) converters, which provide numerical representation of physical events, and by digital to analogue (D/A) converters that provide for the physical interpretation of calculation results.

The tool box of the Western navigator contains scales and compass roses on charts, dividers, sextants, and chronometers. These are all A/D and D/A converters. In our tradition, the operations of observation, computation, and interpretation are each a different sort of activity and they are executed serially. The Micronesian navigator's tool box is in his mind. There are no A/D or D/A converters because all of the computations are analogue. The interpretation of the result (bearing of the reference island, for example) is embedded in the computation (construction of the horizon image) which is itself embedded in the observation (time of day).

The two techniques for solving navigation problems evolved in very different intellectual environments. The Micronesian technique is elegant and effective. It is organized in a way that allows the navigator to solve in his head, problems that a Western navigator would not attempt without substantial technological supports. Other nonliterate cultures, applying themselves over the course of millenia to their own important problems, must have evolved systems that organize the thinking of the problem solver in equally elegant and efficient ways. It is likely, however, that many if not most of these systems have been lost to us. The European colonization of the world must have lead to the extinction of many species of ideas. This would happen not so much by direct refutation, although religions often take this route, as by the destruction of habitat—the removal of the contexts in which the ideas evolved and functioned. This was the fate of navigation knowledge in Polynesia when long distance voyaging there was suppressed.

When one considers documenting the range of mental models mankind has developed, other problems arise. The history of attempts to understand Micronesian navigation shows how difficult it can be to get away from the fundamental assumptions of one's own cultural tradition.

An obvious beginning for this sort of endeavor is to ask the question: "Given the nature of the task they are facing, what would one have to do to accomplish it?" But there are nearly always many ways to solve any complex problem, and the solutions most likely to occur to the cross-cultural researcher are those that arise from the assumptions of his own cultural tradition. In this chapter I have tried to show how easily that can happen, and how convincing such an explanation can be to its formulator even in the face of relatively serious anomalies. What we want to do is not to model a theory of the task, but to model the problem solver's theory of the task. In doing this we identify the real task to be solved as an internal one. It is the set of operations required to operate on the problem solver's representation of the task, rather than the set of operations required in the world. This means that we need to look first at what the problem solver thinks the task is and then ask the question: "How could one operate on that representation to produce the decisions required to accomplish that task?"

Failure to take the utility of alien mental models seriously cheats us out of important insights. Akerblom (1968) ends his discussion of Polynesian and Micronesian navigation with the following passage:

> Polynesians and Micronesians accomplished their voyages, not thanks to, but in spite of their navigational methods. We must admire them for their daring, their enterprise and their first rate seamanship [p. 156].

I hope this chapter succeeds in laying such notions as Akerblom's to rest. In fact, it seems more likely to me that we who have studied Pacific navigation have accomplished what understanding we have, not thanks to, but in spite of our own cultural belief systems.

ACKNOWLEDGMENT

Support in the form of a visiting scholarship was provided by the Program in Cognitive Science, University of California, San Diego while the ideas presented here were being developed. I wish to acknowledge the contributions of my then fellow Fellows in Cognitive Science, Christopher Riesbeck and Geoffrey Hinton, who joined me in the search for a system which could account for the navigator's skills. I am also grateful to David Lewis for convincing me that an earlier model was incorrect. Additional guidance was provided by James Levin, Ian Moar, and Larry Carleton. Figures 9.2, 9.3, 9.4, 9.5, 9.6, 9.8, 9.13, 9.14, and 9.17 were drawn by Shelley Camp. Passages from articles originally in German were translated by Dom Bouwhuis.

REFERENCES

Akerblom, K. *Astronomy and navigation in Polynesia and Micronesia.* The Ethnographical Museum, Stockholm (Ethnografiska Museet) Monograph Series. Pub. No. 14, 1968.

Aveni, A. F. Tropical Archeoastronomy. *Science,* 1981, *213:*4504, 161–170.

Bowditch, N. *The American practical navigator, Vol. 1.* Washington, D.C.: Defense Mapping Agency Hydrographic Office, 1977.

Finney, B. R. *Hokulea the way to Tahiti.* N.Y.: Dodd, Mead & Company, 1979.

Gladwin, T. *East is a big bird.* Cambridge: Harvard University Press, 1970.

Goodenough, W. H. *Native astronomy in the Central Carolines.* Museum Monographs. Phila.: The University Museum, University of Pennsylvania, 1953.

Lewis, D. Polynesian navigational methods, *Journal of the Polynesian Society,* 1964, *73,* 364–374.

Lewis, D. *We the navigators.* Honolulu: The University Press of Hawaii, 1972.

Lewis, D. A return voyage between Puluwat and Saipan using Micronesian navigational techniques. In B. R. Finney (Ed.), *Pacific navigation and voyaging.* Wellington: the Polynesian Society (Inc.), 1976.

Lewis, D. *The voyaging stars: Secrets of the Pacific Island navigators.* N.Y.: W.W. Norton and Company, 1978.

Maloney, E. *Dutton's navigation and piloting.* 13th edition, Anapolis, Md.: Naval Institute Press, 1978.

Riesenberg, S. H. The organization of navigational knowledge on Puluwat. *The Journal of the Polynesian Society,* 1972, No. 1, *81,* 19–55.

Sarfert, E. Zur kenntnis der schiffahrtskunde der Karoliner. *Korrespondenzblatt der Deutschen Gesellschaft fuer Anthropologie, Ethnologie, und Urgeschichte, 42,* 1911.

Schück, A. Die astronomischen, geographischen und nautischen kenntnisse der Bewohoner der Karolinen und Marshall Inseln im Westlichen Groben Ozean, *Aus Allen Welttheilen,* 1882, *13,* 51–57, 242–243.

10 Conceptual Entities

James G. Greeno
University of Pittsburgh

Representations of a problem can differ in several ways. In this essay, I discuss one quite general attribute that can differentiate problem representations: the kinds of entities that are included. By *the entities in a representation,* I refer to the cognitive objects that the system can reason about in a relatively direct way, and that are included continuously in the representation.

A system reasons directly about an object if it has procedures that take the object as an argument. In this regard, entities can be distinguished from attributes and relations, which have to be retrieved or computed using the entities as cues or arguments.

Continous inclusion is often achieved by creating an entity in the initial interpretation of a situation, and revising it whenever the situation is changed. Inclusion in the initial representation is not required; entities can be created in the course of working on a problem as well. The important feature is that an entity is maintained once it is created; this distinguishes entities from intermediate results that are removed from the representation after they have been used.

It seems appropriate to use the term *ontology* to refer to the entities that are available for representing problem situations. Therefore, by the *ontology of a domain* (for a representational system), I refer to a characterization of terms used in describing situations and problems in the domain. The ontology of the domain says which terms can refer to entities, and which only refer to attributes or relations.

I hypothesize that the ontology of a domain is significant for four reasons.

The first hypothesis is that ontology is a significant factor in forming analogies between domains. An analogy is a mapping between objects and relations in two domains. If the domains are represented with entities that have relations that are similar the analogy might be found easily, but if either domain's representation lacks those entities, the analogy might be difficult or impossible to find.

A corollary of the first hypothesis is that an analogy can be used in facilitating the acquisition of representational knowledge in a domain. If an instructional goal is the learning of a representation that includes a specified set of conceptual entities, then that may be facilitated by providing an analogy with a domain for which a natural representation includes entities that correspond to those that are to be acquired in the target domain.

The second hypothesis is that ontology determines the kinds of information that are available for reasoning using general methods. It seems reasonable to suppose that human problem solvers have some very general reasoning procedures that can be used when appropriate information is available. Examples include reasoning about combinations of quantities that are related as parts and wholes, or comparisons of quantities in ordered sets. The ontology of a domain determines the kinds of information that will be available in the representation, and therefore will be available for use in general reasoning methods.

Third, the ontology of a domain has an obvious consequence for computational efficiency. Ontology determines which kinds of information will be available directly whenever they are needed, and which kinds of information will have to be computed. It clearly is an advantage to keep those items of information available that will be needed frequently, and this is achieved by creating entities corresponding to those items of information.

The fourth hypothesis is an extension of the third. It seems likely that ontology should be a significant factor in planning. A reasonable conjecture is that procedures of planning operate primarily on the entities that are formed in the initial representation of a problem. Thus, representational knowledge that includes an appropriate set of conceptual entities should enable a problem solver to evaluate problem information and choose among alternative goals and plans efficiently.

The fourth hypothesis applies especially to problem solving in domains where formulas are used to solve problems presented in text, such as physics problems and word problems in mathematics. Problem solving should be facilitated if representational knowledge that is applied to problem texts forms conceptual entities that correspond directly to variables in formulas. One way for this to occur would be for knowledge of formulas to include schemata that can be instantiated on the information in problem texts. Schemata that enable an integrated representation of problem information will facilitate judgments about the sufficiency and consistency of problem information and choice of problem goals.

In the remainder of this chapter, I discuss examples in which empirical findings are interpretable in terms of these four hypotheses about conceptual entities in problem solving.

I. ANALOGIES BETWEEN DOMAINS

I will discuss two examples involving mapping of problem-solving procedures between domains. The first example is from high-school geometry, and provides an analysis of knowledge acquired in the context of one domain of problems that can provide a basis for transfer to another domain of problems. The second example is from primary-grade arithmetic, and provides an analysis of instruction that uses an analogy between procedures in two domains in order to facilitate acquisition of knowledge and understanding of multidigit subtraction.

Geometry Proofs

The analysis that I discuss first was concerned with an issue in the psychology of learning, discussed by Wertheimer (1945/1959). The issue is whether when students learn to solve problems their knowledge enables them to understand the problems or merely to carry out rote, mechanical solutions.

An example that Wertheimer discussed is in Fig. 10.1. Wertheimer contrasted two ways in which the theorem of vertical angles can be proved. One method, which Wertheimer characterized as mechanical, uses an algebraic representation. Quantites in the problem, the sizes of angles, are translated into algebraic terms and a proof is derived using equations. The algebraic steps are indicated in solution (a) in Fig. 10.1.

The second method, which Wertheimer characterized as a solution with understanding, uses a geometric representation to a greater extent. The representation includes part-whole relations between angles, as indicated in solution (b) of Figure 1. The two whole structures, *x* with *w* and *x* with *z*, are equal because they are both angles formed by straight lines. Furthermore, they share a common part, *x*. The proof rests on the principle that if the same thing is removed from two equal quantities, then the remainders are equal.

The solution that Wertheimer preferred uses a representation that includes geometric entities that are not included in the more algebraic solution. In the more geometric solution, the straight-line angles are entities; that is, they are cognitive objects whose relationships are used in the solution. The only geometric entities that are needed in the algebraic solution are the labeled angles *w*, *x*, and *z*.

In geometry courses in high school, problems about angles, like the vertical angles theorem, are preceded by instruction in solving problems about line segments. A model was developed that simulated learning from three example problems about line segments. The model has been discussed previously, in another context (Anderson, Greeno, Kline, & Neves, 1981). The example problems are shown in Fig. 10.2. Note that the third problem has the same structure as the theorem of vertical angles, but is about lengths of line segments rather than

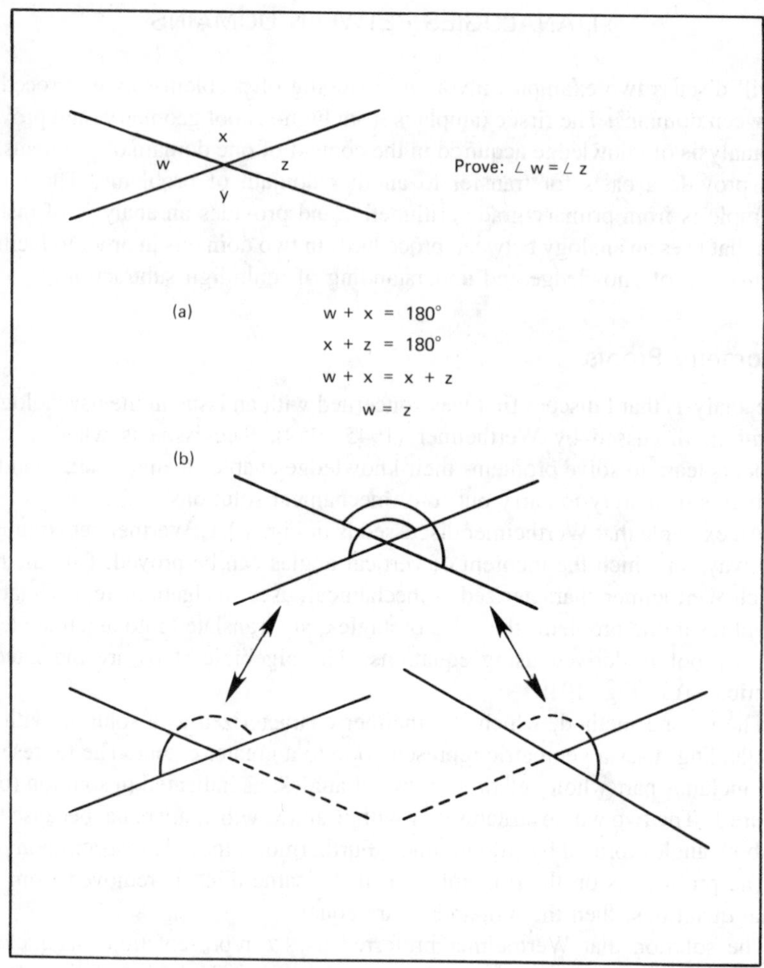

Fig. 10.1. The vertical angles problem with two solutions, from Wertheimer (1945/1959).

sizes of angles. The theoretical goal was to develop a hypothesis about knowledge structures that could be acquired in learning to solve the problems in Fig. 10.2 that would provide a basis for transfer to the vertical-angles problem.

Two simulations of learning were implemented. In one version, called stimulus-response learning, new problem-solving procedures were acquired by associating actions from the example problems with a representation of the problem situations in which the actions occurred. The knowledge acquired in this simulation was very limited in its applicability; however, if mechanisms of stimulus generalization and discrimination like those discussed by Anderson et al. (1981)

were provided, they probably would give a fairly accurate simulation of the knowledge that many students acquire from examples like these.

The second version, called meaningful learning, simulated learning with structural understanding. In meaningful learning, new problem-solving procedures were associated with schematic knowledge about part-whole relationships. The model's initial knowledge included a schema for representing situations involving whole quantities made up of parts, and making inferences about one of the quantities when the others were given.

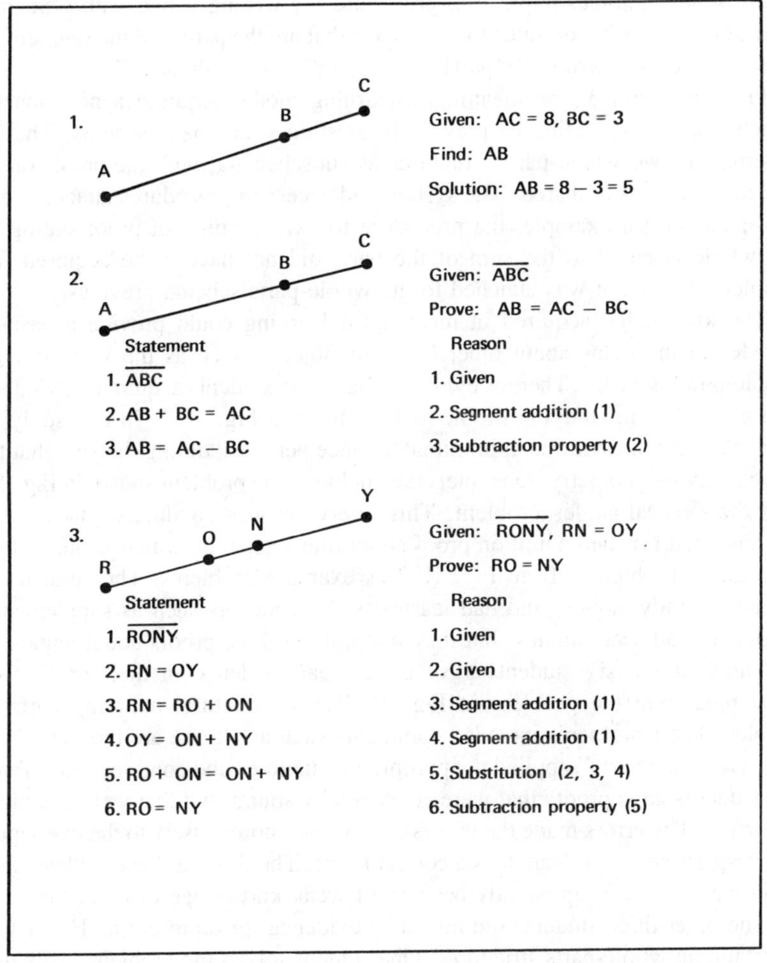

Fig. 10.2. Example problems used for simulations of learning.

From Problem 1, the meaningful-learning model acquired a production for applying its whole-parts schema in situations involving line segments. This knowledge enabled the model to represent problems about lengths of line segments in terms of their part-whole relations, and to use its general procedures for making quantitative inferences about parts and wholes in solving these problems.

From Problem 2, new problem-solving procedures were acquired, with actions of writing lines of proof corresponding to the steps in the example solutions. In meaningful learning, these were acquired as procedural attachments (in the sense of KRL, Bobrow & Winograd, 1977) associated with the whole-parts schema. The arguments of the acquired procedures are objects that occupy slots in the schema; for example, the procedure for writing a line with "Segment Addition" as the reason finds the segments that are the parts and the segment that is the whole, and writes "<part1> + <part2> = <whole>."

From Problem 3, the meaningful-learning model acquired a new schema, which it composed using its previously existing whole-parts schema. The new schema has two whole-parts structures as subschemata, with the provision that one of their parts is shared. The system had access to procedures attached to the subschemata; for example, the procedure for writing lines of proof stating that the whole is equal to the sum of the parts did not have to be acquired from Problem 3, since it was attached to the whole-parts schema previously.

The knowledge acquired in meaningful learning could provide a basis for transfer to problems about other kinds of objects, such as the vertical-angles problem in Fig. 10.1. There is evidence that some students acquire knowledge of that generality in studying problems like those in Fig. 10.2. In one study, six students were interviewed approximately once per week during the year that they were studying geometry. One interview included the problem shown in Fig. 10.3 and the vertical-angles problem. This interview was conducted just after the students had finished a unit on proof about line segments, which included Problem 2 and Problem 3 from Fig. 10.2 as example problems. The students had begun to study angles, and had learned some concepts such as supplementary angles and adjacent angles, but they had not yet done proofs about angles.

Three of the six students gave quite clear evidence in their protocols of conceptualizing the problem in Fig. 10.3 as a structure involving parts and wholes. Their protocols included comments such as "these are the same," and "I have to subtract," applied to appropriate quantities and combinations. Two of the students gave proofs that were conceptually sound, but that were technically incorrect. The errors made the proofs correspond more closely to the overlapping whole-parts structure than does a correct proof. The third of these students failed to prove Fig. 10.3, apparently because of weak knowledge of procedures.

The other three students did not show evidence for representing Fig. 10.3 as overlapping whole-parts structures. One student solved the problem easily using a theorem about supplementary angles. Another student worked out a proof that was technically correct, and appeared to involve applying a procedure for sub-

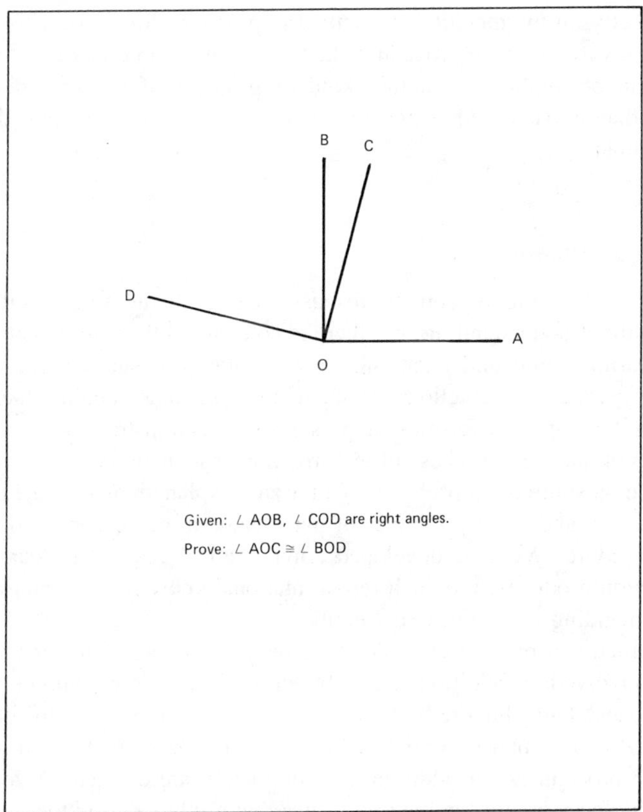
B
C
D
A
O
Given: ∠ AOB, ∠ COD are right angles.
Prove: ∠ AOC ≅ ∠ BOD

Fig. 10.3. Transfer problem given to students.

stitution in an equation. The sixth student was unable to make progress on Fig. 10.3, and in further questioning it seemed that this student had not learned how to solve the segment problems.

A similar variety of responses was obtained when the vertical-angles problem was presented. One of the students who solved Fig. 10.3 with the schema said, "This is the same problem again. You know something? I'm getting sort of tired of solving this problem." The student who appeared to apply the substitution procedure for Figure 3 failed to prove the vertical-angles theorem; this student got caught in a perceptual difficulty in the vertical-angles problem, where w and x are considered as a pair, and y and z are considered as the other pair.

The knowledge acquired in meaningful learning illustrates the role that conceptual entities can play in a problem representation. With the representational knowledge that enables line segments to be represented as parts and wholes, the model's general procedures for making inferences about parts and wholes can operate directly on the quantities presented in problem situations. This analysis also shows a way in which procedures that are acquired in one kind of problem situation can be applied in another kind of problem, if the procedures take arguments that are specified as the slots of a schema that can be applied to both problem domains.

Subtraction Procedure

The analysis of learning in geometry discussed earlier includes models that learn with and without understanding, but there is no analysis there of conditions that facilitate learning with understanding. In the domain of subtraction, we have analyzed a method of instruction that seems to make understanding likely. The method was developed by Resnick (in press); she calls it instruction by mapping. The instruction has been successful in correcting systematic errors in children's performance on subtraction problems. Children's explanations indicate that they also gain understanding of principles of place value in numeration and the subtraction procedure. We have developed a hypothetical analysis of learning that this instruction produces, in which representational knowledge of subtraction is acquired, including new conceptual entities.

The instructional method uses blocks to facilitate students' understanding of principles involved in addition and subtraction of multidigit numbers. Place values of ones, tens, hundreds, and thousands are represented by blocks of different sizes and shapes. Representations of numbers are formed with the blocks, and procedures for addition and subtraction are defined. A correspondence can be formed between the procedures that use blocks and the procedures that use ordinary written numerals. For example, carrying and borrowing with numerals correspond to trading with blocks, where one block of a certain size is traded for ten blocks of the next smaller size. Use of blocks in the teaching of arithmetic is quite common. The distinctive feature of Resnick's instruction is that the correspondence between procedures in the two domains is spelled out in detail, and steps are taken to ensure that the student realizes which components of each procedure correspond to components of the other.

In Resnick's empirical research, the recipients of instruction have been children who needed remedial work on subtraction. The work has been done with fourth grade students who performed subtraction with bugs, according to Brown and Burton's (1978) analysis. Figure 10.4 shows two examples. The first problem is solved with a procedure called the smaller-from-larger bug; the answer in each column is found by subtracting the smaller from the larger digit in that column, regardless of which is on the top. The second and third problems illustrate another bug, called don't-decrement-zero. When borrowing is required and a zero is encountered, a *one* is added where it is needed, but nothing is decremented to compensate for that.

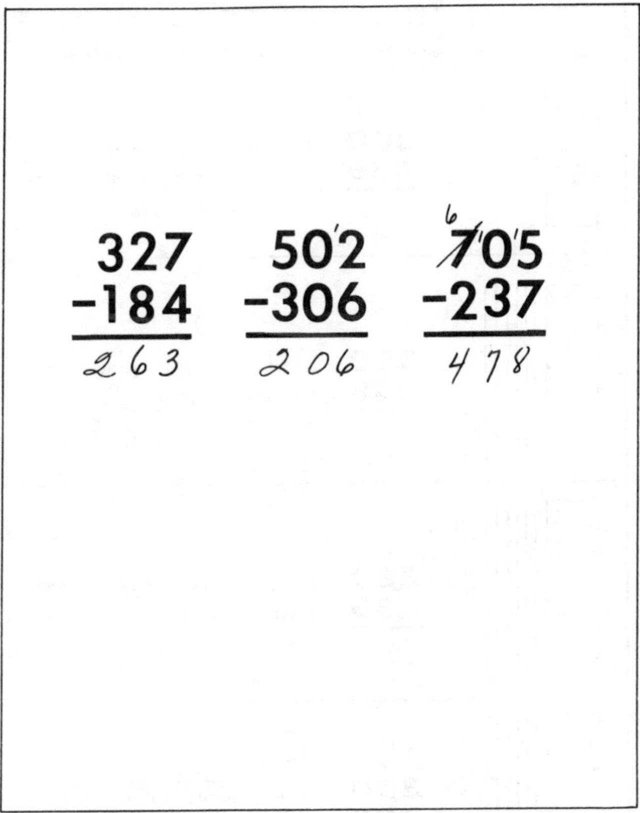

Fig. 10.4. Subtraction problems solved with buggy algorithms.

In Resnick's instruction, children are taught a procedure for subtracting with blocks. In this procedure, the top number in the subtraction problem is represented with blocks, and the number of blocks indicated by the bottom number of the problem is taken away, column by column. When there are too few blocks in one of the top-number piles, a block from the next pile to the left is traded for ten blocks of the size needed. If there are no blocks in the next pile to the left (corresponding to a zero in the top number) a block is taken from the next nonempty pile, traded for ten of the size to its right, one of those is traded for ten of the next smaller size, and so on, until the pile is reached where the extra blocks were needed.

After the child has learned to subtract with blocks, the correspondence between blocks and numerals is taught. For each action performed with blocks, a corresponding action is performed with the written numerals. An example is shown in Fig. 10.5. When a block is removed in borrowing, the corresponding

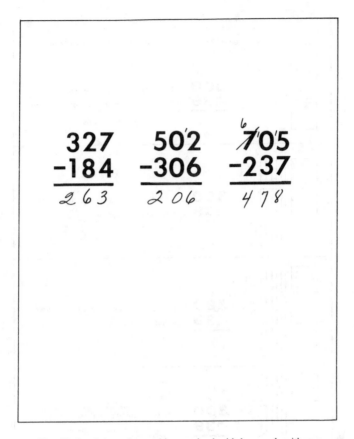

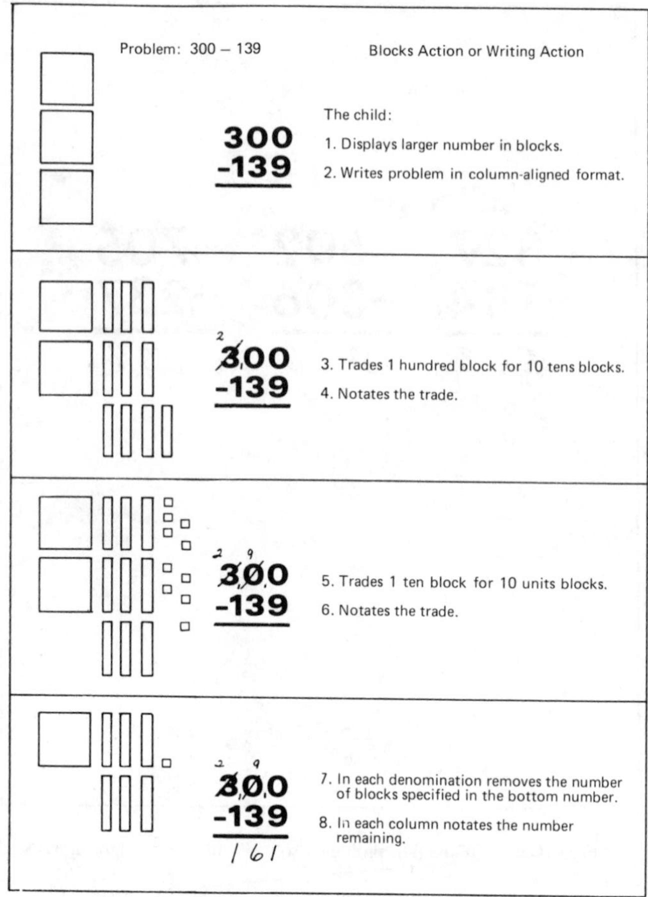

Fig. 10.5. An outline of mapping instruction for borrowing.

numeral is decremented. When ten blocks of the next size are put into the display, the digit for that column is increased by ten. When the number of blocks in a bottom digit are taken away from a pile, the remaining number of blocks is written as the answer for that column.

This instructional sequence can be quite effective. Resnick has recorded several successful cases in which children with bugs like those illustrated in Fig. 10.4 have learned to subtract correctly. Research on the instructional effectiveness of the method is continuing, but the data in hand are sufficient to establish that the instruction can provide effective remediation of subtraction bugs.

There also is evidence that children acquire a better understanding of general principles as a result of mapping instruction. This evidence is provided in part by explanations that children are able to give after the instruction. One child, whom we call Laura, started with the smaller-from-larger bug. She learned the correct procedure, and three weeks later she still remembered how to subtract correctly. She was asked whether she remembered how she used to subtract, and what the difference was. Her answer was, "I used to take the numbers apart. Now I keep them together, *and* take them apart." This remark seems to indicate that Laura came to understand an important principle; that the set of digits that are on a line collectively represent a single number.

Another wise explanation was given by a student who started with a bug involving borrowing when a zero is encountered. This student, whom we call Molly, learned to subtract correctly, and in a posttest solved the problem 403 − 275, correctly decrementing the *four,* replacing the *zero* with a *nine,* and placing a small *one* next to the *three* in the top number. She mentioned that she changed the *four* to a *three* "because I traded it for 10 *tens.*" Then she was asked, "Do you know where the *nine* came from?" Molly answered, "It's 9 *tens* and the other *ten* is right here," pointing to the *one* near the *three*. Molly's remark seems to indicate that she appreciated the requirement of keeping the value of a number the same during borrowing.

In theoretical research in which I have collaborated with Lauren Resnick, Robert Neches, and James Rowland, we have tried to characterize the knowledge that is acquired in mapping instruction, and some of the learning processes that occur when students receive this instruction. We are working with two general ideas, one of which has been implemented as a simulation of learning, based on the protocol given by Molly. A simulation of the other idea is still being developed.

In both of these ideas, we assume that the effect of mapping is to elicit a generalization across the two procedures that are learned by the student. The generalization involves entitites that are abstractions over the domains in which the procedures are defined. In the case of blocks and numeral subtraction, the entities that are acquired in our simulation are quantitative concepts for which both the numerals and the blocks provide symbolic representations.

The main structures involved in the simulation are shown in Fig. 10.6. We assume that initially, the knowledge structure includes the whole-parts schema, including a procedure for adjusting the sizes of the parts while keeping the whole quantity constant. Instruction in the procedure with blocks has resulted in acquisition of a procedure called Trade, where a block of one size is removed and ten blocks of the next smaller size are put back in its place. The amounts that are taken away and put back are understood to be equal, since there is a ten-to-one ratio of the sizes of the blocks.

In mapping instruction, a procedure of borrowing is taught, and explicit connections are made between the components of Trade, and the components of Borrow; that is, Take-Away corresponds to Decrement, and Put-In corresponds to Add. We hypothesize that this correspondence influences the acquisition of Borrow, through the mediation of a third structure which we call Exchange.

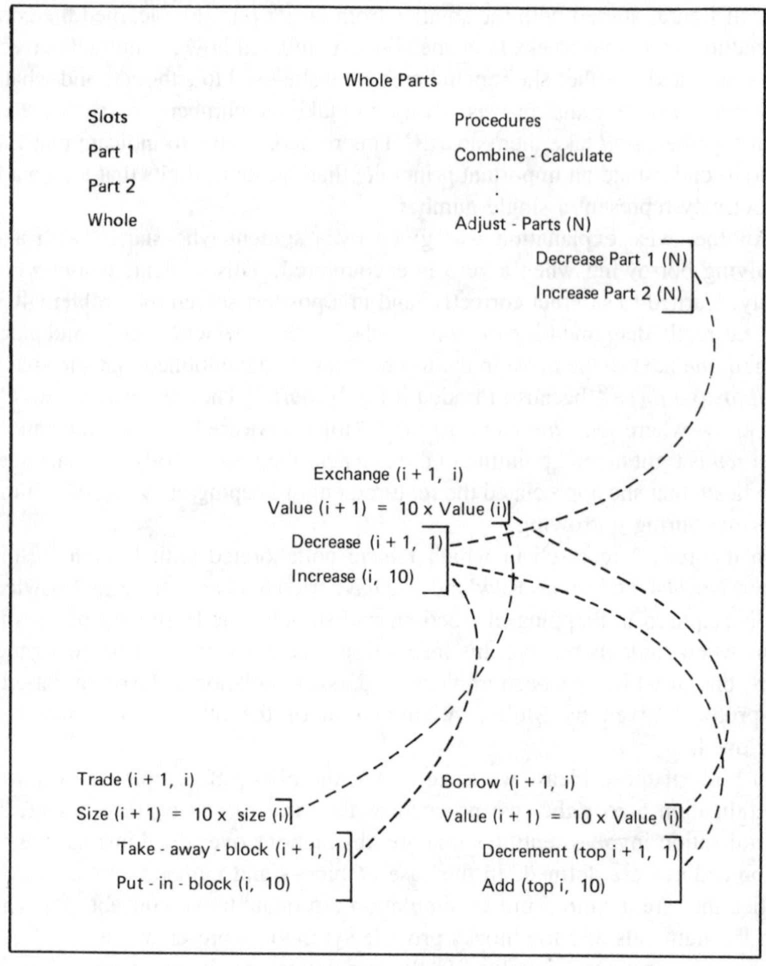

Fig. 10.6. Structures in simulation of learning from mapping instruction.

Exchange is a generalization across Trade and Borrow, and its components are propagated into the Borrow procedure. Decrease (i+1) and Increase (i) are generalizations of the surface-level actions Take-Away, Put-In, Decrement, and Add. The whole-parts schema provides a constraint that the amounts of increase and decrease should be equal. This is satisfied in Trade by the property of block size. We assume that a generalization of block size is included in Exchange as the property of Value, and that this is propagated into the Borrow procedure as a Value associated with the place of each digit.

The structures that our simulation acquires were designed to provide information of the kind needed for explanations like those given by Laura and Molly.

One important component is the concept of value, included in the Borrow procedure. This is an important general principle of numeration. Another important principle is that when borrowing occurs, the value of the number should remain the same. In our simulation, this principle is represented by the procedure's connection to the whole-parts scheme, and the constraint of its Adjust-Parts procedure. We provided our system with some primitive question-answering capability, and it can answer the question, "Where did the *nine* come from?" after it has borrowed through *zero* in a problem like 403 − 275. It finds the value of the block that it took away from the hundreds column, identifies the value of the nine *tens* as being part of the ten *tens* that it put back, and locates the other ten *ones* that it exchanged for one of the *tens*. Laura's answer about keeping the numbers together involves a more subtle use of information, which we have not simulated. However, we conjecture that the answer depends on conceptualizing the value of the numeral as a whole quantity, made up of parts corresponding to the values of the digits, and the concepts needed for this conceptualization are all included in our simulation.

The conceptual entities in this analysis are similar to those acquired in meaningful learning of geometry. In both cases, representations of problem situations include conceptual units that are interpreted as elements with part-whole relationships. In geometry, a conceptual entity represents a structure composed of two segments or angles that are combined in a whole segment or angle. In subtraction, there is a conceptual entity that represents the value corresponding to two adjacent digits, the sum of the values of the separate digits.

II. REASONING WITH GENERAL METHODS

The second function of conceptual entities that I propose is that they provide arguments on which general reasoning procedures can operate directly. In this section, I discuss findings that can be interpreted with this idea. First, analyses of processes in solving physics text problems suggest that experts' representations include entities that provide arguments to general procedures for reasoning about parts and wholes. Then, two experiments involving instruction provide further information about conditions that facilitate acquisition of representational knowledge that includes conceptual entities.

Physics Problems

In physics text problems, experienced problem solvers use representations in which forces, energies, momenta, and other abstractions are treated as entities. An example is in force diagrams, in which the collection of forces acting on an object in the problem is shown as a set of labeled arrows. The diagram shows various relations among these entities, such as opposition between pairs of forces acting in opposite directions. Chi, Feltovich, and Glaser (1981) have shown that abstract concepts such as conversion of momentum are salient for expert physicists when they are asked to classify problems into groups and when they are deciding on a method for solving a problem. McDermott and Larkin (1978) have simulated the process of forming representations based on abstract conceptual entities, such as forces.

I will discuss two specific examples in which representation using conceptual entities enable general reasoning procedures to be used. In both of these examples, the general procedures involve relationships between quantities that can be considered as parts of a whole. Tables 10.1 and 10.2 show partial protocols that were kindly made available by D. P. Simon and H. A. Simon. They were among the protocols obtained from a novice and an expert subject working on problems from a high school text (Simon & Simon, 1978). The problem for these protocols was the following: "An object is dropped from a balloon that is descending at a rate of four meters per sec. If it takes 10 sec for the object to reach the ground, how high was the balloon at the moment the object was dropped?"

In the novice's protocal, shown in Table 10.1, the process was one of search guided by a formula. Quantities in the problem text were interpreted as the values of variables. The subject applied some general constraints, such as a requirement that distances have positive values, but the protocol lacks evidence that velocities and accelerations functioned as conceptual entities.

In the expert's protocol, Table 10.2, there is a rather clear example of a conceptual entity, the "total additional velocity." The expert apparently represented the velocity that would be achieved at the end of a 10-sec fall as the sum of two components: the initial velocity, and the amount that would be added during the fall. The added amount can be found easily, because it is proportional to the time. Then the velocity at the end of the fall was found by combining its two components. The average velocity during the fall, needed to compute the distance, was found by averaging the initial and terminal velocities. Finally, the distance was found by multiplying the average velocity by the given duration.

A reasonable interpretation of this solution is that three general procedures for making quantitative inferences were used. One is a procedure for finding a whole quantity by adding its parts together. The second is a procedure that finds the average value of a quantity that undergoes linear change. The third is a procedure that finds the total amount of a quantity by multiplying its average rate during a time interval by the duration of the interval. All of these procedures correspond to physics formulas, but there is no evidence in the protocol that formulas were used in the solution. A plausible hypothesis is that the solution was obtained by forming representations of quantities that served as arguments for general inferential procedures. That inference seems particularly well justified in the case of the "total additional velocity," a quantity for which there is no specific variable in the formulas that are usually given.

Another example from physics is in the discussion in this volume by Larkin, regarding the loop-the-loop problem that deKleer (1975) discussed earlier.

TABLE 10.1
Novice Protocol

1. "An object dropped from a balloon descending at 4 meters per second."
2. 4 meters per second is v zero.
3. "lands on the ground 10 seconds later."
4. t equals 10 seconds.
5. "What was the altitude of the balloon at the moment the object was dropped?"
6. Now we want s equals v zero times the time plus one half of . . .
7. . . . a equals g equals in this case, minus 32. . . .
8. Oh, minus 9 point 8 meters a second.
9. It's descending at the rate of 4 meters per second.
10. One half g t squared,
11. that equals v zero,
12. which is 4,
13. times 10,
14. plus one half of minus 9 point 8,
15. equals minus 4 point 9 times,
16. . . . . Oh, we're going to come out with a minus number?
17. It was descending at 4 meters per second.
18. Oh, great.
19. "How high was the balloon?"
20. "An object dropped from a balloon descending at 4 meters per second"
21. "lands on the ground 4 seconds later."
22. It was already going. . . .
23. The initial velocity was 4 and not zero, that's it.
24. minus 4 point 9 times 100,
25. But this is its absolute . . . um . . .
26. We want its absolute value, don't we?
27. That equals 40 minus 49 hundred, that, obviously. . . .
28. . . . 4 . . . 4 hundred and 90 . . .
29. . . . 'cause it drops. . . .
30. Its initial velocity was 4. . . .
31. and starting from zero,
32. Now we've got something we really don't know how to handle.
33. Now we really don't know how to handle this.
34. Because it doesn't start from zero;
35. it started from 4 meters per second,
36. and the first second accelerates . . . so each one . . .
37. that initial velocity . . . starts at 4 and not zero.
38. So, I think it's 40 plus, because although it's a negative . . .
39. no, no, it's increasing.
40. Oh no, it's increasing, it's not slowing down.
41. Okay. So the distance equals 40 plus 4 hundred and 90
42. equals 5 hundred and 30 meters.
43. That's my answer.

TABLE 10.2
Expert Protocol

1. "An object dropped from a balloon descending at 4 meters per second.
2. lands on the ground 10 seconds later.
3. What was the altitude of the balloon at the moment the object was dropped?"
4. So it's already got a velocity of 4 meters per second
5. and it accelerates at 9.8 meters per second per second
6. so its final velocity 10 seconds later,
7. well, let's say its total additional velocity 10 seconds later
8. would be 98 meters per second per second
9. and that . . . ah . . . plus the 4 that it had to start with
10. would be 102 meters per second per second
11. so its average velocity during that period
12. would be 106 over 3 or 53 . . . ah . . . 53 meters per second
13. and at 10 seconds that would mean it had dropped 530 meters.

Larkin notes that in place of the sequential envisionment procedure that deKleer described and analyzed, experts frequently represent the problem using the conservation of energy. In this representation, there is a quantity, the total energy, that remains constant. The total energy is made up of two components: the potential energy (associated with height) and the kinetic energy (associated with speed). As the ball moves downward, potential energy is converted to kinetic energy, which is then reconverted to potential energy as the ball moves up the other side. The requirement of the problem is satisfied if the amounts involved in the two phases are equal.

A reasonable interpretation of this solution includes another general inferential procedure involving additive combinations. If a whole quantity is constrained to be a constant, then one of its parts can be increased by a transfer from the other part. The use of a general procedure for inferring quantitative changes based on that principle in the loop-the-loop problem seems a reasonable conjecture.

Distance, Time, and Velocity

The interpretation that I proposed in the last section regarding expert problem solving in physics includes conceptual entities that are available as arguments for general methods of reasoning. A question that arises is how representational knowledge of that kind is acquired. Some suggestive findings were obtained in an instructional study conducted at Indiana University in 1967 (Greeno, 1976). The suggestion is that new conceptual entities can be acquired when procedures are learned that use those entities as arguments.

In the experiment, seventh-grade students were given instruction in solving problems about simple motion using the formula: distance = speed × time. Different groups received differing pretraining prior to the instruction. The pretraining that was effective included training in two kinds of procedures. One was observational: students were shown examples of simple linear motion and were given procedures for manipulating distance and velocity and for measuring distance and time. The other procedures were computational: students had practice in calculating one of the three quantities given the other two. Results of the study suggest that from these experiences students acquired representational knowledge in which distance, duration, and velocity were conceptual entities about which the students could reason in a direct, flexible manner.

The experiment took place in three consecutive daily sessions. In the first session a pretest was given. The second session was an instructional treatment that varied among groups of students. In the third session all of the students received some instruction in solving problems about motion and a posttest was given.

The instructional group of greatest interest was given experience with simple motion in a setup shown in Fig. 10.7. Model railroad tracks were marked at one-foot intervals. A timer, visible to the students, ran as an engine moved along the track. Velocity was variable from .5 to 3 feet per sec. A regulator was available to the students for one of the tracks.

In the instruction, a series of problems was presented to groups of four or five students. In each problem, two of the three quantities—distance, velocity, and duration—were given, and students calculated the third. When the unknown was distance or velocity, students performed the operations that determined the quantity, either by adjusting the transformer or by placing the photocell that stopped the timer. Each result was tested by running an engine. The correspondence between distance and time was noted as the engine moved along the track, a

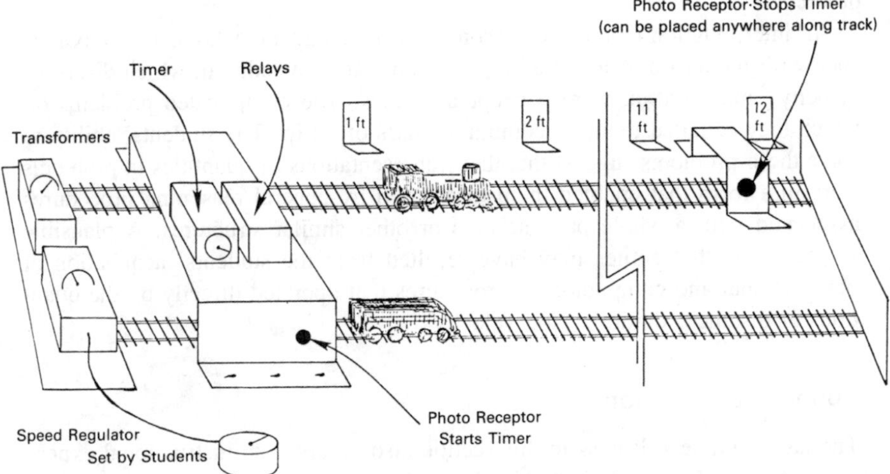

Fig. 10.7. Apparatus for distance-duration-velocity demonstrations (from Greeno, 1976).

record of results on all the problems was kept, and results of different combinations of quantities were discussed. A few problems with two engines moving simultaneously at different velocities were given at the end of the session.

The effect of this experience was compared with two other instructional groups and a control group. The other two instructional groups received experience of a more mathematical kind, involving the inverse relation of multiplication and division or use of ratios in solving problems. The fourth group went to a study hall.

The instruction that all students received on the third day was a straightforward presentation of the formula, distance = speed x time, with examples of its use in solving simple problems.

The tests that were given before and after instruction consisted of seven problems. Three were easy, requiring calculation of one of the three quantities from the other two, for example, "A man drove at a speed of 60 mile per hour for 4 hours. How far did he drive?" The other four problems were more complicated, requiring analysis of motions into components, either of durations or of distances. An example is, "The distance between Bloomington and Chicago is 240 miles, and there are two airline flights between the two cities. One flight is nonstop and takes 1½ hours. The other flight stops for ½ hour in Terre Haute, but also takes 1½ hours. How fast does each plane fly?" Pretest and posttest problems were variants of each other, involving different kinds of moving objects and different numbers.

The best posttest performance was given by the group with experience with the model trains. On the four complicated test problems, that group improved by an average of 1.21 problems between pretest and posttest, the control group improved by .57 problems, and the other instructional groups improved by .21 problems.

An interpretation that seems reasonable is that students who received experience with model trains acquired representational knowledge in which distance, velocity, and duration were conceptual entites. The complicated problems on which they excelled required combining parts of a trip. The students' ability to solve these problems suggest that their representations of quantities in problems were in a form that enabled them to be used by general reasoning procedures associated with a whole parts schema or other similar structures. A plausible conjecture is that entites may have resulted from the students' acquisition of observational and computational procedures that operated directly on the quantities of distance, duration, and velocity.

Sound Transmission

The last example I discuss in this section also involves an instructional experiment. This study was motivated by discussions of mental models as mechanisms of reasoning. In analyses such as Stevens and Collins' (1978) discussion of inferential reasoning about weather, knowledge about the detailed internal structure of processes enables individuals to generate conjectures about the behaviors of the processes in new conditions. In a study in which I collaborated with Gregg T. Vesonder and Amy K. Majetic, we investigated the question whether instruction regarding the detailed causal structure of sound transmission would enhance students' ability to reason about properties of that process. A full report of this experiment is available in another study (Greeno, Vesonder, & Majetic, in prep.).

We designed two instructional units about transmission of sound. One was patterned after the usual textbook sequence, focusing on amplitude and frequency of sound waves. We refer to this instruction as a Steady-State unit, since it focused on temporal properties of sound waves at a single point in space: alternating compressions and rarefactions varying in amplitude and frequency. We gave a simpler discussion than is often used in texts. We made no attempt to discuss longitudinal waves, restricting our discussion to transverse waves consisting of alternating compressions are rarefactions. We also related the properties of waves to concrete phenomena, using a guitar to produce tones varying in loudness and pitch. The mechanism of transmission was discussed, mainly in the context of these properties. A Slinky toy was used to show transmission of a transverse wave, and a piece of plastic foam with dots painted on it was used to model compressions and rarefactions. Waves with varying amplitudes and frequencies were illustrated with both of these models and related to differing sounds made with a guitar.

We refer to the other instructional unit that we designed as a Transmission unit. It focused on the causal mechanism of sound transmission. The idea of a pulse was modeled using a row of dominoes and was reinforced using a tube covered on both ends with balloon rubber, so that pressing on one end caused the other end to bulge. A Slinky toy was used to show a pulse moving through a medium, and foam rubber with painted dots was used to model compression of molecules. Finally, a shallow round dish containing water was used to show that a pulse moving from the center is distributed over a greater area and therefore becomes weaker at any single point. After showing all these aspects of transmitting a pulse, we discussed sound waves as alternating increases and decreases in pressure caused by a vibrating source, and illustrated the effects of that with each of the models.

Our two instructional units can be considered as containing a common core of information, elaborated in different ways. The common information was about the components of sound transmission: the requirements of a source, a medium, and a detector, and some basic causal relations involving vibrations, compressions, and rarefactions. In the Steady-State unit, this information was elaborated by discussing attributes of sounds, identifying properties of pitch and loudness that vary between different sounds and relating these to variables of frequency and amplitude in the theoretical system of sound transmission.

In the Transmission unit, the basic information was elaborated by a more detailed discussion of the causal mechanism of sound, using the simpler case of a pulse to make the causal system easier to understand. This instruction was designed to teach the microstructure of the causal system. We anticipated that this might enable students with Transmission instruction to reason more successfully about situations involving transmission of sound than their counterparts, whose instruction focused more on attributes and less on the causal structure. This anticipation was not borne out in the results.

We tested our sixth-grade student subjects by asking a set of 12 questions. Their answers were tape recorded and transcribed, and we evaluated them using an analysis of propositions that would constitute correct knowledge and understanding. We were particularly interested in four questions that required inferences about sound transmission. One involved a simple application of knowledge that sound will be softer at a greater distance. A second question required the inference that sound will not be transmitted through a vacuum, but that it will be transmitted through water. The other two questions required conjectures about rates of transmission: one that sound could travel faster through one medium than another, and the other that one form of energy might travel faster than another.

To our surprise, scores on these inferential questions were not significantly different among students who had different units of instruction. Indeed, students who received either or both units did not differ from students in a control condition who received neither unit. The trend favored the students in the Steady-State condition, in opposition to our expectation of an advantage due to the Transmission unit.

This finding was reinforced by a more detailed analysis of evidence for knowledge of specific propositions. We divided propositions into four sets, judging whether each proposition was included explicitly in the Transmission unit, the Steady-State unit, both units, or neither unit. On propositions that were in both units, there was a nearly significant difference favoring the Steady-State unit. On propositions that were in only the Transmission unit, students with only Steady-State instruction did as well as students with Transmission instruction. This was not a symmetric finding: on propositions that were only in the Steady-State unit, Steady-State students were much better than Transmission students.

The students' responses to questions suggested that most of them learned about the requirements for sound transmission: a source, a medium, and a receptor. All except four of the 20 students correctly said that sound would not be transmitted through a vacuum when air was pumped out of a jar with a bell in it. Thirteen of the 20 students correctly said that sound would be transmitted if the jar were filled with water. The number of correct answers about either the vacuum or the water did not depend on the instruction that students received.

On the two questions requiring conjectures about velocities of transmission, correct answers were given by only six, and four of the 20 students, and there was no relationship between the answers and the instruction that students had received. Apparently the knowledge that they acquired about sound did not make contact with their general concepts about faster or slower motion. Several students gave answers indicating that the concepts of source, medium, and receptor were applied in answering the questions. One question asked why lightning is seen before thunder is heard; six students conjectured that lightning occurs earlier. The other question asked why a train is heard sooner if your ear is close to the railroad track; 15 students conjectured that the rail becomes a source of sound, being caused to vibrate by the wheels of the train.

The conclusion that we reach is that both of our instructional units probably led to acquisition of conceptual entities corresponding to the components of sound transmission: a source, a medium, and a receptor. This acquisition did not seem to be strengthened substantially by explanation of the detailed causal structure of the system. Of course, we may have chosen poor questions in trying to tap that knowledge. The main opportunity to show improved performance require conjectures about speed of transmission, a global property. The difficulty could have been in children's making contact between their knowledge of sound and their general knowledge about motions with differing speeds, rather than a lack of representational knowledge about sound. Even so, we are led to conclude that knowledge of the detailed causal structure of a mechanism may not be as useful an instructional target as knowledge of attributes that are directly relevant to question-answering and other target tasks.

III. COMPUTATIONAL EFFICIENCY

The hypothesis that appropriate conceptual entities can enable more efficient computation is probably obvious. I present a single example in which the point is illustrated with unusual clarity.

Monster Problems

An example in which alternative representations of problems have been analyzed in detail is a set of puzzles about monsters and globes that are isomorphs of the Tower of Hanoi problem, analyzed by Simon and Hayes (1976). The entities that are involved in this example are sets of objects, and the procedures for which the entities are arguments are operations on sets, such as finding the largest member of a set.

Simon and Hayes classified problems into two categories, called Transfer and Change problems, which differ in the way that applicability of operators depends on attributes and entities. The distinction was very significant empirically: Change problems were about twice as difficult as Transfer problems.

To illustrate the problem categories, consider two problems in which there are three monsters each holding a globe. The monsters and globes both vary in size:

the sizes are small, medium, and large. Initially, the small monster holds the large globe, the medium monster holds the small globe, and the large monsters holds the medium globe. The goal is a situation in which the size of each monster matches the size of the globe that it is holding.

In the Transfer problem, globes are moved from monster to monster. Only one globe can be moved at a time, a monster can only give away its largest globe, and the transferred globe must be larger than any the receiving monster is holding prior to the transfer.

In the Change problem the sizes of globes are changed by shrinking and expanding. To change a globe from its initial size to some terminal size, the monster holding the globe must be the largest monster currently holding a globe of its initial size, and no larger monster may be holding a globe of its terminal size.

To explain the greater difficulty of Change problems, Simon and Hayes suggested a plausible hypothesis about the representation of states and operators. In the representation of a state: (1) there is a list of the monsters; (2) each monster's size is an attribute; (3) a list of the globes held by each monster is a second attribute; and (4) each globe's size is an attribute of the globe. The operator for the Transfer problems has the form Move(GS, MS1, MS2), which means "Move the globe of size GS from the monster of size MS1 to the monster of size MS2." The operator for the Change problems has the form Change(MS, GS1, GS2), which means, "Change the globe held by the monster of size MS from its present size GS1 to size GS2."

The problems differ in a way that involves conceptual entities. The list of globes held by each monster is an entity in the representation; the lists are included in the initial representation of the problem, and are modified after each change in the problem state. These entities are used directly in the Transfer problems. To test whether move(GS, MS1, MS2) can be applied, the solver retrieves the lists of globes held by monsters MS1 and MS2 and determines whether globe size GS is the largest of both sets. The corresponding test in the change problems does not use entities in the representation, and requires construction of lists that are to be tested. Testing applicability of change(MS, GS1, GS2) involves retrieving the monsters holding globes of size GS1 and GS2, and testing whether monster size MS is the largest of both of these sets. The sets have to be constructed, since the lists of monsters holding globes of the three sizes are not entities in the representation.

Simon and Hayes' suggested explanation has not been confirmed empirically, and they are continuing their experimental research on the problem (H. A. Simon, personal communication). There probably are several factors that contribute to the difference in difficulty between the two kinds of problems. Even so, their hypothesis is plausible and provides an especially clear example of the importance of conceptual entities in problem representation.

IV. PLANNING

The final hypothesis considered in this essay is that the ontology of a problem domain has important effects on goal definition and planning. This point is illustrated by results of another set of instructional studies.

Binomial Probability

In the early 1970s, Richard Mayer, Dennis Egan, and I conducted a series of experiments (Egan & Greeno, 1972; Mayer, 1974; Mayer & Greeno, 1972; Mayer, Stiehl, & Greeno, 1975) in which we gave instruction in the formula for binomial probability:

$$P(R|N) = \binom{N}{R} p^R (1\text{-}p)^{N-R},$$

where N is a number of trails, R is a number of success outcomes, and p is the probability of success on each trial. The studies involved comparisons between alternative instructional conditions. In most of the experiments we compared two sequences of expository instruction. One sequence focused attention on calculation with the binomial formula. The other sequence emphasized meanings of concepts, providing definitions of variables in relation to general experience and giving explanations about how the concepts combine to form components of the formula. The conceptual instruction discussed outcomes of trials and sequences of trials with different outcomes, and defined the probability of R successes as the sum of probabilities of the different sequences that include R successes. We also compared expository learning that emphasized the formula with discovery learning, and obtained similar results to those we found with formula and conceptual emphases.

Our interpretation of these studies was that conceptual expository instruction and instruction by discovery led to knowledge that was more strongly connected to the students' general knowledge than the knowledge that was acquired in expository instruction that emphasized the formula. That still seems a correct interpretation, but a more specific hypothesis may be warranted. It seems likely that conceptual instruction and discovery learning may have facilitated formation of conceptual entities corresponding to the variables and that these were less likely to be acquired by students whose instruction emphasized calculation with the formula.

Several of the findings of our experiments are consistent with this interpretation. First, students with conceptual or discovery instruction were able to solve story problems nearly as easily as they could solve problems with information presented in terms of the variables of the formula, whereas for students with formula instruction story problems were considerably more difficult. This is consistent with the idea that conceptual entities facilitate interpretation of problem information in novel contexts.

Three further findings can be interpreted as indications that conceptual entities facilitate planning. First, some of the problems that we presented had inconsistent or incomplete information and hence were unsolvable. For example, one problem gave $R = 3$, $N = 2$, and $p = ½$ and asked for $P(R|N)$. The information is inconsistent, because there cannot be more successes than trials. The students with conceptual instruction identified these as unsolvable problems more frequently than students with formula instruction. Students with conceptual instruction also were better at solving problems in which the probability of a specific sequence of outcomes was requested, rather than the probability of a number of success outcomes. We called a third kind of problem Luchins problems, because Luchins (1942) studied performance on similar problems extensively. These were problems in which the answer could be found by simple direct means, but if students tried to apply formulas they could be led into a complicated sequence of fruitless calculations. An example was the following: "You play a game five times in which the probability of winning each time is .17, and the probability of winning three games out of five is .32. What is the total number of successes plus the total number of failures?" Luchins problems were almost as easy as ordinary problems about binomial probability for students who had discovery learning, but they were much harder than ordinary problems for students with expository learning.

All three of these findings are consistent with the idea that a representation with conceptual entities corresponding to the variables enables a problem solver to reason directly about the quantities rather than simply through the medium of the formula. The conceptual instruction gave more emphasis to discussion of sequences of their outcomes and their properties. Thus, it seems likely that in conceptual instruction, students gained representational knowledge enabling them to interpret problems and questions in terms of individual sequences when that was appropriate. This would provide information that could be used directly to determine the problems were incoherent, to identify problem goals involving individual sequences rather than the quantity given by the binomial formula, and to find direct solution methods.

V. CONCLUSIONS

In this essay I have explored hypotheses about ways in which representational knowledge can influence problem solving. The discussion has been focused on effects of an aspect of representation that I have referred to as the ontology of a problem domain, the kinds of conceptual entities that are included in representations of problem situations. I have presented interpretations of several empirical findings and theoretical analyses that indicate four ways in which ontology can influence problem solving: by facilitating the formation of analogies between domains, by enabling use of general reasoning procedures, by providing efficiency, and by facilitating planning.

The idea of problem ontology raises significant issues relevant to instruction and the acquisition of cognitive skill. It seems important to design instruction so that students will acquire the conceptual entities that are needed for representing problems in the domain, as well as acquiring the procedures needed to make the calculations and inferences required for solving problems. Three studies described in this essay provided evidence of successful instruction that can be interpreted as acquisition of conceptual entities. In each of these the procedures that were taught were related to other information of various kinds. In mapping instruction for arithmetic, the procedure of multidigit subtraction with numerals was related to an analogous procedure of subtraction with place-value blocks. In instruction for solving problems about simple motion, the procedures for calculating answers were related to observational experience and procedures for manipulating and measuring values of the variables. And in instruction for solving problems using the binomial formula, the instruction that led to better understanding provided relationships between the computational formula and general concepts of trials, outcomes, and sequences. These findings suggest a general principle: perhaps the acquisition of cognitive entities is most effective when variables in procedures are related to other entities in cognitive structure. The kinds of relationships that can be useful in this way are clearly quite variable; on the other hand, we cannot expect everything to work, as evidenced by the results of our experiment on sound transmission. A detailed theory of learning will be required to characterize the favorable conditions specifically, but it seems reasonable to propose that the acquisition of the ontology of a domain is one of the significant issues to be addressed in our study of learning processes.

ACKNOWLEDGMENT

This research was supported by the Personnel and Training Research Programs, Office of Naval Research, under Contract Number N00014-79-C-0215. Contract Authority Identification Number NR 667-430.

REFERENCES

Anderson, J. R., Greeno, J. G., Kline, P. J., & Neves, D. M. Acquisition of problem-solving skill. In J. R. Anderson (Ed.), *Cognitive skills and their acquisition.* Hillsdale, N.J.: Lawrence Erlbaum Associates, 1981.

Bobrow, D. G., & Winograd, T. An overview of KRL, a knowledge representation language. *Cognitive Science,* 1977, *1,* 3–46.

Brown, J. S., & Burton, R. R. Diagnostic models for procedural bugs in basic mathematical skills. *Cognitive Science,* 1978, *2,* 155–192.

Chi, M. T. H., Feltovich, P., & Glaser, R. Categorization and representation of physics problems by experts and novices. *Cognitive Science,* 1981, *5,* 121–152.

deKleer, J. *Qualitative and quantitative knowledge in classical mechanics* (Tech. Rep. AI-TR-352). Cambridge, Mass.: Artificial Intelligence Laboratory, Massachusetts Institute of Technology, December 1975.

Egan, D. E., & Greeno, J. G. Acquiring cognitive structure by discovery and rule learning. *Journal of Educational Psychology,* 1972, *64,* 86–97.

Greeno, J. G. Some preliminary experiments on structural learning. In J. M. Scandura (Ed.), *Structural learning II. Issues and approaches.* New York: Gordon and Breach Science Publishers, Inc., 1976.

Greeno, J. G., Vesonder, G. T., & Majetic, A. K. *Conveying knowledge about a process.* In preparation.

Luchins, A. S. Mechanization in problem solving: The effect of Einsrellung. *Psychological Monographs,* 1942, *54* (6, Whole No. 248).

Mayer, R. E. Acquisition processes and resilience under varying testing conditions for structurally different problem-solving procedures. *Journal of Educational Psychology,* 1974, *66,* 644–656.

Mayer, R. E., & Greeno, J. G. Structural differences between learning outcomes produced by different instructional methods. *Journal of Educational Psychology,* 1972, *63,* 165–173.

Mayer, R. E., Stiehl, C. C., & Greeno, J. G. Acquisition of understanding and skill in relation to subjects' preparation and meaningfulness of instruction. *Journal of Education Psychology,* 1975, *67,* 331–350.

McDermott, J., & Larkin, J. H. Representing textbook physics problems. In *Proceedings of the Second National Conference, Canadian Society for Computational Studies of Intelligence.* Toronto, Canada: University of Toronto, 1978.

Resnick, L. B. A developmental theory of number understanding. In H. P. Ginsburg (Ed.), *Children's Knowledge of arithmetic,* in press.

Simon, D. P., & Simon, H. A. Individual differences in solving physics problems. In R. S. Siegler (Ed.), *Children's thinking: What develops?* Hillsdale, N.J.: Lawrence Erlbaum Associates, 1978.

Simon, H. A., & Hayes, J. R. The understanding process: Problem isomorphs. *Cognitive Psychology,* 1976, *8,* 165–190.

Stevens, A. L., & Collins, A. *Multiple conceptual models of a complex system.* (BBN Report No. 3923). Cambridge, Mass.: Bolt Beranek and Newman, Inc., August 1978.

Wertheimer, M. *Productive thinking* (Enlarged ed.). N.Y.: Harper & Row, 1959, (originally published 1945).

11 Using the Method of Fibres in Mecho to Calculate Radii of Gyration

Alan Bundy
Lawrence Byrd
University of Edinburgh

I. INTRODUCTION

This chapter describes recent developments in the Mecho project. The aim of the project is to build a computer program, Mecho, which solves Mechanics problems stated in English, in order to understand how it is possible for experienced mathematicians to form a formal specification of a problem (e.g. equations) from an informal specification (e.g. English sentences). We hope that building this computer program will serve as a vehicle for gaining a detailed understanding of the processes involved, and that this enhanced understanding will suggest improvements in the teaching of Mechanics. A summary of the project can be found in (Bundy, Byrd, Luger, Mellish, Milne, & Palmer, 1979).

The Mecho program can solve problems from a wide range of areas of Mechanics, e.g., pulleys, motion under constant acceleration, levers, motion on a smooth path, statics, Hooke's law, etc. We draw our examples from English, GCE A-level, applied mathematics papers, intended for 16–18 year old pre-university entrants. We are constantly attempting to extend Mecho to new areas of Mechanics, especially those that require new kinds of problem solving or knowledge representation techniques.

Cohen (1974) identifies a method of solving Mechanics problems which he calls the Fibres heuristic. It consists of dividing a body into an infinite collection of subbodies and considering a typical one of these. In this chapter we describe work in progress to extend the Mecho program so that it is capable of applying the method of Fibres.

The standard technique for calculating the radius of gyration of a complex body is a classic application of the method of Fibres. We chose it as a suitable domain for the study of this method. The radius of gyration is a property of a body spinning on an axis which is useful for calculating the body's moment of inertia about the axis. The moment of inertia, I, of the body is the sum over all the particles which make up the body of $m.r^2$ where m is the mass of the particle and r is its perpendicular distance from the axis. The radius of gyration, k, is chosen so that

$$M.k^2 = I$$

where M is the mass of the whole body.

The standard technique for calculating k is

To divide the body into an infinite collection of subbodies, which we will call fibres, in such a way that the radius of gyration of each fibre with respect to the axis is easier to calculate than the radius of gyration of the whole body.

Calculate the moment of inertia of each fibre.

Using integration calculate the moment of inertia and hence the radius of gyration of the whole body.

The hard parts of extending Mecho to deal with these problems were:

Representing the division of a body into an infinite collection of fibres.

Automatically choosing a division which facilitates the solution of the problem.

The solution to these problems forms the topic of the remainder of this chapter. Not surprisingly the solutions turn out to be intimately related.

II. CONTINUOUS MEASURE SYSTEMS

The key to the representation of a body as an infinite collection of fibres is the concept of a continuous measure system. A continuous measure system is used to measure an entity with the aid of a parameter varying between limits. It consists of 6 parts, which may be thought of as the entries in 6 slots of a frame. These parts are:

1. the entity on which the measure system is erected;
2. the parameter which constitutes the measure;
3. the subentity from which the measurements are made;
4. the fibre or typical subentity to which the measurements are made;
5. the first limit or initial value of the parameter and
6. the second limit or final value of the parameter.

We will represent a continuous measure system with a 6 argument predicate, cont-meas(Entity,Parameter,Origin,Fibre,Limit1,Limit2).

Continuous measure systems are useful, not just in radius of gyration problems, but wherever a measuring parameter is erected on an entity. We will give some examples from various problem areas.

Circular Disc

Let dsc be a 2 dimensional, circular disc with radius a and centre c. Let dsc be divided into an infinite collection of concentric rings with centre c and radius r0, and let typ-ring be a typical such ring (see Fig. 11.1). Then the situation is described by the assertion

cont-meas(dsc,r0,c,typ-ring,0,a)

together with various assertions describing the shapes of dsc, c and typ-ring and their relations to r0 and a.

point(c)	
disc(dsc)	ring(typ-ring)
centre(dsc,c)	centre(typ-ring,c)
radius(dsc,a)	radius(typ-ring,r0)

Time Period

Let 1st-session be a period of time and suppose we wish to associate times measured on a clock with each moment of the period. The conventional way to do this is to measure in hours, minutes and seconds from the previous midnight, thus the moment, midnight, forms the origin. If the 1st-session starts at 9.45 and lasts until 11.55 and if t is the time of some typical moment, typ-mom, then the situation (see Fig. 11.2) is described by the assertion

cont-meas(1st-session,t,midnight,typ-mom,9.45,11.55)

together with various assertions describing the nature of 1st-session, midnight and typ-mom and their relation to t, 9.45 and 11.55.

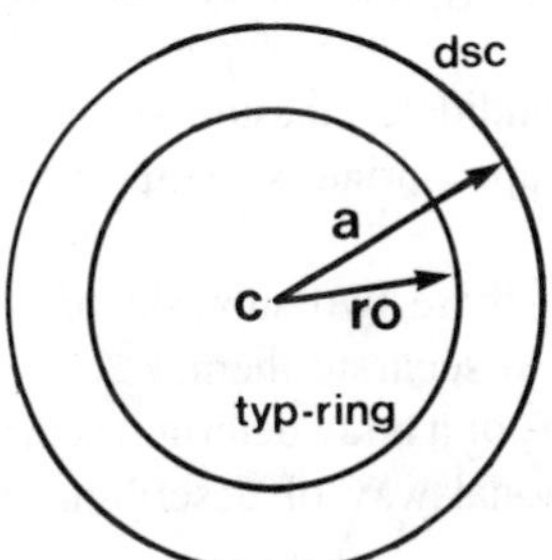

Fig. 11.1. A circular disc divided into an infinite collection of rings.

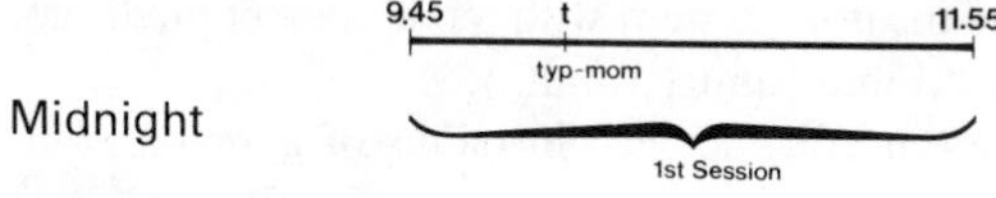

Fig. 11.2. A time period divided into an infinite collection of moments.

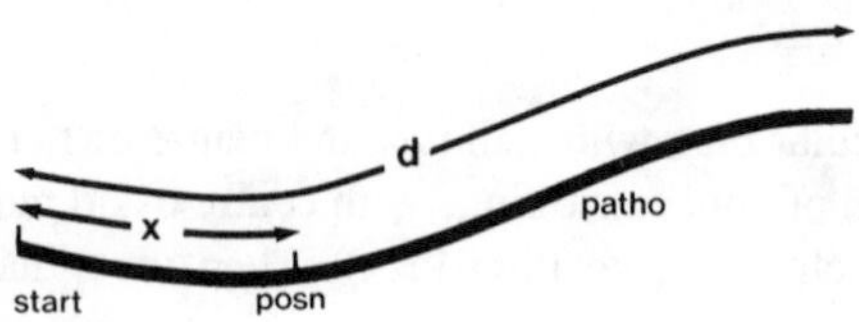

Fig. 11.3. The trajectory of a particle showing its typical position.

Trajectory of Particle

Suppose $path_0$ is the trajectory of a particle. Let start be the initial position of the particle and posn be its position at some arbitrary moment in time. Let the distance along $path_0$ from start to posn be x and the distance to the end of $path_0$ be d then the situation (see Fig. 11.3) is partially described by the assertion

cont-meas($path_0$,x,start,posn,0,d)

III. CHOOSING CONTINUOUS MEASURE SYSTEMS

The division of a body into an infinite collection of fibres can be represented using the cont-meas predicate. We now turn to the problem of choosing a division which facilitates the calculation of a radius of gyration.

For any given entity, especially a 2 or 3 dimensional one, there are several ways of erecting a continuous measure system on it, i.e., several ways of dividing it into an infinite collection of fibres. Fig. 11.4 shows how a disc may be divided into a series of concentric rings or radial, horizontal or vertical lines.

The task of dividing a body into a collection of fibres, so that its radius of gyration can be calculated, consists of two subtasks:

the generation of candidate measure systems and
the choosing of an appropriate system.

In the Mecho program these two subtasks are interleaved, but for purposes of exposition it is useful to separate them.

Obviously, the shape of a body determines the ways in which it can be divided into fibres. The traditional way of describing the shape of a body is by using algebraic expressions in some coordinate system, for instance, a disc, of radius a, may be described with the expressions,

$0 \leq r \leq a$
$0 \leq \theta < 2.pi$
in polar coordinates

or by

$x^2 + y^2 \leq a^2$
in cartesian coordinates

Notice the central role of inequalities in these descriptions. Pairs of such inequalities can be used to define a system of fibres. Consider, for instance, the pair of inequalities,

$0 \leq r \leq a$

above. This allows r to vary between two limits, 0 and a. If we fix the value of r to, say, r0, by replacing these two inequalities with an equation between r and r0,

$0 \leq r \leq a$
$0 \leq \theta < 2.pi$
| $\quad 0 \leq r \leq a => r = r0$
v
$r = r0$
$0 \leq \theta < 2.pi$

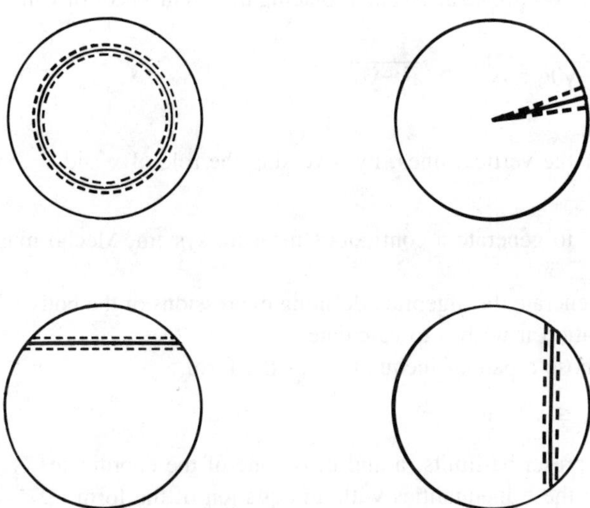

Fig. 11.4. Alternative measure system on a disc.

then the resulting equations define a ring with the same center as the disc, but radius r0. If this ring is regarded as a fibre of the disc and r0 as the parameter of a continuous measure system varying between 0 and a then we have generated the system of concentric rings (see Fig. 11.1 above.)

The system of radial lines can be generated by allowing the r coordinate to vary between 0 and a, but fixing the θ coordinate at say, θ0, that is by replacing the second pair of inequalities in the polar definition of a disc with an equation between θ and θ0,

$0 \le r \le a$
$0 \le \theta < 2.pi$
$\quad 0 \le \theta < 2.pi \Rightarrow \theta = \theta 0$
V
$0 \le r \le a$
$\theta = \theta 0$

and using θ0 as the parameter of a continuous measure system.

The remaining systems of figure 3-1, the horizontal and vertical lines can be generated from the cartesian coordinate system. The same technique, of replacing a pair of inequalities by an equation, can be used provided the cartesian expressions are first rewritten into an appropriate form. For instance, the horizontal lines can be generated from

$$-\sqrt{a^2-y^2} \le x \le \sqrt{a^2-y^2}$$
$$-a \le y \le a$$

by fixing the y coordinate at y0 and replacing the occurrences of y in the limits of x by y0, i.e.

$$-\sqrt{a^2-y0^2} \le x \le \sqrt{a^2-y0^2}$$
$$y = y0$$

Similarly, for the vertical lines, by reversing the role of x and y above.

Therefore, to generate a continuous measure system, Mecho must

1. first, generate the algebraic defining expressions of the body whose radius of gyration it wishes to calculate;
2. then chose a pair of inequalities of the form

$$a \le v \le b \qquad \text{(i)}$$

   which prescribe limits, a and b, on one of the coordinates, v;
3. replace these inequalities with an equation of the form
   $v = v0$
   where v0 is the new parameter of the continuous measure system;

4. replace any occurrences of v elsewhere in the expression by v0;
5. recognize the type of object defined by these new algebraic expressions;
6. use this object as the fibre of the continuous measure system, v0 as the parameter and a and b as the limits.

Note that the fibres generated by this technique are always of one dimension less than the original body.

We have seen that step 2 of this process may involve manipulating the algebraic description of a body so that a pair of inequalities with the form of (i) is produced. Some algebraic manipulation may also be required at step 5 to put the new expressions into a form which may be recognised as the standard algebraic description of a body. The current version of Mecho does no algebraic manipulation at step 2, but does translate the coordinate system at step 5, if necessary, to put the new expressions into standard form. For instance, when finding the radius of gyration of a sphere about a diameter, Mecho divides the sphere into a system of parallel discs and then moves the coordinate origin to the point where the diameter intersects the plane of the typical disc.

Given that it is possible to generate a wide range of measure systems for a body, how can one be chosen which will facilitate the calculation of the radius of gyration? Mecho employs two tests that either weed out or postpone consideration of those measures systems that it considers are unlikely to lead to success.

The first test is designed to postpone consideration of any fibre whose radius of gyration is not already known, e.g., in the case of the disc, the system of concentric rings passes the test because the radius of gyration of a ring with respect to a perpendicular axis is known to Mecho. Mecho makes two passes at choosing the fibres: in the first it tries to find a fibre whose radius of gyration is already known; in the second it relaxes this constraint and allows a recursive process of solution. This recursive process will terminate because a fibre is always of dimension one less than the body it is part of.

The second test ensures that the thickness of the fibre in the parameter dimension is constant. This test was introduced to eliminate various conceptual difficulties in the calculation of radii of gyration reported in earlier versions of this study. It is discussed more fully in the next section.

IV. UNIFORMITY

The investigation of radii of gyration problems uncovered two conceptual difficulties, whose resolution required a deep analysis of the assumptions underlying the solution process.

The first conceptual difficulty is the necessity to idealize a fibre in two different ways, for instance as both a 1 dimensional and a 2-dimensional object. Consider the system of concentric rings in a disc in Fig. 11.4 shown earlier. In order to calculate the mass of one of these rings it is necessary to regard it as having a nonzero area and hence a nonzero thickness of d(r0). Thus, the ring is idealized as a 2-dimensional object. However, in order to calculate the ring's radius of gyration this thickness must be neglected and the ring seen as a 1-dimensional object. Not to do so would necessitate the calculation of the radius of gyration of an annulus—a special case of a disc—and the problem solver would descend into an infinite regress. Similar difficulties arise in all these problems. In the personal experience of both authors, as school students, this "double thinking" was a stumbling block when learning how to solve these problems. The second conceptual difficulty concerns the generation of continuous measure systems. Consider the system of radial lines in Fig. 11.4. Although this is one of the measure systems generated by our technique (by freezing the Θ coordinate) it cannot be used in the calculation of the radius of gyration of the disc, because it would lead to the wrong answer. In fact, a continuous measure system obtained by freezing the Θ coordinate seems only to be useful when the body being subdivided is 1 dimensional. The problem is that the area of the line fibre is not uniformly distributed along its length. The fibre is more accurately idealized as a narrow sector (see Fig. 11.5). However, since the sector is a special case of the disc, using this idealization would at best lead to a nonoptimal solution and might plunge the problem solver into an infinite regress.

This difficulty seems to be avoided in Mechanics textbooks by not considering this way of subdividing a body. We have found no explanation of why such subdivisions should not be used and think it likely that the unprepared student may easily try to use them. In this case (s)he will require a principled explanation of why they fail to generate the correct answers.

The explanation embodied in the current version of Mecho is that, initially, fibres have the *same* dimensionality as the body they compose, that is, in the formation of a measure system from the algebraic defining expressions of a body a pair of inequalities of the form

$$a \leq v \leq b$$

are initially replaced by the inequalities

$$v0 \leq v \leq v0 + d(v0)$$

where d(v0) is an infinitesimal quantity, rather than the equation

$$v = v0$$

(Compare the prescription on p. 258.) Thus the concentric rings and radial lines are to be considered, initially, as 2-dimensional objects: annuli and sectors respectively: albeit with one infinitesimal dimension. This infinitesimal dimension can only be neglected if the fibres are of uniform thickness in the parameter dimension. The concentric rings pass this test as they have uniform thickness

Fig. 11.5. A circular disc divided into an infinite collection of sectors.

d(r0), but the radial lines fail the test as they have a thickness r.d(Θ0), which increases with r.

A fibre is no use in the calculation of radii of gyration unless its infinitesimal thickness can be neglected. It leads to nonoptimal solutions or infinite regression. Thus nonuniform measure systems are rejected by Mecho and uniform ones re-idealized as being composed of fibres of one dimension less than the body they compose, i.e., the radial lines are rejected and the concentric rings are re-idealized as 1-dimensional rings by replacing

$$r0 \leq r \leq r0 + d(r0)$$

with

$$r = r0$$

Mecho's uniformity test is based on the knowledge that freezing angular coordinates, e.g., Θ, always leads to nonuniform fibres, unless the body being subdivided is 1 dimensional, in which case the fibre is trivially uniform. Freezing distance coordinates, e.g., r, x, etc., always leads to uniform fibres.

As a result of this re-idealization process, the mass per unit length of the concentric ring fibre can now be inferred to be d(r0).mu, where mu is the mass per unit area of the disc. Similar inferences can be made for other fibres. This enables both the mass and the radius of gyration of the ring fibre to be calculated from its 1-dimensional idealization, so eliminating the necessity for double idealization.

V. A WORKED EXAMPLE

Let us see how this process works in a particular case. We will show how Mecho can calculate the radius of gyration of a circular disc about a perpendicular axis through its centre. The problem is described to Mecho with a series of assertions.

```
disc(dsc).              center(dsc,c).     radius(dsc,a).
mass(dsc,m).            line(axis).
meets(axis,dsc,c).                         rad-of-gyr(dsc,axis,k).
given(a).               given(m).          sought(k).
```

The first three of these describe the disc whose radius of gyration is sought. They give the type of object, its radius and centre. The fourth gives it mass. The fifth and sixth describe the axis about which the radius of gyration is to be calculated and state (using the ''meets'' predicate) that it is perpendicular to the plane of the disc, intersecting it at point c. The seventh defines the radius of gyration itself. The last three assertions say which of the various quantities mentioned in the problems are to be solved for (i.e., k) and which quantities can be involved in the solution (i.e., a and m).

The standard techniques of Mecho, as described in Bundy et al., 1979, are then brought to bear. A list is made of the quantities whose value is sought, i.e., [k]. An equation is then formed for each of the quantities in this list in terms of the ''given'' quantities, if possible, otherwise the equations may introduce new ''intermediate'' unknowns. Currently, Mecho knows only two formula which contain a radius of gyration: the parallel axis theorem and the ''Fibre'' formula given below. It chooses the ''Fibre'' formula because the axis passes through the centre of gravity of the body.

```
isform(moment-of-inertia, situation(Obj,Axis,Fibre),
   M.RG^2 = integrate(Mf.RGF^2, A, B, X),
            (mass(Obj,M) &
            rad-of-gyr(Obj,Axis,RG) &
            cont-meas(Obj,X,Origin,Fibre,A,B) &
            mass(Fibre,Mf) &
            rad-of-gyr(Fibre,Axis,RGf)) ).
```

The predicate isform takes 4 arguments:

1. the name of the formula, 'moment of inertia';
2. the situation in which the formula is to be used, consisting of, the name of the object whose radius of gyration is sought, the axis about which it rotates and the fibre into which it is subdivided;
3. the formula itself, containing variables, M, RG, etc., which must be filled with the names of particular entities in order to make an equation[1] and
4. a conjunction of relations between these variables and the entities in the 'situation' argument slot.

Further explanation can be found in Bundy et al., 1979.

Filling in the variables of this formula to make an equation involves:

---

[1]Note that we are using the PROLOG convention where identifiers beginning with a capital letter are variables and the rest are constants

accessing the mass and radius of gyration of the disc from the initial assertions;

erecting a continuous measure system on the disc and

calculating the mass and radius of gyration of the fibre thus created.

The continuous measure system is chosen by inferring an algebraic description of the disc from its type and then applying the method described in section III. The first system discovered is the system of concentric rings. These rings are found to be uniform and the rings are re-idealized as 1-dimensional bodies. Using the Mecho schema system, (see Bundy et al., 1979), various assertions about the shape of a typical such ring are then put in the database.

```
ring(typ-ring).             centre(typ-ring,c).
radius(typ-ring,r0).        meets(axis,typ-ring,c).
```

The mass of the typical ring is now known and cannot be inferred by Mecho. However, because mass is a function of an object, Mecho knows that it can create a new intermediate unknown, mf, to fill the variable slot, and this is what it does. A subsequent round of equation forming is now needed to find an equation which solves for mf in terms of a, m and k.

A successful attempt is then made to calculate the radius of gyration of a ring. In fact, this is prestored in Mecho in the inference rule

```
ring(R) & centre(R,C) & radius(R,A) & meets(Axis,R,C)
-> rad-of-gyr(R,Axis,A)
```

which is satisfied by accessing the recently asserted facts about the typical ring.

If this information had not been prestored in Mecho, a new intermediate unknown could have been created to fill the variable in the equation, as with mf above. This would have initiated a recursive attempt to calculate the radius of gyration of a ring. It is nice that Mecho has this ability, but it should only be initiated as a last resort. Fortunately, Mecho discourages the introduction of new unknowns unless there is no alternative and the effect of this is that before creating one, Mecho first backtracks through the possible continuous measure systems looking for a fibre whose radius of gyration is already known. Thus an existing, general purpose, mechanism finds an unexpected application in helping to make a sensible choice of measure system for radius of gyration problems.

The result of all this inference is the "filled in" equation,

$$m.k^2 = \text{integrate}(mf.r0^2,\ 0,\ a,\ r0) \qquad \text{(ii)}$$

integrate is a four argument function of: the expression to be integrated; the lower and upper limits of integration and the variable to integrate with respect to.

Because equation (ii) could only be formed by introducing a new intermediate unknown, mf, an equation must now be formed which relates this unknown to the givens. The equation found by Mecho relates the mass of the ring to its mass per unit length and hence the mass per unit area of the disc.

```
isform(mass-per-length, situation(Obj),
    M = L.Mu,
    (mass(Obj,M) &
    length(Obj,L) &
    mass-per-length(Obj,Mu)) )
```

Filling in the variables in this formula to make an equation involves: accessing the mass of the ring, inferring its length and its mass per unit length.

The length of the ring is inferred using the inference rule.

```
ring(Ring) & radius(Ring,R) -> length(Ring,2.pi.R)
```

The mass per unit length of the ring is inferred to be the same as the infinitesimal thickness of the ring, d(r0), multiplied by the mass per unit area of the disc, but no further progress can be made, as this latter quantity is not known to Mecho. In consequence, the mass per unit area of the disc is introduced as a new unknown, mu.

The resulting equation is,

$$mf = 2.pi.r0.d(r0).mu \qquad \text{(iii)}$$

Finally, an equation must be formed which expresses the new unknown, mu, in terms of known quantities. Mecho decides to use the "mass-per-area" formula, a 2-dimensional version of the "mass-per-length" formula, with the disc playing the role of the Obj(ect). Filling in the variables in this version of the formula, involves: accessing the values of the mass and mass per unit area of the disc, and inferring the area of the disc from its type and radius. The resulting equation is,

$$m = pi.a^2.mu \qquad \text{(iv)}$$

Equations (ii), (iii) and (iv) are now passed to the algebra package Press, (Bundy & Welham, 1981), which has been extended by David Skinner to do symbolic integration (Skinner, 1981).

VI. CONCLUSION

We have shown that Mecho can be extended so that it is capable of using the method of Fibres identified by Cohen. Mecho has used the method to calculate the radius of gyration of a disc about a perpendicular axis through its centre, as described in section V above. It has also calculated the radii of gyration of several other objects, e.g., inclined line, solid and hollow sphere, cone, etc. We are exploring further applications of continuous measure systems and the method of Fibres.

Cohen himself might well pejoratively categorise Mecho's use of the Fibre method as "Formula Cranking." In (Cohen, 1974) he describes how the method can be used, in a highly imaginative way, to solve some hard problems, which he calls dragons. Mecho is not yet capable of solving such problems, but the current paper describes some of the ground work necessary to do so.

We have shown how the notion of dividing a body into an infinite collection of fibres can be represented using the concept of a continuous measure system (section II).

We have shown how such measure systems can be automatically generated and chosen (section III).

We have shown how the method can be smoothly integrated with the existing Mecho system (section V) to enable the calculation of the radii of gyration of some simple bodies.

What Mecho lacks, which prevents it from solving Cohen's dragons is a sophisticated idealization mechanism. Idealization is the process whereby complex real world objects, e.g., a milk bottle, are mapped to "ideal" objects, e.g., a cylinder, which Mecho can deal with, and in which certain properties, e.g., color, are neglected and others, e.g., pressure, are considered.

The radius of gyration problems are input in preidealized form, i.e., the objects involved are already ideal ones. Thus no idealization mechanism is called for. In other problems Mecho does do some simple idealization, but there is usually little ambiguity about what the idealization should be, nor is there any need for the idealization and problem solving processes to interact. Chris Mellish is currently investigating more sophisticated idealization mechanisms.

Extending Mecho to deal with radius of gyration problems has entailed a detailed investigation of the problem solving processes involved. As we saw in section IV, this investigation has uncovered conceptual difficulties in these processes and has suggested a principled way of avoiding the difficulties employing the notion of a uniform fibre. We hope our analysis may lead to the improvement of teaching in this area. The discovery of such applications is one of the major motivations of our work.

ACKNOWLEDGMENTS

Harvey Cohen's analysis inspired us to implement the Fibres method. Richard O'Keefe and Bob Fisher led us to the definition of uniformity. The work was supported by SRC grant GR/A/57954.

REFERENCES

Bundy, A., & Welham, B. Using meta-level inference for selective application of multiple rewrite rules in algebraic manipulation. *Artificial Intelligence*, 1981, *16(2)*.

Bundy, A., Byrd, L., Luger, G., Mellish, C., Milne, R., & Palmer, M. Solving Mechanics Problems Using Meta-Level Inference. In *Proceedings of 6th International Joint Conference of Artificial Intelligence*, Tokyo, 1979. (Also available from Edinburgh as DAI Research Paper No. 112.)

Cohen, H. A. *The art of snaring dragons*. Technical Report, La Trobe University, 1974. (A revised version of LOGO Working Paper No. 28 AI Lab MIT.)

Skinner, D. *A computer program to perform integration by parts*. Working Paper 103, Dept. of Artificial Intelligence, Edinburgh, 1981.

12 When Heat and Temperature Were One

Marianne Wiser
Susan Carey
Massachusetts Institute of Technology

There is now a large and exciting body of work on the differences between the beginners and the expert practitioners in some domain of science. The shift from naive to expert is a shift from one system of beliefs about the physical world to another, one set of concepts to another, one set of problem solving capabilities to another. As such, this shift resembles theory change in the history of science. As of yet, the two fields of study have made very little contact, although several chapters in this volume begin to bring the two endeavors together.

On the whole, work on the naive-expert shift has been characterized by two complementary approaches, both focusing on problem solving. First, the errors of novices while solving problems are diagnosed to reveal systematic misconceptions (e.g., Caramazza, McCloskey, & Green, 1981; Clement, in press; White, in press). Other data as well, such as interview protocols, provide further evidence for the misconceptions so revealed. In the second approach, the emphasis is on the information processing analyses of problem-solving procedures themselves, and how experts and novices differ in this regard (e.g., Larkin, McDermott, Simon, & Simon, 1980; Simon & Simon, 1978).

Novices' misconceptions are often interpreted as false beliefs. A crucial assumption underlies this interpretation: that the novice's concepts are the same as the expert's. The claim that the novice holds a false belief about "force" presupposes that both novice and expert have the same concept of force (the expert's concept) but attach different properties to it and relate it to other concepts differently. Indeed, if as we assume, the naive-expert shift involves the same kinds of conceptual change as does theory change in the history of science, we should expect the opposite. On some views of the history of science (e.g., Kuhn, 1962), it is a truism that the concepts of an earlier period differ from those of a later period.

Successive conceptual systems differ in three salient respects: (1) in their domain—the phenomena explained by the theory and the problems solved by it; (2) in their structure—the laws, models and other explanatory mechanisms, by which the system accounts for the phenomena in its domain; and (3) in their concepts. The chapters in this volume begin to focus on the nature of mental models and the comparison of the models of naive subjects and experts. Relatively little attention has been paid to the difference between successive conceptual systems at the level of individual concepts.

How, at the level of individual concepts, might successive conceptual systems differ? Later repertoires often include concepts not even available earlier (e.g., entropy, specific heat, inertia). But then in other cases, some version of the later concept is available to the earlier practioners; the crucial question is how concepts may differ in those cases where there is the clear relation "precursor." Historians of science and developmental psychologists alike appeal to one ubiquitous form of change at the level of individual concepts—differentiation. For example, Galileo's advances in mechanics involved drawing the distinction between instantaneous and average velocity. These distinctions did not come easily; in each case, making the distinction was part and parcel of a major theoretical change. Unfortunately, a precise characterization of differentiation is lacking not only at the dynamic level (i.e., understanding the process itself, its causes and time course) but even at the structural level (i.e., understanding the structure of the undifferentiated concept relative to its descendants). Developmental psychologists have appealed to vague metaphors (the embryological metaphor of Werner or the perceptual differentiation metaphor of Gibson) when describing differentiation. In both instances, the parent concept is seen as globally diffuse, an unstructured, syncretic whole, in which some of the properties of each descendant are present but are not distinguished or articulated. Such descriptions imply that the undifferentiated concept is different in kind from its descendants, and somehow deficient with respect to them. Also implied is that the relation between parent and descendant concepts can be understood irrespective of other concepts. Kuhn (1977a) provides a dramatically different picture of an undifferentiated concept—Aristotle's concept of velocity, which conflated the concepts of average and instantaneous velocity. According to Kuhn, whether a concept is differentiated from another or not can be judged only in the context of the theories in which the concepts are embedded. Aristotle's concept was undifferentiated in the sense that his physics required only one concept where today's physics requires two; otherwise, Aristotle's *velocity* was a theoretical concept in physics, in no way inferior to modern concepts such as *force* in Newtonian mechanics. Clearly, the notion *undifferentiated concept* requires further explication before it can be useful in the characterization of conceptual change.

There are, of course, other kinds of change at the level of individual concepts besides differentiation, e.g., coalescence and the shift from property to relation.

As an example of coalescence: In Einsteinian mechanics, the Newtonian categories of gravitational and inertial mass are collapsed into a single category. Similarly, Galileo collapsed the Aristotelian categories of natural and violent motion together, seeing that the distinction did not correspond to a real difference in nature. As an example of the shift from property to relation: Before Newton, weight was thought of as a property an object had intrinsically, i.e., independently of other objects. But according to Newtonian mechanics, an object's weight involves a relation between it and objects that exert a gravitational force on it. Obviously, pointing to examples of such changes at the level of individual concepts is not the same as providing an analysis of these "precursor" relations between successive concepts.

In this chapter we present part of an historical case study. We describe the theory change at all three levels—domain, model and individual concepts—and analyze the relations among these three levels of description. While we will raise more questions than we answer, we will conclude with implications for the study of the naive-expert shift.

The case we have chosen for study is the evolution of thermal theories, starting with the first systematic use of the thermometer by the Accademia del Cimento (Academy of Experiments) around 1650 and ending with Black around 1750. We chose this particular case for several reasons. First, it involves the beginning of a new science. Because the transition from naive to expert also involves the mastery of a new science (for the student) we felt that this case might be more relevant to the comparison of the two types of conceptual change than a case of transition between two advanced theories such as from Newtonian to Einsteinian mechanics. Second, although this case involves an early stage of theorizing, it happened late enough to be well documented. Third, and most important, is the claim that before Black, scientists did not distinguish between heat and temperature (cf. McKie & Heathcote, 1935). What evidence do historians of science consider relevant for such a claim? How can two concepts as different as heat and temperature *not* be distinguished? What single concept, encompassing heat and temperature, could there be? To our dismay, although historians of science, like developmental psychologists, speak about differentiation as a species of conceptual change, the secondary sources we could find did not answer these questions for us. We had to do a case study for ourselves.

This chapter is a report on one endpoint of the period of change—the beginning. To set the stage, we must briefly characterize the other end of the period—the conception of heat and temperature achieved by Black and held from him through the caloric theory of the 18th and 19th centuries, up to modern thermodynamics. We call the view of thermal phenomena common to the period from 1750 to the present "the modern view."

Central to the modern view is the principle of thermal equilibrium. When two bodies at different temperatures are left in contact long enough, the hotter one cools off and the colder one warms up until they eventually reach the same temperature. The equilibrium state is achieved through heat exchange: Heat leaves the warmer body and enters the cooler one. This conception of thermal equilibrium requires that heat and temperature be separate, and indeed, on the modern view, they are firmly distinguished. Temperature is an intensive variable, measured with a thermometer. It is measured at one spatial point of a body and is the same at all points (if the body is in thermal equilibrium with its environment). If two separate cups of water, each at 50°C are mixed together, the resulting water will also be at 50°C—such is one property of intensive physical quantities.

Heat on the other hand, is an extensive variable. One speaks of quantity, or amount, of heat, and measures it in units such as calories or BTUs. A calorie is the quantity of heat required to raise one gram of water from 0°C to 1°C. If 1 cup of boiling water melts 100g of snow, 2 cups of boiling water will melt 200g of snow—such is one property of extensive physical quantities.

Heat and temperature are not merely different kinds of physical entities—they are not even perfectly correlated. That is, it is not true that adding a given quantity of heat to a given mass (or volume) of any substance yields a fixed increase of temperature. This correlation breaks down in two ways, both discovered by Black. First, different substances have different specific heats. For example, less heat is required to raise 1 gram of mercury 1°C than to raise 1 gram of water 1°C. Second, even with a single substance, the correlation breaks down during phase changes (from solid to liquid, liquid to gas, and vice versa). These changes require heat input or output but take place at constant temperatures. In the modern view, then, a final respect in which heat and temperature are completely different is the role each plays in the characterization of phase changes. Stating these roles requires the concept of latent heat, the quantity of heat required to melt or boil substances.

Notice that the modern view, so characterized, is neutral with respect to the *nature* of heat and temperature. Black, who first articulated all of the elements of the modern theory sketched above, was expressly noncommittal and referred to heat as "this substance *or* modification of matter." Following Black came the caloric theory, in which heat was a fluid (caloric) and temperature the amount of caloric per molecule of substance, (corrected for specific and latent heat). And in modern thermodynamics, heat is a form of energy and temperature is the mean translational energy of the molecules of the substance.

Having seen what view Black achieved, let us return to the beginning. In this chapter we present the analysis of one document - the *Saggi di Naturali Esperienze dell' Accademia del Cimento.*[1] The Accademia del Cimento (Academy

[1]The *Saggi* have been translated into English twice, by Waller (1684), a contemporary of the Experimenters, and by Middleton (1971). Middleton's translation contains notes from unpublished diaries and interpretations of their intentions. However, Middleton has changed the Experimenter's

of Experiment) was a society formed under the financial and political support of Prince Leopold de Medici, and under the scientific leadership of the most eminent scientists and mathematicians of the Tuscany of the day. Its members called themselves the Experimenters. One, Viviani, had been Galileo's last student, and had performed, under Torricelli, the famous experiment showing that it was air pressure that supported a column of water or mercury in an inverted tube. The years after Torricelli and Galileo witnessed the development in Italy of both the thermometer and the barometer—the Experimenters were at the forefront of both developments.

The Experimenters did not state their thermal theory explicitly, they took most of their concepts and beliefs for granted; in this sense, the *Saggi* are more similar to a collection of experimental articles than to a physics textbook. Moreover, they constitute an extensive, spontaneous and unbiased protocol in which the Experimenters explained the rationale of their experiments and observations, described their experimental procedures and instrumentation, and accounted for their findings or lack thereof. From a protocol analysis of the *Saggi* we have abstracted the scope of their research, the models they used to understand thermal phenomena, and the concepts underlying their work. Whether we have correctly captured their conceptual framework is, of course, open to criticism. Our goal is to analyze the relation between the characterization of their model and the characterization of heat and temperature as undifferentiated concepts.

THE EXPERIMENTERS' ENTERPRISE

Middleton shows that insofar as the Experimenters had theoretical goals, they were carrying on Galileo's program of discrediting the neo-Aristotelian physics of the late middle ages. One example can give a flavor for this aspect of their work. Aristotle held heat and cold to be qualities, akin to hue. Just as the green of a green patch is intensified by being surrounded by red, Aristotle held that cold, surrounded by heat, was intensified, and vice-versa. He used this principle, called antiperistasis, to "explain" why caves were cool in hot weather and warm in cold weather. In the course of the Experimenter's endless descriptive studies on the effects of heat and cold on the expansion of water (see following), they noted that when a vessel such as A (Fig. 12.1) was immersed in a container of ice

---

usage in accord with the modern terms "heat" and "temperature." Waller, in contrast, did not have the modern concepts available to him; he faithfully uses "degree of heat," "temperament," and "heat" where the *Saggi* uses Italian equivalents. Waller's translation provides linquistic evidence about the Experimenter's concepts, in English, saving the necessity of learning to read 17th century Italian. Here, we report only our analysis of Waller's translation, although we began with, and were very much aided by, Middleton's. In our descriptions of the Experimenters' work, we will use "heat," "cold," "degree of heat," and "degree of cold" as we understand they would have done.

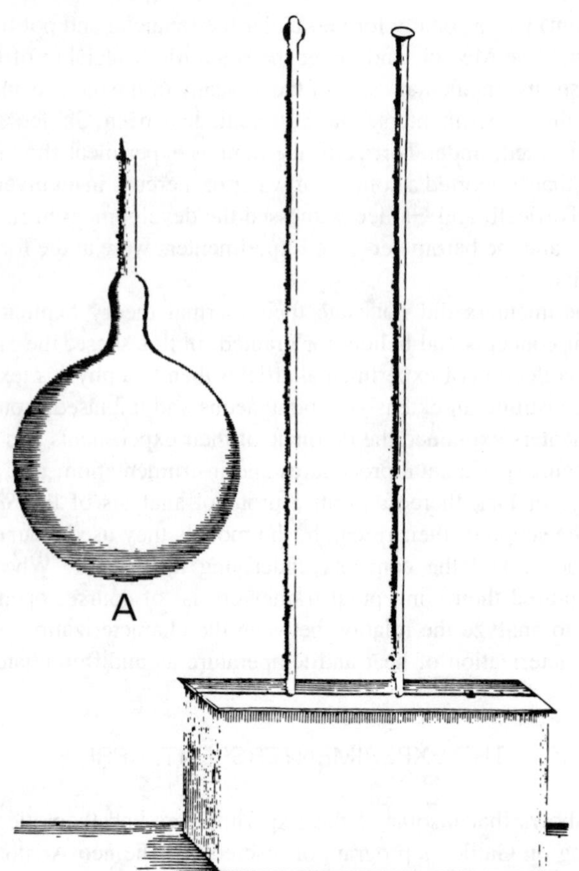

Fig. 12.1. The instruments used in the artificial freezing experiments.

water, the level of liquid first rose a small bit, then fell to a minimum, hovered for a short time, rose a bit, then shot up again as the water froze. (Their interest in the expansion of water in freezing was itself partly due to the Aristotelian flat denial of this fact.) The initial rise seemed consistent with the doctrine of antiperistasis—the liquid initially expanded upon being immersed in ice because the heat of the water was initially intensified by being surrounded by cold, and water was expanded by the heat. The reverse phenomenon was observed when the vessel was plunged into near boiling water; an initial fall preceeded the expected rise in water level. (Ask yourself for the correct explanation of this phenomenon before you go on the next paragraph.)

The Experimenters easily saw that the water only *appeared* to expand, because the cold contracted the glass container before it affected the water. The apparatus in Fig. 12.2 was used to show this was the correct explanation. Small hollow enamel balls were sealed with air in them so that they had approximately the same specific gravity as water. The Experimenters knew that cooling the water would make it more dense, causing the beads to rise; conversely, heating the water would dilate it, causing them to fall.

To show antiperistasis was not the correct explanation of the initial rise, the Experimenters plunged the container into a bath of ice water and observed that during the initial rise of the water level, there was no movement of the balls. The only movement of the balls was upwards as the water level subsequently began to fall. Therefore, the initial rise could not be due to expansion of the water, but rather was due to the contraction of the glass. Parallel results were obtained when the container was placed in hot water; there was no movement of the balls during the initial fall—only during the subsequent rise. (The Experimenters were the first to systematically establish thermal expansion of solids.)

Let the Experimenters speak for themselves (Waller, 1684):

> but rather (to speak first of the subsiding upon the immersion of vessels in hot water) their thoughts are, that it comes from the fixing of several volatile corpuscles of the fire (evaporated from the hot water) into the external pores of the glass, which as so many wedges, forcing and separating the parts thereof, must necessarily distend, and enlarge the internal capacity thereof; till they find a way through the hidden passages of the glass to the liquor therein contained...In fine, that the vessel being first sensible of cold or heat, by shrinking or enlarging it self also first, is the true cause of that phenomenon of the rise or fall; as it becomes more strait, or large, to the contained liquors, yet not vitiated by the quality of the ambient [p. 105].

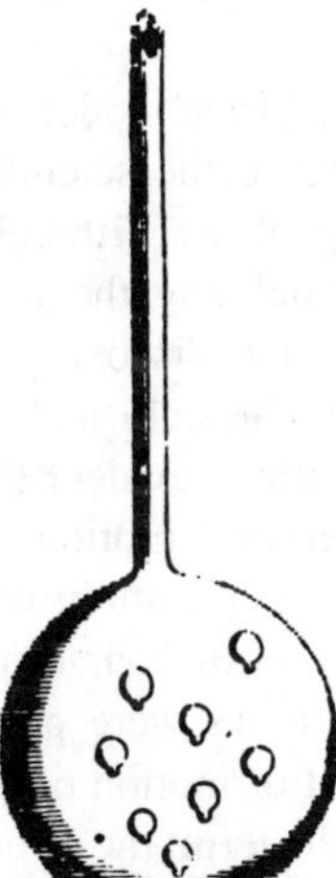

Fig. 12.2. Instrument used in an experiment designed to reject antiperistasis. The vessel is filled with water; the enamel balls float in water in its natural state.

We hope that this example demonstrates the Experimenters' cleverness as experimental scientists, and their technical skill, as well as their anti-Aristotelian goals. Middleton (1971) provides an excellent summary of other aspects of their anti-Aristotelian program. However, Middleton goes so far as to deny that the Experimenters had a positive program of research. There certainly is no explicit model or theory that articulate the studies of heat and cold in the *Saggi,* but we will argue that it is possible to discern a model underlying their work. The characterization of the model cannot be dissociated from the characterization of the Experimenters' thermal concepts. After presenting our analysis of the model underlying their research program, we present the evidence for this analysis and conclude with a discussion of their thermal concepts.

SOURCE-RECIPIENT MODEL

The Experimenters' model of thermal phenomena was directly inspired by mechanics. Heat and cold were conceived of as having intrinsic force or strength. To heat (cool) a substance was to apply to it the force of heat (cold), which caused motion in the substance. The thermal effects that concerned the Experimenters most were thermal dilation and freezing. Freezing interested them not so much as the transition from liquid to solid, but rather as involving changes in volume, dramatic for most of the substances they studied.

Their observations and measurements were articulated in terms of mechanical variables: extent and rate of displacement, weight, and force. For example, one finds them measuring the changes in the length of an iron bar being heated, measuring the speed at which the water level moved in a vessel placed in ice, and attempting to measure the force with which water expanded and broke vessels upon freezing.

It is not surprising that the first model of thermal phenomena would be mechanical. This corresponded to the scientific mood, discoveries, and main achievements of the beginning of the 17th century, particularly the impressive success of Galileo in conceptualizing the motions of celestial and terrestrial bodies. Two recent advances, the discovery of air pressure (and how it was affected by heat and cold) by Torricelli and the invention of the thermometer (probably by Galileo himself) made evident the relation between heat and cold and mechanical variables (pressure, motion) and suggested that thermal phenomena were amenable to systematic study within a mechanical model.

Force in the 17th century was of course not the (Newtonian) concept with which we are now familiar. Forces were pushes, pulls, thrusts, and impacts, which modified the state of rest or motion of bodies. Force was the "cause" of motion in the narrow sense of the term: the direct action of one body or substance upon another one, when the two came in contact. "Causing" motion of a body simply referred to displacing it. The extent and rate of displacement were believed to be larger when the force was greater but there was nothing like Newton's laws relating force to acceleration in a quantitative way.

Thus the Experimenters' mechanical model led them not only to concentrate upon the mechanical effects of heat and cold but also to adopt a causal explanatory stance of thermal phenomena, in the narrow agent-effect sense: Heat and cold "pushed" on substances and their effects were directly related to their "strength." Unlike in a modern model, there was no intervening variable to formally link heat to volume expansion (e.g., temperature, thermal coefficients).

For the Experimenters, heat and cold were emitted by hot and cold sources. All sources, even hot water, were viewed as spontaneous emitters. When studying the mechanical effects of heat and cold, they used only sources that were much hotter or colder than the body on which they acted (mixtures of ice and salt, baths of near-boiling water, fire). These sources had strong effects on the bodies placed in contact with them, whereas they were not visibly affected themselves by the heat exchange. When changes did occur in the source, such as the ice melting, they were not attributed to the recipient's losing heat to the source, but as due to the passing away of the cold of the source, occurring independently of the recipient. Thus, the body receiving the heat or the cold had a very different status from the source; one was passive receiver, the other active emitter.

This emitter view of the source required that the Experimenters have two separate concepts of heat and cold. Cooling and freezing were explained in terms of the entry of cold emitted by the source (mixture of ice and salt) into the recipient (generally a substance in its natural state).[2] They could not conceive of cooling and freezing as due to heat leaving the recipient, since heat was only emitted by hot sources and the recipient was not hot. In terms of their model, the same object could not simultaneously be a source and a recipient. Clearly, the emitter view of heat exchange is very different from the modern principle of thermal equilibrium.

We will call the Experimenters' model the "source-recipient" model. This denomination, throughout our analysis, refers to the mechanical aspect of their model (descriptions of phenomena in terms of the forces of heat and cold causing motions) and to its asymmetrical aspect (the source and the recipient had different status).

---

[2] "Natural state" in the Experimenters' work refers to the state of substances when not influenced by any source, their "proper" or normal state. Aspects of natural state were felt hotness or coldness, density, hardness, and other properties of substances. In the context of the *Saggi* it is clear that the Experimenters considered substances to be in their natural state when at room temperature, although they never used this locution, nor did they measure the degree of heat or cold in the recipient substances.

EVIDENCE FOR THE SOURCE-RECIPIENT MODEL

Our evidence that we have correctly captured the Experimenters' model is of three types: the goals and procedures of their experiments, their language, and their omissions—what they did not do when studying any particular phenomenon.

We illustrate the role of the source-recipient model in the Experimenters' thought with a detailed description of one series of studies on the process of freezing. We then provide further support for our analysis with other examples of their work, briefly described.

STUDIES OF ARTIFICIAL FREEZING

The freezing in these studies was "artificial" because the source of cold was a mixture of ice and salt rather than the winter air. The apparatus in Fig. 12.1 was used in each experiment. It consisted of a vessel containing the liquid being studied, a thermometer, a vat filled with a mixture of ice and salt and a pendulum clock (not shown in the figure). The thermometer contained alcohol (called "spirit of wine" by the Experimenters), and unlike modern thermometers it was not calibrated for the freezing and boiling points of water (nor any other fixed points). Its neck was marked in arbitrary, although equal, units. The vessel was similar to the thermometer in shape and size: a big bulb joined to a thin long neck, marked off in arbitrary, equal length units. The main difference between the two was that the thermometer was closed at the top, while the vessel was open.

Liquids in their natural state were put in the vessel to some height in the neck, expressed in degrees, the bulb plunged into the ice bath, and the course of freezing described. The thermometer was placed in the ice bath at the same time as the vessel, and the clock was started.

In stating the goal of these studies, the Experimenters commented that they were aware, as indeed most people were, of the basic phases of the process of freezing, "but we were yet ignorant, what period these several alterations (produced by cold) observed" (Waller, 1684, p. 79). The phases of freezing which were the units of their analysis (Waller, 1684):

> State natural, signifies, the degree whereat the water, or other fluid stood (before glaciation) in the neck of the vessel.
>
> Rise upon immersion, is the first leap made by the water upon the balls first touching the freezing mixture.
>
> Abatement, or fall, denotes the degree to which the water is reduced (after the rise upon immersion) when it just begins to receive the impression of cold.

Rest is the degree whereat the water stands for some time after its fall, without any apparent motion.

Remounting, shows likewise the degree to which the water is raised from its lowest fall, by means of rarifaction, with a very low, and seemingly equal motion, altogether like the first, wherewith it subsided.

Spring upon glaciation, signifies the degree to which the water rises with that extream velocity upon the very point of glaciation [pp. 81-82].

The Experimenters expected certain qualitative and quantitative regularities in their observations. First of all, they expected a given liquid to always go through the same phases of motion, each phase describable in terms of extent (degrees on neck of vessel), rate, acceleration, and duration. They also expected each phase to correspond to a certain degree of cold on the thermometer. Secondly, they expected that liquids would differ systematically from each other in these respects.

Thus, the focus of these studies was explicity on mechanical variables. The phases of freezing were motions, and these studies would go beyond earlier knowledge in providing detailed descriptions of these motions for various liquids.

They were pleased to find qualitative consistency in the motions of each liquid. For example, the freezing of water was described (Waller, 1684):

> Upon the first immersion of the ball, as soon as ever it touched the freezing mixture, we observed in the water in the neck a little rising, but very quick, which soon subsiding, it fell in the neck, with a motion regular enough and moderate velocity retiring to the ball, till arriving at a certain degree, it stopped for some time, as far as our eyes could judge, immovable. Then by little and little it remounted, but with a very slow motion, and apparently equal, and then of a sudden without any proportionate acceleration it flew up with a furious spring: at which time it was impossible to follow it any longer with the eye, instantaneously running through the decades of degrees. And as this fury began of a sudden, so of a sudden it ceased, changing from that great swiftness to a movement though very fast, yet incomparably less swift than the precedent: and with this it continued to rise most commonly, till it ran over the top of the neck [pp. 78-79].

The Experimenters reported that the same qualitative phases were also found during the freezing of distilled myrtle flower water, distilled rose water, distilled orange flower water, distilled strawberry water, distilled cinnamon water, melted snow, fig water, "the best red Florence wine," white muscadine and distilled vinegar. There were quantitative differences among the liquids, some contracting or expanding more than others, and at different rates. And the freezing of some liquids did not match that of water even qualitatively. The juice of lemons and spirit of vitriol did not rest nor spring upon glaciation, but "rose again with a very small motion, gently freezing.'' Oil of vitriol froze but without dilating and spirit of wine simply contracted, without freezing.

In order to establish the precise quantitative description of the motions of liquids during the freezing process, the Experimenters presented 2 or 3 tables from repeated measurements on the freezing of each liquid. Tables 1, 2, and 3 present the data for the first, second, and third freezing of distilled spring water. To interpret these tables and the way in which the Experimenters describe them is not easy. They do not always make sense from the point of view of modern physics. However, when they are understood in the light of the source-recipient model, the reasons why these particular data were collected and the conclusions the Experimenters drew from them become much clearer. Conversely, the very existence of these tables is evidence for the validity of the source-recipient model.

As can be seen from Table 12.1, the basic data were the levels of the liquid (in degrees) in the vessel at the beginning and the end of each phase of the freezing process (column 1), the times at which each phase began and ended (column 5) and the thermometer readings at the beginning and end of each phase (column 3). The phases are those defined above (pp. 276-277). The Experimenters compared the displacement of the water level during each phase (column 2), the displacement of the thermometer during each phase (column 4), and the duration of each phase (column 6) in the first freezing (Table 12.1) to the corresponding values obtained in the second and third freezings (Tables 12.2 and 12.3). To their satisfaction, the values in column 2 ''differ very inconsiderably'' from one freezing to the next. For example, during the remounting phase (i.e., the expansion water underwent just before freezing), the level rose by 10° the first time, and by 11 and ½° and 10° the second and third times, it was set to freeze. Similar regularities were found for all of the other phases of freezing of distilled spring water.

The Experimenters found, then, part of what they expected: that the kinematic description of the motions of substances during freezing was invariant for each

TABLE 12.1
The First Freezing of Spring Water (Waller, 1684, p. 83)

	1 *Degree of the Vessel*	*2* *Differ.*	*3* *Degree of Therm.*	*4* *Differ.*	*5* *Vibra.*	*6* *Differ.*
State natural	142		139			
Rise upon immersion	143½	1½	133	6	23	23
Abatement	120	23½	69	64	255	232
Rest	120		49	20	330	75
Remounting	130	0	33	16	462	132
Spring upon glaciation	166	36	33			

TABLE 12.2
The Second Freezing of the Same Spring Water
(Waller, 1684, p. 83)

	1 *Degree of vessel*	*2* *Differ.*	*3* *Degree of Therm.*	*4* *Differ.*	*5* *Vibrat.*	*6* *Differ.*
State natural	144		141½			
Rise upon immersion	146½	2½	118	23½	25	25
Abatement	119½	27	38	80	280	255
Rest	119½		28	10	415	135
Remounting	131	11½	17	11	882	467
Spring upon glaciation	170	39	17			

liquid, at least with respect to the extent of the motion, and therefore correctly captured one way in which cold affected substances. However, two of their expectations were not met—there were no constancies in columns 4 and 6. One could not find "the period" (i.e., duration) of each phase, for the periods varied from one freezing to another. They noticed that the second freezing (for all liquids) always took much longer than the first. They wondered whether this was due to a difference in the ice/salt mixture or to a difference in the liquids as a result of having been frozen. They settled this matter in the series on the freezing of distilled orange water. Between the first and second freezing of orange water, the vat was emptied and new ice and salt put in: Now a second freezing gave results very close to the first. The Experimenters concluded that the differences between Tables 12.1 and 12.2 for spring water in column 6 was due to an external passing of the increase of cold obtained from the salt. This explanation is consistent with their mechanical model: If the force of the source is weaker, it requires more time to produce a given effect (fixed displacement). Moreover, they did not attribute the weakening of the source to the recipient's taking cold from it, a symmetrical view of a thermal phenomenon, but to the spontaneous

TABLE 12.3
The Third Freezing of the Same Spring Water
(Waller, 1687, p. 54)

	1 *Degree of vessel*	*2* *Differ.*	*3* *Degree of Therm.*	*4* *Differ.*	*5* *Vibrat.*	*6* *Differ.*
State natural	143		141½			
Rise upon immersion	145	2	125	16½	23	23
Abatement	119½	25½	51	74	369	346
Rest	119½		44	7	565	196
Remounting	129½	10	38	6	933	368
Spring upon glaciation	169	39½	38			

"passing" of the cold of the source, an emitter view of the process, in which what happens to the source is independent of its action on the recipient.

The other regularity expected but not forthcoming concerned degree of cold as measured by the thermometer (column 4). There was no fixed degree of cold associated with each phase of freezing, even of a single liquid. They explained the failure to find such a regularity as due to experimental artefact—they claimed that it was impossible to apply the same proportion of cold to the bulb and to the thermometer. The ice/salt mixture provided uneven sources of cold to the vessel and to the thermometer, because powdered ice froze up unevenly when salt was strewn over it.

In sum, they did not find stable relations among all of the variables they sought to relate. However, they did not consider these experiments failures, because they found constancies in column 2 from one freezing to another in a single liquid, and qualitatively similar phases in the freezing of a wide variety of substances.

By making displacement the invariant descriptor of the freezing process, the Experimenters missed the "true" regularities in their data: the absolute levels in column 1. The reader will have noticed that the levels (in degrees) at the end of each phase are as much in accordance in the three Tables as are the "differences" in column 2. For example, the levels after abatement are 120°, 119 and 1/2°, and 119 and 1/2° in the first, second and third freezings, respectively. Similarly, the levels after remounting are 130°, 131°, and 129 and 1/2° and after glaciation the values are 166°, 170° and 169°. In a sense the Experimenters had the data necessary to conclude that the specific volumes of water at its minimum and when it froze were fixed. To a modern physicist, the absolute values in column 1 are the correct descriptors because they are lawfully related to other physical variables (e.g., temperature); the displacements in column 2 are constant, of course, but as the result of being differences between constant levels. These displacements figure in no basic laws in modern theory. Exactly the opposite is true of the Experimenters. The effects of cold, for them, were motions, caused by the force of the cold, and thus displacements were the natural descriptors. The absolute heights, being static positions, were not seen as directly related to forces and therefore not treated as relevant descriptors. Displacements were so much at the center of the Experimenters' conceptualization of freezing that having noticed that the initial levels ("natural states") differed by a few degrees in the three Tables, they claimed that all the other levels also did, because the displacements were what was constant. Of course, this is simply false, even of their own data, although deviations from their generalization were obscured by noise. If initial states had differed more, the amount of abatement would have varied correspondingly, while the endpoint of the abatement at the point of rest would have remained constant.

The "degrees of the thermometer" data are the hardest to interpret. The Experimenters wrote that the thermometer was used "to see at what degree of cold each change happened to the liquor.'' To the modern eye it is odd, and therefore important, that the thermometer was placed next to the vessel in the ice bath, rather than in the vessel. Their statement of goals implies that they were expecting regularities in the thermometer readings, but they did not say which ones. Their only disucssion of the thermometer data concerned the technical difficulties which precluded meaningful results, so there are no clues to their intentions in their writing about results. Finally, they did not justify setting the thermometer in the ice bath rather than the vessel, although they apparently found this procedure perfectly legitimate.

There is little doubt that the degree of cold the thermometer was intended to reflect was that of the liquid in the vessel. The source-recipient model allows us to see why this is so, in spite of the fact the thermometer was placed in the ice bath. Since the thermometer and the vessel were put in the ice simultaneously, the same cold (at least ideally) was applied to both at the same time. Although the motions resulting from the force of cold were a function of the particular recipient, as the studies on artificial freezing amply demonstrated, the force of the cold from the source itself was thought independent of its effects on different recipients. The thermometer, then, was probably intended to play the role of a standard recipient, its level an indication not only of the degree of cold acting on the alcohol, but also of the cold acting on the liquid in the vessel. Given the regularities displayed by the motions of the liquid, regularities in the measure of the causes of these motions were expected. That the Experimenters calculated ''differences'' for thermometer readings (column 4 on the Tables) suggests that they expected the distance moved by the alcohol to be regularly related to time elapsed (column 6) and to the phases of freezing in the vessel.

The Experimenters' comment that the vessel itself was a kind of thermometer bolsters our interpretation: ''. . . taking the whole instrument for a nice thermometer, by reason of the largeness of the ball and proportion of the neck'' (Waller, 1684, p. 80). Further, the vessel and thermometer were apparently identical in size and shape (Fig. 12.1) and in initial level (Tables).[3] This ensured that not only would the source apply the same degree of cold to both, but it would act on identical volumes and areas. Finally, there is the Experimenters' explanation of their failure to find useful data: ''...all our diligence was fruitless through the difficulty and impracticableness of applying an equal proportion of cold to the ball and to the thermometer; by reason of the inequality of the pieces of ice, and the quantity of salt sprinkled'' (Waller, 1684, p. 82).

In sum, the studies in artificial freezing support both components of the source-recipient model. The model's emphasis on the mechanical effects of the force of cold is needed to explain the Experimenters' fixation on the distance covered in the various phases of freezing and the asymmetry between source and

---

[3]The relevance of this fact was suggested to us by T. Kuhn.

recipient is required to explain the attempted use of the thermometer in these studies.

Other Evidence for the Source-Recipient Model

Approximately 60 of the 162 pages of the *Saggi* are devoted to the study of heat and cold (Table 12.4) and the source-recipient model plays a role in the Experimenters' conception of all this work. We will confine our demonstration that this is so to several examples.

Studies of artificial freezing (No. 4 on Table 12.4). The studies of artificial freezing discussed above are 4d on Table 12.4. They were part of a much larger series designed to prove that water expanded while freezing, to demonstrate and measure the force with which it expanded and to measure the extent of the expansion.

TABLE 12.4

1. The description of some instruments to discover the alterations of the air caused by heat and cold (pp. 1–8).
2. An experiment, showing the effect of heat and cold, applied externally to the void space (pp. 41–44).
3. An experiment examining what may be the motion of the invisible effluvia of fire in vacuo (pp. 46–47).
4. Experiments of artificial freezing (pp. 69–94).
    a. Experiments to know, if water dilates itself in freezing (n=6).
    b. An experiment, to measure how great the force of rarefaction may be in water shut up is close vessels, to freeze.
    c. Experiments, to measure the utmost expansion of water in freezing (n=3).
    d. Experiments, touching the procedure of artificial freezings, with their wonderful accidents.
5. Experiments of natural freezing (pp. 95–103).
6. Experiments, touching an effect of heat and cold, lately observed as to the alteration of the inward capacity of glass, and metalline vessels (pp. 104–107).
7. Experiments in the dilation of solids (pp. 107–113).
    a. The first experiment, showing the alteration of the size of a brass ring put in the fire, and in ice, its figure still remaining unaltered.
    b. The second experiment, whereby it appears that bodies are dilated by the imbibing of moisture, as well as by the insinuation of heat.

(*continued*)

Table 12.4—*Continued*

c. The third experiment, which discovers more evidently the readiness of glass to contract and dilate itself upon heat and cold.
d. The fourth experiment, to find the same effect in metals.
e. The fifth experiment, to observe by the sound the like dilation in a stirrup of glass.
f. The sixth experiment, discovering the same effect more clearly to the eye.
g. The seventh experiment, showing the same effects in wire strings.
h. The eighth experiment, whereby from the appearance of a contrary effect 'tis confirmed, that the first motion of liquors comes from the capacity of the vessels being altered in the instant of immersion.
i. The ninth experiment, to show, that a vessel may be distended, not only by heat, or by soaking up of moisture, but also by weight.

8. Experiments touching some effects of heat and cold (pp. 149–154).
a. The first experiment. Of a steel wire seeming to grow lighter by being heated.
b. The second experiment. Of the vast force of heat in raising up an included liquor.
c. The third experiment, about antiperistasis.
d. The fourth experiment, whether cold is caused by an intrusion of frigorific atoms.
e. The fifth experiment. Of heating and cooling of water by salts, etc. And of hot and cold ebulletions.

The proof that water expands upon freezing (No. 4a on Table 12.4). Galileo had argued that ice floated and therefore its specific gravity was less than water, so water must expand during freezing. The Experimenters accepted this argument, but wanted to show the great force of the expansion. They performed six experiments in which water was confined in metal and glass balls and then put in mixtures of ice and salt to freeze. They then described the manner in which the containers broke. They started with a silver container with a screwed-on cover; the container broke and the ice inside was found to have a convex shape. This provided them with an important counter to the Aristotelian explanation of the breaking of containers of frozen water. Aristotle held that it was due to the water drawing the walls of the container inward as it shrank, for the metaphysical reason that "nature abhors the vacuum." The Experimenters then went on to try to find a vessel that would resist the force of the cold. They made a ball of much thicker silver, and also tried bronze, thick glass, brass, and gold. The gold ball did not break because of its malleability, but it expanded with the ice.

In trying balls of increasing thickness, the Experimenters were conceiving of the force of cold as pitted against the resistance of the vessel in exactly the same way as the force of impact of a moving object might or might not break its target. In sum, these studies reveal the mechanical aspects of the source-recipient model; a mechanical variable (expansion of water) is at question, as well as the causal powers of the force of cold.

The attempt to measure the force of expansion of water (No. 4b on Table 12.4). The Experimenters' intent was to measure the force of expansion during freezing by equalling it to a weight. First, they hoped to determine the thickness of the walls of a metal ball such that it would be broken by freezing water, but any thicker ball would not. Then, they would make a ring of the same metal and the same thickness and determine the weight required to break the ring. Technical difficulties rendered this experiment impossible, but their plans show that for them the force causing the water to expand was a kind of mechanical force; measuring it by equalling it to another mechanical force was therefore a legitimate scientific enterprise.

Measuring the extent of expansion during freezing (No. 4c on Table 12.4). In three straightforward experiments, they established that the amount of expansion when water froze was about 1/8. They performed the measurements in two ways: by weighing two equal volumes of water and ice, and by measuring the volume of ice that came from a known volume of water freezing. Both measures gave the ration 9:8.

The title of this study itself is informative (Table 12.4)—the water received the expansion; cold was the agent and the liquid the passive recipient. And of course, this study was just part (along with 4a, 4b, and 4d) of the project of a quantitative description of the process of freezing in terms of mechanical variables—length, force, time, and their derivatives.

Experiments on natural ice (No. 5 on Table 12.4). Of all the studies on heat and cold in the *Saggi,* those on natural ice are the most chaotic and seemingly pointless. The central question was whether water frozen in the winter air (natural ice) differed in fundamental ways from water frozen by the cold of ice/salt mixtures (artificial ice). To this end, the Experimenters placed water of various sorts (spring water, sea water, distilled water) in vessels of various sorts (different shapes, materials, volumes) and set them out to freeze on a cold night in winter. They observed in which vessels the water froze fastest, most completely, and also what the ice looked like. The results were entirely inconclusive. They themselves acknowledged: "But as to the rest, we have found nothing so constant, as the perpetual irregularity of the accidents; and among others, there have some vessels stood all night without the least coat of ice, where some next to them have been frozen in an hour. Moreover, in the same sort of vessels set to freeze, in the same night, we have observed the like varieties, whether placed north, south, east or west; and as well those vessels which have stood more southwardly have been frozen first, as at other times, those that stood more northwardly, tho the cold generally comes from that tract with us'' (Waller, 1684, p. 96).

The premise of these studies was that cold from different sources might have different effects. Different sources, different colds, different ice. Indeed, the Experimenters found that the ice resulting from the cold of the winter air was ''not so suddenly made, but begin from a thin coat, or hair-like vein, scarce discernable; yet those veins, or coats are more firm, and hard bodies, and as it were more cristaline, and solid ice,'' (Waller, 1684, p. 95-96). Similarly, when ice was made in a vacuum the ice was ''more equal and hard, and less transparent and porous than the other.'' The source imported some of its fundamental characteristics to the ice it was making. Of all the Experimenters' thermal studies, these provide the least support for the source-recipient model. The effects of cold highlighted here were non-mechanical—the appearance of the ice, its consistency, transparency, hardness, and so on. Although the time of freezing was noted, it was not measured systematically. There was, of course, a strong asymmetry between the source and recipient—properties of the air affected the freezing process, whereas properties of vessels and water had no effect on the air. However, the asymmetry in the natural freezing studies is not so clearly between the force of cold and the recipient. Rather it seems to be between the source overall (winter air) and the recipient. This is shown by the Experimenters noting that natural ice resembled air more than did artificial ice (it was drier). Also, they never measured the degree of cold in the air, nor even speculated whether the cold of winter air was more effective than the cold of ice/salt mixtures.

In sum, although these studies clearly show the asymmetry between source and recipient, plus the causal role of the source, they are not particularly concerned with mechanical variables.

Thermal expansion of solids (No. 7 on Table 12.4). In what Middleton calls the Experimenters' most elegant and influential series of studies, they illustrated that heat expanded and cold contracted glass, bronze, brass, and copper. They claimed to be measuring the different expansions produced by different degrees of heat; however, they provided no quantitative results. Qualitatively, they found that the longer the recipient stayed in contact with the source, the more dilated (or contracted, if the source was ice water) it became.

These studies provide exactly the same sort of support for the source-recipient model as do those on the expansion and contraction of water described above. Two studies are of special interest in this regard (see Table 12.4). In one, (7b), they showed that wood expanded when it absorbed moisture. The parallel effects of moisture and heat were meant to support their claim that heat was a substance. In the other, (7i), they showed that a metal vessel was expanded by the weight of mercury. The parallel effects of heat and weight were meant to support their view of heat and cold as having mechanical force.

Effects of heat and cold on a vacuum (2 on Table 12.4). The question in this study was whether heat and cold affected the vacuum mechanically; that is, did they expand and contract it? The Experimenters placed a barometer inside the vacuum chamber, reasoning that if heat affected the vacuum, the vacuum would expand like a substance. If the vacuum expanded, it would press on the mercury and make it go down. And this was what they found (because their "vacuum" contained some air). They measured the strength of the source of heat and cold: "The hot water made use of in this experiment raised a thermometer of 50 degrees to 48° and with the same heat shortened the mercurial cilinder one 146th part of the whole height. And that of the cold water increased to one 50th part, when in the same water the thermometer came to 11 degrees 1/2" (Waller, 1684, p. 44).

This study provides exactly the same kind of support for the source-recipient model as do those on artificial freezing and on the thermal expansion of solids. One further point may be added. The Experimenters did not worry about the propagation of heat through the vacuum; it was in the nature of heat that sources emitted it, the only question was whether the vacuum would be affected as were substances. This is why a barometer, rather than a thermometer, was placed inside the vacuum.

The Thermometer

The Experimenters used three types of thermometers in their experiments, which differed primarily in their sensitivity to heat and cold and in reliability. They were called the 50 degree, 100 degree and 300 degree thermometers in reference to the number of degrees marked on their neck. As mentioned before, thermometers were not calibrated for fixed points. For each type of thermometer, the dimensions of the bulb, the bore and height of the neck and the quantity of alcohol were established by trial and error so that the full range of the thermometer would be used. For example, the 100° thermometer was designed so that its level would be around 20° when placed in snow and around 80° when placed in the sun in mid-summer. It was important that all the thermometers of a given type give the same reading when placed in identical sources, so that meaningful comparisons could be established when more than one thermometer was required. The Experimenters noted: "The rule of making these, so as they shall keep such a correspondence is only obtained by practice, teaching how to proportionate the ball to the cane, and so to adjust the quantity of liquor, as they shall not vary in their motions" (Waller, 1684, pp. 4-5). This was easily done for the 50° thermometers, less easily for the 100° ones and impossible in the case of the

300° thermometers, because "the smallest inequality and error committed in making one with a large ball, and small neck, being very easy to be discovered: so that they will show great disagreement and inequality when compared together" (Waller, 1684, p. 5). The correspondence between the 50° and the 100° thermometers, the two most frequently used in the experiments, was arbitrary; for example, "at the greatest cold of our winter [the 100° thermometer] subsiding to 17 or 16 degrees [, the 50° thermometer] usually to 12, or 11" (Waller, 1684, p. 4).

Thus the Experimenters had instruments that would give the same or corresponding readings when placed in identical sources. But the actual reading of any particular thermometer was meaningless: "One degree" represented a certain length on the neck, not a unit of thermal variable. This was because the degree was not defined in reference to any other physical variable or phenomenon.

The analysis of the Experimenters' use of the thermometer plays two roles in our argument—providing support for the source-recipient model and diagnosing their thermal concepts. We consider the former in this section and the latter in the next section.

The Experimenters' description of the workings of the thermometer provide what may be the clearest support for the model as we have laid it out. For example, they mentioned that spirit of wine was used rather than water "because it is sooner sensible of the least change of heat and cold, and by reason of its extreme lightness, it more readily contracts itself, quickly falling or rising" (Waller, 1684, p. 3). The principle[4] behind this statement is purely mechanical. Combined with the principle that greater degrees of heat or cold created larger motions, it is consistent with the mechanical principles known at the time: Greater forces had greater effects, and heavier recipients provided greater resistance to the effects of forces.

The thermometer worked because the liquid in it was a recipient and therefore registered changes of heat and cold in its ambient medium, viewed as a source. Often the simple registration of the presence of heat or cold (by the direction the liquid in the thermometer moved) was the only role the instrument played in an experiment. For example, the Experimenters wondered if a concave mirror would reflect cold as well as heat, so they put a sensitive thermometer at its focus and placed a large piece of ice so that cold would be reflected on the thermometer. They noted only that it fell[5], diagnostic of the presence of cold. Similarly, a chemical reaction that produced boiling-like bubbling (a mixture of ammonia and

---

[4]Although mercury was used in the Experimenters' barometers, it was not used in their thermometers. Mercury, of course, is a counterexample to this principle—its specific gravity is much greater than water yet it is more responsive to heat. It was not until Black that the notion of specific heat was developed.

[5]They realized that this study was inconclusive; the thermometer might have been affected by the ice directly.

an acid) paradoxically produced "a marvelous cold," which felt cold to the touch. The Experimenters checked that cold was actually being produced by noting that the level of a thermometer placed in the mixture fell.

As a recipient of heat or cold from the source, the thermometer reflected the degree of heat or cold imparted to it by the source and thus the strength of the source itself. These were most often assessed by the rate at which the spirit rose or fell in the thermometer, or by the number of degrees changed (as in the experiments on artificial freezing). For example, the thermometer was used in the comparison of different salts' powers to increase the force of cold in ice-salt mixtures. The relative rates at which the thermometer fell, when placed in vessels in different ice-salt mixtures, were compared. Also noted was which water froze faster. These two measures of relative strengths of two sources of cold were merely checks on each other.

In another case, the Experimenters wondered whether heat radiated equally in all directions, or rose, as the Aristotelian doctrine held. To factor out convection of air, they attempted to perform the experiment in a vacuum (No. 3 on Table 12.4). Two thermometers were placed in the vacuum, one much higher than the other. A glowing coal was placed on the outside, midway between the thermometers and it was noted that the top thermometer heated up faster than the lower one, and also changed more degrees, although the effect was much less than in air[6]. Again, these two measures (rate and displacement) were merely alternative indicators of relative degrees of heat applied to the thermometers.

Only rarely did the Experimenters wait for the thermometer to reach a steady state before reading its level, in marked contrast to the modern uses of the thermometer. In all such cases, such as the effect of heat and cold on the vacuum (No. 2 on Table 12.4), the degree of heat or cold of the source was at issue and the height at which the level stopped was seen as representing how far a source of a given strength would be able to move the liquid.

Also in contrast with the modern use, in experiments in which thermal dilation was the object of study, the thermometer was either not used or placed outside the recipient. For example, the studies of the thermal expansion of solids took for granted that, since the recipient was above the fire, its heat was necessarily increasing in time. The goal of the experiments was to demonstrate that the specific volume of solids did increase with heat but no attempt was made to look at volume as a function of thermometer reading for the metal or glass. And we have already discussed the case of artificial freezing, in which the thermometer was placed outside the recipient.

Thermometers, as used by the Experimenters, registered the effects of heat and cold and therefore could reflect their presence and relative strength. Howev-

---

[6]The Experimenters realized that this study was inconclusive, since convection of air outside of the vacuum chamber could account for the effect.

er, they did not "measure" anything in the proper sense because their "degree" was not a unit of any physical variable.

THE EXPERIMENTERS' THERMAL CONCEPTS

The Experimenters' concept of heat had three aspects: substance (particles), quality (hotness) and force. As we have shown, their experimental program centered on the force of heat. However, all three aspects of the concept were important, and were intimately related to each other.

On the Experimenters' emitter view of heat sources, it was particles of heat, atoms of fire, that were emitted by hot bodies. Thermal expansion was explained in terms of the atoms of fire forcing the atoms of the substance apart. The Experimenters took this view of heat seriously; they attempted to weigh heat (No. 8a on Table 12.4), and noted that heat expanded substances just as did moisture. Thermal expansion was also described as the effect of the force of heat. For example, one of their experiments is entitled: "Of the vast force of heat in raising up an included liquor" (No. 8b on Table 12.4). The causal axioms of their day required all explanation of change to be mechanical, that is, resulting from the physical impact of one group of particles on another (see Kuhn, 1977b). The particles of fire provided the Experimenters with a material support for the force of heat. Lacking the notion of thermal equilibrium, the Experimenters had no account of the circumstances under which particles of fire left one body and entered another, except for their view of sources as spontaneous emitters. Thus, particles provided material support for the causal powers of heat and the nature of emitters provided (by stipulation) an important key—the conditions under which particles of fire moved at all.

The particle aspect of the Experimenters' concept of heat should not be identified with the later concept of caloric, which dominated thermodynamics through the 18th and some of the 19th century. The Experimenters did not measure amount of heat, nor even mention number of particles. The caloric theory, in contrast, postulated that the total amount of caloric was conserved; what was lost by one body was gained by another, and amount of heat was measured in units of the same type as modern calories or BTUs.

The sensory quality, hotness, was also an aspect of the Experimenters' concept of heat. Indeed, an essential property of heat was hotness, which was one reason heat emitters (sources) had to themselves be hot. However, the quality aspect of heat played a minor role in the Experimenters' scientific endeavor. Their anti-Aristotelian program included the denial that heat was merely a quality, one reason that the mechanical effects of the force of heat was the center of their enterprise.

Cold, like *heat,* had both a force aspect and a quality aspect. As to whether cold was a substance—as to whether there were atoms of cold, the Experimenters acknowledged their ignorance. They raised this question explicily, tried to answer it on an experimental basis and ended up noncommittal.

This asymmetry between heat and cold also emerges in their discussion of the ultimate sources of heat and cold. Whereas the sun is cited as the ultimate source of heat and light, the Experimenters were agnostic about there being an ultimate source of cold, and questioned scholastic speculations about such a source, deep in the earth. However uncertain about the ultimate relation between heat and cold, their experimental program provided for no doubt. In the model guiding their experiments, heat and cold were definitely treated as separate entities, each existing by itself and bearing its own force. Heat and cold were emitted by different kinds of sources (i.e., hot ones such as fire and cold ones such as ice, respectively), and had complementary mechanical effects.

WERE HEAT AND TEMPERATURE DIFFERENTIATED?

We began this paper with the question of whether the Experimenters had differentiated the concepts of heat and temperature. By this question, we meant: Did the Experimenters' conceptualization of thermal phenomena rest on two distinct thermal concepts, one of which had at least some of the important properties of modern heat and the other at least some of the important properties of modern temperature, and differing from each other in at least some of the important respects by which modern heat and modern temperature differ? The reader may have noticed that in our descriptions of the Experimenters' model, experiments and concepts, we never used the word "temperature" and discussed only their concepts of heat and cold.[7] The question of differentiation between heat and temperature can be rephrased accordingly: Was heat the only thermal concept in the Experimenters' repertoire and if so, can we claim that it was not differentiated, in the sense outlined above, from temperature? The answer is yes to both counts.

The Experimenters' program was to study the mechanical effects of heat. As can be seen from the titles of their experiments (Table 12.4), this involved relating only one thermal variable, heat, to a series of mechanical ones. It was simply not part of this program to seek any relation between two thermal variables.

Two lines of argument show that their single variable was neither modern heat nor modern temperature, but a mixture of both. First, they lacked critical components of both modern concepts, components necessary to distinguish the two. Second, in those cases where they had knowledge of properties that do now

---

[7]As established above, heat and cold were parallel concepts, playing the same roles in their model. In this section "heat" is contrasted with temperature and stands for both heat and cold.

distinguish the two, these properties were then aspects of the same thermal concept.

A crucial component of modern temperature is a scale defined by two fixed points, usually the freezing and boiling points of water, such that a "degree" is a fixed portion of the interval between the two. As we have seen, the Experimenters' thermometers were not so constructed. An important ingredient in the concept of heat, on the other hand, is the notion of amount. Although the Experimenters conceived of heat as made of particles, they had no measure for heat that enabled them to firmly consider heat as an extensive quantity. They never spoke of quantity or number of particles, nor of "much heat." Rather, it was always "intense heat," "strong heat," and so on. Thus, the Experimenters lacked measures for both heat and temperature.

Another crucial component of modern temperature and heat is the principle of thermal equilibrium. The Experimenters' thermal variable did not have the property of being equalized when two bodies are brought in contact. Without this notion, the question could not even arise as to the conditions under which equalization occurs (temperature difference) and what is exchanged (heat).

The Experimenters' concept of heat had both intensive and extensive aspects. Heat was intensive in the sense that the effects of heat were the same at every point of a homogeneous body; in a bath of hot water, for example, the hotness felt with the hand or the heat measured with a thermometer were the same at all points. According to our interpretation of the artificial freezing studies, the Experimenters also believed that the ice applied the same cold at every point in it—that is why a thermometer placed in one part of the ice mixture was relevant to the degree of cold affecting the vessel in another part of the ice mixture. Heat was extensive in the sense that the Experimenters thought that increasing the volume of the source increased its heat—the bigger the source, the larger its effect. This is why adding boiling water to tepid water increased its heat and why a bigger fire heated a room faster than a smaller fire.

The Experimenters' occasional puzzlement over some findings often reflects their not having differentiated heat and temperature. In an unpublished experiment, described by Middleton (Middleton, 1971), the Experimenters heated 2 lbs. of iron until it ignited sulphur, placed it into a container of water, and recorded the level of the thermometer placed in the water. They repeated the experiment with a jar containing a mixture of 1/2 lb. of tin and 1 1/2 lbs. of nitric acid and noted that although the heat of this mixture did not ignite sulphur, it heated the water more than had the iron, "so that it seemed possible to conclude that this heat although more powerful was not of the same nature as that taken up by the iron held under the ignited coals [p. 273]." This experiment is interesting in more than one respect, but the point we want to make here is that, had the Experimenters differentiated between heat and temperature, they would have expressed their puzzlement in other terms. Rather than wondering about heats of different nature, they would have wondered how a mass at a lower temperature (not igniting sulphur) could produce more heat. Similarly, in one of their artificial freezing studies, they were surprised to find that adding more ice and more salt to the source did not influence the course of freezing of the water in the vessel. This would not have been puzzling, of course, had they distinguished the temperature of the ice-salt mixture from the total heat capacity of the mixture.

Finally, the Experimenters' language reflects the non-differentiation. They had three terms, ''heat,'' ''degree of heat,'' and ''temperament,'' where the modern theory has two, and the usage of none of the three corresponded just to that of modern ''heat'' or ''temperature.'' The contexts in which ''heat'' and ''degree of heat'' and the adjectives and adverbs qualifying these terms were thoroughly ambiguous with respect to their intensive and extensive aspects. For example, the Experimenters described the calibration of a thermometer (Waller, 1684): ''If the heat of the room is not sufficient to make the thermometer rise to 60, it may be helped, by putting the vessel in a bath of warm water, increasing the heat by gradual pouring in boiling water, if needful'' (pp. 7-8). ''Degree of heat'' was always used in the context of attempts to quantify heat, but the quantification was equally ambiguous. For example, in their studies of the dilation of solids, the Experimenters wanted ''to observe the different increasings, caused by different degrees of heat given to the same, or several conical rings of metal'' (Waller, 1684, p. 113).

''Temperament'' is the concept most foreign to the modern ear. It is used only 13 times in the Waller translation[8], in contrast with hundreds of uses of ''hot,'' ''cold,'' ''heat,'' ''warm,'' ''cool,'' and so on. ''Temperament'' had several meanings, centered around the notion of composition and balance of qualities and the state of substances relative to those qualities. Being concerned with thermal effects, the Experimenters focused on temperament with respect to heat and cold. But even in this restricted sense temperament was not a purely thermal concept. ''Temperament of heat and cold'' meant, approximately, ''state as affected by heat and cold.'' The qualities of a substance which were part of its ''temperament of heat and cold'' were not only its hotness or coldness but also its hardness, as evidenced by a passage about the possibility of a subterranean ultimate source of cold, in which the Experimenters marvelled that ''cold reduces the pure water to such a temperament that it turns it into even the hardest rock-crystal'' (Waller, 1684, p. 20). The meaning of temperament quite often also included the notion of density. For example, in their studies of antiperistasis, the Experimenters hypothesized that the brief motion of a liquid in the neck of a vessel plunged into a bath of ice or hot water ''was not really from any

---

[8]Waller's translation also contains two instances of the word ''temperature.'' Temperature, in the 17th century, had the same basic meaning as temperament. Middleton mentions that the Experimenters used the locution ''tempera di calore e di freddo''; we believe that both ''temperature'' and ''temperament'' are the translation of the Italian word ''tempera.''

intrinsic alteration of rarity, or density at that moment wrought in their natural temperament by the outwardly applied ambient'' (Waller, 1684, pp. 104-105).

Thus, although ''temperament'' was never used in the extensive sense (i.e., it was always independent of volume), it certainly did not correspond to modern temperature. Temperament was not a thermal variable; the thermometer did not measure temperament, and temperament played no role in the Experimenters' causal model, except as an aspect of the effects of heat and cold upon density.

In conclusion, the only truly thermal variable in the Experimenters' repertoire was their concept of heat. In denying that the Experimenters had the concept of temperature, we do not deny them the notion of felt hotness nor the knowledge of the fact that applying heat to a body made it warmer to the touch. However, to state this fact did not require two separate concepts because it was the direct consequence of hotness being a property of heat.

One can draw an interesting analogy between this case and the case of instantaneous and average velocity in Aristotelian physics discussed by Kuhn (1977a). Just as instantaneous velocity was part of Aristotle's concept of speed but lacked the status of physical variable in his description of motion, so hotness was part of the Experimenters' concept of heat but played no important role in their conceptualization of thermal effects.

About the case of velocity, Kuhn says ''Aristotle's concept of speed, in which something like the separate modern concepts of average and instantaneous speed were merged, was an integral part of his entire theory of motion and had implications for the whole of his physics.'' An analogous statement could be applied mutati mutandis to the Experimenters' thermal theory. The nondifferentiated state of the Experimenters' thermal concept can be related to their model and domain of enquiry in two ways. First, the conceptualization of the mechanical effect of heat and cold within the source-recipient model captured important physical regularities: specific volumes of gases, liquids, and solids do increase upon being heated, and exposure to cold does have regular effects on substances (although these vary from substance to substance, as described by the Experimenters). Therefore, there was no need for revising the model nor being dissatisfied with the concept of heat on which the model was based. The dual intensive/extensive aspect of heat, for example, was not self-contradictory (as it might appear at first to a modern physicist) but consistent with viewing thermal dilation as caused directly by the force of heat. And the Experimenters' belief that thermometers measured heat, as well as the ways in which they used thermometers, made sense from the point of view of the source-recipient model.

Second, certain properties of heat and temperature (e.g., thermal equilibrium, amount of heat, and the notion of fixed points) that would have helped or might have forced the differentiation not only were not part of the Experimenters' conceptual repertoire, but were sometimes inconsistent with the source-recipient model. Thus, even in the face of paradoxical results or inconsistencies, the differentiation could not be achieved within this model. It would have required giving up a purely mechanical account of thermal phenomena, restoring quality as a valid primitive, and ceasing to think of heat and cold as separate entities, emitted spontaneously and therefore necessarily from very hot and very cold sources.

WHAT NEXT?

Currently we are trying to understand the period between the Experimenters and Black, a period that witnessed change in domain, model and thermal concepts. We know that the source-recipient model played little or no role in any systematic work after the Experimenters. The mechanical effects of heat were assimilated and did not become a focus of study again until the much later work on thermal coefficients. Immediately after the Experimenters, the principle of thermal equilibrium and knowledge of fixed points allowed the development of today's thermometer, which set the stage for a new domain in the study of thermal phenomena. In the years between 1730 and 1750, Boerhaave, Krafft, and Richman worked on the quantitative description of the resulting temperature when two quantities of water at different temperatures were mixed together. Black solved this problem in 1759 for the case of two different substances, discovering specific heat.

According to McKie and Heathcote (1935), Boerhaave, Krafft and Richman also failed to distinguish heat and temperature. The domain of their study required only one thermal variable; as long as only one substance was involved it did not matter whether one considered heat to be exchanged in the mixture, or temperature itself, or some entity with properties of both. Thus, although inconsistent with conceiving of cold and heat as forces emitted by sources, the discovery of thermal equilibrium and fixed points and the investigation of new thermal phenomena (heat/temperature exchange and phase change), did not guarantee the differentiation of heat and temperature. This is most clear in the work of Wilcke, who independently performed exactly the same experiments on melting snow as did Black, but who failed to formulate the concept of latent heat and who failed to distinguish heat and temperature (McKie & Heathcote, 1935). A new distinction as fundamental to a developing science as that between heat and temperature is a major achievement. We do not expect to be able to give necessary and sufficient conditions for Black's success, but we do hope to trace the steps he took in enlarging the domain of enquiry and the conceptual repetoire available for the development of thermodynamics.

HISTORY OF SCIENCE AND THE NOVICE-EXPERT SHIFT

Larkin (this volume) contrasts the novice's and the expert's representations of physical problems. The expert has physical representations, in which the entities are the concepts of modern physics, the properties of these entities are localized to them (i.e., independent of the particular circumstances instantiated in the problem), and the inference rules are time-independent. In contrast, the entities of the novice's representations are common objects. Insofar as the novice has physical concepts at all they are diffusely distributed over the concrete objects in the representations, and inference rules follow a real-time flow.

Although Larkin describes models for particular problems and we have described the Experimenters' model for thermal phenomena in general, there are striking similarities between her novices' model and the Experimenters' model. The Experimenters' model was articulated partly in terms of concrete objects—the sources such as fire, the sun, and ice—and heat and cold as forces were not completely separate from the sources themselves (especially in the experiments on natural ice). The asymmetry between source and recipient crucially involved time-dependent causal reasoning in Larkin's sense. Today, in contrast, thermal expansion is thought of in terms of state equations that relate density of substance to temperature: time-independent causal reasoning in Larkin's sense.

Such similarities raise the generality of such a progression: Will we always see these features in change from earlier conceptual systems to more advanced ones? Are these similarities superficial or deep? Until now, we have assumed that the novice-expert shift involves conceptual change of the same kind that occurs in the history of science, and that the analogy between a first scientific model such as the Experimenters' and a contemporary novice's model is therefore revealing. These assumptions are by no means obviously correct.

The *Saggi* were the result of several years of systematic work by scientists consciously engaged in theory building. Scientists, even at the earliest stages of their science, bring to bear whatever models are current in other domains of science, mathematical knowledge, and a general abstract and systematic approach. The uneducated beginner's models and concepts are not the result of such conscious theory building.

We cannot know whether the similarities between Larkin's novices and the Experimenters, or more generally between novices' conceptual systems and first theories in the history of science, are deep or superficial until a case study of the novice's conceptualization of some domain is completed. Students of the novice-expert shift have not, in general, been engaged in such case studies. Rather, naive students have been diagnosed for their knowledge of the expert system and for their methods of solution of the problems in the domain of the expert system. Although the misconceptions of the novice are often attributed to his naive theory of the world, the research to back up this attribution has not yet been done. What is the domain of the novice's theory, what problems does it solve, what are its explanatory mechanisms, and what are its concepts? The case study of the *Saggi* presented here illustrates how difficult it is to answer these questions for conceptual systems different from our own.

The analogy we are exploring is structural and licenses comparisons across different domains of science (as between Larkin's novices on mechanics and the Experimenters on thermal phenomena). Students of the novice-expert shift have begun to use the history of science in another way—in claiming that naive physics is similar in content to the physics of an earlier age. For example, diSessa (in press) claims that the novice's physics is Aristotelian in some senses, and Clement (in press) relates the naive physics of today to the developed physics of the time immediately before Galileo.

It is not inconceivable that ontogeny recapitulates phylogeny in this sense. After all, scientists are people in the world before they are physicists. However, it is more likely that analogies such as those pointed to by diSessa and Clement hold only for isolated misconceptions, and are therefore somewhat misleading. Aristotelian physics crucially involved an elaborate cosmology, a ''final cause'' type of explanation (e.g., bodies fell because they seeked their natural resting place at the center of the cosmic order), and a view of matter as being composed of qualities. Dijksterhuis (1961) provides a comprehensible characterization of Aristotle's physics, a formidable task given how foreign Aristotle's system is to the modern mind. It is extremely unlikely, although not impossible, that today's novice begins with a conceptual framework like Aristotle's, or the impetus theory of the middle ages for that matter, if the whole system is at issue.

We plan to explore the conception of thermal phenomena of nonphysicist adults and to relate their conceptions to the theories in the time before Black. Thus, we do not wish to imply that the ways in which ontogeny recapitulates phylogeny is not an important one. But to address it one must do an analysis of the domain, explanatory mechanisms, and concepts of each conceptual system that enters into the comparison.

ACKNOWLEDGMENTS

The research reported here is part of a larger collaborative effort with Carol Smith and Ned Block. Both commented on this chapter and contributed ideas to it. We would also like to thank Dedre Gentner and Al Stevens for valuable comments on an earlier draft. We are especially grateful to T. S. Kuhn for detailed comments that saved us from some grave historical and conceptual errors. Any remaining are of course our responsibility. We were supported by NSF Award Number SED-7913278 in the joint NIE-NSF Program of Research on Cognitive Processes and the Structure of Knowledge in Science and Mathematics.

REFERENCES

Caramazza, A., McCloskey, M., & Green, B. Naive beliefs in ''sophisticated'' subjects: Misconceptions about trajectories of objects. *Cognition*, 1981, *9*, 117–123.

Clement, J. Students' preconceptions in introductory mechanics. *American Journal of Physics*, in press.

Dijksterhuis, E. J. *The mechanization of the world picture*. (C. Dikshoorn, trans.). Oxford: Clarendon Press, 1961.

diSessa, A. Unlearning Aristotelian physics: A study of knowledge-based learning. *Cognitive Science,* in press.

Kuhn, T. S. *The structure of scientific revolutions.* Chicago: University of Chicago Press, 1962.

Kuhn, T. S. A function for thought experiments. In T. S. Kuhn (Ed.). *The Essential Tension.* Chicago: University of Chicago Press, 1977 .(a)

Kuhn, T. S. Concepts of cause in the development of physics. In T. S. Kuhn (Ed.), *The essential tension.* Chicago: University of Chicago Press, 1977.(b)

Larkin, J. H., McDermott, J., Simon, D. P., & Simon, H. A. Expert and novice performance in solving physics problems. *Science,* 1980, *208,* 1335–1342.

McKie, D., & Heathcote, N. H. V. *The discovery of specific and latent heats.* London: Edward Arnold & Co., 1935.

Middleton, W. E. K. *The experimenters: A study of the Accademia del Cimento.* Baltimore: Johns Hopkins Press, 1971.

Simon, D. P., & Simon, H. A. Individual differences in solving physics problems. In R. Siegler (Ed.), *Children's thinking: What develops?* Hillsdale, N.J.: Lawrence Erlbaum Associates, 1978.

Waller, R. *Essayes of natural experiments made in the Academie del Cimento under the protection of the most serene Prince Leopold of Tuscany.* London: Printed for Benjamen Alsop at the Angel and Bible in the Poultrey, over-against the Church, 1684.

White, B. Sources of difficulty in understanding Newtonian dynamics.*Cognitive Science,* in press.

13 Naive Theories of Motion

Michael McCloskey
The Johns Hopkins University

Everyday life provides people with countless opportunities for observing and interacting with objects in motion. For example, watching a baseball game, driving a car and even dropping a pencil involve encounters with moving objects. Thus, everyone presumably has some sort of knowledge about motion. However, it is by no means clear what form or forms this knowledge may take. Everyday experience may lead only to the acquisition of concrete facts about the behavior of specific objects in specific situations (e.g., when a moving billiard ball strikes a stationary ball head on, the moving ball often stops). Alternatively, experience may result in the induction of descriptive generalizations that summarize a variety of observations (e.g., moving objects eventually slow down and stop). Finally, experience might even lead to the development of implicit theories of motion that provide explanations for, as well as descriptions of, the behavior of moving objects (e.g., changes in the speed or direction of an object's motion are caused by external forces).

In this chapter we describe research aimed at determining what sorts of knowledge are in fact acquired through experience with moving objects. We first present some basic findings from experiments in which subjects solved simple problems concerning objects in motion. We then show that these and other findings imply that people develop on the basis of their everyday experience remarkably well-articulated naive theories of motion. Further, we argue that the assumptions of the naive theories are quite consistent across individuals. In fact, the theories developed by different individuals are best described as different forms of the same basic theory. Although this basic theory appears to be a reasonable outcome of experience with real-world motion, it is strikingly inconsistent with the fundamental principles of classical physics. In fact, the naive theory is remarkably similar to a pre-Newtonian physical theory popular in the 14th through 16th centuries.

In addition to considering the nature of the knowledge acquired through experience with moving objects, we briefly discuss the ways in which the experience-based knowledge interacts with knowledge acquired through classroom instruction in physics. Finally, we discuss the relationship of our work to other research concerning knowledge and reasoning about physics, and mention several important issues for future research.

MISCONCEPTIONS ABOUT MOTION

We first attempted to probe people's knowledge about motion in a series of experiments employing simple, nonquantitative problems concerning the behavior of moving objects. Subjects were undergraduate students at the Johns Hopkins University. In each experiment three groups of subjects were employed: (1) students who had never taken a high school or college physics course; (2) students who had taken high school but not college physics; and (3) students who had completed at least one college physics course.

In one experiment we asked 48 subjects to solve thirteen simple problems. Each problem consisted of a diagram, with instructions that explained the diagram and asked the subject to make a qualitative prediction about the motion of an object. Two of the problems are shown in Fig. 13.1. For problem A the subjects were given the following instructions:

> The diagram shows a thin curved metal tube. In the diagram you are looking down on the tube. In other words, the tube is lying flat. A metal ball is put into the end of the tube indicated by the arrow and is shot out of the other end of the tube at high speed.

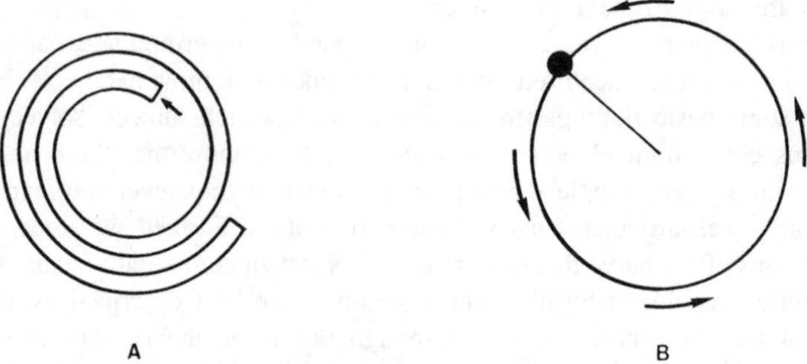

Fig. 13.1. Diagrams for the spiral tube problem (A) and the ball and string problem (B).

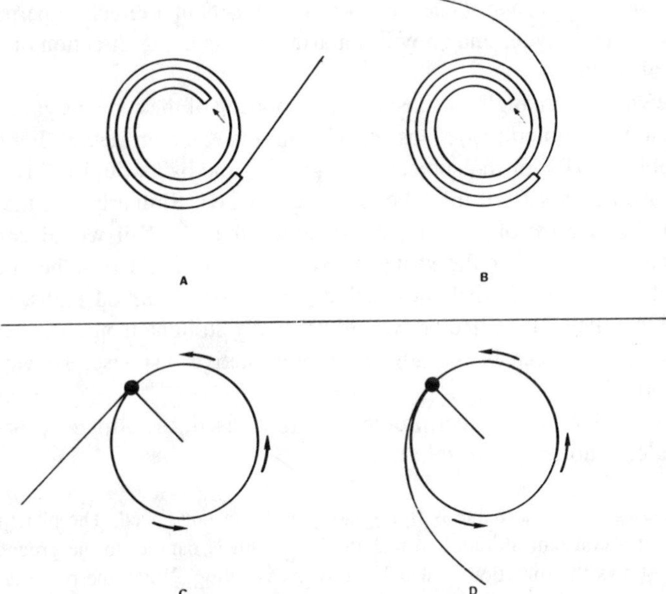

Fig. 13.2. Correct response and most common incorrect responses for the spiral tube problem and the ball and string problem. The correct responses appear in (A) and (C).

The subjects were then asked to draw the path the ball would follow after it emerged from the tube, ignoring air resistance and any spin the ball might have.

For problem B, the subjects were told:

> Imagine that someone has a metal ball attached to a string and is twirling it at high speed in a circle above his head. In the diagram you are looking down on the ball. The circle shows the path followed by the ball and the arrows show the direction in which it is moving. The line from the center of the circle to the ball is the string. Assume that when the ball is at the point shown in the diagram, the string breaks where it is attached to the ball. Draw the path the ball will follow after the string breaks. Ignore air resistance.

Newton's first law states that in the absence of a net applied force, an object in motion will travel in a straight line. Thus, the correct answer to the spiral tube problem is that after the ball leaves the tube it will move in a straight line in the direction of its instantaneous velocity at the moment it exits the tube (see Fig. 13.2A).

The correct answer to the ball and string problem is similar. As shown in Fig. 13.2C, the ball will fly off in a straight line along the tangent to the circle at the point where the ball was located when the string broke. In other words, the ball will travel in a straight line in the direction of its instantaneous velocity at the moment the string broke. (The force of gravity acts in a direction perpendicular to the horizontal plane, and so will not affect the speed or direction of the ball's horizontal motion.)

Somewhat surprisingly, a substantial proportion of the subjects gave incorrect answers to the problems (McCloskey, Caramazza & Green, 1980). For the spiral tube problem, 51% of the subjects thought that the ball would follow a curved path after emerging from the tube (see Fig. 13.2B). Similarly, for the ball and string problem 30% of the subjects believed that the ball would continue in curvilinear motion after the string broke (Fig. 13.2D). One other interesting aspect of the results is that most subjects who drew curved paths apparently believed that the ball's trajectory would gradually straighten out. This straightening of trajectories can be seen in the representative responses shown in Figs. 13.2B and 13.2D.

Figure 13.3 shows another problem we have used, the airplane problem. For this problem subjects were told that

> In the diagram, an airplane is flying along at a constant speed. The plane is also flying at a constant altitude, so that its flight path is parallel to the ground. The arrow shows the direction in which the plane is flying. When the plane is in the position shown in the diagram a large metal ball is dropped from the plane. The plane continues flying at the same speed in the same direction and at the same altitude. Draw the path the ball will follow from the time it is dropped until it hits the ground. Ignore wind or air resistance. Also, show as well as you can, the position of the plane at the moment the ball hits the ground.

The correct answer to the problem, which is shown in Fig. 13.4A, is that the ball will fall in a parabolic arc. The airplane will be directly above the ball when it hits the ground. This answer may be understood by noting that the total velocity of the ball may be decomposed into independent horizontal and vertical

Fig. 13.3. Diagram for the airplane problem.

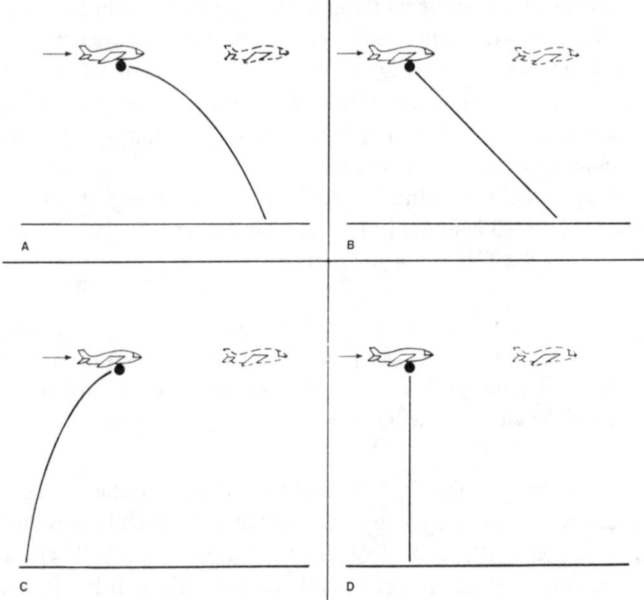

Fig. 13.4. Correct response (A) and incorrect responses (B-D) for the airplane problem.

components. Before the ball is dropped, it has a horizontal velocity equal to that of the plane, and a vertical velocity of zero. After the ball is released, it undergoes a constant vertical acceleration due to gravity, and thus acquires a constantly increasing vertical velocity. The ball's horizontal velocity, however, does not change. In other words, the ball continues to move horizontally at a speed equal to that of the plane. (The force of gravity acts in a direction perpendicular to that of the ball's horizontal motion, and consequently does not influence the ball's horizontal velocity. Further, no other forces are acting on the ball. Thus, according to the principle of inertia, the ball's horizontal velocity will remain constant.) The combination of the constant horizontal velocity and the continually increasing vertical velocity produces a parabolic arc. Finally, because the horizontal velocity of the ball is always the same as that of the plane, the plane will remain directly above the ball until the ball hits the ground.

When we presented the airplane problem to 48 subjects, we obtained a variety of responses (Green, McCloskey & Caramazza, 1980). Nineteen subjects, or 40%, drew forward arcs that looked more or less parabolic (see Fig. 13.4A). Fifteen of these 19 subjects indicated that the plane would be directly over the ball when the ball hit the ground. However, four subjects indicated that at the moment the ball hit the ground, the airplane would be well ahead of it horizontally.

Thirteen percent of the subjects thought that the ball would fall in a straight diagonal line (Fig. 13.4B), whereas another 11% indicated that the ball would move backwards when released (Fig. 13.4C). However, the most common incorrect response, which was made by 36% of the subjects, was that the ball would fall straight down (Fig. 13.4D). These results suggest that many people have little understanding of projectile motion.

Consider finally the very simple problem shown in Fig. 13.5, which we recently presented to 135 students in an introductory psychology class. The subjects were given the following instructions:

> The diagram shows a side view of a cliff. The top of the cliff is frictionless (in other words, perfectly smooth). A metal ball is sliding along the top of the cliff at a constant speed of 50 miles per hour. Draw the path the ball will follow after it goes over the edge of the cliff. Ignore air resistance.

The correct answer for the cliff problem is similar to that for the airplane problem. After the ball goes over the edge of the cliff, it will continue to travel horizontally at a constant speed of 50 mph. However, the ball will acquire a constantly increasing vertical velocity, and consequently will fall in a parabolic arc.

Seventy-four percent of the subjects drew trajectories that appeared more or less parabolic (see Fig. 13.6A). However, as shown in Figs. 13.6B and 13.6C the drawings of 22% of the subjects clearly showed the ball moving in an arc for some time and thereafter falling straight down. These subjects apparently believed that the ball's horizontal velocity, instead of remaining constant, would gradually decrease to zero. Several of the subjects who believed that the ball would eventually be falling straight down drew particularly interesting trajectories. In these trajectories, one of which is reproduced in Fig. 13.6C, the ball continues to travel in a straight horizontal line for some time after it goes over the edge of the cliff. The ball then turns rather abruptly and falls straight down.

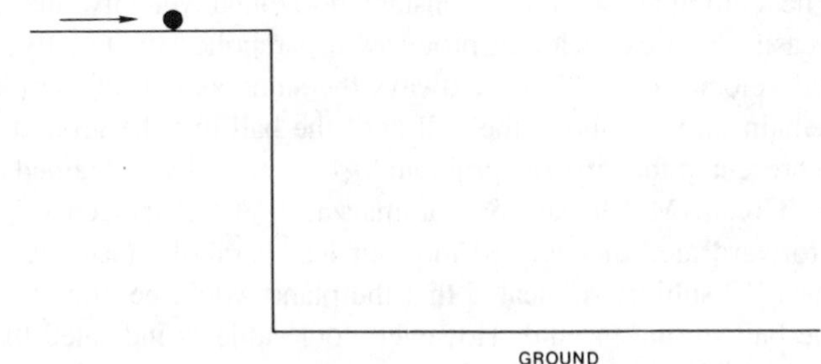

Fig. 13.5. Diagram for the cliff problem.

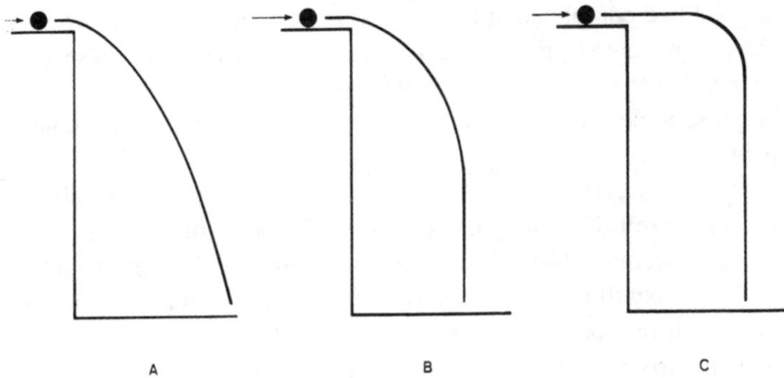

Fig. 13.6. Correct responses (A) and most common incorrect responses (B and C) for the cliff problem.

Other problems have produced results similar to those obtained for the four problems discussed here. In other words, although some subjects gave the correct answer, a large percentage made errors of various sorts.

For most of the problems we have employed, classroom physics instruction appears to affect the number but not the types of errors. In other words, subjects who have never taken a physics course make the most errors, subjects who have completed a high-school course do somewhat better, and subjects who have taken college physics make the fewest errors. However, the same sorts of errors are made by subjects in all three groups.

At first it appeared to us, as it must also appear to the reader, that the errors obtained for the various problems reflected a wide variety of separate and perhaps idiosyncratic misconceptions held by the subjects. However, as we show in the next section, additional research revealed that this was not the case.

A NAIVE THEORY OF MOTION

In an attempt to uncover the bases for the errors observed on our simple problems, we conducted an experiment in which subjects were tested individually. The subjects first solved several problems, and were then interviewed at length about their answers. During the interviews, the subjects were asked to explain their answers to the problems presented initially. They were also asked to solve additional problems when there was need to clarify a point. The subjects were encouraged to talk about what they were thinking as they attempted to arrive at an answer to a question or problem. The interviews, which lasted 1.5 to 2.5 hours per subject, were tape recorded and later transcribed verbatim.

Subjects were 13 students at Johns Hopkins University. Four of the subjects had never taken a physics course, three had taken high school physics, and the remaining six had completed at least one year of college physics. The results for the problems presented prior to the interviews suggested that these 13 subjects were comparable to those from the earlier experiments. In particular, the subjects from the present experiment made the same sorts of errors as the subjects tested previously.

The interviews clearly indicated that at least 11 of the 13 subjects relied heavily upon a well-developed naive theory of motion in arriving at answers to the problems. Remarkably, all 11 subjects held the same basic theory. This theory, which we will refer to as a naive *impetus theory,* makes two fundamental assertions about motion. First, the theory asserts that the act of setting an object in motion imparts to the object an internal force or "impetus" that serves to maintain the motion. Second, the theory assumes that a moving object's impetus gradually dissipates (either spontaneously or as a result of external influences), and as a consequence the object gradually slows down and comes to a stop. For example, according to the impetus theory, a person who gives a push to a toy car to set it rolling across the floor imparts an impetus to the car, and it is this impetus that keeps the car moving after it is no longer in contact with the person's hand. However, the impetus is gradually expended, and as a result the toy car slows down and eventually stops.

In the following discussion we present evidence that our subjects do indeed hold a naive impetus theory. Further, we show that many of the errors observed for our problems follow from this basic theory and the specific elaborations of it developed by the subjects. However, before discussing these points we digress briefly to consider the differences between the impetus view and the principles of classical physics.

According to the impetus theory, an object set in motion acquires an internal force, and this internal force keeps the object in motion. This view, which draws a qualitative distinction between a state of rest (absence of impetus) and a state of motion (presence of impetus), is inconsistent with the principles of classical physics. Classical physics argues that in the absence of a net applied force, an object at rest remains at rest and an object in motion remains in motion in a straight line at a constant speed. Just as no force is required to keep an object at rest, no force is required to keep an object in motion. In fact, no qualitative distinction is made between a state of rest and a state of constant-velocity rectilinear motion. Any object that is not accelerating (i.e., not undergoing a change in speed and/or direction) can be described as at rest or as in constant-velocity motion, depending on the choice of a frame of reference. For example, a person riding in a car that is moving in a straight line at a constant speed may be described as at rest if the car is chosen as the frame of reference, or in motion if the ground is taken as the reference frame. According to classical physics, neither of these descriptions is any more valid than the other. Another way of saying this is that, within classical physics, states of absolute rest and absolute motion do not exist. Thus, it is not correct to say, as the impetus theory does, that moving objects have an internal force or impetus while objects at rest do not, because an object may be simultaneously described as at rest or in motion depending upon the choice of a frame of reference.

With this discussion in mind, let us now consider the results of the experiment in which subjects were interviewed about their answers to problems. Several aspects of these results provide strong support for the claim that many people espouse a naive impetus theory.

In the first place, several subjects stated the impetus view rather explicitly during the course of the interview. For example, one subject, who had completed one year of college physics, used the term *momentum* in explaining his answer to a problem involving the motion of a metal ball. When asked to explain what he meant by momentum, the subject stated:

> I mean the weight of the ball times the speed of the ball.... Momentum is...a force that has been exerted and put into the ball so this ball now that it's travelling has a certain amount of force....The moving object has the force of momentum and since there's no force to oppose that force it will continue on until it is opposed by something.

In a similar situation another subject, who had also taken college physics, defined momentum as

> a combination of the velocity and the mass of an object. It's something that carries it along after a force on it has stopped.... Let's call it the force of motion.... It's something that keeps a body moving.

The belief that motion is maintained by an impetus impressed on an object is quite clear in these statements.

The belief that moving objects slow down and stop due to the dissipation of impetus can also be seen in subjects' statements. For example, one subject, who had never taken a physics course, was asked to explain why a ball rolling along a floor would eventually come to a stop. The subject stated that friction and air resistance slow the ball down, and was then asked to explain how these factors affect the ball. He replied as follows:

> I understand that [friction and air resistance] adversely affect the speed of the ball, but now how. Whether they sort of absorb some of the force that's in the ball...I'm not sure. In other words, for the ball to plow through the air resistance or the friction if it has to sort of expend force and therefore lose it, I'm not sure.... That seems to be a logical explanation.

The subject's assumption that the ball slows down because friction and air resistance sap its impetus is clear, although the subject is unsure whether this assumption is correct.

The naive impetus theory was also used by subjects to explain the behavior of objects in more complex situations. One subject, who had completed both high school and college physics courses, was asked to draw the path followed by a ball thrown upward at a 45 degree angle. The subject drew a parabolic arc, which is correct, and was then asked to explain why the ball follows this sort of path. The subject responded by drawing force vectors at various points along the path of the ball (see Fig. 13.7), and explaining that

> The ball when it was first thrown was provided with a certain amount of force.... What's happening is that the force is basically being counterbalanced by gravity, and at this point [labeled 1 in Fig. 13.7] the upward force is still stronger than gravity, while here [point 2] they're both equal and here [point 3] gravity has become stronger.

In response to further questioning the subject stated that the upward force steadily decreased due to the constant force of gravity.

Two other subjects gave virtually identical explanations for the behavior of a projectile shot from a cannon. For example, one subject explained that the cannonball slows down as it moves from the cannon to the peak of the arc, and speeds up thereafter

> Because as it [the cannonball] comes up the force from the cannon is dissipating and the force of gravity is taking over. So it slows down.... As it makes the arc and begins to come down, gravity is overcoming the force from the cannon.

The subject further argued that the cannonball accelerates on the way down due to the continuing dissipation of the force from the cannon. Clement (1982) has obtained similar results with the same sort of problem.

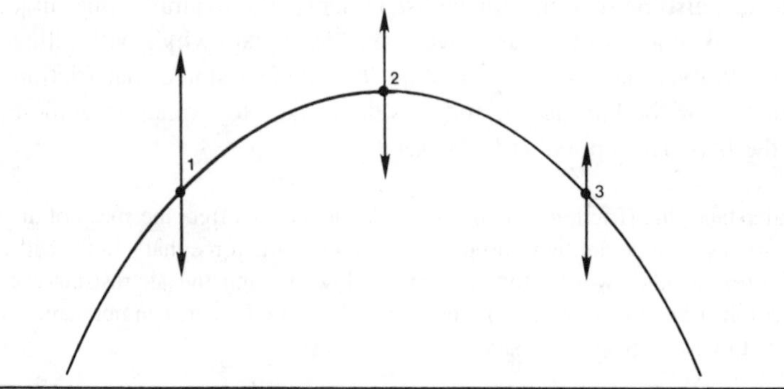

Fig. 13.7. Subject's drawing of the trajectory of a thrown ball, with vectors drawn by the subject to represent the "upward force" and the force of gravity at three points on the trajectory.

The view that many people espouse a naive impetus theory offers an interpretation for many of the errors made by subjects on the problems described in the preceding section. Consider, for example, the problem in which a moving ball goes over the edge of the cliff. As discussed earlier, many subjects indicated that the ball would move in an arc for some time and thereafter fall straight down (see Figs. 13.6B and 13.6C). This response seems to reflect a belief that the ball's impetus, which causes it to keep moving horizontally for some time after it goes over the edge of the cliff, gradually dissipates. When the original impetus is entirely gone, the ball has no forward motion and thus falls straight down. This interpretation is supported by statements made by several subjects in the interview experiment. One subject, who indicated that a ball going over a cliff would continue in a straight horizontal line for a short time and would then turn and fall straight down, said

> When it leaves the cliff the inertia force—the horizontal force—is greater than the downward motion force. When the horizontal force becomes less the ball would start falling...eventually the horizontal force would no longer have an effect, and it would be a straight downward motion.

Another subject who believed that the ball would eventually be falling straight down said that after the ball went over the cliff, its velocity would gradually be expended, so that

> It will come to a point.... where there's no longer any forward movement and the fall translates into a 90 degree fall, straight down.

The curved trajectories drawn for the spiral tube and ball and string problems (see Fig. 13.2) also stem from the impetus theory. The subjects who drew curved paths apparently believed that an object constrained to move in a curved path (e.g., by being shot through a curved tube) acquires a ''curvilinear impetus'' that causes the object to retain its curved motion for some time after it is no longer constrained. However, the curvilinear impetus gradually dissipates, causing the object's path to straighten out (see Figs. 13.2B and 13.2D). Support for this interpretation once again comes from statements by subjects during interviews. One subject, who had never taken a physics course, explained a curved trajectory drawn for a ball shot through a curved tube in the following way:

> The momentum from the curve [of the tube] gives it [the ball] the arc.... The force that the ball picks up from the curve eventually dissipates and it will follow a normal straight line.

Similarly, a subject explaining a curved trajectory for the ball and string problem stated that the ball would follow a curved path

> because of the directional momentum. You've got a force going around and [after the string breaks, the ball] will follow the curve that you've set it in until the ball runs out of the force within it that you've created by swinging.

It is interesting that the subjects argue that when curvilinear impetus dissipates, the ball will continue in rectilinear motion rather than stopping. This argument seems to imply that in addition to the rapidly-dissipated curvilinear impetus, the ball has a longer-lasting impetus for straight-line motion.

Consider finally the problem shown in Fig. 13.8A, the pendulum problem. The diagram represents a side view of a metal ball swinging back and forth at the end of a string. Subjects are told that when the ball is in the position shown and moving from left to right, the string is cut. They are then asked to draw the path the ball will follow as it falls to the ground, ignoring air resistance. The correct answer to the problem is shown in Fig. 13.8B.

Several manifestations of the naive impetus theory were observed in the context of the pendulum problem (Caramazza, McCloskey, & Green, 1981). First, a number of subjects used the impetus concept to explain the back and forth motion of the ball before the string was cut. One subject, for example, stated that "the gravity that pulls it (the ball) to the center gives it enough force to continue the swing to the other side." Another subject indicated that the ball stops at the ends of the pendulum's arc because "the force has been expended."

The impetus view was also evident in many subjects' ideas about how the ball would behave after the string was cut. Several subjects indicated that when the string was cut the ball would continue along the original arc of the pendulum for a short time, and would then either fall straight down, as in Fig. 13.8C, or would describe a more or less parabolic trajectory, as in Fig. 13.8D.

The interpretation of these responses in terms of a naive impetus theory is rather obvious. The response shown in Fig. 13.8C reflects a belief that the motion of the pendulum before the string is cut imparts a curvilinear impetus to the ball. When the string is cut, this impetus carries the ball along the original path for a short time. However, the impetus eventually dissipates, and the ball falls straight down. The response in Fig. 13.8D can be interpreted in a similar fashion. One subject who made this sort of response explained that when the string is cut, the ball has

> the momentum that is has achieved from swinging through this arc and should continue in a circular path for a little while.... then it no longer has the force holding it in the circular path, and it has the force of gravity downward upon it so it's going to start falling in that sort of arc motion because otherwise it would be going straight.

This subject apparently believes that when the curvilinear impetus has been expended, the ball will still have an impetus that in the absence of gravity would

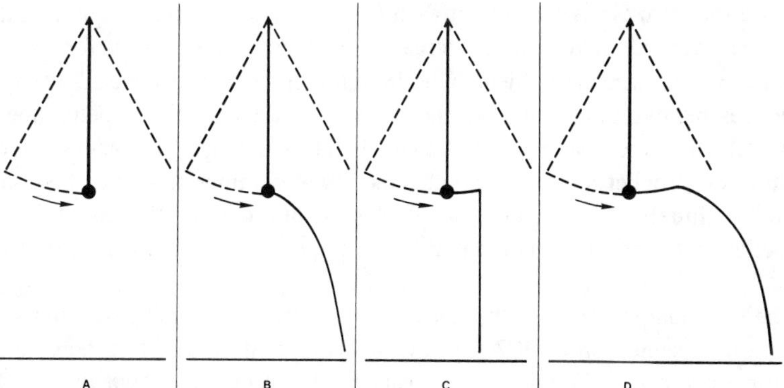

Fig. 13.8. Diagram for the pendulum problem (A) with the correct response (B) and two incorrect responses (C and D).

cause the ball to move in a straight line. Because of this additional impetus, the ball falls in an arc rather than straight down.

We have argued in this section that most of the subjects we have questioned in detail hold the same naive theory of motion, an impetus theory. However, several different forms of the impetus theory may be distinguished on the basis of the subjects' responses. In the next section we discuss these individual differences.

INDIVIDUAL DIFFERENCES

The individual differences we have observed in the naive impetus theories represent differences among subjects in the position taken on four important issues. First, subjects differ on the issue of the existence of curvilinear impetus. As discussed earlier, many subjects believe that an object constrained to move in a curved path acquires a curvilinear impetus that causes it to follow a curved trajectory for some time after the constraints on its motion are removed. However, other subjects who hold the basic impetus theory do not postulate the existence of a curvilinear impetus.

The second important issue on which subjects differ concerns how impetus is dissipated. Some subjects believe that impetus is self-expending (i.e., dissipates spontaneously). These subjects argue that even in the absence of any external influences on a moving object, the object's impetus steadily decreases, causing it to slow down and stop (in the case of rectilinear impetus), or (in the case of curvilinear impetus) causing its path to become progressively straighter. A more common view, especially among students who have completed physics courses, is that impetus is sapped by external influences like friction and air resistance.

(We use the term *influences* rather than *forces* because students do not naturally view the external factors that decrease an object's impetus as forces in the classical physics sense.) Subjects who hold that impetus is decreased by external influences believe that in the absence of such influences the impetus does not dissipate. Thus, these subjects state that a ball moving on a frictionless plane in a vacuum, or a rocket moving through space, will continue to move at a constant speed indefinitely. Although this sort of statement is correct, the basis for it (i.e., the belief that motion is maintained by an impetus in the object) is, of course, not.

The view that impetus is sapped by external influences can be seen in the third quotation presented on p. 307. This view also manifests itself in the context of curvilinear impetus. Consider, for instance, the problem shown in Fig. 13.9, which involves a ball shot through a tube shaped like a circle with a 90 degree segment removed. One subject argued that in a vacuum, the ball would curve around and re-enter the tube, whereas in air the ball's path would be less curved and would eventually straighten out. This response suggests a belief that the curvilinear impetus dissipates in the presence of air resistance but not in a vacuum.

A third issue on which different subjects adopt different positions involves the interaction of impetus with gravity. Most subjects believe that gravity affects a moving object regardless of how much impetus it has. Thus, for example, most subjects state that a moving ball going over the edge of a cliff will immediately begin to fall. Some subjects, however, believe that gravity does not affect an object until its original impetus falls below some critical level. These subjects argue, for example, that a ball that goes over the edge of a cliff continues to

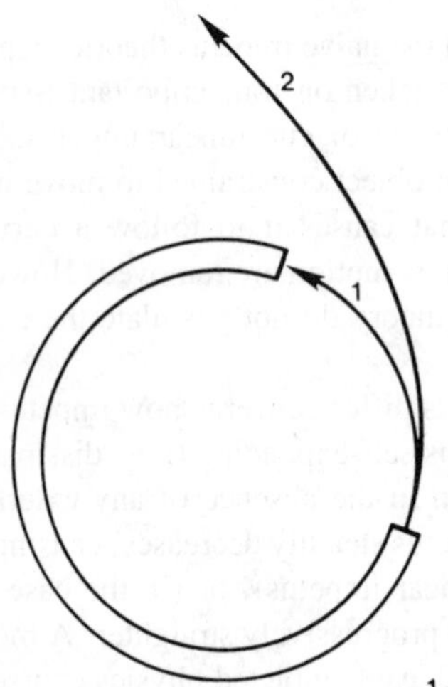

Fig. 13.9. Responses by one subject for a problem in which a ball is shot through a circular tube that is lying flat. The subject indicated that in a vacuum the ball would follow the trajectory labeled 1, while in air the ball would follow path 2.

travel in a straight horizontal line for some time before it begins to fall (see Fig. 13.6C). One subject, who gave this sort of response for a problem in which a ball launched by a spring-loaded piston goes over a cliff, explained that

> as it comes out at a certain force and speed it's going to eventually lose its horizontal momentum and as the momentum decreases it will begin to fall because gravity will begin to take over...your initial force—the spring—pushes it out, but it can't keep going at that speed indefinitely, sooner or later it's going to slow down. So as it slows down it begins to fall and somehow this line [the part of the trajectory where the ball begins to fall] is the relationship between the force of the spring and the force of gravity.

Subjects who believe that a moving object is immune to the effects of gravity until its impetus falls below a critical level differ in their views about just what this critical level is. Some of the subjects argue that gravity begins to affect the object when the object's internal force becomes weaker than the force of gravity. Thus, as we mentioned earlier, one subject who claimed that a ball going over a cliff would travel in a straight horizontal line for some time before starting to fall stated that

> when it leaves the cliff the inertia force—the horizontal force—is greater than the downward motion force[gravity]. When the horizontal force becomes less, the ball would start falling.

A few subjects, however, believed that gravity would not affect a moving object until its impetus had been entirely expended. For example, one subject, whose response to the cliff problem is shown in Fig. 13.10, stated that "gravity isn't going to affect it until it stops moving."

The last major issue on which subjects differ is perhaps the most interesting. This issue concerns how impetus is imparted to an object. Most subjects believe that any agent that sets an object in motion imparts to the object an impetus that will keep the object moving after the agent is no longer acting upon the object. However, some subjects believe that an object must be directly pushed or pulled to acquire impetus. According to these subjects, an object that is merely carried by another moving object does not acquire impetus.

Consider, for example, the airplane problem, in which a metal ball is dropped from a moving airplane. Many subjects indicate for this problem that the ball will fall straight down (see Fig. 13.4D). One subject explained this response by stating that the carrying of the ball by the airplane

> would give the ball no force in the x [horizontal] direction...the only force acting on the ball would be in the y direction, which is downward.

Consequently, the subject said, the ball would fall straight down.

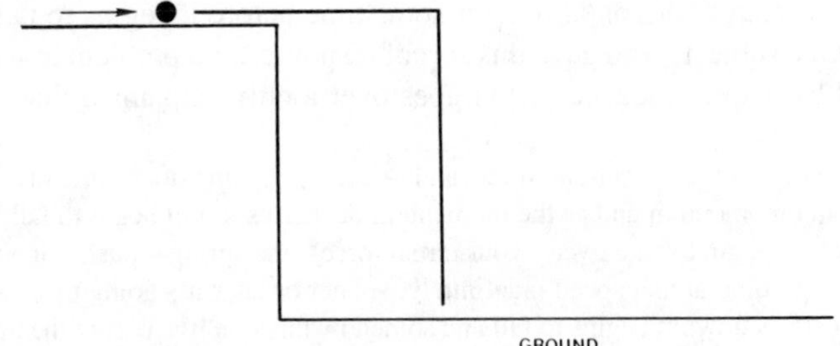

Fig. 13.10. One subject's response to the cliff problem.

The belief that impetus is acquired by a pushed but not by a carried object is revealed rather clearly by the problems shown in Fig. 13.11. For the problem shown in Fig. 13.11A, subjects are told that a ball is given a push to set it in motion, and that the ball slides along the top of the cliff at a constant high rate of speed. For the problem in Fig. 13.11B subjects are told that a ball is held by an electromagnet at the end of a metal rod, which is carried along by a conveyor belt at the same speed as the ball that was pushed. Subjects are further told that when

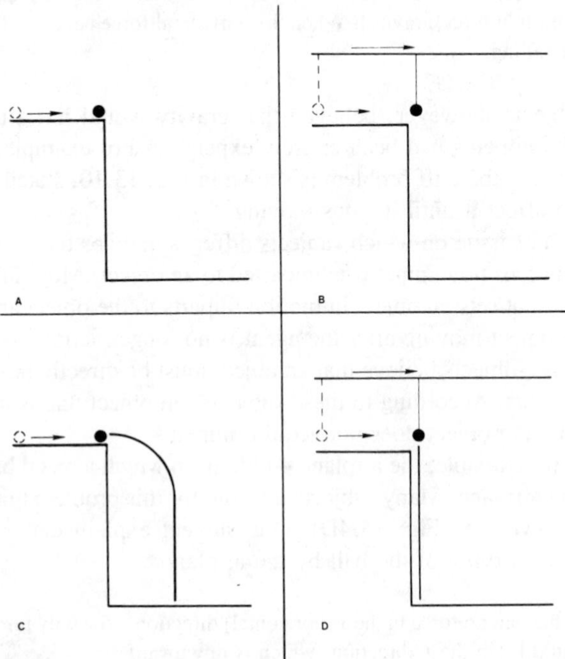

Fig. 13.11. Diagrams for the cliff problem (A) and the conveyor problem (B), with one common pattern of responses (C and D).

the ball reaches the position shown in the diagram, the electromagnet is turned off, releasing the ball. The conveyor belt continues to move. For both problems subjects are asked to draw the path the ball follows as it falls.

These two problems were presented to 7 of the 13 subjects in the experiment in which subjects were interviewed about their answers. Three of the subjects indicated that while the pushed ball would fall in some sort of arc (as shown in Fig. 13.11C), the carried ball would fall straight down (Fig. 13.11D). One of these subjects explained that with the pushed ball

> You've got a lot of force behind it, which would give it some motion straight out.

However, she continued, the carried ball, although it is moving at the same speed as the pushed ball, does not have any force behind it. She concluded that

> speed is not what controls the fall—it's the force behind it....To me speed and force are two different things, so it [the carried ball] is going to fall straight down.

Another subject who gave the same response explained that the carried ball would fall straight down "because the ball *itself* isn't moving, it's just moving because it's attached to that [the conveyor]." A person with whom we have discussed these problems informally expressed a similar view by saying that the pushed ball has its own motion and therefore will continue to move after it goes over the cliff. However, she said, the ball on the conveyor is being carried and therefore does not have its own motion. Thus, it will fall straight down.

HISTORICAL PARALLELS: THE MEDIEVAL IMPETUS THEORY

The naive theory held by our subjects is strikingly similar to the theory of impressed force or impetus discussed by Philoponus in the 6th century and developed in detail by John Buridan and others in the 14th century. (For detailed discussion of this theory, see Butterfield, 1965; Clagett, 1959; Dijksterhuis, 1961; and Franklin, 1976.) Like our subjects' naive theory, the medieval impetus theory assumes that the act of setting an object in motion impresses in the object a force, or impetus, that serves to keep the object in motion. Buridan (Clagett, 1959) for example, states that a mover

> in moving a moving body impresses in it a certain impetus or a certain force...[which impetus acts] in the direction toward which the mover was moving the body, either up or down, or laterally, or circularly...It is by that impetus that the stone is moved after the projector [i.e., mover] ceases to move [it]. But that impetus is continually decreased by the resisting air and by the gravity of the stone [pp. 534–535].

The parallels between the medieval impetus theory and our subjects' conception of motion extend far beyond the basic claim that motion is maintained by an impressed force. First, as the quotation from Buridan suggests, many impetus theorists postulated a circular impetus that served such purposes as maintaining the motion of a wheel or sustaining the rotation of the celestial spheres. This circular impetus is clearly very similar to our subjects' curvilinear impetus.

Further, just as our subjects differed on the question of whether impetus dissipates spontaneously or as the result of external forces, so did the earlier proponents of the impetus theory (Clagett, 1959; Dijksterhuis, 1961). Buridan, for instance, argued that impetus is not self-expending. However, others, including Franciscus de Marchia, Oresme and, much earlier, Avicenna, asserted that while an object's impetus could be depleted by air and other factors, the impetus would dissipate even in the absence of these factors.

The impetus theorists also resemble our subjects in their views on the interaction of impetus and gravity. Some theorists, like some of our subjects, believed that gravity would affect an object's motion regardless of how much impetus the object had. Other proponents of the impetus theory, however, held different views. Avicenna, for example, argued that only a single impetus could reside in an object an any one time. According to this view, a stone thrown upward at a 45 degree angle would acquire an impetus that would cause it to travel along a straight line at a 45 degree elevation until the impetus was exhausted and the stone came momentarily to rest. The stone's natural gravity would then impart a natural impetus to the stone, causing it to fall straight down (Clagett, 1959). This view is similar to that of the subjects who believed that gravity would not affect an object until its impetus had been entirely expended. As we have seen, for example, one subject, in discussing a ball going over the edge of a cliff, said that "gravity isn't going to affect it until it stops moving."

Several of our subjects held the less extreme view that gravity will not affect an object until its impetus falls below some critical (nonzero) level, but will thereafter cause the object to begin to fall. This viewpoint echoes the argument made centuries earlier by Albert of Saxony, who asserted that a projectile's impetus initially overpowers its natural gravity (Crombie, 1952). Thus, for example, a projectile fired horizontally will for some time follow a straight horizontal trajectory. However, the projectile's impetus gradually weakens and at some point the projectile, while still moving forward, will begin to fall.

One can also find some hint in the writings of Buridan and others of the belief held by several of our subjects that an object carried by another moving object will not acquire impetus. Buridan, for example, offers several arguments in favor of the view that the earth, rather than the heavens, rotates (Clagett, 1959; Franklin, 1976). However, he ultimately rejects this viewpoint on grounds that if the earth turned, an arrow shot straight upward should hit the ground some distance away from the point at which it was launched, rather than returning directly to the launch point (which is, to a close approximation, what it actually does). The implicit assumption is that the arrow would not acquire any impetus by virtue of being carried along by the moving earth. Thus, when shot upward it would not continue moving laterally in the direction of the earth's rotation. Rather it would travel straight up and down, while the original launch point moved out from under it.

The close correspondence between the medieval impetus theory and the naive theory held by our subjects can also be seen in the remarkable similarity between medieval explanations for certain phenomena, and the explanations given by our subjects. Galileo (Galilei, 1632/1967) who in his early writings endorsed the impetus theory, provides one simple example:

> I have put forth the observation of the pendulum so that you would understand that the impetus acquired in the descending arc…is able by itself to drive the same ball upward by a forced motion…in the ascending arc. [p. 227].

This explanation is virtually identical to that given by the subject who stated that "the gravity that pulls it [the ball] to the center gives it enough force to continue the swing to the other side."

The correspondence between the explanation for projectile motion given by some of our subjects and that given by several impetus theorists is even clearer. Recall that two of our subjects explained the behavior of a projectile fired from a cannon by saying that the impetus from the cannon is initially stronger than the force of gravity, and consequently the cannonball moves upward. However, the impetus progressively weakens and the cannonball slows down. At the peak of the trajectory the impetus and the force of gravity are equal. Thereafter, the impetus from the cannon continues to weaken, so that gravity is now the stronger force. Consequently, the projectile begins to fall, accelerating as it does so because the original impetus is still being dissipated.

Compare this explanation with that given in Simplicius's description of a theory proposed by Hipparchus (Clagett, 1959):

> Hipparchus…declares that in the case of earth [i.e., an object] thrown upward it is the projecting force that is the cause of the upward motion…then as this force is diminished, (1) the upward motion proceeds but no longer at the same rate, (2) the body moves downward under the influence of its own internal impulse [i.e., gravity], even though the original projectory force lingers in some measure, and (3) as this force continues to diminish the object moves downward more swiftly [p. 543].

Galileo, in *De Motu* (ca. 1590/1960) offers a similar explanation:

> the body moves upward, provided the impressed motive force is greater than the resisting weight. But since that force….is continually weakened, it will finally become so diminished that it will no longer overcome the weight of the body and

> will not impel the body beyond that point...as the impressed force characteristically continues to decrease, the weight of the body begins to be predominant, and consequently the body begins to fall...there still remains...a considerable force that impels the body upward...[that] force continues to be weakened...and the body moves faster and faster [p. 89].

Clement (1982) has also pointed out the resemblance between students' explanations of projectile motion and that of Galileo.

These strong parallels between our subjects and the earlier impetus theorists suggest that the impetus theory is a very natural outcome of experience with moving objects in the real world.

In this context it is worthwhile to comment briefly on the claim made recently by several researchers that students' beliefs about motion are Aristotelian (e.g., Champagne, Klopfer & Anderson, 1980). These researchers have pointed out that many students, like Aristotle, believe that a force is required to keep an object in motion. There is, however, an important difference between the Aristotelian view and that of modern students. Specifically, Aristotle held that an object remains in motion only so long as it is direct contact with an *external* mover. Thus, for example, in the Aristotelian view a projectile is kept in motion by air pushing on it from behind. In contrast, modern students, as we have shown in this paper, believe that motion is maintained by a force impressed in the object itself. In other words, students believe that objects are kept in motion by internal and not external forces. Thus, the students' naive conception of motion is most similar not to the Aristotelian theory, but to the later impetus theory, which was developed in reaction to the Aristotelian view.

NAIVE THEORIES AND PHYSICS INSTRUCTION

It is beyond the scope of this paper to consider in detail the interaction of students' naive theories with information presented in a physics course. However, we should note briefly that the naive theories seem to create a number of difficulties for students taking physics. In particular, information presented in the classroom may frequently be misinterpreted or distorted to fit the naive impetus view, with the result that many students emerge from physics courses with their impetus theories largely intact. Indeed, we found in the experiment in which subjects were questioned in detail that most of the subjects who had taken physics courses still held some form of impetus theory.

An example of the distortion of information to make it fit the naive impetus theory is provided by the definitions of momentum given by two subjects who had taken college physics (see p. 307). Both subjects knew that an object's momentum is defined as the product of its mass and its velocity. However, the subjects also believed that "momentum is...a force that has been exerted and put into the ball" and "it's something that keeps a body moving."

The concepts of energy and inertia seem also to lend themselves to misinterpretation. For example, one subject, who had completed a college physics course, defined inertia in the following way:

> when you throw something that's what keeps it going...you put a little force behind it and it'll just keep going...inertia is...just the force that's on it when you let it go—sort of a residual force on it.

Distortion may occur even for very explicit information about the behavior of a moving object. For example, a subject presented with the ball and string problem (see Fig. 13.1B) stated that he knew the ball would fly off in a straight line tangent to the circle at the point where the string broke, because this situation had been discussed in his college physics course. However, he further stated that when the string broke, the ball would curve along its original path for a very short time, and would then turn rather abruptly and follow a path parallel to the tangent to the circle at the point where the string broke.

These examples make it very clear that the naive impetus theory is very strongly held and is not easily changed by classroom physics instruction. Thus, it may be useful, as several researchers have suggested (e.g., Champagne et al., 1980; Clement, 1982; Minstrell, 1982), for physics instructors to discuss with students their naive beliefs, carefully pointing out what is wrong with these beliefs, and how they differ from the views of classical physics. In this way students may be induced to give up the impetus theory and accept the Newtonian perspective.

A BRIEF REVIEW OF RELATED RESEARCH

The studies described in this paper contribute to a growing body of recent research concerning knowledge and reasoning in physics and related domains. In this section we mention briefly a few of the studies that are relevant to the issues we have discussed.

Several research groups have investigated the difficulties that students have with basic principles of mechanics (e.g., Champagne et al., 1980; Champagne, Klopfer, Solomon & Cahn, 1980; Clement, 1979, 1982; diSessa, 1979; Minstrell, 1982). Champagne et al., (1980) have reported that on problems involving free fall, many college students indicate that objects fall at a constant speed. Clement (1982) and Viennot (1979) have noted impetus-like beliefs in students attempting to describe the forces acting on objects in simple situations (e.g. a coin thrown straight up). Minstrell (1982) has also discussed difficulties that students have in understanding forces. Further, he has described an intensive demonstration-discussion method which appears to be successful in overcoming these difficulties.

Other researchers have attempted to characterize people's knowledge of mechanics concepts (e.g., mass, acceleration). Piaget (1970) studied children's understanding of movement and speed, reporting that these seemingly simple concepts are actually quite complex, and are poorly understood by young children. More recently, Trowbridge and McDermott (1980, 1981) have argued that the concepts of velocity and acceleration pose some difficulty even for adults. Finally, several studies have used proximity analysis methods (e.g., multidimensional scaling) to reveal the subjective organization of mechanics concepts (see Preece, 1978, for a review).

A number of interesting results have been obtained in studies of physics problem-solving by experts and novices (e.g., Chi, Feltovich & Glaser, 1981; Bhaskar & Simon, 1977; Larkin & Reif, 1979; Larkin, McDermott, Simon & Simon, 1980a; Novak & Araya, 1980). For example, Larkin et al. (1980) have reported that beginning physics students solving textbook problems use a strategy quite different from that employed by experts. Specifically, experts work forward from the quantities given in the problems to the desired unknown quantity, while novices work backward from the unknown to the givens.

The research on problem-solving has stimulated a number of attempts to develop explicit models of knowledge representation and processing in mechanics (e.g., Larkin, McDermott, Simon & Simon, 1980b; Novak, 1976, 1977; de Kleer, 1975, 1977). Novak, for example, has developed a program that diagrams and solves statics problems stated in English.

Other research has examined knowledge and reasoning in areas of physics other than mechanics, as well as in other branches of science. Fredette and Lochhead (1980), for example, have discussed students' misconceptions about electric circuits, and Nussbaum and Novak (1976) have described children's conceptions of the earth. In addition, Collins, Stevens and Goldin (1979; Stevens & Collins, 1980) have examined students' misconceptions about the complex physical systems involved in climate and rainfall.

More general aspects of scientific thinking have also been examined (e.g., Inhelder & Piaget, 1958; Gentner, 1980, in press; Kuhn, 1977; Siegler, 1978). Gentner (1980, in press) for example, has discussed the role of analogies (e.g., atoms are like miniature solar systems) in scientific thinking, and Kuhn (1977) has considered the function of thought experiments in scientific development. In addition, Carey (this volume) and her colleagues are examining the processes by which scientific concepts such as heat and temperature come to be differentiated.

The recent research on scientific knowledge and reasoning has produced many important insights, and should provide a firm foundation for the development of more complete and detailed descriptions of the scientifically naive individual, the expert, and the process by which the former is transformed into the latter.

CONCLUDING REMARKS

We have argued in this paper that people develop on the basis of their everyday experience remarkably well-articulated naive theories of motion. These theories provide not only descriptions of, but also causal explanations for, the behavior of moving objects. In particular, many people believe that the act of setting an object in motion impresses in the object an internal force or impetus. This impetus is assumed to keep the object in motion after it is no longer in contact with the original mover. According to this view, moving objects eventually slow down and stop because their impetus gradually dissipates. This naive theory is, as we pointed out, strikingly similar to the medieval theory of impetus.

Although we have focused in this paper on naive theories of motion, we should note that people reasoning about the behavior of moving objects use, in addition to naive theories, several other sorts of knowledge. For example, some subjects in solving our simple problems made use of analogies, memories for specific experiences (e.g., throwing a rock with a sling), isolated facts about mechanics (e.g., Galileo found that heavy and light objects fall at the same rate) and knowledge acquired through formal instruction in physics (e.g., a projectile's motion can be analyzed into independent horizontal and vertical components). However, for most subjects a naive impetus theory played a prominent role in attempts to solve problems.

The findings of the present study suggest a number of interesting directions for subsequent research. First, there is need to characterize in greater detail people's naive theories in mechanics and in other scientific domains. Second, future research should seek to determine how the naive theories develop. Addressing this issue may involve exploring in children as well as in adults, what sorts of information people glean from observing and interacting with moving objects, and how they generate from this information a theoretical framework for explaining the behavior of moving objects. For example, the assumption that carried objects do not acquire impetus may stem from a frame of reference confusion in the observation of moving objects. Consider, for instance, a person who has seen a film taken from an airplane of bombs dropped from the plane. From the frame of reference of the plane, the bombs will drop nearly straight down. The person observing this may confuse frames of reference and consequently may believe that the bombs hit the ground at the point that was directly beneath the airplane when the bombs were released. From this faulty datum the person may conclude that a carried object does not acquire impetus. Other assumptions of the naive impetus theory may perhaps represent deductions made from observations that focused on salient aspects of an event (e.g., a push given to an object) and ignored less salient factors (e.g., air resistance). Additional research will be required to determine whether these speculations are reasonable.

Finally, future research should seek to determine what role, if any, naive theories of motion play in everyday life. An acquaintance of ours was recently stepping onto a ladder from a roof 20 feet above the ground. Unfortunately, the ladder slipped out from under him. As he began to fall he pushed himself out from the edge of the roof in an attempt to land in a bush about three feet out from the base of the house (in the hope that the bush would break his fall). However, he overshot the bush, landing about 12 feet from the base of the house and breaking his arm. Was this just a random miscalculation, or did our acquaintance push off too hard because of a naive belief that he would move outward for a short time and then fall straight down (rather than continuing to move outward throughout the fall)? Research in which people interact with actual moving objects may shed some light on the question.

In research currently in progress, we are attempting to address these other issues. It is to be hoped that this research will enable us to acheive a better understanding of naive conceptualizations of motion.

ACKNOWLEDGMENTS

This research was supported by NSF Award No. SED 7912741 in the Joint National Institute of Education - National Science Foundation Program of Research on Cognition Processes and the Structure of Knowledge in Science and Mathematics. Any opinions, findings, conclusions or recommendations expressed herein are those of the authors and do not necessarily reflect the views of the National Science Foundation or the National Institute of Education. We would like to thank Deborah Jira and Alfonso Caramazza for their assistance with the experiments. We would also like to thank Robert Kargon and Jeffrey Santee for their helpful comments.

REFERENCES

Bhaskar, R., & Simon, H. A. Problem solving in semantically rich domains: An example from engineering thermodynamics. *Cognitive Science,* 1977, *1,* 193–215.

Butterfield, H. *The origins of modern science 1300–1800*. New York: Free Press, 1965.

Caramazza, A., McCloskey, M., & Green, B. Naive beliefs in "sophisticated" subjects: Misconceptions about trajectories of objects. *Cognition,* 1981, *9,* 117–123.

Chi, M. T. H., Feltovich, P. J., & Glaser, R. Categorization and representation of physics problems by experts and novices. *Cognitive Science,* 1981, *5,* 121–152.

Champagne, A. B., Klopfer, L. E. & Anderson, J. H. Factors influencing the learning of classical mechanics. *American Journal of Physics,* 1980, *48,* 1074–1079.

Champagne, A. B., Klopfer, L. E., Solomon, C. A., & Cahn, A. D. *Interaction of students' knowledge with the comprehension and design of science experiments*. Unpublished manuscript, University of Pittsburgh, 1980.

Clagett, M. *The science of mechanics in the middle ages*. Madison, Wisc.: University of Wisconsin Press, 1959.

Clement, J. Mapping a student's causal conceptions from a problem-solving protocol. In J. Lochhead & J. Clement (Eds.), *Cognitive Process Instruction*. Philadelphia: Franklin Institute Press, 1979.

Clement, J. Students' preconceptions in introductory mechanics. *American Journal of Physics,* 1982, *50,* 66–71.

Collins, A. M., Stevens, A. L., & Goldin, S. Misconceptions in students' understanding. *International Journal of Man-Machine Studies,* 1979, *11,* 145–156.

Crombie, A. C. *Augustine to Galileo: The history of science A.D. 400–1650.* London: Falcon Press, 1952.

deKleer, J. *Qualitative and quantitative knowledge in classical mechanics.* Technical Report, Massachussetts Institute of Technology, 1975.

deKleer, J. Multiple representations of knowledge in a mechanics problem solver. *Proceedings of the Fifth International Joint Conference on Artificial Intelligence.* Cambridge, Mass.: 1977.

Dijksterhuis, E. J. *The mechanization of the world picture.* (C. Dikshoorn, trans.) Oxford: Clarendon Press, 1961.

diSessa, A. On learnable representations of knowledge: A meaning for the computational metaphor. In J. Lochhead & J. Clement (Eds.), *Cognitive process instruction.* Philadelphia: Franklin Institute Press, 1979.

Franklin, A. *The principle of inertia in the middle ages.* Boulder: Colorado Associated University Press, 1976.

Fredette, N., & Lochhead, J. Student conceptions of simple circuits. *The Physics Teacher,* 1980, *18,* 194–198.

Galilei, G. *De Motu.* (I. E. Drabkin, trans.) In I. E. Drabkin & S. Drake (trans. and ed.), *Galileo Galilei: "On Motion" and "On Mechanics".* Madison: University of Wisconsin Press, 1960 (Originally written ca. 1590).

Galilei, G. *Dialogue concerning the two chief world systems.* (S. Drake, trans.) Berkeley: University of California Press, 1967 (Originally published, 1632).

Gentner, D. *The structure of analogical models in science.* Unpublished manuscript, Bolt Beranek & Newman, Cambridge, Mass., 1980.

Gentner, D. Are scientific analogies metaphors? In D. S. Miall (Ed.), *Metaphor: Problems and perspectives.* Brighton, Sussex: Harvester Press, in press.

Green, B., McCloskey, M., & Caramazza, A. The relation of knowledge to problem solving, with examples from kinematics. *Proceeding of the NIE-LRDC Conference on Thinking and Learning Skills,* Pittsburgh, Pa.: October 1980.

Inhelder, B., & Piaget, J. *The growth of logical thinking from childhood to adolescence.* New York: Basic Books, 1958.

Kuhn, T. S. A function for thought experiments. In P. N. Johnson-Laird & P. C. Wason (Eds.), *Thinking: Readings in cognitive science.* Cambridge: Cambridge University Press, 1977.

Larkin, J., McDermott, J., Simon, D. P., & Simon, H. A. Expert and novice performance in solving physics problems. *Science,* 1980, *208,* 1335–1342. (a)

Larkin, J. H., McDermott, J., Simon, D. P., & Simon, H. A. Models of competence in solving physics problems. *Cognitive Science,* 1980, *4,* 317–345. (b)

Larkin, J. H., & Reif, F. Understanding and teaching problem-solving in physics. *European Journal of Science Education, 1979, 1,* 191–203.

McCloskey, M., Caramazza, A., & Green, B. Curvilinear motion in the absence of external forces: Naive beliefs about the motion of objects. *Science,* 1980, *210,* 1139–1141.

Minstrell, J. Explaining the "at rest" condition of an object. *The Physics Teacher,* 1982, *20,* 10–14.

Novak, G. S., Jr. *Computer understanding of physics problems stated in natural language.* Technical report NL-30, Department of Computer Sciences, University of Texas at Austin, 1976.

Novak, G. S., Jr. Representations of knowledge in a program for solving physics problems. *Proceedings of the Fifth International Joint Conference on Artificial Intelligence,* Cambridge, Mass.: August 1977.

Novak, G. S., Jr., & Araya, A. A. Research on expert problem solving in physics. *Proceedings of the First Annual National Conference on Artificial Intelligence,* Stanford, Calif.: August 1980.

Nussbaum, J., & Novak, J. D. An assessment of children's concepts of the earth utilizing structured interviews. *Science Education,* 1976, *60,* 535–550.

Piaget, J. *The child's conception of movement and speed.* London: Routledge & Kegan Paul, 1970.

Preece, P. F. W. Exploration of semantic space: Review of research on the organization of scientific concepts in semantic memory. *Science Education,* 1978, *62,* 547–562.

Siegler, R. S. The origins of scientific reasoning. In R. S. Siegler (Ed.), *Children's thinking: What develops?* Hillsdale, N.J.: Lawrence Erlbaum Associates, 1978.

Stevens, A. L., & Collins, A. Multiple conceptual models of a complex system. In R. Snow, P. Federico & W. Montague (Eds.), *Aptitude, learning and instruction: Cognitive process analyses of aptitude.* Hillsdale, N.J.: Lawrence Erlbaum Associates, 1980.

Trowbridge, D. E., & McDermott, L. C. An investigation of student understanding of the concept of velocity in one dimension. *American Journal of Physics,* 1980, *48,* 1020–1028.

Trowbridge, D. E., & McDermott, L. C. An investigation of student understanding of the concept of acceleration in one dimension. *American Journal of Physics,* 1981, *49,* 242–253.

Viennot, L. Spontaneous reasoning in elementary dynamics. *European Journal of Science Education,* 1979, *1,* 205–221.

14 A Conceptual Model Discussed by Galileo and Used Intuitively by Physics Students

John Clement
University of Massachusetts

Galileo's works are notable for their use of two interesting techniques: the use of qualitative thought experiments for presenting basic concepts and theories, and the inclusion and consideration of theories Galileo considered to be wrong, as voiced by Simplicio in the *Dialogues*(Galileo, 1960). One wonders why Galileo did not do as modern physics texts do and simply present mathematical results. Presumably, Galileo recognized that it was going to be difficult to present his views convincingly to his colleagues, since they subscribed to a more Aristotelian approach that essentially amounted to a very different "world view." It is plausible that he felt it necessary to discuss and counter the preconceptions of his colleagues explicitly, and to use qualitative arguments in presenting his own theory, because he sensed the strong resistance of their world view to change.

We have collected data that indicate many students have a significantly different view of certain aspects of mechanics than the now standard Newtonian view. Furthermore, this view, like those of Galileo's colleagues, appears to be fairly resistant to change and persists even after taking college physics. Specifically, many students have an alternative mental model for the relationship between force and motion, probably based on their own intuitions about how to move objects around in the world. This model conflicts with the qualitative model of the physicist underlying the equation F = ma. When a constant force is applied to an object, the physicist thinks of this as producing a constant acceleration in the same direction as the force. Such a model is a "conceptual primitive" in the sense that it is a basic prerequisite for learning many higher-order principles in physics.

The student's intuitive model is usually structured differently than the physicist's. In the real world, where friction is present, one must push on an object to keep it moving. Because friction is often not recognized by the beginner as a force, the student may believe that continuing motion, even at a constant speed, implies the presence of a continuing force in the same direction, as a necessary cause of the motion. We call this the ''motion implies a force'' misconception. Empirical evidence is presented indicating that many beginners apply this view to various simple mechanics problems. In fact, the misconception shows up in a wider diversity of problem situations than one would expect, and appears to still be present in many students after they have completed a course in mechanics. It therefore appears to be a major stumbling block in the physics curriculum. Related misconceptions have been studied by Driver (1973), Viennot (1979), Lawson, Trowbridge, and McDermott (1979), and DiSessa (1979). In this study it is shown that preconceptions can be studied using problems of minimum complexity which help to isolate the source of the errors. It was discovered that the motion implies a force preconception and is remarkably similar to a conception discussed by Galileo. This is illustrated by a comparison of his writings to transcripts of student interviews.

THE "MOTION IMPLIES A FORCE" PRECONCEPTION

The error pattern described in the following example was observed in a large number of course laboratory write-ups from students taking introductory mechanics after they had worked with pendulums in the lab. A typical incorrect solution to the Pendulum Problem is shown in Fig. 14.1.

Example 1: Pendulum Problem

Question: (1) A pendulum is swinging from left to right as shown below. Draw arrows showing the direction of each force acting on the pendulum bob at point A. Do *not* show the total net force and do not include frictional forces. *Label each arrow* with a name that says what kind of force it is.

(2)In a similar way, draw and label arrows showing the direction of each force acting on the pendulum bob when it reaches point B.

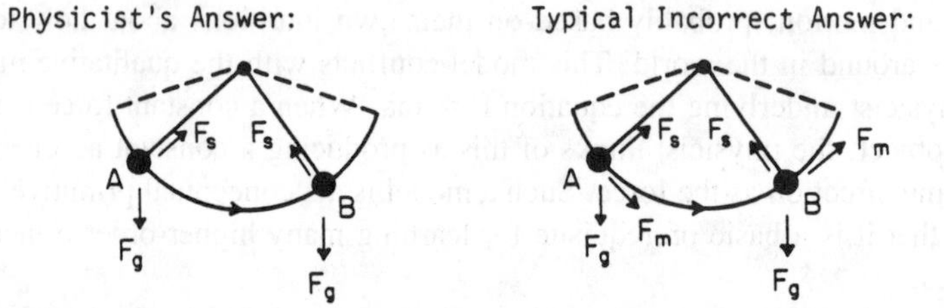

Fig. 14.1. Correct and incorrect answers to pendulum problem.

Typical Incorrect Explanation. F_m is the force that makes the pendulum swing upward. If F_m weren't there, the pendulum could never move up to the top of its swing.

Here, F_m is seen as one of the forces acting on the bob and is often described as the force that "makes the pendulum go up on the other side." We also noticed that students drawing force diagrams for an object sliding down a track, or for an object in orbit, would often include a force in the direction of motion. These classroom observations led us to suspect that many students were applying the idea that continuing motion implies the presence of a continuing force in the same direction as the motion. This type of belief shows up in pre-Newtonian theories of motion such as an impetus force injected into an arrow and travelling with it, or the Aristotelian explanation of the horizontal motion of an arrow after release from the bow via forward forces from air currents. What is surprising is the pervasiveness of the belief and the wide diversity of situations in which it shows up, once one begins to listen to students' common-sense theories. [For a summary of different impetus theories, see Dyksterhuis (1961) or Franklin (1978).]

In an effort to further isolate the source of this type of error, we designed the problem shown in Fig. 14.2, and predicted that it might trigger the "motion implies a force" misconception in spite of its extreme simplicity.

Example 2: Coin Problem

A coin is tossed from point A straight up into the air and caught at point E. On the dot to the left of the drawing draw one or more arrows showing the direction of each force acting on the coin when it is at point B. (Draw longer arrows for larger forces.)

Typical Incorrect Answer. While the coin is on the way up, the "force from your hand", F_h, pushes up on the coin. On the way up it must be greater than F_g, otherwise the coin would be moving down.

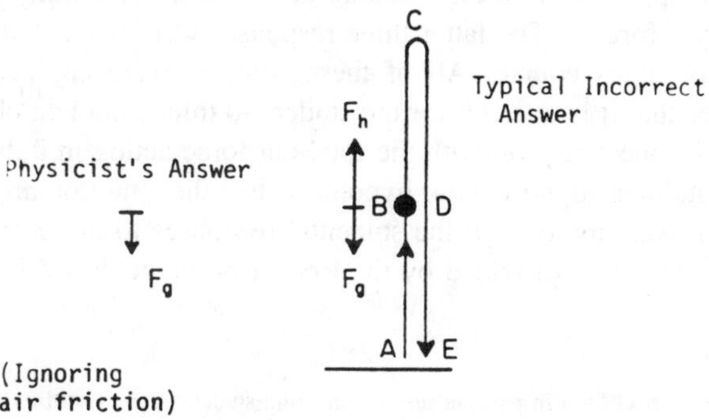

Fig. 14.2. Correct and incorrect answers to coin problem.

TABLE 14.1
Performance on Coin and Rocket Problems. Scores From Three Separate Groups of Engineering Majors Before and After Taking Mechanics

		Percentage Correct Before Course	*Percentage Correct After Course*	*Percentage Correct (For engineers with 2 semesters of Physics at a Second Institution)*
COIN PROBLEM		12% (N = 34)	28% (N = 43)	30% (N = 37)
ROCKET PROBLEM	Part 1	11% (N = 150)	23% (N = 43)	35% (N = 37)
	Part 2	38% (N = 150)	72% (N = 43)	65% (N = 37)

On a diagnostic test we gave the coin problem to a representative group of engineering students early in their first semester before they had taken physics. We also gave it to two groups of engineering students after they had taken mechanics.[1] The results are shown in Table 14.1. Eighty-eight percent of the prephysics students gave an incorrect answer. Virtually all (90%) of the errors in this case involved showing an arrow labeled as a force pointing upwards at position B. Eleven students were interviewed while solving this problem aloud: five of these had taken a physics course in mechanics for scientists and engineers. Three students solved this problem correctly, whereas seven students drew an upward arrow at point B, referring to it as the "force of the throw," the "upward original force," the "applied force," the "force that I'm giving it," "velocity is pulling upwards, so you have a net force in this direction (points upwards)," the force up from velocity," and "the force of throwing the coin up." Another student gave a questionable response, referring to "a momentum force...acting up", which doesn't belong in "a formal free body diagram" but "is definitely a force." The latter three responses were from students who had taken the mechanics course. All of these students were engineering majors. Again, we see that it is difficult for the student to think about an object continuing to move in one direction with the total net force acting in a different direction. These findings supported our hypothesis that the "motion implies a force" preconception was involved in the students' responses to these problems.

Another example is provided by the Rocket problem shown in Fig. 14.3.

---

[1]This sample was chosen in part because engineering students comprise the largest clientele of physics departments at many universities.

Example 3: Rocket Problem

(1) A rocket is moving along sideways in deep space, with its engine off, from point A to point B. It is not near any planets or other outside forces. Its engine is fired at point B and left on for two seconds while the rocket travels from point B to some point C. Draw in the shape of the path from B to C. (Show your best guess for this problem even if you are unsure of the answer).

(2)Show the path from point C after the engine is turned off on the same drawing.

Typical Incorrect Answer. The force of the rocket engine combines with whatever was making it go from A to B to produce path BC. After C, whatever made it go from A to B will take over and make it go sideways again, causing the rocket to return to its original direction of motion.

Results from written testing on this problem with a representative group of 150 prephysics engineering students are shown in Table 14.1. Eighty-nine percent drew an incorrect path for part 1 of the Rocket problem whereas 62% missed part 2. A summary of the responses to the Rocket problem is given in Table 14.2.

The curved path from B to C is a detailed aspect of the motion that the uninitiated student will rarely reproduce. A more surprising and significant difficulty than this, however, is the tendency in many students to actually draw the rocket's motion returning to a horizontal direction after the engine is shut off at point C. The student's prediction that the rocket will return to a horizontal path is usually accompanied by a reference to some influence acting on the rocket from A to B which "takes over" again after C. This behavior can be explained by assuming that, for the student, the presence of constant motion from A to B implies the presence of a continuing force in the same direction, even though the problem states that no outside forces are present. Note also that students usually show the direction of motion changing instantaneously in a noncontinuous manner, apparently to correspond to instantaneous changes in the direction of applied force.

Taped interviews were conducted with 18 of the above students. Five of the seven students who had responses of type 3 or 4 in Table 14.2 made a specific reference to the idea that "whatever was making it go to the right before will take

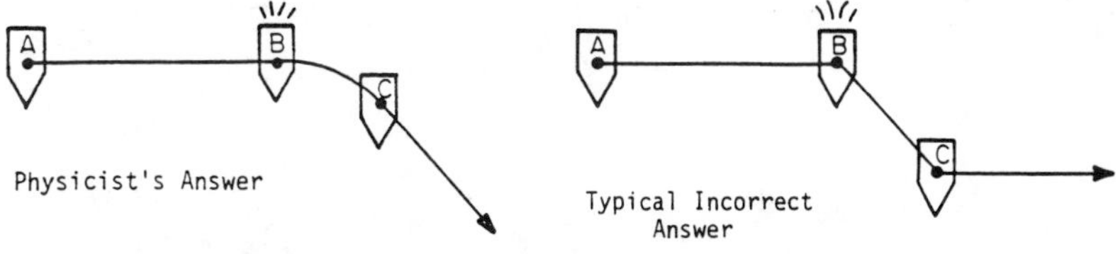

Fig. 14.3. Correct and incorrect answers to rocket problem.

TABLE 14.2
Types of Responses Given for Rocket Problem by Freshman Engineering Majors Before Taking Physics

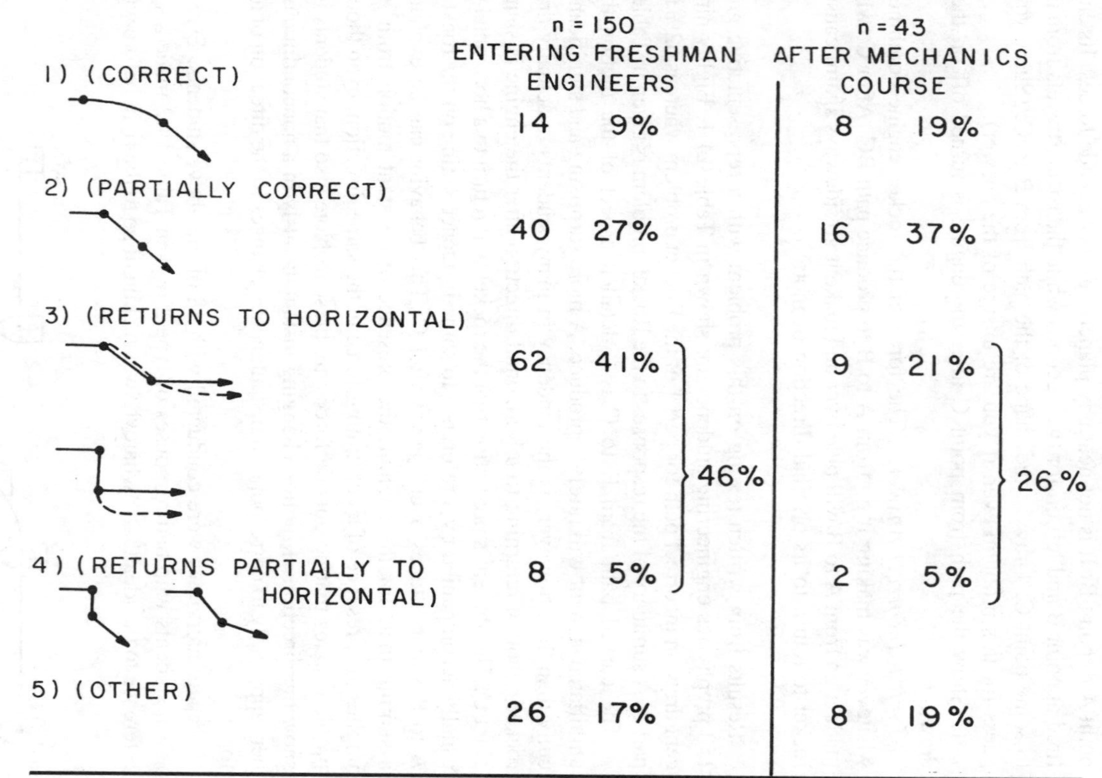

	n = 150 ENTERING FRESHMAN ENGINEERS			n = 43 AFTER MECHANICS COURSE		
1) (CORRECT)	14	9%		8	19%	
2) (PARTIALLY CORRECT)	40	27%		16	37%	
3) (RETURNS TO HORIZONTAL)	62	41%	46% (3 + 4)	9	21%	26% (3 + 4)
4) (RETURNS PARTIALLY TO HORIZONTAL)	8	5%		2	5%	
5) (OTHER)	26	17%		8	19%	

over again after point C.'' (See Appendix 1 for example of a Rocket problem transcript.) These interview results, and the consistent error pattern both within each problem and across the problems indicate that most errors are not due to random mistakes but rather are based on a stable misconception that is shared by many individuals.

DISCUSSION OF SIMILAR ARGUMENTS IN GALILEO'S WRITINGS

Two typical transcript excerpts from freshman engineering students working on the Coin problem are shown below:

Transcript of S1

S1: *So there's a force going up* and there is *the force of gravity pushing* it down. And *the gravity is less* because the coin is still going up until it gets to C. (Draws upward arrow labeled ''force of the throw'' and shorter downward arrow labeled ''gravity'' at point B in Fig. 14.2.)...if the dot goes up *the force of throw gets to be less and less because gravity is pulling down on it, pulling down.*

Interviewer: Okay, what about the length of this arrow [''force of the throw'']. If we use that to represent how strong the force is, would it be stronger than gravity at point B?

S1: Yeah, because the ball is still going up, so the force of the throw is still overcoming the force of the gravity that wants to make it go down.

Transcript of S2

S2: At B there'd be two—that I could think of. The upward force—the *upward original force* that was given to the coin to make it fly in the air...(Draws upward arrow at B). . .and the gravitational. (Draws downward arrow at B.) But the *reason that the coin is going up is because the original is greater than the gravitational.*

The italicized statements indicate that the students believe that a force is acting upwards on the coin at Point B, and that the coin is continuing to rise because the upward force is greater than the gravitational. This is evidence for the ''motion implies a force'' belief, in this case with reference to the sum of forces acting on the body.

After these student explanations were analyzed we discovered that Galileo (1960) had made some similar arguments in his manuscript *De Motu* (*On Motion*). In explaining the motion of an object thrown upwards he states:

> The body moves upward, provided the impressed motive force is greater than the resisting weight. But that force, as has been shown, is continuously weakened; it will finally become so diminished that it will no longer overcome the weight of the body and will not impel the body beyond that point.... As the impressed force characteristically continues to decrease, the weight of the body begins to be predominant, and consequently the body begins to fall.... This is what I consider to be the true cause of the acceleration of motion [p. 89].

His explanation that ''the impressed motive force is greater than the resisting weight'' is similar in many ways to the students' explanations. S2 explains that the ''upward original force...is greater than the gravitational,'' and S1 explains that the ''force of the throw...is...overcoming the force of gravity.'' In fact, it is remarkable how similar the statements are, given the fact that the speakers are separated culturally by over 300 years. In each case, they describe a continuing upward force acting on the coin as a cause of motion, and state that the upward motion requires that this force be larger than the force of gravity.

Of course, Galileo thought much more deeply about these issues in his ingenious thought experiments than students do. When he published *Two New Sciences* much later in his career, Galileo (1974) presented essentially the aforementioned argument, but was unwilling to endorse or refute it.[2] He assigned the argument to Sagredo, the ''middleman'' in the dialogues, rather than to either Salviati, the spokesman representing himself, or to Simplicio, whose views are closest to Galileo's Aristotelian adversaries. Following Sagredo's presentation, in *Two New Sciences* (1974), Salviati says:

> The present does not seem to me to be an opportune time to enter into the investigation of the cause of the acceleration of natural motion...it suffices our Author that we understand him to want us to investigate and demonstrate some attributes of a motion so accelerated (whatever be the cause of its acceleration) that the momenta

[2]Sagredo:...it seems to me that a very appropriate answer can be deduced for the question agitated among philosophers as to the possible cause of acceleration of the natural motion of heavy bodies. For let us consider that in the heavy body hurled upwards, the force impressed upon it by the thrower is continually diminishing, and that this is the force that drives it upward as long as this remains greater than the contrary force of its heaviness...The diminutions of this alien impetus then continuing, and in consequence the advantage passing over to the side of the heaviness, descent commences...And since this [force] continues to diminish, and comes to be overpowered in ever greater ratio by the heaviness, the continual acceleration of the motion arises therefrom. (pp. 157–158)

> of its speed go increasing, after its departure from rest, in that simple ratio with which the continuation of time increases [p. 159].

One of Galileo's strengths, in contrast to the philosophical generalists of his age, was that he was able to make deep progress by intentionally restricting his field of inquiry (in this case to kinematics.) But the quotations from Galileo indicate that real conceptual change in this area is an extremely difficult task which should not be underestimated.[3] The fact that Galileo propounded a careful and well-articulated impetus theory during part of his career, and the fact that present day students give explanations that are very similar in their basic aspects to that theory, is supporting evidence for the strong, intuitive attraction of the ''motion implies force'' belief. The students' errors appear not to be simply capricious; the belief appears to be an informal but plausible theory which has been constructed by students on the basis of experience. This historical comparison makes the high error rates for students on these problems somewhat less surprising.

SUMMARY OF CHARACTERISTICS FOR THE "MOTION IMPLIES A FORCE" PRECONCEPTION

By studying the error patterns discussed so far, we can summarize what appear to be the most common characteristics of the ''motion implies a force'' preconception:

1. Continuing motion, even at a constant velocity, can trigger an assumption of the presence of a force in the direction of motion which acts on the object to cause the motion.
2. Such invented forces are especially common in explanations of motion that continues in the face of an obvious opposing force. In this case the object is assumed to continue to move because the invented force is greater than the opposing force.
3. The subject may believe that such a force ''dies out'' or ''builds up'' to account for changes in an object's speed.

The diversity of situations in which this preconception surfaces suggests that it is a major source of the difficulties encountered by students in understanding the physical principles associated with the equation F = ma.

---

[3]Although there is wide agreement on the fact that Galileo never stated Newton's second law, the extent to which he progressed toward a statement of the first law of inertia has been a point of discussion. See Drake (1964, 1980); Losee (1966).

POST COURSE RESULTS

In order to determine the effect of a physics course on these misconceptions we also tested two groups of students who had taken mechanics. The students in post group A were paid volunteers who agreed to take a diagnostic test before their final exam in a standard, one semester introductory mechanics course for engineers and science majors. Most of these students were sophomores and were from the same institution as the freshman group reported on earlier. The teacher of the course has received consistently high praise in written evaluations from students for his clarity of presentation, helpfulness, and genuine interest in teaching. The average grade in the course for these volunteers happened to be significantly higher than the course mean. The students in post group B were sophomore, junior, and senior engineering majors enrolled in an upper level engineering course at a second institution. All had previously taken mechanics.

Scores of the post course students were somewhat better than those of the prephysics students, but an alarmingly high number of students still gave wrong answers of the same kind on these very basic problems, as shown in Table 14.1. This was in spite of the fact that none of the problems required advanced mathematical skills. What they did require was adequate knowledge of the basic qualitative model for how forces affect motion.

On the Rocket problem, these students did somewhat better in avoiding the most blatant error: the misconception that the rocket will return to a horizontal path. However, on the Coin problem, the percentage of error only changed from 88% to 75% for group A, a rather disturbing result. In this problem, almost all errors were again in the form of an upward arrow. Additional data for this group show 44% drawing forces incorrectly on the Pendulum problem, with a 51% error rate at the second institution. Sixty-eight percent and 78% of these errors, respectively, included arrows drawn horizontally or tangential to the motion. Possibly, these error rates are lower than for the Coin problem because the opposition between the direction of motion and the gravitational force is more pronounced in the Coin problem. This is consistent with the fact that more invented forces were shown on the upswing of the pendulum than on the downswing.

Although the precourse and post-course tests were given to different groups, the two independent results indicate what can be expected of students before and after the introductory course, and the fact that post group A was an above average sample from the course leads us to be concerned about the level of understanding that is generally attained. In conclusion, the data support the hypothesis that for the majority of these students, the "motion implies a force" preconception was highly resistant to change. This conclusion applies to the extent that the students could not solve basic problems of this kind where the direction of motion does not coincide with the direction of the net force.

IMPLICATIONS FOR INSTRUCTION

These findings lead us to suspect that it may be necessary to devote more attention to conceptual primitives at the qualitative level than is currently practiced, and that teaching strategies limited to expository presentation may be unlikely to succeed in this area. The "motion implies a force" preconception is not likely to disappear simply because students have been exposed to the standard view in their physics courses. More likely, Newtonian ideas will simply be misperceived or distorted by students so as to fit their existing preconceptions; or they may be memorized separately as formulas with little or no connection to fundamental qualitative concepts. Attempts to "cover" a very large syllabus, and to present physics primarily in a formal mathematical language, may preclude students from learning basic qualitative concepts that give them an intuitive understanding of the subject. Discouraging as these implications may seem, it should be remembered that historically, pre-Newtonian concepts of mechanics had a strong appeal, and scientists were at least as resistant to change as students are.

Serious difficulties with conceptual primitives have also been documented for undergraduates in several other areas of physics, including relative motion, torque (Barowy & Lochhead, 1980), simple circuits (Fredette & Lochhead, 1980), and acceleration (Trowbridge & McDermott, 1981). In addition, preconceptions producing consistent error patterns have been identified in the areas of Newton's Third law, centrifugal force (Viennot, 1979), velocity (Trowbridge & McDermott, 1980), elastic forces, and curvilinear motion (McCloskey, Caramazza & Green, 1980). These involve beliefs such as assuming that a stronger person experiences a smaller force than a weaker person when they push away from each other on an ice rink, drawing radially outward forces in circular motion, assuming that an object passing another moving object is travelling at the same speed when it is next to the object, believing that passive objects like tables cannot be sources of force, and believing that objects projected from a curved tube will continue to follow a curved path. Not all of these error patterns are as strong as the ones discussed here, but they do show up in a significant percentage of students.

Preconceptions need not be viewed exclusively as obstacles to learning, however. They constitute micro-theories that students have constructed on their own, and should be respected as such. Because they ordinarily have some predictive power in certain practical situations, they can be thought of as "zeroth-order models" which the students possess. Some preconceptions can be built upon or modified by students in order to increase the precision and generality of their theories.[4] In this approach the goal is to find teaching strategies that encourage

---

[4]Impetus theory, for example can be seen historically as an important intermediate step between Aristotle's antipersperis theory and the modern concept of inertia. For a discussion of how more formal physical principles may be connected to physical intuitions, see Clement (1979a).

students to articulate and become conscious of their own preconceptions by making predictions based on them. A second goal is then to encourage them to make explicit comparisons between these preconceptions, accepted scientific explanations, and convincing empirical observations. Similar strategies have been advocated by Fuller, Karplus, and Lawson 1977; Fuller, 1977, and Arons (1977) among others. In one attempt to develop this approach we are designing laboratory activities for introductory mechanics in which students are asked to give a large number of qualitative predictions and explanations about elementary phenomena such as the motion of the simple pendulum or of the tossed coin[5]. We have found that questions about the direction and relative magnitudes of forces, velocities, and accelerations at different points of the motion are quite challenging to introductory students. In the absence of formulas to ''plug into,'' such questions are an effective way of getting students to think about their own preconceptions. In general, when qualitative misconceptions arise, it is necessary for students to express them and to actively work out their implications in order to see the advantages of the Newtonian point of view. Class discussions and arguments between pairs of students are especially helpful in this regard. Further development of innovative instruction techniques that emphasize the understanding of qualitative principles should be encouraged. Most importantly, instructional strategies that do not discourage students from making their own conjectures in the future should be sought.

Galileo was apparently aware of this type of teaching strategy, for his dialogues represent a marvelous attempt to deal directly with the common preconceptions and prevailing theories of his time at a qualitative level. The enormous conceptual breakthroughs that were achieved by Galileo were not easy to communicate to his peers. His writings appeal to the reader's intuitions by using concrete, practical situations to illustrate his theories (Galileo, 1960, 1962). He also took pains to present and discuss the Aristotelian theories he considered to be wrong, showing *why* he believed them to be wrong. One might do worse than to take these aspects of Galileo's teaching technique as a model for pedagogy today.

Another possible instructional strategy for teaching these concepts involves the use of analogies and kinesthetic intuitions. VanLehn and Brown (1979) have proposed an approach for teaching mathematical models underlying subtraction based on partial analogies between successively more complex models. The use of analogies to generate scientific models has been documented in thinking aloud interviews with scientists (Clement, 1981), and with students (Clement, 1979b). The latter study shows a college freshman spontaneously generating several analogies in a series of thought experiments in order to arrive at a fairly abstract understanding of Newton's third law and the concept of inertial mass. It may be

[5]Draft available from the author on request.

that sequences of analogies could be generated for fostering the understanding of other physical principles as well. Studies also indicate that at least some students have a useful set of physical intuitions that could be used as starting points for instruction (Clement, 1979a; 1979b). In addition, spontaneous hand motions produced by students in these studies indicate that ''developed'' physical intuitions underlying an understanding of such physical principles can involve a rather rich set of kinesthetic images. Further research is needed to determine how this mode of representation and the use of analogies might be tapped in instruction.

THEORETICAL IMPLICATIONS

Apparently one cannot consider the student's mind to be a ''blank slate'' in the area of force and motion. Many of the concepts presented in this area must displace or be remolded from stable intuitive concepts that the student has constructed over a number of years.

An important problem for future research is to determine the origin of the persistance of the ''motion implies a force'' preconception. Presumably the conception is rooted in everyday perceptual-motor experiences with pushing and pulling objects. We have seen that deeply seated mental models in the form of physical intuitions can be very compelling and resilient, even in the face of potentially contradictory evidence and/or earnest teaching. They have a power and ''momentum'' of their own quite unlike a memorized rule or a passive set of verbal propositions which would presumably be easy to ''delete.'' They appear to have become ''embedded into the system'' at a perceptual-motor (''gut'') level rather than at an abstract level.

However, it is not yet clear how we are to go about modeling the way such deep notions are represented mentally. The usual method is to represent them as lists of symbols in the form of rules or propositions; this leaves unanswered the question of the locus of meaning underlying each symbol. Such models fail to capture the representational richness that is suggested by the resistence of preconception to change, by subjects' references to ''picturing,'' ''imagining,'' and ''feeling,'' by spontaneous hand motions simulating forces and movements, and by expressions of necessity and intuitive conviction during explanations (Clement, 1979a, 1979b, 1982). These phenomena may eventually be more fruitfully modeled in terms of visual and kinesthetic representations of a more analogue character.

A more general theoretical implication of these findings is that although various general reasoning skills are important in physics, domain-specific knowledge is also crucial. Knowledge structures that represent specific types of physical interactions must be structured in a particular way if they are to embody Newtonian concepts; but the preconceptions found in students are often structured very differently. When students with these alternative knowledge structures produce incorrect answers in the classroom, the instructor may in many cases assume that the cause is "low intelligence" or poorly developed reasoning skills, when in fact the cause is the stability of the student's alternative knowledge structures. It is important for teachers to become sensitive to such distinctions because the indicated teaching strategies are quite different in each case. Avoiding this confusion might have an impact on the way teachers view students and, in turn, on the way students view themselves.

ACKNOWLEDGMENT

Research reported in this paper was supported by NSF Award No. SED 78-22043 in the Joint National Institute of Education/National Science Foundation Program of Research on Cognitive Processes and the Structure of Knowledge in Science and Mathematics. Some of the material presented in this paper appears in "Students' preconceptions in introductory mechanics." *American Journal of Physics,* 1982, *50(1),* 60–71.

REFERENCES

Arons, A. *The various language*. New York: Oxford University Press 1977.

Barowy, W., & Lochhead, J. Abstract reasoning in rotational physics. *American Association of Physics Teachers Announcer,* 1980, *10(2),* 74.

Clement, J. Mapping a student's causal conceptions from a problem solving protocol. In J. Lochhead & J. Clement (Eds.), *Cognitive process instruction*. Philadelphia, Pennsylvania: Franklin Institute Press, 1979.(a)

Clement, J. *The role of analogy in scientific thinking: Examples from a problem solving interview*. Technical Report, Cognitive Development Project, Department of Physics and Astronomy, University of Massachusetts at Amherst, 1979.(b)

Clement, J. *Analogy generation in scientific problem solving*. Third Annual Meeting of the Cognitive Science Society, Berkeley, CA, August 1981.

Clement, J. Students' preconceptions in introductory mechanics. *American Journal of Physics,* 1982, *50(1),* 66–71.

diSessa, A. On learnable representations of knowledge: A meaning for the computational metaphor. In J. Lockhead & J. Clement (Eds.), *Cognitive Process Instruction*. Philadelphia, Pa.: Franklin Institute Press, 1979.

Drake, S. Galileo and the law of inertia. *American Journal of Physics,* 1964, *32,* 601.

Drake, S. Newton's apple and Galileo's dialogue. *Scientific American,* 1980, 243, 151.

Driver, R. P. *The representation of conceptual frameworks in young adolescent science students*. Unpublished doctoral disseration, University of Illinois, 1973.

Dyksterhuis, E. J. *The mechanization of the world picture*. Oxford: The Clarendon Press, 1961.

Franklin, A. Inertia in the middle ages. *The Physics Teacher,* 1978, *16,* 4.

Fredette, N. & Lochhead, J. Student conceptions of simple circuits. *The Physics Teacher,* 1980, *18,* 194.

Fuller, R. G., Karplus, R., & Lawson, A. Can physics develop reasoning?. *Physics Today,* 1977, *30(2),* 23–28.

Fuller, R. *The ADAPT book*. Lincoln, Nebraska: ADAPT Program, University of Nebraska, 1977.

Galilei, G. *De motu*. Madison, Wisconsin: University of Wisconsin Press, 1960. Trans. by I. E. Drabkin.

Galilei, G. *Dialogue concerning the two chief world systems*. Berkeley: University of California Press, 1962. Trans. by S. Drake.

Galilei, G. *Two new sciences*. Madison: University of Wisconsin Press, 1974. Trans. by S. Drake.

Lawson, R. A., Trowbridge, D. E., & McDermott, L. C. Students' conceptions of dynamics. *American Association of Physics Teachers Announcer*, 1979, *9*, 87.

Losee, J., & Drake, S. Galileo and the law of inertia. *American Journal of Physics*, 1966, *34*, 430.

McCloskey, M., Caramazza, A., & Green, B. Curvilinear motion in the absence of external forces: Naive beliefs about the motion of objects. *Science*, 1980, *210*, 4474.

Trowbridge, D., & McDermott, L. An investigation of student understanding of the concept of velocity in one dimension. *American Journal of Physics*, 1980, *48*, 12.

Trowbridge, D., & McDermott, L. An investigation of student understanding of the concept of acceleration in one dimension. *American Journal of Physics*, 1981, *49*, 2242.

VanLehn, K., & Brown, J. S. *Planning nets*: A representation for formalizing analogies and semantic models of procedural skills. In R. Snow, P. Frederico, & W. Montague, (Eds.), *Aptitude learning and instruction: Cognitive process analyses*. Hillsdale, N.J.: Lawrence Erlbaum Associates, 1979.

Viennot, L. Spontaneous reasoning in elementary dynamics. *European Journal of Science Education*, 1979, *1*, 205.

APPENDIX I

EXAMPLE OF A TRANSCRIPT FROM THE ROCKET PROBLEM

Student S3

One student answered the rocket problem as follows:

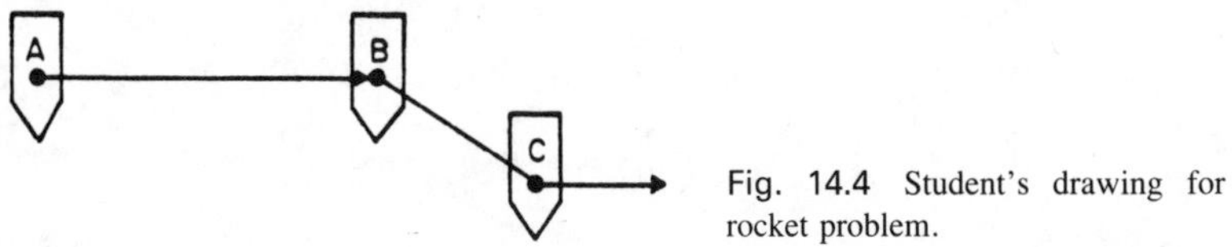

Fig. 14.4 Student's drawing for rocket problem.

I: Ok, can you describe the motion and tell me what the rocket did?

S: Ok. The rocket was moving towards here (points to right) a force acting upon it here (points to B) to drive it down—so in effect it would be driving it at an angle because there's two forces acting upon it.

I: And after the engine shuts off?

S: Right here (points to C) and with the same force acting upon it—motion—it'd continue along this path (horizontally to the right).

This subject apparently believes that a force is needed to cause the initial movement at a constant velocity with the engine off. After the engine is fired and turned off, this "same force acting upon it" horizontally causes the rocket to return to the horizontal path. Notice that the student's ideas are quasi-consistent in this case. A belief that a constant force causes a constant velocity implies that there must be a constant horizontal force; these two ideas then predict both the straight diagonal path during the burn, and the return to a horizontal path afterwards.

Author Index

Italics denote pages with bibliographic information.

Y,Z

Subject Index

A

B

C